ean in religion, or partisan in

Department of the Institute, an

t be used in the election of

the Institute, nor shall any such test ever be used in selecting, for any purpose

understood as the fundamental c

Endpapers

Top: An ornamental detail over the Brookings Hall archway in the Quadrangle carries the University's motto: "Per Veritatem Vis" — "Strength Through Truth."

Joe Angeles, WU Photographic Services

Bottom: Article VIII of the original Constitution drawn up by William Greenleaf Eliot and Samuel Treat assured that the institution that has become Washington University in St. Louis would always be nonsectarian.

WU Archives

ℬEGINNING A GREAT WORK
WASHINGTON UNIVERSITY
IN ST. LOUIS
1853-2003

BY CANDACE O'CONNOR

In praise of Wayman Crow

"[The passage of the University's Charter] was obtained by the
exertions of Hon. Wayman Crow, at that time Senator from this district...As he
was the sole originator of the design and himself prepared the charter, the
existence of the university is primarily due to him."

–William Greenleaf Eliot, address at the Inauguration of
Washington University, April 23, 1857

Crow and Eliot were the co-founders of Washington University

Previous pages:
Brookings Hall in springtime.
The best-known building at the University, Brookings
serves as a "front door" to the Hilltop Campus.
Joe Angeles, WU Photographic Services

Left: **Ivy-covered walls.**
In the autumn, the Virginia creeper on Washington
University's buildings turns a vivid red.

Pages iv-xx:
Photos by David Kilper, Washington University
Photographic Services, unless otherwise noted

CONTENTS

Detail on Cupples I.
Many buildings feature
limestone grotesques.

JOSEPH GIBSON HOYT
1st Chancellor • 1858-1862

"St. Louis, the geographical centre, not only of this valley, but of the whole country, will be, to a fearful extent, responsible for the intellectual and moral character which shall be impressed upon the American people. It was in view of considerations like these, that a few far-sighted and large-hearted men…laid the foundation of Washington University."

Inaugural address, October 4, 1859

WILLIAM CHAUVENET
2nd Chancellor • 1862-1869

"The question — What shall we teach, and how shall we teach it? — when proposed in relation to a community, involves the whole question of life. What kind of lives shall we live? What shall be our aims, our occupations? What kind of beings shall we be? What shall be the form of our intellectual and moral existence? What is its relation to our physical existence? How shall we employ our faculties?"

Inaugural address, June 17, 1863

Left: **The Brookings Quadrangle framed by the January Hall arch.**
In many ways, the Quadrangle serves as the heart of the Hilltop Campus.

Above: **Fountain and roses.**
The Margaret Talbott Thomas Fountain, on the north side of Brookings Hall, was donated in 1977. Thomas, who died in 1975, was a charter member of the Women's Society, and her husband, the late Charles Allen Thomas, was a life trustee.

WILLIAM GREENLEAF ELIOT
3rd Chancellor • 1870-1887

*"I*n the beginning of every enterprise we should know, as distinctly as possible, what we propose to do, and the means of doing it....We should also make up our minds...whether it is, upon the whole, worth the doing, and if so, whether it is our part to do it....The enterprise which we now contemplate is one of this sort. It is not only the beginning of a great work, capable of indefinite extension, but each step in its progress and the first step in its commencement involve the sacrifice both of time and money."

Address to the board of Washington Institute of St. Louis, February 22, 1854

Over the Brookings archway.
University Hall, completed in 1901, was renamed Brookings Hall in 1928 in honor of Robert S. Brookings, who served as president of the University's board of directors from 1895 to 1928 and who sponsored the building's construction.

Laboratory Science Building for Arts & Sciences.
The 129,500-square-foot building on the north side of campus, completed in 2002, includes classrooms, a 350-seat lecture hall, and laboratories — particularly for the chemical sciences.

Francis Field gates.
In 1904, Francis Field served as the venue for the Olympic games — the third of the modern era and the first held in the Western Hemisphere.

WINFIELD SCOTT CHAPLIN
4th Chancellor • 1891-1907

"*I* have a vision of a great university. Its structures are grand and its surroundings are beautiful. The public esteem it, because its high aims, its great utility, its magnificent results are known. To support it is considered a duty, to aid in its development a pleasure, and to have one's name connected with it an honor."

Inaugural address, January 11, 1892

The Village.
One of the newest housing complexes, which opened in fall 2001 on the northwest corner of the Hilltop Campus, the Village provides living quarters for groups of undergraduate students sharing similar interests, classrooms, and gathering spaces.

Treasuring the Past • Shaping the Future

DAVID F. HOUSTON
5th Chancellor · 1908-1917

"No great university can be built up and sustained unless the university can secure and keep a fair number of the strongest, greatest, most creative and inspiring of the world's teachers and investigators....In addition to these things there must be a mature university student body, considerable leisure on the part of professors for research, a sympathetic environment, and absolute freedom in subject and method."

"A University for the Southwest," address to the Commercial Club of St. Louis, October 30, 1908

Center for Advanced Medicine.
Completed in 2001 to bring together outpatient services previously scattered across the Medical Center, the Center for Advanced Medicine houses the National Cancer Institute-designated Siteman Cancer Center.

Joe Angeles, WU Photographic Services

Anheuser-Busch Hall.
Completed in 1997, Anheuser-Busch serves as a state-of-the-art home for the School of Law.

Simon Hall.
Completed in 1986 for the Olin School of Business with funds from the ALLIANCE FOR WASHINGTON UNIVERSITY campaign, the 100,000-plus-square-foot structure was the largest building on the Hilltop Campus at the time.

FREDERIC ALDIN HALL
6th Chancellor • 1913-1923

"The war has helped in bringing about a solidarity of interests at the University previously unknown. It has helped more than any single thing to identify all the schools of the University as parts of a whole....In France, in the various cantonments, wherever graduates of Washington are, they now speak of themselves as Washingtonians regardless of whether they come from the Law School, the Medical School, or any other department."

"Address at the Meeting of the Alumni Association of Washington University," City Club, March 8, 1918

Treasuring the Past • Shaping the Future

Keeping watch.
This beautiful figure has seen generations of students pass beneath the Ridgley Hall arches.

HERBERT S. HADLEY
7th Chancellor • 1923-1927

"Ours is the typical American city…that belongs neither to the East, West, North, or South, but which exemplifies American life as a whole. Here are to be found the culture and refinement of the East, the courage and vigor of the North, the frankness and freedom of the West, and the courtesy and chivalry of the South. We have sunshine enough for sentiment and snow enough for courage, and we have the substantial foundations of industrial and agricultural wealth to justify our claim to leadership in material as well as in spiritual achievements."

Laying of the cornerstone for Newton R. Wilson Memorial Hall, May 19, 1924

GEORGE R. THROOP
8th Chancellor • 1927-1944

"*P*rivate institutions, not partisan, not sectarian, not political, not beholden to party or creed, are needed now more than ever in our history to guard without fear or favor a knowledge without bias, and the complete privilege of the search for and the expression of truth. The compelling picture of this responsibility cannot be overdrawn. In a world oppressed by intolerance, by partyism, and other constricting pressures, a free institution is indeed a rock in a weary land."

"A University's Responsibility," May 1941

Eads Hall.
The building that was home for the Department of Physics in Arts & Sciences when Arthur Holly Compton did his Nobel Prize-winning work on the X-ray scattering effect (which has become known as "the Compton effect") today serves as a teaching and learning facility for students in the College of Arts & Sciences.

Graham Chapel.
A gift from Christine Blair Graham, widow of paper distributor Benjamin Brown Graham, made possible the construction of Graham Chapel in 1909. Renovations to the chapel, begun in 2001, will continue in 2004 when the organ will be refurbished.

Left: **McMillan Hall.**
Built initially as a dormitory for women students, McMillan houses several departments in Arts & Sciences today.

IAM A SHADOW·SO ART THOU.
I MARK TIME·DOST THOU

CLASS OF 1908

Treasuring the Past • Shaping the Future

ARTHUR HOLLY COMPTON
9th Chancellor • 1945-1953

"The goal before us is education for a greater destiny. Our nation is setting a pattern for the world. Here at our nation's heart the pattern selected by Washington University can thus shape the growth of man. With the cordial support of the Corporation and friends of the University, the loyal cooperation of the faculty, and the earnest effort of the students, this University will take an ever greater part in building our community and our world."

"Education for a Greater Destiny," inaugural address, February 22, 1946

Left: **Sundial.**
This embellishment on Cupples I Hall was a gift from the class of 1908. It bears the inscription, "I am a shadow/So art thou; I mark time/Dost thou?"

ETHAN A.H. SHEPLEY
10th Chancellor • 1953-1961

"The University that Eliot founded and Brookings so notably developed is moving forward today in the ennobling cause of truth. It is only through truth that man can build with strength. As the University motto has it, 'Per veritatem vis.'"

Address to Newcomen Society, October 14, 1958

Duncker Hall towers.
Completed in 1924 to house the School of Commerce and Finance and named for Charles H. Duncker, Jr., who was killed in World War I, Duncker Hall today houses the English department in Arts & Sciences.

CARL TOLMAN
11th Chancellor • 1961-1962

"As a private institution, we have the independence to be able to determine our own objectives and philosophy and to follow through toward them. We have settled on quality education as our goal. We have made tremendous progress toward it….In this emphasis in quality we are trying — and doing — nothing which was not in our tradition from the beginning."

Commencement address, June 4, 1962

Givens Hall.
In 1930 Joseph Givens, whose father had been an architect and builder for the University's former downtown campus, gave funds for a new building to house the School of Architecture, making possible the construction of Givens Hall in 1932.

Left: **Ridgley Hall.**
Initially built in 1902 as the University's library, Ridgley is the only building facing the Quadrangle designed in the English Renaissance style.

THOMAS H. ELIOT
12th Chancellor • 1962-1971

"*I* want to say one reassuring word. The University still stands. It stands: and, as it always has, it stands for the unterrified and unconfined search for truth....As we gird to protect our beloved institution from the felonies of the few, we must also protect the freedom of the many — professors and students alike — to dissent, to criticize, to engage in intellectual controversy, to work together with minds unfettered and unafraid."

Founders Day remarks, February 28, 1970

Grotesques.
The many bosses and grotesques that adorn the buildings are a prominent architectural feature on the Hilltop Campus.

East Asian Library.
The library with its Tudor-style oak ceiling, in January Hall, was initially the library and reading room for the School of Law.

WILLIAM H. DANFORTH
13th Chancellor • 1971-1995

"*I* believe that Washington University is one of this community's contributions to mankind. A successful university is a noble institution. It is a statement of faith; faith that human beings can be educated and that human thought is worthwhile, that the thinking, analyzing animal called man can use his unique talents for the benefit of himself and his fellows; that we can learn from our past; that we can change; that by intelligence we can improve our lot and the lot of our children and their children."

Founders Day address, 1972

Right: **Psychology Building.**
With a nod to the towers of Brookings Hall, the Psychology Building was completed in 1995 at a cost of $28 million, making possible an expansion of the Department of Psychology in Arts & Sciences and its research programs.

MARK S. WRIGHTON
14th Chancellor • 1995–present

FOREWORD

Great universities respond to the needs of the society they serve. Washington University in St. Louis was founded by St. Louisans for St. Louis, and as the needs of our community have changed, the University has changed, too. From its founding as a vision of Wayman Crow in 1853 and its early development by William Greenleaf Eliot, the University has grown in scope and impact, serving not only St. Louis, but also the nation and world. The University's mission today is to conduct programs for people to learn what is known; to create new knowledge; to contribute creative works in music, art, performing arts, and literature; to steward scholarly resources; to advance human health through research and patient care; and to serve our community.

From lofty ideals but modest beginnings in 1853, Washington University in 2003–04 is one of America's finest research universities with an operating budget of more than $1.3 billion, involving approximately 12,000 full-time students and more than 1,200 faculty in its eight schools. In addition, the University mission is enabled by more than 8,000 staff members. During its 150-year history more than 150,000 students have earned degrees at Washington University, and more than 100,000 are living today in all 50 states and 129 countries. Through the work of its graduates, the impact of the University has been felt in all sectors of society and all around the world.

By the standard of the great European universities, Washington University has a short history. However, the

Whitaker Hall for Biomedical Engineering.
Built to house one of the newest, quickly expanding programs at the University (which draws on strengths of the School of Engineering & Applied Science and the School of Medicine), Whitaker Hall opened for classes in spring 2003.

preeminence of American higher education in the world and the University's high standing in the United States places Washington University among the world's leading research universities. The current population of students and faculty is drawn from more than 100 countries of the world, illustrating the University's visibility and impact internationally. Today, about ten percent of the students come from countries other than the United States. Continuing to attract students and faculty from other countries is a vital contribution to the educational experience of all members of the Washington University community.

Washington University is an American university, however. Located in America's heartland, the University largely serves American students, and has been generously supported by Americans, American corporations and foundations, and the United States government. Indeed, these elements of support have contributed to building programs and facilities of extraordinary quality and value. These programs have attracted talented people from other parts of the world who want to study in America with Americans, and who want to learn about America. Washington University provides one of the most attractive settings for learning and discovery, and the international participation enhances the experience for students from the United States. Increasingly, our international alumni are providing support to enhance the University's value to society.

At its founding Washington University served students from St. Louis. Today, nearly 90 percent of first-year undergraduates are from outside the state of Missouri. As the 18th largest metropolitan region in the United States, St. Louis will continue to be an important source of many talented students who aspire to attend Washington University. But with the ease of movement among major urban centers, students today enjoy many more choices than did the students of 1853. In consciously and thoughtfully changing from a "streetcar" college to a national university, Washington University continues to maintain its commitment to St. Louis. Importantly, the University has taken steps to remain attractive to the most talented students, and the results for St. Louis are important and impressive. Some of the nation's and the world's most talented students come to St. Louis for their studies, providing St. Louis with an opportunity to retain them as they take up their lives

The Quadrangle seen through the Ridgley arches.
A rare quiet moment is depicted of one of the most-used spaces at Washington University.

and careers. Approximately one third of the University's living graduates live in the greater St. Louis region. They contribute much to our community, and the University's new graduates continue to be well represented in all walks of life. Recruiting talented students, faculty, and staff to Washington University and St. Louis is a vital contribution to our community,…arguably, the most important contribution in this era. The University's impact is enhanced by the work of its students, faculty, alumni, and staff. The "products" from the University include its scholarly and creative works, and these certainly also have impact. During my tenure as chancellor we have contributed significantly, for example, to sequencing the human genome, and the results will certainly have enduring consequences. But this and other scholarly products stem from the efforts of the people of the University. The graduates are the key

products of the University; they amplify dramatically the importance of the faculty, students, and staff of our day. Because they have been educated in a way and in a setting that prepares them to be leaders of society, our graduates are making critical contributions in St. Louis, the nation, and the world. Every class of new graduates enters a society facing challenges and problems that will yield to approaches learned or inspired by the educational experiences at Washington University.

Every 150-year period in recorded history is rich in advances in the human condition. Washington University's history documented in this book reveals a remarkable record of accomplishment in bringing benefits to society. From a humble academic mission to today's comprehensive undergraduate, graduate, and professional programs in Architecture, Art, Arts & Sciences, the John M. Olin School of Business,

Engineering & Applied Science, Law, Medicine, and the George Warren Brown School of Social Work, the University has made contributions across a broad spectrum of society's interests and needs. The scholarly resources include great books, media, and prized works of art, and an information infrastructure to access them. Indeed, University leaders of the past and present have maintained a good balance between focusing on the work of the present and building the infrastructure and resources to support future advances. The promise for the future has grown even as the integral of achievement and the scope of current activities have grown. In financial terms the University enjoys one of the strongest endowments among American research universities. The campus itself, located in downtown St. Louis at our founding, was moved to its current location at the western edge of Forest Park through the foresight of one of our most significant leaders, Robert S. Brookings. In its 100-year history the Hilltop Campus that Brookings and his colleagues envisioned has been developed into one of the most beautiful university campuses in America. Opportunities for continued expansion of campus facilities exist and will be needed to fulfill future needs.

Chancellor Mark S. Wrighton

The Medical Campus on the eastern edge of Forest Park has grown dramatically, too. This era promises a rich future for the University, because this is widely regarded as the age of biology, a time rivaling in impact the revolutionary advances in chemistry and physics of the era unfolding about 100 years ago. Today, the University is positioned to emerge as a world leader in the life sciences, especially human and plant biology, owing to its remarkable achievements of the past 50 years in medicine, biomedical research, and plant science. A current goal is realization of the promises to help people and to preserve the environment through advances in molecular-level understanding of living systems. The School of Medicine's research emphasis as we begin the 21st century is to be on diagnosing, managing, and curing disease. For example, the recent launch of the Alvin J. Siteman Cancer Center with our partners BJC HealthCare and Barnes-Jewish Hospital represents one major step toward world leadership in cancer research and patient care. The academic medical centers associated with major American research universities illustrate well the value of our work to the people we serve and who support us. Our School of Medicine is among the largest and strongest in education, research, and patient care.

Our sesquicentennial theme is *Treasuring the Past. Shaping the Future.* Indeed, a great university becomes so because of great people, and our current well-being and future strength have been developed by many who preceded us and shaped our University as we know it today. The work we now do will contribute to shaping the University to serve future generations. I am immensely grateful to all those who have shaped our present and who are now working to shape the future. My predecessor, Dr. William H. Danforth, who served as chancellor for 24 years and a term as chairman of the board, is due our special thanks, for it is he who built our considerable momentum and brought so many together toward common goals and purposes. His work was transforming in a manner exhibited by our founders and by Robert S. Brookings. His legacy is one that has positioned us as one of America's finest research universities. He created a tradition of community and mutual respect, even in the midst of aggressive pursuit of truth, understanding, and new knowledge. He continues to provide inspiration through his work with the University and in our community.

It is a privilege to have had the opportunity to serve as chancellor in an era of such remarkable progress for Washington University, and to be a part of the family of more than 120,000 students, faculty, alumni, and staff who are continuing to make the world a better place. This book illustrates the history of a great university that serves the world and has touched the lives of many who have never been directly involved in its life. But 150 years is just a beginning. Our challenge is to continue to provide that best balance of effort to execute current programs while building future potential. The future of the world is made brighter by all those who work and contribute to the progress of Washington University.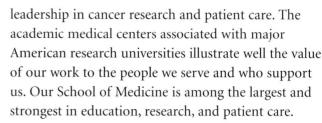

Right: **Archway between January and Ridgley Halls.**
The University's shield appears over the archway with the Latin motto, Per Veritatem Vis, "Strength Through Truth."

Photos, Joe Angeles, WU Photographic Services

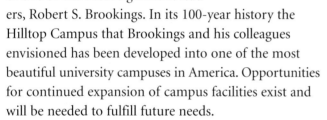

VISION FOR
A UNIVERSITY

1853-1857

———

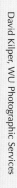

View of St. Louis in 1854.
Drawn by George Hofmann from a daguerreotype by Thomas M. Easterly, engraved by Emille B. Krausse, printed in
New York by W. Pate, and published in St. Louis by Charles A. Cuno, Emille B. Krausse, and George Hofmann in 1854.
Collection of A.G. Edwards and Sons, Inc., St. Louis, Missouri

Vision for a University

On February 13, 1854, ten men gathered in the parlor of a fashionable St. Louis home owned by merchant Wayman Crow. They were meeting as a group for the first time, yet they knew each other well and had a great deal in common. Like Crow, a Kentuckian by birth, most had come to the city as young adults, eager to make their fortunes. Now in early middle age, they were comfortable if not yet wealthy; they had households to support, businesses to nurture, and growing families to educate. Few had much formal education themselves, but they were all generous, altruistic, civic-minded. They were also members of the same Unitarian church, and their pastor, William Greenleaf Eliot, Jr. — a small, delicate man with a colossal social conscience — was their spiritual leader and moral inspiration. On a visit to St. Louis, Ralph Waldo Emerson had met Eliot and called him "the Saint of the West."

1853 ✦ 1857

1853 On February 22, Missouri Gov. Sterling Price signed into law the Charter incorporating Eliot Seminary.

1854 The directors named in the 1853 Charter met for the first time on February 13. O'Fallon Evening School opened on October 22.

1856 On September 8, the University's first new building opened for classes at 17th Street and Washington Avenue.

1857 On February 12, Gov. Trusten Polk signed into law the amended Charter renaming the young school "Washington University."

Wayman Crow (1808-1885). Oil on canvas, c. 1854.
Courtesy of Andrew Leighton and Isabella C. Smythe

William Greenleaf Eliot, Jr. (1811-1887). c. 1850
Missouri Historical Society, St. Louis

Eliot, then 42 years old, had earned this title through a life devoted to good works. In 1834, he had arrived from civilized Boston, a young and untried graduate of Harvard Divinity School, to build a congregation in the rough-and-tumble West. By 1851, he had succeeded so well that his Church of the Messiah, flush with 1,200 members, had just dedicated a new sanctuary at the corner of 9th and Olive in St. Louis. But the church was only the beginning of his labor. Amid his endless pastoral duties, he was deeply involved in community causes, particularly education. In 1841, he had prodded his congregation into founding a Mission Free School for poor, homeless boys. Soon he was serving as board member, then president, of the St. Louis public schools, and instigating passage of a city property tax to give them adequate funding.

CO-FOUNDERS OF THE UNIVERSITY

A new educational venture was what brought him to this wintry meeting at the home of Wayman Crow, his parishioner and close friend for nearly 20 years. Their friendship was unlikely, given their many differences. While Eliot was diminutive, Crow was tall, with a commanding manner; while Eliot was an intellectual, who had traded ideas with Boston transcendentalists, Crow was a self-educated man, whose schooling had ended when he was 12 years old; while Eliot was a man of the cloth, Crow was a man of business, who was rapidly building one of the largest wholesale dry goods companies in St. Louis. Yet Crow and Eliot shared other, more binding qualities. They were both energetic and large-spirited, with strong mutual respect and an

Letter to Eliot from Wayman Crow.
This postscript first informed William Greenleaf Eliot of the Charter to incorporate Eliot Seminary.
WU Archives

Home of Wayman Crow on Olive.
The first meeting of the Eliot Seminary directors took place here on February 13, 1854.
WU Archives

unshakable dedication to public service. Crow, who had helped Eliot organize the Mission Free School and reorganize the public schools, had twice been elected to the Missouri state senate.

In the previous year, near the close of his last term of office, Crow had presented Eliot with a most surprising gift. At the end of a February 2, 1853, letter to Eliot about assorted bills and bits of news, he added a postscript:

"If you see notice of a charter to incorporate the 'Eliot Seminary' — don't condemn me for using the title — it is rather a favorable time to get acts of incorporation and I avail of it, as our Society may desire to have the privilege of establishing such an institution at some day, and this can be partially organized and held in reserve."

Years later, reflecting on this action, he said that he had drawn up the Charter of this new seminary "without consultation with others." Eliot remembered that Crow had modeled his bill on another charter, drawn up by a fellow senator, which had struck him as particularly good. Certainly he had not discussed the matter in advance with Eliot, who noted in his journal on February 22, 1853, that: "An 'Eliot Seminary' has been incorporated by [the] present legislature, but I know nothing of it." Just as certainly, Crow must have known from long association with Eliot that such an action would be acceptable, even welcome. On the same day that Eliot made this notation in his journal, Gov. Sterling Price signed Crow's Charter into law, and Eliot Seminary was born.

His senate session concluded, Crow returned to St. Louis on March 1, 1853, with three items involving Eliot: a large grant from the legislature for another of Eliot's cherished projects, the State Institute for the Blind; a commission for Eliot as a curator of the State University at Columbia; and

the new seminary Charter. Eliot must have read this last document quickly and with interest, for on March 2 he wrote in his diary that "it is very liberal and full and will be worked up in some way before long." Much later, he recalled that:

"It took us by surprise, and, at first thought, caused some amusement; for none of us had dreamed of such a thing, and an educational enterprise seemed quite beyond our strength. But, upon examination of the charter, it was found to be a document of extraordinary merit, and capable of the grandest use. Its possession constituted a divine call; and, after talking it over for a year, we determined to organize it, and go to work."

The "we" of Eliot's recollection were 17 men whom Crow had named in the Charter as directors of this nascent institution. Ten of them made up the group that assembled in Crow's home, almost exactly a year after the Charter was adopted, for their first official meeting as a board of directors. During this year, they had not been idle; as Eliot said, they had been talking among themselves and discussing what to do next. Characteristically, Eliot had done most of all. In a July 1853 journal entry, he noted that he was in the midst of founding "an Educational Institute under charter of 'Eliot Seminary': to consist of Male and Female and Industrial Departments. It will require large Endowment."

All of these men, even Eliot, must have had some qualms about embarking on this new venture; they had little time and heavy responsibilities. But they saw a need for an institution of higher learning, and they were intrigued by the breadth of the Charter, which gave them exciting scope for their plans. As Eliot later put it:

"The puzzle at first was where to begin. The whole educational field was open before us, unoccupied except by the public schools, a few indifferent private seminaries....Our charter authorized us to establish anything we pleased, to hold an unlimited amount of property free from all taxation, and direct our affairs according to our own judgment. We determined not to let such privileges die for want of use. It looked like rashness or over-ambition, but has proved to be of the highest prudence."

Gov. Sterling Price (1809-1867).
When the Missouri governor signed Wayman Crow's Charter into law on February 22, 1853, he made possible the establishment of Eliot Seminary — and Washington University.
Missouri Historical Society, St. Louis

A "DAY OF SMALL BEGINNINGS"

The ten men in attendance that evening quickly went to work. One of them was Samuel Treat, judge of the U.S. Court for the District of Missouri. Years afterwards, he called that eventful evening a "day of small beginnings," and remembered, with a touch of nostalgia, the exciting conversation that took place.

"With what distinctness, at this moment, the consultations of that hour well up in the memory! — the free interchange of views concerning the educational wants of the West and of the age, the proper mode of giving force and living energy to the practical thoughts entertained — the policy or impolicy of an early effort, — whence would come the necessary funds to place such an enterprise beyond the reach of failure."

As men of business, they were thoroughly pragmatic, but they were also concerned about the future of the Mississippi Valley in the absence of powerful civilizing forces that could tame the diverse, fast-growing population. The West, Treat added, was "a seething caldron into which so many ingredients have been thrown." It was urgently necessary to develop "some directing and re-creative power to preside over and give shape, beneficent vitality and healthfulness to the resulting compound."

Finally, though, it was the promise of preliminary funding that carried the day. Col. John O'Fallon, one of the city's wealthiest residents but not yet a director, had pledged two prime blocks of land — worth $25,000 already and rapidly gaining in value — for the proposed Industrial School. This generous gift, recalled Treat, "coming as it did at the turning point in the enterprise, gave it the required firmness and certainty. What only a few evenings before no one had probably regarded, save as a good to be slowly and cautiously reached in the uncertain future, had most unexpectedly received vitality and proportions."

So the assembled board members began to plan in earnest. They listened to a reading of the school's new Constitution, which had been drafted by Eliot and Treat, the only two college graduates on the board; next they elected their officers. As president, they named William Greenleaf Eliot; as vice president, Wayman Crow. No election for either office was necessary again for decades, since each man would fill this role for the rest of his life.

President Eliot proceeded quickly to a plan of action. He asked his directors to agree that a Collegiate Department should be established whenever they could raise the first $50,000 of an endowment. An Industrial School, named for Colonel O'Fallon, would open, too, as soon as they could secure $10,000 to supplement his gift of land. And, in an optimistic touch, three board members were empowered to create a subscription fund to support Eliot Seminary.

Eliot had another, more personal matter to settle. He appointed a subcommittee of two — again himself and Treat — to choose a name other than his own for this fledgling seminary. Modesty must have played a large part in his resistance; Eliot would spend a lifetime deflecting credit from himself to others. He also believed to his core that church was the proper place for religious instruction, and that narrow, sectarian influences must not taint educational truth. If his name were associated with this new venture, it would have a sectarian cast from the outset. He and Treat were to report back at the next board meeting with a new name in mind.

For this second meeting, held only nine days later, they chose an auspicious date: February 22nd, the first anniversary of incorporation. Once

"An 'Eliot Seminary' has been incorporated by [the] present legislature, but I know nothing of it."

–William Greenleaf Eliot, Jr.

Samuel Treat (1815-1902).
One of the 17 original directors, Judge Treat drafted the new school's constitution with William Greenleaf Eliot, and — again with Eliot — proposed that the name be changed from Eliot Seminary to Washington Institute.
Missouri Historical Society, St. Louis

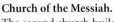

Church of the Messiah.
The second church building of Eliot's growing congregation, located at the northwest corner of 9th and Olive, was dedicated on December 7, 1851.
First Unitarian Church Archives

more the new board assembled, this time with different questions. It was no longer a matter of *whether* to proceed with this new institution — now the directors were wondering *how*? Firmly, Eliot announced the result of his subcommittee's deliberation: The new school should be renamed "Washington Institute," a name suggested, he said, by the coincidence that its Charter had received approval on the anniversary of George Washington's birth.

To a man concerned about implied sectarianism, this new name was the proper antidote. It would set the school on a higher plane, he later said, "upon the broad foundation of Republican and Christian principles, free from the trammels of sect and party" and free from any possible hint of sectionalism or divisiveness. Like most Americans, Eliot stood in awe of George Washington, and par-

ticularly admired Washington's large-spirited 1796 Farewell Address. Inspired by his name, they could "educate the rising generations in that love of country and of our whole country, which the Farewell Address of Washington inculcates, and in that faithfulness to God and Truth which made Washington great," Eliot said.

ELIOT SEMINARY BECOMES WASHINGTON INSTITUTE

It must have been hard for the other board members — as anxious as they surely would have been to honor their pastor and friend — to oppose Eliot's call to pay tribute to Washington, widely revered as the "Father of his Country." Inserting the new name in the proper place within the Constitution, they approved the document unan-

O'Fallon encourages early medical education

John O'Fallon (1791-1865).
WU Archives

A t its February 22, 1856, meeting, the Washington Institute board named two new directors: lawyer Thomas T. Gantt and Dr. Charles A. Pope, eminent surgeon and

St. Louis Medical College.
This neoclassical structure, located at Clark and 7th Street, housed the St. Louis Medical College from 1855-92. The building was commonly referred to as "Pope's College."
WU Becker Medical Library

faculty member at St. Louis Medical College and already a lecturer in the O'Fallon Evening School. Pope, who had received his M.D. from the University of Pennsylvania, was a medical prodigy who joined the College at age 25 as professor of anatomy and physiology. By 29, he was chair of surgery, then dean two years later. By 36, he was president of the American Medical Association.

He married Caroline O'Fallon, the only daughter of one of the wealthiest St. Louisans of his day, Col. John O'Fallon, who admired his son-in-law. O'Fallon financed construction of a new College building at 7th and Clark, which Pope then owned until his death in 1870. The St. Louis Medical College later became the Medical Department of Washington University.

Charles Pope (1818-1870).
WU Archives

Thomas T. Gantt (1814-1889).
WU Archives

imously. Together with the Charter, it would soon be issued in a slim booklet that represented the first publication of this new Washington Institute.

As this booklet demonstrates, the Charter was a concise but sweeping document. It was made up of three sections: one naming the 17 "incorporators" and conferring tax-exempt status upon the corporation; a second establishing those incorporators as a board of directors; and a third authorizing these directors to prescribe the course of instruction, hire faculty and staff, and make the school's bylaws.

The Constitution, on the other hand, contained 11 sections dealing with such details as endowing scholarships. Overall, it said, the new Institute would aim to provide "a thorough and complete education, with particular view to practical usefulness." Already its scope had expanded from Eliot's earlier notion of "Male and Female and Industrial Departments." Now the new school would include "a Collegiate Department, a Female Seminary, a Practical and Scientific Department, an Industrial School, and such other departments as devised by the Board." In Eliot's view, the Practical and Scientific side should be particularly prominent, lending "character to all the rest."

At the heart of this Constitution was Article VIII, a clause that Eliot would always refer to with pride. It was designed to guarantee that the new school would remain forever nonsectarian and nonpartisan: that no such test would be used in the hiring of faculty or officers, and that no such restrictions would be allowed in any additions to the endowment. In fact, the board felt so strongly about this matter that in 1857 it would ask the state to amend the original charter to include this provision.

During this February 22 meeting, Eliot gave his first speech as board president and mentioned Article VIII. That rule, he said, "has now become, by our solemn act, unalterable forever." And he spoke broadly and frankly about the drawbacks of embarking on such an important educational

venture. "It is not only the beginning of a great work, capable of indefinite extension, but each step in its progress and the first step in its commencement involve the sacrifice both of time and money," he said.

So why undertake the difficult work of establishing this new Institute? Eliot, like other board members a parent himself, outlined three key motives. First, he said, they needed to educate their own children in a school that offered the best advantages but was also located in St. Louis. Second, they should provide for children in the community who would benefit from a practical education. To accomplish this purpose, Eliot suggested the idea — admittedly experimental — of founding an Industrial School that would give these children a sound, basic education and teach them "such employments as will enable them to earn a respectable living."

Third, he proposed that they would be founding this Institute "for the public benefit." St. Louis was likely to become, he said, "one of the largest and most influential [cities] in the Western Valley. The necessity of laying a broad and substantial foundation for educational…institutions is, therefore, strong and imperative."

AN EVENING PROGRAM OPENS

By 1854, St. Louis was already a very different place in size and appearance from the rough young city of 8,000 that Eliot had first encountered in 1834. Over the succeeding two decades, waves of immigrants had flooded into the city, increasing the population more than tenfold. In 1849, a great fire had destroyed 15 downtown blocks on the riverfront; a cholera epidemic had killed thousands. In the wake of these disasters, St. Louis had responded by rebuilding its business district out of brick and cast iron, installing

George Washington (1732-1799).
The original Eliot Seminary was renamed Washington Institute — and ultimately Washington University — because Washington's name was free from any divisiveness and the Charter was signed into law on George Washington's birthday: February 22.

Painting attributed to J.J. Paradise
WU Gallery of Art

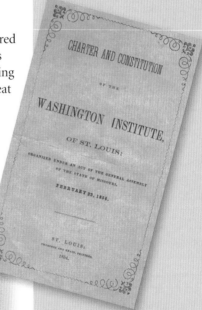

Charter and Constitution.
The first publication of Washington Institute in 1854 contained the Charter drawn up by Wayman Crow and the Constitution detailing the new school's organization. Article VIII assured that the institution would always be nonsectarian.
WU Archives

Article VIII

No instruction. either sectarian in religion, or partisan in politics. shall be allowed in any Department of the Institute, and no sectarian or partisan test shall be used in the election of professors, teachers, or other officers of the Institute, nor small any such tests ever be used in any wise whatever, for any purpose whatsoever. This Article shall be understood as the fundamental condition on which all endowments, of whatever kind, are received.

Famed sculptor Harriet Hosmer learns anatomy at Missouri Medical College with the help of Wayman Crow

In 1850, Harriet Hosmer traveled to St. Louis from her Massachusetts home to visit a former schoolmate, Cornelia Crow, whose father, Wayman, helped Hosmer achieve a long-held goal. With the support of Crow and Joseph N. McDowell, the Missouri Medical College's founder, she gained access to an anatomy course at the college, later part of Washington University School of Medicine, where she received training that helped her become a neoclassical sculptor. In 1854, she gave Crow her first original marble from Rome, *Daphne*, and he commissioned her first monumental marble, *Oenone*

(1854-55). In 1868, she sculpted a bust of Crow, which was unveiled at the 1868 Commencement by Henry Ware Eliot, A.B. '63, son of William G. Eliot. All three Hosmer sculptures are now in the University's Gallery of Art collection.

Harriet Hosmer (1830-1908).
Watertown Free Public Library, Watertown, Massachusetts

Wayman Crow, Sr.
WU Gallery of Art

Oenone, 1854-1855.
Marble, 33⅜ x 34¾ x 26¾"; gift of Wayman Crow, Sr., 1855
WU Gallery of Art

Benton School.
When O'Fallon Evening School opened in 1854, classes were held on 6th Street in the Benton School House, which belonged to the St. Louis public schools.
Missouri Historical Society, St. Louis

a sewer system, and adding civic improvements such as street lighting. Business was growing vigorously, with factories, a bustling levee, new railroads.

With the vast number of newcomers to the city, many of them foreign-born, there was a pressing need for education — both industrial training and basic general courses — conducted outside of normal working hours. As businessmen, the Washington Institute board members were acutely aware of this need. So it is not surprising that the first educational step of the young school, taken by Eliot then approved after the fact by the board, was to open the O'Fallon Evening School on October 22, 1854.

However, the criteria set at the February 13 board meeting had to be met first. The board needed $10,000 in hand, along with Colonel O'Fallon's gift of real estate, before it could launch such a school. In a move that would establish a pattern of support for the young institution, the board members donated the necessary amount themselves. Wayman Crow gave $2,000, five others pledged $1,000 each, and Eliot — who could probably least afford it — made up the last $3,000 out of his own pocket.

Even so, nearly everything required for this new enterprise had to be borrowed from somewhere else. The four faculty members, including Principal Nathan D. Tirrell, came from the public schools and so did the building: the Benton School House on 6th Street, between Locust and St. Charles. Promising a course of instruction that "will embrace mental and written Arithmetic, Algebra, Reading, Grammar, Declamations, and if desirable writing and spelling," newspaper ads invited young men to sign up for classes held on Monday, Tuesday, and Friday evenings. Best of all, tuition was free.

Ninety men registered on the first evening; another 40 on the second. By the end of the first winter session in February 1855, the program had attracted a respectable 270 students, ranging in age from eight to 46. Sixty percent were foreign-born — mostly from Germany, Ireland, and England — and the majority were semi-skilled workers or laborers. The cost of this session, largely for faculty salaries, was $830.

In remarks at the close of the program, Principal Tirrell praised this first attempt and made an impassioned plea to the Institute board to fund another session. "It remains for you to say whether you will cut off the supplies from the fountain, from which so many thirsty souls have taken but *one* draught, or open new and deeper springs that shall well up a purer and more refreshing drink." It must have been hard to resist such rhetoric; the board rated the experiment a success and future sessions went forward.

Eliot must have been pleased at this outcome, though he was disappointed by one piece of the program. As the ads proclaimed, he had contracted with a Professor A. W. Sprague, "well known in the East as a most able lecturer," to give a series of talks on natural philosophy and astronomy. The equipment Sprague needed for his demonstrations was expensive and arrived late; then he charged a hefty fee for his work. While Eliot made the best of the matter to the board, claiming that these lectures had "given dignity to the Evening School," he admitted in his journal: "At tea, Mr. Sprague, to whom I gave check for $500…[I] couldn't help grudging it."

THE SEVENTEEN ORIGINAL DIRECTORS OF ELIOT SEMINARY

Hudson E. Bridge, 1810-1875, stove manufacturer and railroad president

Mann Butler, c.1783-1855, attorney, killed in Gasconade disaster

John Cavender, ?-1863

Wayman Crow, 1808-1885, dry goods merchant; state senator; University co-founder

Nathaniel J. Eaton, 1807-1883, captain, West Point graduate, father was a close friend of George Washington

William G. Eliot, Jr., 1811-1887, minister, Church of the Messiah; University co-founder

William Glasgow, Jr., 1813-1892, wine manufacturer

John How, 1812-1885, businessman; three-time St. Louis mayor

John M. Krum, 1810-1883, lawyer; judge; taught at law school 1868-78

Phocion R. McCreery, 1816-1861, Crow's business partner and nephew

George Partridge, 1810-1890

George Pegram, c. 1816-1877

Seth A. Ranlett, c. 1808-1881, long-time University secretary/treasurer

Christopher Rhodes, 1801-1858

Samuel Russell, c. 1802-1859, wholesale grocer

James Smith, 1820-1877, Smith Academy benefactor

Samuel Treat, 1815-1902, judge, U.S. Court for the District of Missouri

O'FALLON POLYTECHNIC INSTITUTE FOUNDED AS MECHANICS' TRAINING SCHOOL

Undaunted, he noted in the same entry: "Spent an hour this morning, 1-2, in reading the Rules etc. of Franklin Institute of Phil[adelphia]. To see how far they will suit a Reading Room and library to be established under the Industrial Department of Institute." There must have been times in the coming years when he rued the day that he had ever plunged into this effort or met John How, a prominent businessman, St. Louis mayor from 1853-54, and one of the 17 original Eliot Seminary directors. How, talented but arrogant and impetuous, had once been a Franklin Institute apprentice and was determined to found a similar mechanics' training school in St. Louis. He and some friends had already rented space in a downtown building.

Deciding that his school should affiliate with a larger institution, How approached Washington Institute. In March 1855, the board accepted his offer of a library and reading room, placing them under the aegis of a nine-member board of managers. At the same meeting, the Institute board signaled a small change in its own educational vision by splitting the proposed Practical and Scientific Department into two parts. The new Practical Department, it said, would deal with the "education of those who are preparing for mechanical, agricultural, and other industrial pursuits, or who are already engaged in them." Future sessions of the evening school would fall under this department's jurisdiction, as would John How's new mechanics' institute.

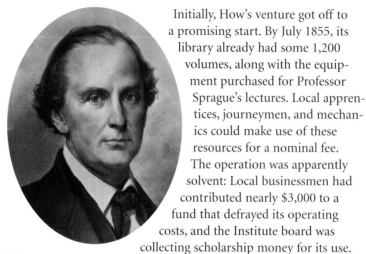

John How (1812-1885).
An original director, How gave Washington Institute a library and reading room. In 1855, he established O'Fallon Polytechnic Institute as part of Washington Institute.

WU Archives

Initially, How's venture got off to a promising start. By July 1855, its library already had some 1,200 volumes, along with the equipment purchased for Professor Sprague's lectures. Local apprentices, journeymen, and mechanics could make use of these resources for a nominal fee. The operation was apparently solvent: Local businessmen had contributed nearly $3,000 to a fund that defrayed its operating costs, and the Institute board was collecting scholarship money for its use. In August, the managers of this new library and reading room decided to call it the "O'Fallon Polytechnic Institute," in honor of Col. John O'Fallon, the Washington Institute benefactor who had been elected a board member.

This name hinted at bigger plans for the new enterprise. Now How and his managers began to dream of an annual manufacturing exhibition, a school of design, and a mathematical class. Without consulting the Washington Institute board, the O'Fallon Polytechnic managers voted in August to expand their membership to 20, adding such prominent citizens as engineer James B. Eads and lawyer Edward Bates, who later served as President Abraham Lincoln's attorney general. Soon they assumed control of Washington Institute's O'Fallon Evening School and, in October 1855, successfully launched its second, four-month session. Volunteer faculty from the St. Louis Medical College offered a new series of practical and scientific lectures, among them chemistry professor Abram Litton and prominent surgeon Charles A. Pope.

At a Washington Institute board meeting in February 1856, President Eliot noted that the once-modest library and reading room venture had changed significantly, greatly enlarging its "general plan of action." First intended as one piece of the Practical Department, it had since, in effect, *become* the department. He recommended, perhaps with some private misgivings, that the board sanction all these steps retroactively. It did so, and by September 1856, he could simply note in his diary: "Industrial Dept., (O'Fallon Institute), doing well."

Seth A. Ranlett (c.1808-1881).
A founding director, Ranlett served as the first secretary/treasurer of the board.

WU Archives

THE BIRTH OF OTHER DEPARTMENTS

While the Practical Department was gaining strength through the O'Fallon Polytechnic Institute, other Washington Institute departments were beginning to take shape. One was the proposed Collegiate Department which, as the undergraduate liberal arts division, would lie at the heart of the young school. In June 1854, four months before the opening of the evening school, the board's scholarship committee reported the joyous news that it had $31,000 in Collegiate Department scholarship funds in hand. Wayman Crow had established the only perpetual scholarship, at a cost of $5,000; James Smith had endowed the only 50-year scholarship, for $2,000. They, along with ten other board members and friends, donated the rest: two dozen 25-year scholarships at $1,000 each.

With this strong beginning toward the minimum requirement of a $50,000 endowment, the board decided to move ahead, authorizing construction of a Collegiate Department building at a cost of $20,000. It would be located on a lot the board had recently purchased at the southwest corner of 17th Street and Washington Avenue, near the fashionable residential district where most of the members lived. They named a subcommittee — including Eliot and Seth Ranlett, who soon became the board's long-standing volunteer secretary/treasurer — and charged it with developing a plan for this new department so that it would be "in full action" a year hence, in September 1855.

This subcommittee must have worked briskly, for in an October 1854 newspaper article, President Eliot described the new curricular plan it had devised. The school, he wrote, would now have a "scientific and classical school…in which a complete collegiate or scientific education can be obtained." At a board meeting several months later, he elaborated further. This new department, which would encompass the Collegiate Department, was intended to provide a strong education for young men in the higher branches of learning. A preparatory school for this department might be added subsequently.

But the building plans hit a snag. Early in 1855, the board reviewed projected costs for the Collegiate Department building and decided it would have to hold off. Then a lower estimate came in — $18,011 — and in July the members voted to begin construction on the plain but substantial three-story brick structure in the Italian Renaissance style. Work progressed slowly, and the building was only ready for its first students a year later, in September 1856. In the end, the cost was more than anyone had expected: $30,000, including furnishings.

And when it was finished, this new building did not house the Collegiate Department after all. A different course was set at a board meeting on February 22, 1856 — the third anniversary of the Charter's approval by the governor — when the members once again discussed plans for Washington Institute. Financially, things were looking up. Not only did the Institute now have an endowment worth $51,000, but it also had real estate holdings valued at $115,000: the O'Fallon gift, now worth $40,000; the new building and its lot worth another $40,000; and a $35,000 home and lot between Washington and Locust previously owned by Eliot's late friend, William Beaumont, a renowned researcher, known for his ground-breaking studies of human digestion.

Accumulating wealth only conferred a stronger moral responsibility for the new venture. The "classical" — or liberal arts — part of the program, Eliot said, was particularly crucial. "Everything depends upon the proper commencement of this

Department, and great care should be taken to avoid any false step." He recommended the appointment of a new Committee on Education to consider such vital questions as the organization of this department, the kind of curriculum it would offer, the faculty it would engage, and its tuition fees.

The committee would also consider the scientific side of the program, he said, but meanwhile he had some recommendations. While eventually he wanted to endow and fill professorships in every branch of theoretical and practical science, he proposed beginning with two: one in civil engineering and the other in chemistry. To fund each fully would take $20,000, but even half that amount, he said, "would make it safe to begin." The board would then have an assured $1,000 return toward the likely $1,500 or $2,000 salary.

This Committee on Education, chaired by Eliot, went on to produce a report whose findings became part of the school's first-ever catalogue in 1856-57.

William Beaumont (1785-1853). A pioneer surgeon and physiologist, Beaumont was among the first American scientific medical researchers. He is best known for the first direct observation of the physiology of digestion.
WU Becker Medical Library

Gasconade train disaster injures co-founder and Washington Institute directors

On November 1, 1855, 600 St. Louisans had boarded a special train to celebrate the completion of the Pacific rail line as far as Jefferson City. En route the train crossed the Gasconade River where the temporary trestle bridge collapsed, plunging the train into the river. Thirty-one St. Louisans were killed and another 70 injured. The mayor declared November 5 a day of fasting and prayer.

The Washington Institute board was seriously affected by this accident. Not only was board member and attorney Mann Butler killed, but

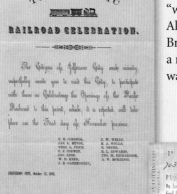

Wayman Crow was "badly hurt and confined to the house two months," wrote Eliot in his journal. Samuel Treat, though injured, had heroically taken command of rescue efforts and "distinguished himself by his labors," while John How "went up to deliver what assistance he could." Although he was in the engine cab, Hudson Bridge, president of the rail line and later a major benefactor to Washington University, was injured but miraculously survived.

Special train. An announcement (left) and ticket for the railroad celebration that ended in disaster.
Missouri Historical Society, St. Louis

Abram Litton (1814-1901). Litton taught chemistry and physics at the University until he resigned in 1892, at 78 years old. He then received the honorary LL.D. degree in recognition of his service. He was so versatile in his teaching ability that Eliot called him a "man of all work."
WU Archives

Joseph J. Reynolds (1822-1899). An 1843 West Point graduate, Reynolds was the first to hold the Eliot Professorship of Mathematics, Mechanics, and Civil Engineering, established by Wayman Crow.
CivilWarIndiana Archive

It described a school with four departments — Academic, Collegiate, Scientific, and the O'Fallon Polytechnic Institute (Practical Department) — and lavished attention on the Academic Department, which would offer an elementary- and secondary-level program. If boys passed a qualifying examination, it said, they could be admitted to the eight-year curriculum beginning at age ten. The course work would be thorough, even daunting; in the area of language, for instance, boys would master German, French, Latin, and Greek. Still, the catalogue announced, without a touch of irony, that this was a liberal system of instruction, "under which neither Pupil nor Teacher will be overworked." Tuition was $40 a term.

The catalogue heralded another aspect of the program: The school had "the advantage of not being encumbered with the dormitory system, which has been proved by experiment to be both expensive and troublesome." Students would continue to live with their parents or, if they came from a distance, board with private families — and in that way stay away from temptation. "It is far better for the young to remain under the parental roof as long as practicable," it said.

The Collegiate Department only received a brief mention — a hint that the Committee on Education had recommended postponing its establishment until enough students had moved up through the Academic Department to create the necessary demand. Plans for a Scientific Department, modeled on Harvard University's Lawrence Scientific School, were moving forward, too. At its April 1856 meeting, board members voted to designate the proposed engineering chair as the "Eliot Professorship," and seek an endowment of $10,000 to support it. They would raise $10,000 for the chemistry

chair and ask Professor Abram Litton to fill it, even though he would demand a suitable laboratory and equipment. Neither was in hand, but they appointed him anyway — and so Professor Litton became, on paper at least, the first member of the faculty.

By the time of the board's June meeting, Wayman Crow had decided to honor his friend by donating a lot at 14th and Olive, worth at least $10,000, to make possible the "Eliot Professorship of Mathematics, Mechanics, and Civil Engineering." The person chosen to fill it was Joseph J. Reynolds, an 1843 West Point graduate and faculty member. At this same meeting, two other men were appointed to the Scientific faculty: Charles A. Pope, the surgeon and board member; and George Engelmann, an obstetrician and botanist, who later advised Henry Shaw on the planning of Shaw's Garden.

When the school's first building was finally ready for students on September 8, 1856, it was the Academic Department — not the Collegiate, Scientific, or Practical departments — that filled it. The initial enrollment was gratifying: 87 boys with "good prospect of increase," reported the Committee on Education. To staff the program, the board had hired two principals, one of them Nathan Tirrell from the evening school. The new department was solvent, barely. On the revenue side of the ledger, tuition would bring in $6,690; on the expense side, salaries totaled $6,600, plus utilities and other things. The cost overrun on the building itself, now known as "Academic Hall," had been made up from scholarship income.

Still, it was a creditable beginning and Eliot was pleased, noting in his journal that the school was "in fair progress…Academic Department is now in operation. Scientific Department organized and goes in operation Oct. 1." He also noted that Litton's laboratory — the institution's second building — was under construction at 17th and Washington, and he had personally guaranteed its financing: "Chemical laboratory in progress at estimated cost of $10,000, which I have undertaken at individual risk."

Much more work remained, as he well knew. In a late-September journal entry, he mentioned, with a touch of weariness but with determination, his plans for fall fundraising campaigns on behalf

Academic Hall. The first building completed on the University's original downtown campus, Academic Hall opened for classes on September 8, 1856.
WU Archives

View of St. Louis in 1853.
Drawn by Frederick Piercy,
engraved by Charles Fenn,
and published in London
by F.D. Richards, Liverpool,
for Jas. Linforth in 1855.

Collection of A.G. Edwards and
Sons, Inc., St. Louis, Missouri

of his church, his ministry to the poor, and finally
Washington University. "University will be a
heavy care, for an immense amount of money is
needed and everything depends on my exertions,"
he wrote. "This year ought to find at least $50,000
of Endowment, and I mean that it shall."

"UNIVERSITY IS A GREAT WORD"

In this entry, he was entitled to use the term "Washington University" because the young school had
recently undergone yet another name change. In
fact, the whole naming issue had been problematic
from the start. First it was called Eliot Seminary,
then Washington Institute, but before the board
could complete the legal process of altering the
Charter, two legislators obtained approval for a rival
institution to be called "Washington College."
Temporarily outflanked, Washington Institute turned
into the "O'Fallon Institute" for a brief period in
1855-56, until these "mean men," as Eliot called
them in his journal, decided to give up their charter,
and the "Washington" name again became available.

So at the same February 22, 1856, meeting
that established the important Committee on
Education, board members wrestled one last time
with the name question. They wanted a name,
they said, that would "express correctly the
breadth and scope of the educational design of
the founders." Clearly the name "Washington"
had grown on them, and perhaps their brief

period without it had given it a special allure. But
Washington *what*? Perhaps in tribute to the growing accomplishments and ambitions of the young
program, Samuel Treat suggested "Washington
University," and his motion passed.

The next step involved amending the Charter
to reflect this new name, which meant applying to
the state legislature at its next session. Meanwhile,
the board adopted Washington University for its
own use, and Gov. Trusten Polk finally signed the
new name into law on February 12, 1857.

Curiously, Eliot himself — who had done more
than anyone else during those first crucial years to
nudge the young school forward — had some qualms
about this change. "University," after all, implied a
much broader, more ambitious undertaking than
terms such as "college" or "school," "seminary" or
"institute" did. Perhaps Eliot worried that he
would be the one largely responsible for making
this broader conception a reality. University-
building was a mighty vision, yet it was a
daunting task.

Years later he recalled the name change and
admitted that he had felt some misgivings then
and for a long time thereafter. "[T]he suggestion of
University was made by Judge Treat.…It seemed
to me, at the time, to savor not a little of Western
grandiloquence, and to say the truth I have not
entirely overcome that feeling yet," he wrote, still
awestruck at the giant task ahead, "for University
is a great word." Ⓦ

CHAPTER TWO

GROWING
PAINS

1857-1871

A treasure trove of early history. In 1992, then-graduate student James Robertson, A.M. '84, Ph.D. '93, found a significant collection of official University records in a seldom-used treasurer's vault in Brookings Hall. These documents cover the first four decades (1850s-1880s) of the institution, prior to its move from downtown to the Hilltop Campus. WU Archives

GROWING PAINS

"With a degree of pleasure which I cannot adequately express, and with feelings of profound gratitude to Him without whose blessing none can thrive, I welcome you here this day, to take part in the Inaugural Exercises of Washington University." With these words, Rev. William Greenleaf Eliot, president of the board of directors, greeted visitors assembled for the University's gala inaugural celebration on April 22, 1857.

He and his fellow board members had spent four years laying the groundwork for this day, but they must have doubted that it would ever arrive. It was a day for exuberance and gratitude, for pride and humility, for reflections on the past and fond hopes for the future. With this crowd of wealthy St. Louisans before him, it was a day on which Eliot could not resist hinting that more money would be welcome.

Previous pages:
Academic Hall.
The University's
first building
was completed
in 1856.

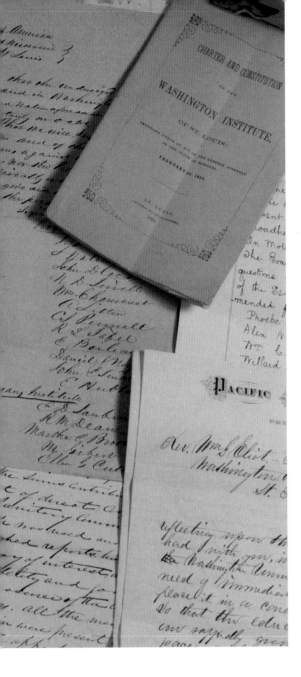

1857   *Washington University held its inaugural celebration on April 22.*

1858   *On October 11, the board of directors approved a resolution creating the office of chancellor.*

1859   *Joseph Gibson Hoyt became the University's first chancellor in February; his inauguration took place on October 4.*

1862   *The first Collegiate Department students received their bachelor's degrees at Commencement, then immediately formed the first Alumni Society.*

1867   *In August, the directors established the "St. Louis Law School" within the University.*

1869   *The Law School admitted its first two women students: Phoebe Wilson Couzins and Lemma Barkeloo.*

Inaugural program.
The University's gala inaugural celebration took place on April 22, 1857.
WU Archives

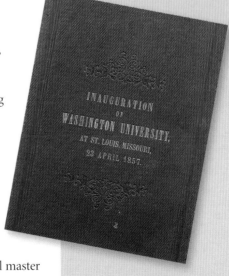

And it was a day on which every speaker could be forgiven a bit of grandiose rhetoric.

The festivities began with morning exercises held in the lecture room of Academic Hall, the University's only building. With the entire board of directors seated on the platform behind him, Eliot traced the University's brief history, praising Wayman Crow warmly as the "sole originator" of its charter and saying that "the existence of the University is primarily due to him." He spoke proudly of the Charter itself as broad and non-sectarian, concluding that:

"The time has now arrived when we may, as we think, without arrogance, claim the right of being inaugurated, — to take a humble place, which we hope may become, in the course of years, an exalted place, among the Educational Institutions of the land."

Next Jeremiah Low, principal of the Academic Department, described his young program, in which 100 boys from age ten on were enrolled in an eight-year course of English, French and German, history, mathematics, the mechanic arts, and physical sciences. Students began Latin in the fourth year and Greek in the fifth; the study of the classics, Low said, imparts a mental discipline that "we cannot afford to lose." He summed up: "We desire not so much that the pupil shall master the book as the subject; not so much to learn many things as to learn much."

Rev. Truman Marcellus Post (1810-1886).
At the University's inaugural exercises, Post — a new history professor — was one of several speakers. His descendants became distinguished ophthalmologists in the medical school.
First Congregational Church of St. Louis (United Church of Christ)

Washington University seal.
This version of the seal was first used in 1866.
WU Archives

Edward Everett (1794-1865).
A noted orator, Everett gave the keynote address, "Academical Education," at the grand inaugural ceremony.
Courtesy of Boston Public Library, Print Department

John How, president of O'Fallon Polytechnic Institute — which constituted the University's Practical Department, a major piece of the young school — spoke next. Over the past three winters, he said, the Institute's evening school had admitted nearly 1,400 scholars. Its daytime session was preparing students to enter the third branch of the University's program: its newly formed Scientific Department. In time, he predicted lavishly, O'Fallon might rival the polytechnic institutes of Berlin and Vienna. Perhaps in sly expectation of a secret to be divulged later that day, he added that a new building for the Institute would be most welcome.

Several more speakers followed, including a new member of the faculty: Rev. Truman Marcellus Post, minister of First Congregational Church. The only full professor in the Academic Department, appointed just a month earlier to teach ancient and modern history, he soon became the first professor in the still-nascent Collegiate Department. On this day, Post touched on two themes dear to Eliot's heart. He was gratified, he said, that "God has bestowed on those among us to whom He has given princely fortunes, a disposition to employ them for princely uses." He was pleased, as well, that the University had no "ecclesiastical" affiliation, but was established on "a catholic and general basis, on which fellow-citizens whose walk in life may be…somewhat different, can unite."

Festive though the morning ceremony was, it paled by comparison with the afternoon session, held in the grand Mercantile Library Hall at 5th and Locust streets. The board had taken no chances with attendance, placing notices in every newspaper. Now 2,000 people were gathered, as Eliot rose to speak. Again he described the University's progress, especially its new chemical laboratory, which would be ready by September. He revealed his broad new vision for the school. Along with a fourth department — the Collegiate or undergraduate department — he now dreamed of fifth and sixth pieces of the program: departments of law and of fine arts.

Then he made three startling announcements. First came the news that banker James Yeatman was giving a "superior equatorial telescope" to the University at a cost of $1,500. Second, Eliot declared that John How himself, one of the city's "mechanic princes," was prepared to spend up to $30,000 on a lot for a new O'Fallon Polytechnic Institute building. But Eliot had saved the latest-breaking news for last: The University's "largest benefactor" — unnamed by Eliot but widely known to be Col. John O'Fallon — had just buttonholed Eliot to say that he was giving the University real estate worth at least $27,000. That meant the University now had an impressive $200,000 in property — though, Eliot added hopefully, "the endowments of professorships…and a general productive endowment… are yet to be obtained."

At last, Eliot introduced the principal speaker for the day, a "national man…who belongs not to one State but to the Union of States: EDWARD EVERETT of America." This was the moment the crowd had been waiting for. Everett, then 63, was a distinguished man at the pinnacle of his career. Like Eliot, he was a Unitarian minister and Harvard Divinity School graduate; just as Eliot would later do at Washington University, Everett had become Harvard's president. He had also been a politician who had served as a congressman, governor, senator, and secretary of state. In 1855, he had decided to help save Mount Vernon, the decaying home of George Washington, and embarked on a nationwide tour to raise money for this project.

Everett ranked, along with Henry Clay and Daniel Webster, among the nation's three greatest orators — the "Cicero of Boston," one newspaper called him. In 1863, he would give a two-hour oration at Gettysburg that was upstaged by President Abraham Lincoln's brief, eloquent address. Invited to this inauguration — probably because of his reputation, his interest in George Washington, his moderate political views amid the building North-South tension, and his longstanding friendship with Eliot — he had prepared another blockbuster speech entitled "Academical Education." In it, he traced the exploration of the West and ended, majestically:

"Go on, then, my friends, in your praiseworthy undertaking….Complete your already liberal endowments. Fill your departments with able and faithful instructors. Establish on a permanent basis a…great school of literature, science, and the arts….Remember… the frugal legacy that gave being to Harvard, the few precious volumes that founded Yale; not doubting…that the seminary you are now founding will take rank hereafter with those venerable patriarchs. Let these tender associations [with the East] give strength to the sacred bond of brotherhood which unites us, and before the dark day shall arrive that witnesses its rupture, may these eyes be closed beneath the sod."

JOSEPH HOYT BECOMES THE UNIVERSITY'S FIRST CHANCELLOR

Perhaps unwittingly, Everett had touched on the very themes that would recur throughout the University's early, difficult years: the wrenching financial worries; the arrival — and departure — of able, underpaid faculty members; the herculean task of establishing a great school devoted to the liberal arts; the struggle to convince the city's elite to educate their sons (and soon their daughters) locally, not in the East; and the growing sectional conflict that was about to engulf the country and have a devastating impact on St. Louis, a deeply divided city within a border state.

A year after the inauguration, Washington University's three departments were doing well. The Academic Department had doubled in size. John How had kept his promise, donating a lot at the corner of 7th and Chestnut streets for a grand O'Fallon Polytechnic Institute building; construction began in the summer, as a major fundraising drive got under way. The Scientific Department, too, had received a boost with the completion of Abram Litton's new laboratory, though at a far greater cost than expected. Out of his own pocket, Eliot had defrayed the additional expense.

In September 1858, Washington University finally launched, a little shakily, its long-awaited Collegiate Department which corresponded, said the catalogue vaguely, "very nearly to the Freshman, Sophomore, Junior, and Senior classes of American Colleges." The Collegiate courses were not listed separately, but were still under the Academic Department, and the only faculty member assigned to this department was still Professor Post. There were several students enrolled, however, including Eliot's oldest son, Thomas Lamb Eliot.

Meanwhile, Eliot had returned to a question that he had first raised in 1856: the need to appoint a full-time chancellor who had no "other laborious occupation to occupy his thoughts." The new head should have a strong reputation, said Eliot, and should be "practical in mind, scientific in attainments, and popular in manners" — a combination, he admitted, "as rare as it would be valuable." On October 11, the board approved a resolution creating the office of chancellor, and a day later, seven of the board members — led by Wayman Crow, Thomas Gantt, James Smith, and J.B. Lucas — pledged to pay the $3,000 salary themselves.

By the December board meeting, the Committee on Education had a candidate in mind: Joseph Gibson Hoyt, a New Hampshire native and brilliant scholar. Despite the refusal of his father to pay for his education, Hoyt managed to attend Yale University and graduate with high honors, sixth in his 100-member class. Afterwards, he spent 18 years as a respected professor of mathematics and natural philosophy at Phillips Exeter Academy in Exeter, New Hampshire, where he became known as an eminent Greek scholar. Educational issues were his special interest. For the town of Exeter, he designed a model schoolhouse, and at Phillips Exeter he played a major role in revising the curriculum.

These skills would come in handy at Washington University, where he assumed the duties of chancellor in February 1859; a professorship of Greek literature was later added to his title. Right away, he found several problems that cried out for a firm hand. The boys of the Academic Department, he wrote to a colleague, were "a fine set of fellows, the very cream of the city," but they were used to bringing "altogether too much of the democracy of their homes and of the streets into the schoolroom. I have already astonished a few of them with slight exhibitions of monarchical authority which would have done no discredit to an eastern despot."

In a city growing so rapidly, with so many "avenues of wealth" open to young men, he wrote, it was hard to impress on students the need for "steady, persistent purpose in pursuing a course of study to the point of graduation." Even the few

Joseph G. Hoyt (1815-1862). After his death, the board passed a resolution expressing deep gratitude for Hoyt's tenure as chancellor: "To his unwearied and cordial devotion…" the directors wrote, "is largely due the success which the University has thus far attained."

Oil on canvas by Ulysses Dow Tenney, gift of Edward R. Hoyt
WU Gallery of Art

1857 Bible. Students gave this Bible to the University during the 1857 inaugural ceremonies. It was rebound by the Class of 1907 and presented to the University as a class gift.
WU Libraries' Special Collections

with a scholarly bent "catch the spirit of the hurrying street and chafe at the thought of an eight-year indoor pupilage." Yet he was determined, he said, to "develop from this academic soil a *College*," despite the shocking state of the curriculum:

"On getting the hang of the Academic Department, the utter want of classification did not so much amaze me as the utter unconsciousness of the fact on the part of the teachers and scholars alike. The number of studies was at least twice as large as it should be, each student apparently thinking it necessary to pursue all the studies taught in the institution in order to get the worth of his tuition fee. Some classes, so-called, of considerable size, contained no two members who recited together in any other class, and all were mixed up like a nest of black snakes in the winter, when you cannot tell to which one of a dozen heads any particular tail belongs."

UNTANGLING SNAKES AND RECRUITING FACULTY

So Hoyt embarked on the job he loved best — educational reform — working to establish the brand-new Collegiate program on a firmer basis with its own full-time faculty. In May 1859, he proposed creating professorships of Greek, mathematics, and rhetoric and oratory, and in June, Washington University appointed its first three assistant professors. One of them, Sylvester Waterhouse, a brilliant but slightly eccentric professor of Greek, had a particular impact on the University.

Waterhouse was Hoyt's former student at Exeter, hired the year before to teach in the Academy. He had physical limitations, due to the loss of a leg and eye in childhood accidents, but a keen intellect. An indefatigable author, he turned out scores of pamphlets on such diverse topics as Mississippi River improvement and the cultivation of jute. He was devoted to Washington University and remained on the faculty for 43 years. Although

The Chauvenet legacy

William Chauvenet (1820-1870).

Oil on canvas by Charles F. von Saltza, gift of Mrs. S. Chauvenet WU Gallery of Art

William Chauvenet, a brilliant mathematician and astronomer and charter member of the National Academy of Sciences, became the second chancellor of Washington University. Sylvester Waterhouse once said of him: "Mr. Chauvenet moved with the ease of genius in the higher walks of mathematical science." His sons, Regis, A.B. '62, A.M. '66, LL.D. 1900; and Samuel, A.B. '71, were graduates. Regis, who had taught mathematics part-time at the University, went on to serve as

Chauvenet plaque.
WU Photographic Services

president of the Colorado School of Mines from 1883-1902; Samuel became president of Universal Road Machinery Co. This plaque (below), a replica of one mounted at the U.S. Naval Academy — which William Chauvenet helped establish — was unveiled on Navy Day, October 27, 1940, and presented to Washington University as a gift of the Academy. It hangs in the arcade near the main entrance to Ridgley Hall.

Samuel (above right) and Regis (above) Chauvenet.
WU Archives

Sylvester Waterhouse (1830-1902).

He taught Greek at the University from 1859 to 1901.

Oil on canvas by Charles F. von Saltza
WU Gallery of Art

his salary never exceeded $2,500, he was a bachelor and lived abstemiously. At his death, he left the University $25,000, stipulating that it be invested for 100 years — and if the value then exceeded $1 million, anything over that first million would be invested for another century.

But Hoyt's greatest coup was snagging William Chauvenet, a Yale College classmate, as the new chair of mathematics and astronomy. Chauvenet, a Pennsylvania native, had mastered Yale's entire mathematics curriculum before matriculating; after graduating Phi Beta Kappa, he did ground-breaking work in astronomy, then became head of the Naval Asylum School in Philadelphia. That school offered only a lean, eight-month course of study, so Chauvenet lobbied for a broader, four-year curriculum. In 1845, his efforts bore fruit when the U.S. Naval Academy in Annapolis was established; he became its first head of mathematics, first librarian, and member of the first Academic Board. For 14 years, he worked to make the Naval Academy the finest institution of its kind in the world.

Other universities were eager to recruit Chauvenet — Yale tried twice, but he turned them down. Meanwhile, his reputation was growing, thanks to seminal treatises on trigonometry and astronomy and his invention of important navigational instruments. Much later he became president of the American Association for the Advancement of Science. After his death, the Naval Academy named a mathematics building for him, and the U.S. Navy christened two ships *Chauvenet*. So why would such an eminent man come to a little-known school in the Mississippi Valley?

On a July 1859 visit to St. Louis, Chauvenet wrote an effusive, slightly giddy, letter home to his wife, Kate, describing St. Louis and his job prospects. The city, he wrote, "is a busy commercial one but yet rapidly refining….It stirs one up to see this city grow." As for the University, he liked its nonsectarian character and saw it as a place to educate his own five children — far better, he told his wife, than "the schools of that congregational mire of New Haven." Clearly, the board had pulled out all the stops to impress him; Dr. Charles Pope ("the pope of Rome is nothing to him," wrote Chauvenet, wryly) drove him out to

University mathematicians receive Chauvenet Prize

In 1925, the Mathematical Association of America named a prestigious award for William Chauvenet: the Chauvenet Prize, which would be awarded annually to one person who demonstrated excellence in mathematical writing. Two University professors have won the award — Guido Weiss (right) in 1967 for an article entitled "Harmonic Analysis" and Steven Krantz (below, second from left) in 1992 for "What is Several Complex Variables?" — as well as a graduate, Kenneth I. Gross, who received his Ph.D. from the University in 1966. Thus, Washington University can claim more Chauvenet Prize winners than any other university.

Guido Weiss.
Now the Elinor Anheuser Professor of Mathematics, Guido Weiss joined Washington University's mathematics faculty in 1961 as an associate professor.
Joe Angeles, WU Photographic Services

Steven G. Krantz.
Chair of the mathematics department in Arts & Sciences, Steven Krantz (second from left) came to Washington University as Professor of Mathematics in 1986.
David Kilper, WU Photographic Services

the palatial country estate of his father-in-law, Colonel O'Fallon. And Chauvenet approved of the board members, whom he called:

"a fine set of men, polished, and yet open and hearty. This Dr. Eliot has himself been the instrument of collecting from the wealthy men of St. Louis not less than five millions of dollars for various charitable and educational institutions. He is…simple and unpretending, but earnest and clear. Everybody seems to love him."

Calvin S. Pennell (1816-?).
When Mary Institute opened in 1859, Calvin Pennell became the headmaster.
Courtesy of MICDS Archives

With Chauvenet and others joining the faculty, Hoyt turned to the thorny curricular problems. He did little to the Scientific Department, but he revamped the Academic Department, now "The Academy," into a six-year program: a two-year preparatory, junior high-type division followed by a four-year high school curriculum offering only four or five classes per term. Next Hoyt tackled the Collegiate Department, establishing it as an independent school with a four-year curriculum leading to a Bachelor of Arts degree. Perhaps because of his own interests, Latin and Greek were still required in seven of the eight semesters; mathematics was strongly represented, as well. To provide a home for the Collegiate Department, he urged the board to consider a new building that would form a "T" with the existing Academic Hall.

On October 4, 1859, Hoyt was inaugurated as the first chancellor of Washington University, and in his address he defined what he meant by a university education. "Of the constituent elements of a true University," he said, "the first and most important is the College," which would give students a solid, liberal arts foundation. With a College at its core, he said, the University could develop other departments, such as art, law, and eventually — a wish that no one else had yet uttered — even a department of medicine.

A FEMALE SEMINARY OPENS

While Hoyt's reorganization was going on, another piece of the University program was just beginning. On May 11, 1859, a new female seminary had been founded: Mary Institute, named for Eliot's beloved oldest daughter, who had died in 1855. The school opened in September 1859, offering a six-year course of instruction much like

that of the Academy, with recitations in the languages, mathematics, and the natural sciences conducted by professors from the Collegiate and Scientific Departments.

Planning for this seminary had begun in earnest in June 1858, when the board authorized Eliot to open a $20,000 subscription for the new program. The campaign was an instant success and soon the fund was oversubscribed. Exchanging the lot donated in 1856 by Wayman Crow for another at Lucas Place (now Locust) and 14th Street, the board moved ahead with construction of a new building, large enough for 100 students, which was ready by the time of the school's opening.

Diploma of Emma Bridge, 1864.
The daughter of Hudson E. Bridge, she was in the first class to graduate from Mary Institute.
Courtesy of MICDS Archives

The rationale for the school, outlined in the 1859 catalogue, was a familiar one. St. Louisans should not have to "send their daughters a thousand miles *away from home for four or five of the most critical years of their life, to be trained by strangers.*" A circular went further: "The design is to…secure an accurate and sound education, not limited or specially directed to the superficial or more showy acquirements, to which too much time is generally devoted in schools for young ladies." This sentiment may reflect the enlightened views of Eliot, who had long advocated treating women as rational beings, capable of intellectual growth. As he wrote in his *Lectures to Young Women*, published in 1854:

> "The limit of education should be fixed not by some arbitrary idea of how much a woman ought to know, or how much it is safe to teach without spoiling her as a…faithful drudge….But the limits of female education should be fixed, as of the man's, by the capacity of the individual scholar and the external means within reach."

1860 FUNDRAISING CAMPAIGN

Since 1857, Eliot had been talking about the need for an endowment to bolster the young University. At Hoyt's inauguration, he became more specific: They would need $100,000 in cash, within the next 12 months. Luckily, Eliot was not alone in his

---

MARY INSTITUTE SCHOLARS WITH FAMOUS NAMES

Mary Institute benefited from the fact that many board and faculty members had young daughters in need of an education. Early catalogues list these students (the father's name is in parentheses):

- Emma Bridge (Hudson)
- Mary Chauvenet (William)
- Harriet Eaton (Nathaniel J.)
- Abby A. Eliot (William G.)
- Mary and Anna Glasgow (William, Jr.)
- Annie Hoyt (Joseph)
- Mary January (Derrick, a board member elected in 1860)
- Anna McCreery (Phocion)
- Caroline O'Fallon Pope (Charles Pope and grandfather Colonel O'Fallon)
- Clara and Kate Post (Truman)
- Miriam A. Tirrell (Nathan, the newly appointed head of the Academy)
- Mary B. Treat (Samuel)

Mary Institute's first building.
Classes opened in 1859 in a building on Lucas Place, at the center of St. Louis's residential area. The building is visible here, adjacent to the steeped church at center. From: *Pictorial St. Louis, the Great Metropolis of the Mississippi Valley: a Topographical Survey Drawn in Perspective, A.D. 1875*. By Camille N. Dry, designed and edited by Richard J. Compton (St. Louis: Compton & Co., 1876).
WU Libraries' Special Collections

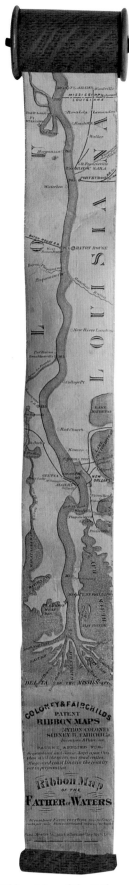

Ribbon Map of the Father of the Waters, 1866.
The linen-mounted map, about 2 inches wide by 129 inches long, shows points along the Mississippi just after the Civil War.
Gift of Mr. Lewis P. Andrews, Jr.
WU Libraries' Special Collections

determination. In a December 1859 letter, board member George Partridge told Eliot that he too considered $100,000 necessary because "of the certainty that for some years to come we cannot hope that…income, if ever, will meet…expences [sic]." Better still, he gave the first $10,000 himself.

That gift was the spark Eliot had been hoping for. A second board member, James Smith, donated $10,000 in real estate, Eliot himself gave $10,000 in cash, and soon four more directors — Wayman Crow, Phocion McCreery, Hudson Bridge, and Thomas Gantt — had given $10,000 each, for a grand total of $70,000. The remainder, however, was more difficult to secure. Eliot approached several wealthy St. Louisans, including one whose sons would go on to graduate from the University — Sarah A. Collier, widow of merchant George Collier — but he had no luck.

At this difficult juncture others might have pulled back, but Eliot responded by increasing the goal of the campaign, aiming for $25,000 more to help pay for the building that Hoyt had suggested.

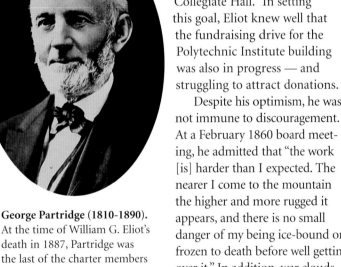

George Partridge (1810-1890).
At the time of William G. Eliot's death in 1887, Partridge was the last of the charter members still serving on the board of directors.
WU Archives

New classrooms, an 800-seat assembly hall, library, offices, and tower to house the Yeatman telescope would all be part of the facility, called "Collegiate Hall." In setting this goal, Eliot knew well that the fundraising drive for the Polytechnic Institute building was also in progress — and struggling to attract donations.

Despite his optimism, he was not immune to discouragement. At a February 1860 board meeting, he admitted that "the work [is] harder than I expected. The nearer I come to the mountain the higher and more rugged it appears, and there is no small danger of my being ice-bound or frozen to death before well getting over it." In addition, war clouds were gathering. "It is a time when prudent men are more prudent than usual, and strong men doubt their own strength," he said. But if they did not press on, Washington University must "begin to be rated…a one-horse college."

Shrewdly, he decided to raise the $25,000 in smaller increments: by offering scholarships at $1,000 each. The strategy worked, and by June

The Collier family connection

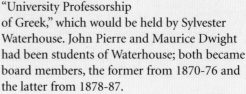

Collier brothers.
WU Archives

In 1860, William Greenleaf Eliot asked Mrs. Sarah A. Collier (1816-1885), widow of tea and coffee importer George Collier (1796-1852), for a donation to the University. She turned him down but later her family was generous. In December 1863, she gave a small gift to commemorate her oldest son's 21st birthday. Then in 1868, four Collier brothers — John Pierre, A.B. '64 (1842-1877); William Bell; Maurice Dwight, LL.B. '69; and Thomas Fassett, A.B. '66 (1848-1868) — gave $25,000 in their father's memory to create a "University Professorship of Greek," which would be held by Sylvester Waterhouse. John Pierre and Maurice Dwight had been students of Waterhouse; both became board members, the former from 1870-76 and the latter from 1878-87.

Two Collier daughters married men with Washington University connections: Mary (1833-1928) married Henry Hitchcock and gave $6,000 to the law school — its first endowment — in 1871; her half-sister Margaret (1839-1912) married Henry's brother, Ethan Allen Hitchcock, grandfather of later University chancellor Ethan A.H. Shepley.

View of St. Louis from Lucas Place.
Color lithograph by E. Sachse and Co., 1865 (with the Collier home in the foreground), and published by Edw. Buehler, St. Louis.
Courtesy of A.G. Edwards and Sons, Inc., St. Louis, Missouri, and Missouri Historical Society, St. Louis

Chester Harding Krum (1840-?).
At his 1860 graduation from the Academy, Krum gave the address, "I am not a Virginian but an American."
WU Archives

the University was near its goal. When the board tried to thank Eliot for his labors, he demurred. True to form, he had a more practical suggestion: raise another $15,000, just to be safe. Instead, the board proceeded with plans to begin the new three-story building, which was completed in September 1861 at a cost of $79,000 — much higher than expected.

In the midst of the 1860 campaign, a costly new venture appeared on the horizon. A group of St. Louis lawyers decided to incorporate a law program, and the board got nervous, believing that the University needed its own law school, they said, to secure "a prestige not otherwise attainable." They charged a committee with studying the matter, and added to it Henry Hitchcock, a prominent lawyer who had joined the board in 1859 and would eventually play a dominant role in establishing the law school.

For the present, political problems were brewing that would postpone such an idea. At the June 1860 Academy graduation, war was already in the air, even in the boys' orations. Charles Heyle spoke on "Pride of Country," while Chester Harding Krum struck a poignantly hopeful note in his address, "I am not a Virginian, but an American."

THE CIVIL WAR BEGINS

On April 12, 1861, the roar of guns at Fort Sumter signaled the start of the Civil War — but sectional rivalry had already reached a minor flashpoint at Washington University. In December 1860, Eliot received a complaint that Chancellor Hoyt had asked his English class to write compositions for and against the South — and had praised the anti-South compositions, while criticizing the anti-North. The matter was "all hum and bosh," grumbled Eliot in his journal.

Still, feelings did run high in St. Louis. In spring 1861, the federal arsenal at Camp Jackson — named for Missouri's secessionist governor Claiborne F. Jackson — was occupied by southern-sympathizing Missouri militia. Then on May 10, Union troops under Gen. Nathaniel Lyon converged on Camp Jackson and captured it, just as an all-school Mary Institute picnic was being held at a park nearby. A group of mothers hurried to the site and whisked their daughters away to safety.

Financially, the University seemed to be entering the war years in a good position, thanks to momentum from the 1860 campaign. On the very day of the Fort Sumter surrender, the board bravely decided to finish paying for the Collegiate building by taking on a $20,000 loan. Six days later, they agreed to buy property from the estate of William Beaumont. In his journal, Eliot said of the purchase: "It is bold at this time of Civil War: but…the University *must not fail*."

Soon the war was affecting academic life at every level. Among the faculty, John M. Schofield — on leave from the army to replace Joseph Reynolds as Eliot Professor of Physics and Civil Engineering — resigned on May 1, 1861, to resume active duty. When General Lyon was killed at the battle of Wilson's Creek in August 1861, Schofield assumed command; later, he was major general and commander of the Union's XXIII Corps during Gen. William T. Sherman's campaign through Georgia. Reynolds himself had a distinguished military career in the Union army, winning honors for gallantry at Missionary Ridge and Chickamauga.

With the city under martial law, the University ended the 1860-61 academic year early. Since donors were now reneging on pledges, the board adopted strong measures to keep the school afloat: trimming two faculty positions, cutting some salaries, freezing Schofield's position, dropping publication of the 1861-62 catalogue. Eliot himself agreed to teach a class in intellectual and moral philosophy, without compensation. Most serious of all, instruction in the Polytechnic Institute was suspended, and construction stopped abruptly on its partly completed building.

John M. Schofield as Major General, U.S.A. (1831-1906). Schofield, briefly a faculty member, was awarded one of the first two honorary LL.D.s at Washington University in 1870. He served as superintendent of West Point from 1876-81 and Secretary of War from 1868-69, retiring in 1895 with the rank of lieutenant general.

Carte de visite photograph by Handy Studio, Washington, D.C., ca. 1865 Missouri Historical Society, St. Louis

Henry Hitchcock (1829-1902). Hitchcock's war experiences, compiled in the book, *Marching with Sherman*, provide an important look at Sherman, whom Hitchcock called "a man of genius." Sherman returned the compliment, saying Hitchcock had been "of infinite assistance." In 2000, Ronald M. Levin was installed as the first Henry Hitchcock Professor of Law.

Daguerreotype by Thomas Easterly. Missouri Historical Society, St. Louis

Camp Jackson.
Lithograph by E. Robyn, c. 1862.
Missouri Historical Society, St. Louis

Enrollment in the other departments did not suffer as much as the board might have feared. By 1862, the student body — largely made up of Academy boys, who were not yet of military age — had only declined by one-third and soon began to recover. However, some students went to war and did not return, among them Daniel F. Chamberlain, a Union corporal who was killed in the battle of Wilson's Creek, and Edward G. Martin, a Confederate soldier killed in other combat. Altogether, three students, said a later report, left school "for the purpose of joining the rebel army, and…one of these was killed in a skirmish within a few days." Charles Branch, an 1862 Collegiate Department graduate, also joined the Confederate Army, serving in the Horse Artillery under Gens. J.E.B. Stuart and Fitzhugh Lee from Gettysburg to Appomatox.

Such divided loyalties among the student body did not reflect any division among the board or faculty members. Led by Eliot, they were a staunchly Union group, and some had personal ties to the Union army. John Cavender worked tirelessly to assist war refugees; his son, John Smith Cavender, was promoted to brevet brigadier general in 1865 for his service at Fort Donelson and Shiloh. Col. Thomas Gantt served on the staff of Gen. George McClellan. Hudson Bridge was a fierce Unionist, who wrote a scathing letter to Mary Institute principal Calvin Pennell when the program for an 1863 event did "not contain a single patriotic song or anthem."

> "In the extraordinary circumstances which surround us, when the very life of our common country is assunder [sic], when traitors and treason abound, it seems to me that whenever occasion offers, we should not fail to renew our devotion to our beloved country…as one of the patrons of the institution under your immediate charge, I take this occasion of expressing my disappointment."

Pennell must have been aghast to receive such blistering criticism from the school's largest donor. His apology, which does not survive, was immediate and likely abject, for Bridge's next letter, written only two days after his first, takes a conciliatory tone. "Your explanation of the cause of the omission complained of is satisfactory," he wrote. "I did not suffer myself for a moment to doubt your patriotism or your loyalty, and am now convinced that I did you injustice."

Board member Henry Hitchcock, an Alabama native, was another strong Union supporter who felt an urgent need to serve. In 1864, his uncle, Gen. Ethan Allen Hitchcock, introduced him to Secretary of War Edwin Stanton, saying, "Here is a young fellow spoiling for a fight." At age 35, Hitchcock joined the Judge Advocate General's staff and was assigned to Gen. William T. Sherman as legal adviser. His letters and diaries, compiled in book form, chronicle Sherman's march to the sea.

Washington University linked to three Civil War generals

Ulysses S. Grant (1822-1885).
Missouri Historical Society, St. Louis

I n August 1859, an unemployed Ulysses S. Grant told his father, who had apparently suggested that he apply to teach at the University, that he stood "no earthly chance. The Washington University…is one of the best endowed institutions in the United States, and all the professorships are sought after by persons whose early advantages were the same as mine, but who have been engaged in teaching all their mature years." He added that the appointment had gone to "the most distinguished man in his department in the country": William Chauvenet.

William T. Sherman, a St. Louis resident after the Civil War, was a great friend of William G. Eliot and remarked once that "The University should have been named for him!" Sherman's son, Thomas Ewing Sherman, graduated from the School of Law in 1878.

William Tecumsah Sherman (1820-1891).
Missouri Historical Society, St. Louis

In October 1947, an *Alumni Bulletin* article reported that Robert E. Lee, a descendant of the Confederate general, had enrolled in the School of Engineering.

ELIOT HELPS ESTABLISH WESTERN SANITARY COMMISSION

Two of the board's most prominent Union men were Eliot and James Yeatman. After the battle at Wilson's Creek, when there was no facility prepared for the wounded arriving in St. Louis, Eliot saw the need for an agency to provide hospitals and other services for soldiers and civilians. At his urging, the Western Sanitary Commission came into being in September 1861, headed by a five-member civilian commission that included four Washington University board members: Eliot; George Partridge; Carlos Greeley, who joined the board in 1864; and Yeatman as president.

Yeatman, a Tennessee native and one-time slave owner, threw himself into this humanitarian work. "If I were called upon to name the six most useful men in St. Louis since 1861," Eliot wrote to him, years later, "I should put you among them, and probably at the head of the list." Under his leadership, the commission built hospitals, maintained hospital ships, assisted civilian refugees, established homes for war orphans, even buried the war dead. Eventually, they focused on freed slaves, helping them find jobs and providing schools for their education. While some support came from the government, the commission relied heavily on private donation — forcing Yeatman and Eliot into heroic new fund-raising efforts.

Against this backdrop of support for the Union, 11 board members and nine faculty signed a loyalty oath in February 1862, as requested by military authorities. They promised to support the Constitutions of the United States and of Missouri, avoid taking up arms against the government, and refrain from giving aid to the enemy.

James Yeatman (1818–1901). He was a merchant, banker, and railroad entrepreneur who headed the Western Sanitary Commission. Gen. William T. Sherman praised the "judicious, sensible and effective way in which he…did his noble work." The epitaph on his gravestone reads: "In Favour with thee, our God, and in perfect charity with the world."
WU Gallery of Art

Overall, day-to-day school life was little disrupted by the war. In October 1862, the administration briefly instituted daily military drills as part of the curriculum. Lacking uniforms or rifles, students were unenthusiastic, and in March 1863 the school abandoned drills in favor of regular physical exercise.

WILLIAM CHAUVENET BECOMES UNIVERSITY'S SECOND CHANCELLOR

Amid these bleak times, the graduation of the first five Collegiate Department students in June 1862 — Henry Anderson; twins Charles and Henry Branch; Eliot's son, Thomas Lamb Eliot; and William Chauvenet's son, Regis Chauvenet — marked a singularly happy moment. The Commencement exercises, held in the new Collegiate Hall, included a heartfelt prayer by Eliot: "From these walls may all party spirit and sectional strife be forever banished, while the duties of Patriotism and Loyalty are faithfully and plainly taught." Immediately afterwards, the graduates met and formed the University's first Alumni Society.

Notably, Chancellor Hoyt was missing from the ceremony. In fall 1860, not long after his arrival, he showed signs of a wasting disease. By spring 1862, he knew he was dying of tuberculosis. In May he wrote to a friend, "My health is no better and probably never will be. At least my physician frankly told me yesterday that my lungs were 'diseased incurably.' It is henceforth simply a struggle to put off the evil day." He tendered his resignation, but the board kindly refused to accept it; instead, it placed him on a leave of absence and paid his usual salary. Eliot, aided by Chauvenet, took over the work of chancellor.

On October 4, Hoyt tried again to resign in a final, poignant letter. "I need not say," he wrote, "that it fills me with inexpressible sadness to feel constrained, at the very noon of life, to ask leave to lay down an office in which I had concentrated every worldly hope and ambition." The board, quietly compassionate, decided to table his request, thus freeing Hoyt's last days of financial worry. The end came on November 26, 1862. In a eulogy, Sylvester Waterhouse recalled that, on his deathbed, Hoyt was still dwelling, "with eloquent regrets, upon the incompletion of his plans and labors…for the advancement of the University."

Not for the last time the board asked Eliot to step into the breach, but he refused, saying that the University was "too young to be left without a recognized head." So it turned to the most distinguished faculty member, William Chauvenet, and he agreed to serve, at a salary of $2,800. His June 1863 inaugural address signaled a sharp change from the classics-centered curriculum favored by Hoyt. Chauvenet,

Henry (1842–c. 1930) and Charles (1842–1915) Branch. Twin brothers, they received A.B. degrees in the first class of Collegiate Department graduates in June 1862. Charles (left) who served in the Confederate Army, received an A.M. degree in 1867, and later became a successful insurance man in St. Louis. Henry (top), who received his A.M. in 1866, became a Presbyterian minister and temperance advocate in Maryland. In 1953, Branch descendants presented Charles Branch's two diplomas to the University.
WU Archives

Charles Branch's 1862 A.B. diploma.
WU Archives

Faculty compensation presents challenges

In 1864, George Howison was a popular and effective teacher at Washington University; his wife, Lois, taught at Mary Institute. In 1868 and 1869, he demanded a salary increase to $2,500 since he had "for the past year been doing not only the work properly falling to me as Professor of Logic and Political Economy, but the whole work of the Latin chair besides, and, in addition, the Mathematics of the Junior class." Late in 1869, the Boston English School offered him $3,000 a year and, after dramatic but unsuccessful last-minute negotiations, he left St. Louis. Eventually, he became Mills Professor of Philosophy at the University of California, where he founded and later headed the department of philosophy.

George (1834-1916) and Lois Howison.
WU Archives

Chauvenet was a man of action, with a slightly sardonic streak. In 1862, a student had mistakenly offered to pay him the semester's tuition, and Chauvenet could have referred the matter to Seth Ranlett, the University secretary — but he decided not to risk having the student change his mind. "I suppose," he wrote to the board with sly humor, enclosing the $35, "it is as well for me to receive the money when it is offered."

As chancellor, he took a forthright, even brusque, approach to under-performing students or faculty. In 1863, he reported that some students had left to make their fortunes in the wartime economy, but they were largely not "distinguished either for good scholarship or correct deportment....Our past losses in this respect will prove our future gain." He also lambasted the teaching of Etienne Boileau, a writing instructor: "Indeed so unfortunate is Mr. Boileau in the matter of discipline that even if we were compelled to omit the instruction in his branch…I should think it necessary to recommend that his services be dispensed with." In florid script, an outraged Boileau complained to Eliot, rather comically, that he had been discharged for "reason of incompetency," and that "somebody must be wrong, but if I can prove that I am not wrong, then somebody else must be wrong." Eliot replied soothingly, offering Boileau a reference and assuring him that he had not been discharged at all — merely "not re-appointed for the next year."

Generally the University was fortunate in its faculty, but it lost some able people because salaries were so low. The first head of Mary Institute, E.D. Sanborn, resigned in 1863 to take a job at Dartmouth, because "my pecuniary affairs… hardly leave me the power of contrary choice." John Crehore, who taught a popular commercial class in the Scientific Department, resigned "owing to the smallness of my present salary." In January 1864, Chauvenet traveled east for a meeting of the National Academy of Sciences and tried to recruit new faculty members, with little success. In a letter, he said bluntly, "The fact is that our salary is not a sufficient inducement to eastern men to leave their present positions…*at this disturbed time especially.*"

who had published his own master work on astronomy since coming to the University, decided to implement a new curriculum, strong in the sciences and in such "practical" subjects as history and modern foreign languages.

Another task was shoring up the school's sagging finances. Only half the $100,000 of the 1860 pledges had come in, the $20,000 loan for Collegiate Hall was still outstanding, and the O'Fallon building was only partly completed. While the Academy and Mary Institute were flourishing, the Collegiate and Scientific Departments were attracting few students: a combined total of 40 in 1862 down to 25 by 1865, with an average senior class of only four or five. Because four of the first five 1862 graduates wished to go on for a master's degree, it was becoming necessary to start a graduate program.

ELIOT SEEKS FINANCIAL STABILITY

Soon the tide of war began to turn. Much fighting still remained, but by early 1864 Union victories had reopened the Mississippi River; by September, General Sherman captured Atlanta, and two months later he embarked on his march to the sea. In March 1864, Eliot decided that it was time to try again to place the University on a firmer footing. Already, he said, of the $478,000 given to the University, four-fifths had come from his own congregation. He would rely on St. Louisans to complete the Polytechnic building — that "premature ruin," he called it — and he would turn to easterners for help in raising $200,000 for the endowment.

Help came from Boston financier Nathaniel Thayer, who had investments in Missouri railroads, and Mary Tileston Hemenway, daughter of a New York banker, each of whom gave $25,000. With these donations, the board created the Thayer Professorship of Mechanics and Civil Engineering in the Scientific Department and the Tileston Professorship of Political Economy in the Collegiate Department, in honor of Mrs. Hemenway's father, Thomas Tileston. Soon local gifts added to the total, including a $25,000 donation from George Partridge and $20,000 from James Smith.

Mary Tileston Hemenway (1820-1894).
A gift from Hemenway in 1864 helped establish a professorship in political economy at the University. She was an honorary member of the Women's Anthropological Society of America, founded in June 1885 because of her contributions. In 2002 Washington University anthropologist Erik Trinkaus was installed as the first Mary Tileston Hemenway Professor in Arts & Sciences.
Peabody Museum, Harvard University

Buoyed by a little solvency, Eliot proposed salary increases for Chauvenet and other members of the faculty. The board named several new faculty members, among them Benjamin F. Tweed as professor of English literature and George A. Howison as assistant professor of mathematics. Howison, a popular teacher who wrote an important book on analytic geometry, soon switched fields and taught political economy; he received the University's new Tileston chair. In 1869 he left for a new job in Boston, amid a flurry of unsuccessful salary negotiations.

With an end to conflict in view, the 1864 Commencement was a joyous affair. Salutatorian Charles Illsley gave one oration in Latin and another in English, "After the War," which dealt with "the probable condition of the country at the termination of the struggle," said a newspaper account. Only five students graduated, down from nine the year before. This class was "originally much larger," added the article, "but has been reduced by the attractions which the military field has offered to the young."

POST-WAR ERA BEGINS AND THE POLYTECHNIC CHANGES HANDS

In 1865, most board members signed the "Ironclad Oath" of allegiance to the Union, as the new Missouri Constitution of 1865 required board members at chartered institutions to do, but in April, the war that had devastated the country for four long years was over. Along with the rest of the nation, Washington University moved into the post-war future.

That spring brought the first ominous hint of problems with William Chauvenet's health. In a letter to Eliot, he admitted having had a hard winter with lung inflammation. By 1866, he was well enough to report that, although no growth had taken place in the Collegiate Department, he was determined not to lower the school's standards in an effort to attract more students. The University's work was "not merely to supply an existing demand but actually to create a demand for higher education," he wrote, adding optimistically that "we can already see our future in the increased and increasing numbers of our Academic Department which acts, to a great extent, as the *feeder* of the College."

Among the 1866 graduates was a student who must have met Chauvenet's high standards: Edward Singleton Holden, a graduate of the Academy and a protégé of Chauvenet, who eventually married his daughter. After Washington University, Holden went on to West Point, then returned to the University to complete an A.M. degree. After several prestigious astronomical appointments, he

Charles Illsley (1842-1914).
Illsley, A.B. '64, A.M. '67, was 1864 class salutatorian. Said one newspaper: "He is…the son of a carpenter of this city [who], not having enjoyed the benefits of a liberal education, had sense, courage, and liberality of mind enough to resolve that his intelligent and promising son should have all the advantages which he himself had lacked." Illsley, who became a civil engineer in St. Louis, served as an instructor in the O'Fallon Polytechnic Institute from 1867-69.
WU Archives

Chauvenet protégé heads University of California, then Lick Observatory

Edward Singleton Holden (1846-1914).
WU Archives

Edward Singleton Holden earned his B.S. degree in 1866, studying astronomy under William Chauvenet. He completed a master's degree in 1875. In 1870, he had graduated from the U.S. Military Academy at West Point, third in his class. Afterwards, he worked at the U.S. Naval Observatory, directed the Washburn Observatory at the University of Wisconsin, and — in 1885 — became the fifth president of the University of California, before moving over to

direct Lick Observatory when it was finished three years later. The much-honored Holden, who published dozens of articles and was a member of the National Academy of Sciences, led the observatory to international prominence before resigning in 1897.

Lick Observatory.
The west front of the observatory.
Mary Lea Shane Archives of the Lick Observatory, University of California-Santa Cruz

---

1867 bond.
The board authorized a $150,000 bond issue to try to reduce the indebtedness of O'Fallon Polytechnic Institute.
WU Archives

became president of the University of California, then head of the new Lick Observatory.

In June 1867, St. Louis newspapers triumphantly reported the dedication of the long-awaited O'Fallon Polytechnic Institute building, describing it as "a noble edifice for a noble purpose." An engraving showed an elaborate structure, four stories high, with an elegant mansard roof; inside was the 1,200-seat Eliot Hall and the extravagant Ames Library. Soon the Institute's evening program had reopened and two new programs had begun: a School of Design and a School of Civil and Mechanical Engineering.

Behind the scenes the story was much different. This building, estimated at $130,000, actually cost $350,000, thanks to many architectural changes and the high price of materials during the Civil War — and John How had assumed a ruinous debt of $134,000 to finance it. Feeling honor-bound to help, the board was saddled with this indebtedness;

it quickly had to liquidate a portion of the endowment and authorize a $150,000 bond issue. Finding that O'Fallon's own board had not met in two years, the University board delivered a vote of "no confidence" in How by taking control of future elections to this group. Worse still, the building itself soon proved radically unsuited to its purpose, with a poorly planned interior.

Valiantly, Eliot tried to raise the necessary funds, but this time he did not succeed. Early in 1868, he admitted that the building was a "millstone [on] our neck" and the board had to agree. In March, when the board decided to dispose of it, John How angrily resigned, "aware that I cannot longer be useful to you." Some faculty members probably breathed a sigh of relief, believing that a mechanics' institute did not belong at the University, but the community, which had long supported this innovative venture, was outraged that O'Fallon was for sale.

In a delicate balancing act, Eliot tried to find a buyer who would preserve O'Fallon's original purpose. In April, he traveled unsuccessfully to Washington, D.C., to see if the government wanted it, then in August ran an ad in a St. Louis newspaper proposing that someone buy it for $300,000 and keep it operating. The school board saw this proposal and struck a bargain with Eliot: They would pay $280,000, enough to liquidate the University's debt, while the University board would spend $6,000 annually to support the Ames Library and technical education in the public schools. While the deal was expensive, the community was pacified, and the O'Fallon venture did give birth to a small engineering program, which now moved back to the University.

LAW SCHOOL BEGINS

Just as the Polytechnic was leaving the University, a new program was arriving. In August 1867, the board finally acted upon its long-cherished dream of establishing a law school, giving it a somewhat confusing name: "The St. Louis Law School." The first dean was Henry Hitchcock and there was a distinguished part-time, unpaid faculty, which included charter board member Samuel Treat.

In fall 1867, the first class of 12 students gathered in two third-floor rooms of the O'Fallon Polytechnic building. They had to be 19 years old, "of good moral character," and have "a good English education." Classes met for an hour in the late afternoon, five days a week; students spent their days clerking and reading law. They attended school six months of the year and received the LL.B. degree after two sessions of study. An examination, given by a committee of the Bar, completed their program.

Two years after it opened, the law school earned a place in history when it admitted Lemma Barkeloo and Phoebe Wilson Couzins, two of the first women law students in the United States. In the liberal tradition of Eliot, Hitchcock told the board, on behalf of the law faculty, that he saw "no reason why any young woman who in respect to character and acquirements fulfilled the conditions applicable to male students, and who chose to attend the law lectures in good faith for the purpose of becoming acquainted with the law of her country, should be denied that privilege."

Barkeloo was not there long. She passed the bar examination during her first year of study and withdrew from the program; then, before her early death in 1870, she became the first woman in the nation to try a case in court. Couzins received her LL.B. in 1871, went on to help found the National Woman Suffrage Association, and in 1887, became the first woman ever named a U.S. marshal when she was appointed to the Eastern District of Missouri.

Dean Hitchcock, an outstanding legal scholar who later became president of the American Bar Association, built the program quickly, advertising aggressively throughout Missouri and nearby states. By 1869, the school had five departments: pleading, practice, evidence, and criminal law; equity; U.S. courts' jurisdiction and practice and admiralty law; real estate and successions; and law of contracts and commercial law. Students attending lectures in all five paid $60 tuition.

Hitchcock helped the University in another crucial way. The new state constitution of 1865 prohibited the legislature from granting tax exemptions to corporations, and in 1866 St. Louis County tried to tax the struggling school. Hitchcock

Phoebe Wilson Couzins (1842-1913).
When Couzins received her law degree in 1871, she became the first woman awarded a University law degree — and one of the first women law graduates in the United States.
Missouri Historical Society, St. Louis

Susan Frelich Appleton.
Installed in April 2000 as the first Lemma Barkeloo and Phoebe Couzins Professor of Law, Susan Appleton is an expert on family law.
Joe Angeles, WU Photographic Services

The Polytechnic building.
WU Archives

33

filed suit on the University's behalf, arguing that its 1853 Charter represented an irrevocable contract with the state. The case pitted Hitchcock against Edward S. Rowse, the St. Louis tax collector and later University board member, as it worked its way through the courts. When it reached the U.S. Supreme Court in 1869, the University was ably represented by Benjamin R. Curtis, a former justice. By a single-vote majority, he won the case.

DEATH OF CHAUVENET

Three months earlier, misfortune had struck the University again. William Chauvenet, whose lung ailment had grown steadily worse despite a long journey west, resigned in September 1869. Reluctantly, the board — minus a weary Eliot, who was spending a year abroad — accepted his resignation, lavishly praising him. Chauvenet wrote again,

expressing gratitude for their kind regard. "In one respect alone am I conscious of deserving it, namely, in the 'earnestness' with which I have labored for the promotion of the interests of Washington University."

Chauvenet died on December 13, 1870 — and, during his final illness, the chancellorship briefly became a kind of revolving door. Benjamin Tweed took over as interim but left the University after a few months. Abram Litton stepped in, though it was understood that his appointment would be temporary.

Meanwhile, there were encouraging signs. The first student organization — the Irving Union Debating Society — had formed in 1858-59, and in 1869 it began producing a monthly publication, *Irving Union*, which included political and social commentary, poems and essays, college news, and student gossip. One of the

Eads Bridge design and construction involved faculty and students

James Buchanan Eads (1820-1887), a member of the O'Fallon Polytechnic Institute board, designed the remarkable Eads Bridge, which opened in 1874. William Chauvenet played a role in this triumph. He checked and revised the mathematical calculations that Eads made in designing it, then certified their correctness. He also invented a revolving mirror for use in measuring the elastic limit of the steel and iron.

Much later, Eads was memorialized on campus when his daughter, Eliza Eads How — the daughter-in-law of board member and O'Fallon founder John How — donated a building in his name, Eads Hall.

The University had other Eads Bridge connections as well. Classes took field trips to watch the construction. In 1872, the University bought the machine used to test structural materials for the bridge and added it to the civil engineering laboratory. And Professor Calvin Woodward later wrote a history of the Eads Bridge, which a leading bridge engineer called "the most important American contribution to engineering literature."

Eads Bridge.
David Kilper, WU
Photographic Services

early editors was a student who would have an illustrious career: David Rowland Francis, later a well-known politician and president of the Louisiana Purchase Exposition Company for the World's Fair in 1904.

Thanks to the largess of Hudson Bridge, Mary Institute had a newly expanded building. In 1868, Bridge had sent Eliot a letter that must have gladdened his heart: the offer of Bridge's former home on 8th Street, worth about $25,000, to provide the funds for enlarging the Institute's original Lucas Place building. Wary of Eliot's tendency to use gifts for unsuspected projects, he said he wanted it "absolutely understood" that this gift be used for Mary Institute "and no other purpose."

After Eliot's Civil War work, one piece of news must have been most gratifying. Using interest on money they had collected for relief work, the Western Sanitary Commission decided to establish four scholarships at the University for descendants of Union soldiers. Soon nominations were coming in. William Torrey Harris, superintendent of public schools, wrote to recommend two students: Michael F. Healy, who went on to earn a B.S. in 1875 and an LL.B. in 1877; and Winthrop Bartlett, who graduated from the civil engineering program in 1874.

Several sent affecting letters on behalf of two brothers: Minard L. and John O. Holman. Their high school principal lamented that these able young men had been forced to drop out of school because of family finances. Their minister supported them as well: "Of their rightful claim to the scholarships on the ground of being soldiers' sons, I need say nothing. For everyone is familiar with their father's heroic and self-denying services in the hour of our country's peril."

Finally, their father himself wrote — John Henry Holman, a brevet brigadier general. "I make this application," he said, "in consequence of not being financially able to otherwise educate my sons." Not only did his sons receive the scholarships, but they also graduated with distinction, and Minard received an honorary master's degree in 1905.

Many things were going well, yet the University had pressing needs. Eliot, who was due to return to St. Louis in May 1870, had foreseen them quite clearly. The University needed more space and a larger faculty; as usual, it needed a larger endowment. Looming on the horizon was an even greater need: the steady hand of a new chancellor to make all these wishes a reality. (WU)

Minard L. Holman (1852-1925).
WU Archives

The first Western Sanitary Commission Scholarships are awarded

Minard, B.S. '74, and John Holman, B.S. '75, were two of the first four recipients of the new Western Sanitary Commission scholarships. Both became civil engineers, and Minard was water commissioner for the City of St. Louis. Their father, John Henry Holman, brevet brigadier general, had served as colonel with the 1st U.S. Infantry Regiment, United States Colored Troops, during the Civil War. Wounded and badly disabled, he found it "necessary that I avail myself of the gratuitous gift."

Letter from John Henry Holman (1824-1883).
WU Archives

In November 1834, after a long steamboat journey, Rev. William Greenleaf Eliot, Jr., landed in St. Louis, eager to establish a Unitarian presence in the untamed West. It was a "wild, unpromising adventure," he admitted later, and at 22 he was "young, inexperienced." Yet, he added, "I never for a moment had a doubt upon the subject! It never entered my head that failure was possible!....My faith in the power of Christian truth was such that I felt [a] sense of gaining [a] foothold."

Already Eliot had the towering moral strength that would inspire people with admiration, even awe, for all the rest of his life. As Rev. James Freeman Clarke, a classmate and friend, remarked in 1839: "One feels rebuked in his presence. William Eliot carries with him this dignity, so that no one would like to trifle with him." Clarke also noted Eliot's playful smile, his luminous eyes, his remarkable sweetness. "He never offends, because he is calm, quiet, kindly....His whole body is full of light."

Eliot was born in New Bedford, Massachusetts, the third child of William Greenleaf Eliot, Sr., and Margaret Dawes Eliot. His family, prominent in New England religious and political circles, believed in living principled lives. His great-grandfather, Rev. Andrew Eliot, was minister for more than three decades at Boston's Old North Church. Offered the presidency of Harvard College in 1773, he refused, feeling honor-bound to remain true to his vocation.

Eliot's own father was a merchant and ship owner, ruined by shipping restrictions imposed by the War of 1812. He moved his family to Washington, D.C., where he became chief examiner in the Post Office. Though not poor, the family was no longer wealthy; young William graduated from Columbian College (later George Washington University) in 1826, then worked for a year in the post office. There, parcels from St. Louis caught his eye, and he decided that, if he should ever go west, St. Louis would be his home.

In 1831, he entered Harvard Divinity School, where he read German philosophers, visited the needy, and preached his first sermon, entitled "Philanthropy." He honed his religious belief — a form of Christianity taught by William Ellery Channing, the founder of Unitarianism — that included devotion to God and Christ, the Bible, the practice of morality, and religious freedom. He decided to follow a "practical" faith, dedicating himself to his flock and his community — and taxing his own frail constitution in the process. "I believe the path of duty," he said, "...soonest leads to the love and perception of truth."

Where to begin that journey? In 1833, he wrote to Clarke, who had settled in Louisville: "I hear that at St. Louis a parish is getting together; is it true, and what about it?" By spring 1834, he wrote again, having made up his mind: "Let them know in some way that a youngster is ready to come there to live, to spend his life among them if they will provide food and lodging — for if I come, I come to remain, and to lay my ashes in the valley of the Mississippi."

Coincidentally, in June 1834, Christopher Rhodes traveled to Boston in search of a Unitarian missionary for St. Louis. During a meeting with Rev. Henry Ware, Jr., a Harvard Divinity School faculty member, he heard that Eliot was already hoping to make St. Louis his home. The two met and Rhodes instantly engaged Eliot for a year's trial period — a decision he would never have the smallest reason to regret.

When Eliot arrived, Rhodes met him and introduced him to James Smith, who became a second friend and ally. From that kernel of support, Eliot worked to build a congregation amid a heavily Catholic community. "It would have been no matter of surprise if we had utterly failed," he later wrote. "....No one expected anything else. With a Boy for a Pastor...and no one man of wealth among us, numbering in all

Rev. William Greenleaf Eliot, Jr. (1811-1887).
Eliot was elected to the prestigious post of secretary of the American Unitarian Association — but he turned it down. "Duty was [the] deciding motive," he wrote, "and to say truth I have felt the sacrifice very deeply." In 1857, he did accept an honorary doctorate from his alma mater, Harvard Divinity School, in recognition of his role as co-founder of Washington University.
Oil on canvas by George P.A. Healey
WU Gallery of Art

but 15 or 20 persons, men and women…what wonder if we had…ceased before we had begun!"

Soon he had help from his new wife, Abby Adams Cranch, whom he married in 1837. She was his first cousin, daughter of a Washington, D.C., judge, and only 20 years old when she left her comfortable home for St. Louis. "Although I had been told much about the smoke and mud, I found it even worse than I imagined," she reminisced in 1895. "No pavement and a very dusty road….Policemen few and *very bad boys*."

In 1837, his Church of the Messiah built its first sanctuary at 4th and Pine, enlarged it only five years later, then dedicated a magnificent new sanctuary at 9th and Olive in 1851. At the same time, Eliot was becoming a civic leader: member, then president, of the St. Louis School Board; founder of the Academy of Sciences of St. Louis; still later a temperance advocate, women's suffrage supporter, and staunch foe of legalized prostitution. On an 1843 visit to St. Louis, novelist Charles Dickens commented: "The Unitarian Church is represented in this remote place...by a gentleman of great worth and excellence."

During the 1849 cholera epidemic that killed thousands of St. Louisans, Eliot demonstrated his worth in his heroic efforts to help the stricken. One week, he was gone day and night, "making himself physician, nurse, pastor, friend, all in one," recalled Clarke. "When Sunday came, he

went into the pulpit and spoke with no mental preparation, feeling that the care of the sick and dying was more important than the sermon. At the close of the service, he remarked to his mother, 'You see, mother, what poor stuff they are willing to take from me.' She answered, 'They know where you have been all the week.'"

Though he abhorred slavery himself, Eliot wished to help avert conflict by steering a moderate political course that favored gradual emancipation. Some of his own church members left when he preached against slavery; some northerners criticized him for not going far enough. But Eliot rejected the interference of people "too distant from the scene of action to know what ought to be done." Rather, he said, "the two texts which reformers need most are these — 'In patience possess your souls'; and 'Let your moderation be known to all men.'" Once the Civil War broke out, however, he became an ardent Union supporter and emancipationist.

In a controversial 1849 sermon, he had declared he would never return a fugitive slave to his master. So in 1863, when his family's new servant, Archer Alexander, proved to be a fugitive slave, Eliot's course was clear. He protected Alexander, even rescued him when slave-catchers tried to steal him back. After the war, he employed Alexander, became his friend, and in 1885 wrote a moving biography, *The Story of Archer Alexander*. Eventually, he gave a photo of Alexander to sculptor

Abby Adams Cranch Eliot (1817-1908).
Despite the difficult journey to St. Louis, she wrote later, she and her new husband were "young and strong and full of hope, and hardships were easily borne."
WU Archives

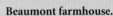

Mary Rhodes Eliot (1838-1855). The beloved first-born child of William Greenleaf and Abby Eliot, Mary Rhodes Eliot died at 16 in January 1855. Her death, in a sudden illness, was a crushing blow. Mary Institute was named for her.
Courtesy of MICDS Archives

Beaumont farmhouse.
From 1861-68, William Greenleaf Eliot and his family lived near Washington, Beaumont, and Locust, in an old farmhouse formerly owned by his friend, physician William Beaumont. Camp Jackson was only a half-mile away, and during the 1861 action, rifle bullets whizzed past Eliot's fence. Afterwards, Eliot built a home, also on the Beaumont property, at 2660 Washington.
WU Archives

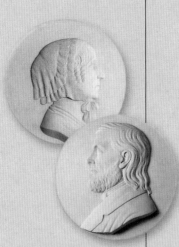

Medallions.
These medallions, on display at Mary Institute-Country Day School, depict Margaret Dawes Eliot and William Greenleaf Eliot.
Courtesy of MICDS Archives

Thomas Ball, who used it in shaping the face of the newly freed slave in his *Freedom's Memorial* statue, still on display in Washington, D.C.

In addition, Eliot published collections of sermons, notably his *Discipline of Sorrow*, which he wrote after the sudden, tragic death of his oldest daughter, Mary Rhodes Eliot, in 1855. In all, the Eliots had 14 children and only five lived to adulthood, but the loss of 16-year-old Mary was a particularly stunning blow. Two months later, he wrote in his journal: "I almost craze myself with work, yet dear Mary is never away from my mind." His surviving children were four boys — Thomas Lamb, Henry Ware, Christopher Rhodes, Edward Cranch — and one girl, Rose Greenleaf. All the boys were graduates of Washington University; Rose was an alumna of Mary Institute.

His extended family also had connections to the University. In 1860, his mother, "desiring to associate her memory with the enjoyment and happiness of the young," donated $1,000 to

Thomas Stearns Eliot (1888-1965). Grandson of William Greenleaf Eliot, T.S. Eliot, Smith Academy '05, was a Nobel Prize-winning poet and playwright. In 1933 and 1953, he lectured at Washington University. The University sponsored an Eliot centenary conference in 1988, and today it is co-sponsor, with the Institute of United States Studies of the University of London, of the annual T.S. Eliot Lecture.
WU Archives

the Mary Institute on condition that the second Friday in May be set aside forever as a holiday; it is still celebrated — called "Grandmother's Day." His brother Thomas, an attorney and Congressman, consulted with Eliot on several University tax issues. After the Civil War, William Greenleaf Eliot endowed a scholarship to honor another brother, Frank Andrew Eliot, who was killed in gallant action at the battle of Chancellorsville.

Eliot's friend, Archer Alexander, serves as model for *Freedom's Memorial* sculpture

I n 1873, with $21,000 in funds collected largely from black Civil War soldiers and newly freed slaves, the Western Sanitary Commission decided to commission a statue honoring the Great Emancipator, Abraham Lincoln. On a trip to Italy in 1869, William Greenleaf Eliot had seen a suitable statue in the studio of sculptor Thomas Ball; later the Commission asked Ball to execute this piece, *Freedom's Memorial*, as a large-size bronze. Eliot provided a photo of his friend, Archer Alexander, so that Ball could use a freedman's likeness in creating the face of the newly freed slave. He did so, and

in 1875 this version was installed in Washington, D.C., where it still stands in Lincoln Park. Eliot gave the University a small, marble version of the Ball statue (left) as it appeared before Ball incorporated Alexander's likeness. This sculpture is now in the collection of the University's Gallery of Art.

Freedom's Memorial.
WU Gallery of Art

Archer Alexander (c. 1810-1879).
Missouri Historical Society, St. Louis

Succeeding generations of Eliots have played a role in University life. Celebrated poet and playwright Thomas Stearns (T.S.) Eliot was the youngest child of Henry Ware and Charlotte Stearns Eliot. He attended the Academy (by then called Smith Academy) where he was an outstanding student; in 1905, at age 16, he left St. Louis for Boston and eventually became a British citizen. In 1933, he lectured in Graham Chapel on Shakespearean criticism, then in 1953, he returned during the University's centennial to receive an honorary degree and give a lecture, "American Literature and the American Language," in which he mentioned William Greenleaf Eliot:

"I never knew my grandfather; he died a year before my birth. But I was brought up to be very much aware of him: so much so, that as a child I thought of him as still head of the family....The standard of conduct was that which my grandfather had set; our moral judgments, our decisions between duty and self-indulgence, were taken as if, like Moses, he had brought down tablets of the Law, any deviation from which would be sinful. Not the least of these laws...was the Law of Public Service: it is no doubt owing to the impress of this law upon my infant mind that, like other members of my family, I have felt...an uncomfortable and very inconvenient obligation to serve upon committees."

Another grandchild was William Greenleaf Eliot, Jr., A.B. '88, honorary LL.D. '32, who married an early woman graduate, Minna Sessinghaus, A.B. '90, summa cum laude. Like his father — Thomas Lamb — Eliot, Jr. became a Unitarian minister in Portland, Oregon; in 1932 he returned to give the University's 75th anniversary Commencement address. In it he mentioned that, when he was born, his father's 1862 class had given him a silver cup inscribed with his future graduation date — indicating, he said, "that I was born an alumnus of Washington University!" Most recently, an Eliot great-great-great grandson has matriculated: Eliot Isaac Sinclair of Mesa, Arizona, Class of 2004. Ⓦ

Rev. Thomas Lamb Eliot (1841-1936).
An 1865 Harvard Divinity School graduate who taught Latin and Greek briefly at Smith Academy, Eliot, A.B. '62, A.M. '66, moved to Portland, Oregon, in 1867 to become pastor of the First Unitarian Church, as well as a civic leader and president of the board of Reed College. He received an honorary LL.D. from Washington University in 1912.

Henry Ware Eliot (1843-1919).
Eliot, A.B. '63, stayed on in St. Louis, where he became chairman of the board of the Hydraulic Brick Company, president of the Academy of Sciences, and trustee of the Missouri Botanical Garden. He was a member of the University's board of directors from 1877 to 1919.

Rev. Christopher Rhodes Eliot (1856-1945).
After teaching for a year in the Academic Department, Eliot, A.B. '76, A.M. '81, graduated from Harvard Divinity School. A distinguished churchman and educator, he served in eastern pastorates, primarily Bulfinch Place Church in Boston. He received an honorary LL.D. from Washington University in 1925.

Edward Cranch Eliot (1858-1928).
A lawyer who stayed in St. Louis, Eliot, A.B. '78, LL.B. '80, A.M. '81, specialized in international law and was a lecturer in the University's law school from 1887 to 1923. In 1898, he served as president of the American Bar Association and president of the St. Louis school board.

All photos, WU Archives

CHAPTER THREE

"CHILD OF HIS HEART":
Chancellor Eliot and Washington University

1871-1887

"Child of His Heart"

As 1870 wore on, Washington University had no permanent chancellor, and everyone was feeling anxious. Editorials in the student publication, the *Irving Union*, fretted that the Collegiate Department's tiny enrollment had dropped further, popular professors had left, and William Greenleaf Eliot was still not back from his year-long tour of Europe. Worse yet, they said, "No Chancellor elected, and all in the unknown future," then added with an almost audible sigh, "the fates will probably decide before long."

In May, this discontent gave way to delighted optimism when Eliot returned, full of energy and new hopes. "[He] brings with him the welcome assurance that…the university will begin the next school year with renewed vigor and enterprise," crowed one student. The board also was jubilant. The directors relieved Abram Litton of his duties as acting chancellor and in September appointed Eliot, who already had resumed his position as board president, to take Litton's place.

Eliot's very presence was a tonic to the University. Within days of his arrival, he promised students that faculty vacancies would soon be filled; within weeks, he made a proposal to the board that must have sounded familiar to old-time members, whose generosity had so often been tested. He wanted to raise $200,000 to finance the expansion of his cherished Scientific (now "Polytechnic") Department. More broadly, he wanted to strengthen the University, making it irresistible to prospective students, top-notch faculty — and a dynamic new chancellor.

Behind the scenes, Eliot's position as interim chancellor troubled him. Since the Civil War, he

had moved into the national spotlight as a Unitarian leader and social reformer. Now, this broader role, combined with his new duties at the University and the approach of his 60th birthday, forced him to a momentous decision: It was time to resign his pastorate at the Church of the Messiah. Yet this wrenching step left him feeling uneasy, ambivalent. To his journal, he confided: "I may get used to [being chancellor] and mean to succeed. But it is a turn in my life which I take unwillingly: [and intend] to return to my proper calling whenever I can."

Acceptance letter.
Eliot's letter of acceptance for the chancellorship.
WU Archives

Left: **William G. Eliot (1811-1887).**
Oil on canvas by George P.A. Healey, 1870.
WU Gallery of Art

1871 ❧ *1887*

1871 *The search committee for a new chancellor chose William Greenleaf Eliot to fill the position.*

1876 *Ada Calista Fisher and Mary Josephine Rychlicki became the first women to graduate from the College.*

1878 Student Life *succeeded* Irving Union *as the student-run publication.*

1879 *The board voted to create a School of Fine Arts under the direction of Halsey C. Ives.*

1880 *The Manual Training School opened in a new building, funded in part by Samuel Cupples.*

1882 *The University, on the 25th anniversary of its inauguration ceremony, had 1,486 students and 87 professors.*

View of downtown St. Louis (left).
Lithograph with hand color. Published by Richard J. Compton and Camille N. Dry in 1875 as Plate 42 in *Pictorial St. Louis: The Great Metropolis of the Mississippi Valley.* Washington University is near the top at 17th and Washington.
Collection of A.G. Edwards and Sons, Inc., St. Louis, Missouri

Previous pages:
Cupples I Hall.
Cornerstones were laid in 1901 for two Cupples buildings, named for Samuel Cupples, a board member for 31 years. In 1872, Cupples made Robert Brookings — later University board president — a partner in his firm.

Marshall S. Snow (1842-1916).
A graduate of Phillips-Exeter Academy, where he was a student of Joseph Hoyt, Snow came to the University in 1870. A specialist in French history, he was dean of the College for nearly 40 years and twice the University's acting chancellor, from 1887-91 and from 1907-08.
Missouri Historical Society, St. Louis

Hudson E. Bridge (1810-1875).
A New Hampshire native, Bridge moved to St. Louis in 1835, where he founded the successful Empire Stove Works. One obituary read: "Few have seemed to so well understand the obligations and responsibilities of wealth."
Courtesy of MICDS Archives

A "Bird out of a Cage"

Soon several things happened to lighten Eliot's burden and sweep him inexorably toward a permanent appointment. One was the arrival of a new humanities faculty member: Marshall S. Snow, a courtly, urbane Harvard graduate who became professor of belles-lettres in 1870. A remarkably versatile teacher, he could lecture widely on literature and history. In 1874, with the departure of Truman M. Post, he was appointed professor of history, a position he held until 1912.

Happily, he was an able administrator as well — a talent that Eliot quickly recognized. In January 1871, the board created a new position for Snow: dean of the Collegiate Department (soon called "the College"), charged with assisting the Chancellor, especially in matters of discipline and student conduct. In his journal, Eliot wrote gleefully, "Out of this I shall work some freedom by putting all details of work upon him." When Snow courteously declined, saying that it sounded more like a registrar's job, Eliot quickly named him registrar, with the same responsibilities. Snow remained registrar until 1876 when he was quietly retitled "dean."

On the science side of the faculty, Snow had a strong counterpart: Calvin M. Woodward, a rough-edged personality but an extraordinary teacher who had, said one admirer, "the power to fire the minds of the students with the will to accomplishment." Another Harvard graduate, he had come to the University in 1865 as assistant principal in the Academy and later headed the evening school at the O'Fallon Polytechnic Institute. When O'Fallon dissolved in 1868, Woodward had moved key elements to the University, merged them with the Scientific Department, and created a new undergraduate division: the Polytechnic

Department, offering courses in mathematics, the sciences, and engineering. In 1870, Woodward became Thayer Professor of Mathematics and Applied Mechanics and dean of the burgeoning Polytechnic Department — a job he held, with one break, until 1910.

The Polytechnic was much on Eliot's mind in 1870 as he planned for a new, four-story building to accommodate it. "University Hall," as it was called, formed a westward extension to the existing three-story building, which underwent renovation, acquiring a fourth-story studio for the art classes previously held at O'Fallon. Altogether, raved the *Irving Union*, "with the opening of this building will commence a new era in the history of Washington University....Its scientific course will then stand unrivaled west of the Alleghenies."

The question, as always, was how to pay for it. On March 7, 1871, Eliot set off — hat in hand — for the home of his old friend and fellow board member, Hudson Bridge, a wealthy stove manufacturer and railroad president. Two days later, he recorded in his journal the outcome of this meeting: Hudson Bridge would give $15,000 toward the new building, $15,000 toward its apparatus, and $100,000 in gold securities to endow the chancellorship — soon renamed the "Hudson E. Bridge Chancellorship" — and ensure a decent salary for its occupant. For once, even Eliot was at a loss for words. He ended his entry with the simple notation: "God bless him."

In a letter to Eliot, Bridge expressed the hope that his gift would "enable the University to assume a commanding position." In addition, he made clear that this was a gesture of friendship, intended

to ease Eliot's mind so that "the evening of your days may be cheered by seeing the Institution to whose interests you have given so much…placed by the friends of popular education upon a sure foundation." Eliot was overjoyed; such munificence, he said, made him feel like a "bird out of a cage."

"God only knows how I thank you….The last year had some very dark days to me, and I have required all the strength of will that I could summon to carry me through….There is an indescribable sense of relief; yet at the same moment I feel that I can do twice as much as I ever did before."

Eliot disclosed this delightful secret at the March board meeting, joyfully proclaiming a "Field Day" because the fund drive had exceeded its goal with a grand total of $212,000. As always, his board members had come through, donating the lion's share of the total. One $40,000 gift had come from an outsider: St. Louis railroad and mining tycoon Thomas Allen, who endowed the Allen Professorship of Mining and Metallurgy for a trial five-year period. A talented young geologist, William B. Potter, accepted this position, establishing mining and metallurgy as a new course of study and attracting valuable mineral collections to the University.

THE SEARCH FOR A NEW CHANCELLOR

Since there was money in hand to pay a chancellor, it was time to get serious about hiring one, so the board appointed a committee of three — James Yeatman, Bridge, and Samuel Treat — and assigned them the task. They were looking, Yeatman wrote later, for "a man of the greatest and at the same time the most versatile and the most dissimilar gifts. He should be one whose scholarship will command respect; and whose good sense, tact and faculty for swaying mankind will be as efficient as if his whole life had been devoted to practical pursuits." Not surprisingly, it was hard to find a qualified candidate.

One eager applicant was John Frazer, president of the University of Kansas, but a recommender whispered that he had "peculiarities" — "he does not excel in tact, is rather choleric, and says things pretty often which in taste and temper might be improved." Others, like Ephraim W. Gurney of Harvard, turned it down flat. By August, a weary committee had made its choice: William Greenleaf Eliot. "We know the deep and abiding interest which he feels in the university," wrote Yeatman. "It is the child of his heart, endeared by long years of anxiety, trial and toil. There is none other that can ever feel for and take the same interest in it which he has done, and can and will continue to do."

The University acquires a mineral and fossil collection

William B. Potter (1846-1914).

In 1870, Washington University was chosen by the State Board of Geological Survey to be the repository of its valuable mineral collection; Eliot had cabinets built for it on the first floor of the new University Hall. When the Survey group moved to Rolla in 1875, the minerals remained, and Professor William Potter, who headed the University's mining and metallurgy program from 1871-93, added to them actively. In 1882, the University acquired a major collection of 15,000 fossils. Many of these specimens are still in the University's collection and will be on display in a museum located in the new Earth and Planetary Sciences building, scheduled to open in 2004.

University Hall mineral display.

Fossils on parade. Fossils, including the skeleton of an Eocene relative of today's crocodiles, are on permanent display in Wilson Hall, which houses the Department of Earth and Planetary Sciences in Arts & Sciences.

All photos: WU Archives

Hale G. Parker becomes the first African-American student

Hale G. Parker, an Ohio native and an 1873 Oberlin College graduate, was the first African American to study law at Washington University. He did not receive a law degree because he scored less than one percentage point under the required total on his exams. However, he passed the Bar exam, went on to a successful law career in St. Louis and Chicago, and was named alternate commissioner-at-large for the 1893 World's Columbian Exposition in Chicago.

In 1916 Dean Richard Goode of the law school asked Chancellor Frederic A. Hall to reconsider the matter, saying that Parker's classmate, David Castleman Webb (1856-1935),

A.B. '80, LL.B. '83, had "become interested in trying to obtain a degree for Parker. He says Parker has done well in the practice in Chicago and has held honorable positions, but that now and then some rival at the Bar makes use of the fact that he failed to graduate to his detriment."

William W. Keysor, LL.B. '83, a law faculty member and another of Parker's classmates, vouched for him, pointing out that Parker had been forced to teach school during his student days and that this had interfered with his studies. Yet, Chancellor Hall refused to reopen the case.

Hale G. Parker (1851-1925).
Oberlin College Archives, Oberlin, Ohio

In September 1871, Eliot yielded to the inevitable — but only for "one or two years to come," he added quickly. To Bridge, he confided that "at my age, to enter upon a new class of duties…is a serious thing, and the insight which the last year has given me into them has not made them more attractive. In fact, it will involve the greatest personal sacrifice I have ever made." But he added — torn as ever — that he would like to help Washington University exert "a deep and progressive influence in promotion of practical science and liberal culture."

At his inauguration on February 29, 1872, Eliot addressed the crowd, recalling heroes from the past: the first chancellor, Joseph Hoyt ("a perfect educator"), and the second, William Chauvenet ("one of nature's noblemen"). As the third chancellor, he would grapple not so much with "how a University may be conducted as how a University may be built." It should be a place, he said, where students were trained in intellectual or mechanical pursuits, according to their ability. A smaller number would pursue the "higher realms of thoughts," he said, but the University should be able to offer

"the best education to the few, as well as a good education to the many." Then he added:

"We would found a University so strong in its faculty of instruction, so generous in its ideas, so thoroughly provided with all facilities of education, so hospitable to all comers and so rich in its benefactions conferred, that it should gather round itself a constituency of learning and science, and give tone to the educational movement of the region in which we live. We would found a University so widely acknowledged in its influence, that St. Louis and Missouri should be honored throughout the world by its being established here."

Women Enter "Golden Gates of Learning"

Among those newcomers were the first female students. The door had opened a crack in 1869 with the admission of Phoebe Couzins and Lemma Barkeloo to the law school. Then in September

1870 came the University's announcement that the program of study at Mary Institute had been extended and women could now take classes in the Collegiate Department alongside the male students. An *Irving Union* editorial praised the idea: "May the young ladies do full credit to themselves and to the institution which has so liberally opened to them the golden gates of learning."

Alice Belcher, the first woman to enroll in a full undergraduate program, certainly did herself credit. In 1870-71, she surpassed all the men in her freshman class with an 84 percent average; her cousin, George, was a star, too, graduating from the University that year as class valedictorian. A second woman, Mary H. Strong, took a partial load of English, Latin, and composition, but neither returned the next fall; Alice Belcher transferred to the University of Michigan.

In 1873, two more women — Ada Calista Fisher, a public school graduate, and Mary Josephine Rychlicki, a Mary Institute alumna — were admitted as sophomores, and they stayed to graduate in 1876, third and fifth, respectively, in their eight-member class. Socially, their tenure was rocky. An 1873 *Irving Union* article teased that they had been missing early-morning chapel, probably because they were "primping," but in a letter signed "Sophomora" one replied tartly that she refused to attend services only to "be stared at by a mob of insolent boys." Further, she did not feel fully accepted by her male classmates and teachers: "No lady has made a speech or read an essay in public," she said, "[or] been honored by an election into that august circle, the Irving Union Debating Society."

Still the women kept arriving, bolstering the College's tiny enrollment. In 1882, there was one woman in a class of three; by 1886, there were three among six. Not all the men were pleased. "The gradual increase in the number of girls — if the fair creatures will allow the expression — entering our University," complained one *Irving Union* letter-writer, "has occasioned numerous discussions among the male students, or boys. Although we are certainly a gallant set of fellows, admiring girls in their proper sphere, yet I fear, had we the management of affairs, the fair maidens would soon be obliged to seek else where for a University education."

Even more tentative was the first expression of interest by a black student. In September 1870, St. Louis attorney George Kellogg asked the law school dean whether an application by a man of African descent would automatically be rejected. Since no such case had yet arisen, replied the dean, the faculty had not considered the question. No application seems to have followed this query, but an African-American student, Hale G. Parker, did attend the law school from 1881-83. On his final exams, he scored less than one percent under the required total, so he did not receive a degree; however, he went on to a successful law career.

HARD TIMES BEGIN

The first year of Eliot's chancellorship passed smoothly. University Hall, completed at the end of 1871, was too large for the handful of College students plus the 36 students who were now taking undergraduate programs in civil engineering, mechanical engineering, chemistry, mining and metallurgy, and a short-lived new course of study — building and architecture. So another Washington University department, the St. Louis

Mary Josephine Rychlicki (?-1916).
A Mary Institute graduate, Rychlicki, A.B. '76, A.M. '79, went on to teach at her alma mater from 1877-87. She and Ada Calista Fisher, A.B. '76, A.M. '81, were the first two women to graduate from the College.
WU Archives

Alice Belcher enrolls as first female undergraduate

A lice Belcher, the first woman in the College, faced pressure to succeed. In a letter to her mother, she wrote: "When…Dr. Eliot observes, 'You are responsible that this experiment should be successful, so study,' then I realize how hard it will be to live up to this." She did so, however, earning better grades than the men in her class. Alice left after one year for the University of Michigan and a year later left Michigan to marry James F. Tweedy. Eventually, she settled in New York City, had five children, and became a part-time journalist, writing articles for popular publications.

Alice Belcher Tweedy (1850-1934).
Photo courtesy of John H. Tweedy

Law School, moved its 56 students in, too — a welcome change from the ill-suited quarters they formerly occupied in the O'Fallon Polytechnic Institute building, far removed from the University's main campus. O'Fallon, now under the auspices of the St. Louis Public Schools, continued to offer free evening courses to the public, which the University still promoted in its own catalogue.

Mary Institute and the Academy, always the University's largest divisions, were thriving. In 1872, the Academy was bursting at the seams with 320 students from the primary grades through the advanced classes, and Eliot reported proudly to the board that Mary Institute, with 240 students, was "altogether in most satisfactory condition. I know of no better school for girls;

no other so good." Even the College had hopes for expansion with the opening of a recently acquired house near campus as a small dormitory for students from outside St. Louis.

Then in 1873 a lingering depression began that had a major impact on St. Louis, a city of nearly 311,000 people in 1870 and the fourth-largest in the United States. Suddenly there were bank failures, railroad strikes, a business slump. At the University, many parents had trouble paying tuition, and Thomas Allen did not renew his funding for the engineering professorship. In this climate, the goal set by Eliot at the start of his term — building an endowment of "one million of dollars" in five years time — proved impossible to reach. In fact, the faculty would have to take a cut in salary by 1877, just to make ends meet.

STUDENT ACTIVITIES FLOURISH

Amid these financially gloomy times, students continued to find diversions. The Irving Union Debating Society, whose membership included four-fifths of all College students, staged an annual exhibition and staffed the *Irving Union* publication until 1878, when it was replaced by *Student Life*. In 1874, the first University sanctioned fraternity — Phi Delta Theta — was organized. Dances were popular; each spring, the junior class held a much-awaited exhibition and "hop." There was a chess club, a boating club, a small choir, and a gymnastic club; students played baseball and exercised in a modest new gym, with its own bowling alley in the basement. "In truth," sighed the *Irving Union* contentedly, "we all drink *deep* of the intoxicating *bowl*."

The oddest activity was the Ugly Club, which staged a farcical, post-exam party each June. To the music of a comb, triangle, and tin horn band, club members marched into the University's crowded main hall, where they were solemnly awarded

Hungry Man.
In 1871, Lyne S. Metcalfe, Jr., A.B. '72, was awarded the title of "Hungry Man." His caricature is pictured here.

All images, WU Archives

Smith family endows the first public lecture series

In 1875, William Henry Smith of Alton, Illinois — brother of board member James Smith — along with his wife, Ellen, endowed a free lecture series at the University. Smith, a close friend of William Greenleaf Eliot, wanted to call it the "Eliot Lecture Fund," but Eliot insisted that it be named for Smith himself. These lectures, offered to the public on Friday evenings, covered subjects ranging from the people of France (given by Marshall Snow) to petroleum (by William Potter).

The Smiths' only son, William Eliot Smith (1844-1909), A.B. '64, A.M. '67, was a namesake of Eliot, valedictorian of his college class, and later president of the Illinois Glass Works. In 1921, his widow, Alice E. Smith, established the William Eliot Smith Professorship in History in his name; today it is held by Derek M. Hirst.

Ellen Smith.

William Henry Smith.

titles: ugly man, pretty man, college fool, solemn man, hungry man, brassy man, wicked man, and ladies' pet. Afterwards, each nominee received a prize: a dunce cap for the fool, for example, and a bologna sausage for the hungry man.

More slowly now, and with greater difficulty, the University managed to make improvements. In 1875, William Henry Smith of Alton, Illinois, donated $25,500 for the endowment of a University lecture series. It was so popular that Eliot named five men "University Professors" — among them William Torrey Harris, the noted St. Louis schools superintendent and later head of the U.S. Bureau of Education — allowing them to lecture occasionally at the University and collect admission fees for themselves.

One of the Smith lecturers was a young physics professor, Francis Nipher, who spoke on "The Interaction of Magnets and Electrical Currents." Only a year into his 39-year tenure at the University, he already showed enough promise that in 1875, when a $25,000 gift from Wayman Crow funded a new chair in physics, Nipher was the first in a talented series of scientists appointed to the position.

Despite the ongoing financial worries, Polytechnic faculty members made remarkable progress in the sciences and benefited the community through their work. In 1877, Nipher organized the Missouri Weather Service, which used volunteer observers around the state to check meteorological data, then telegraph these findings to each other. And in the same year, Calvin Woodward and John K. Rees followed up on an earlier, more limited effort by Chancellor Chauvenet to establish standard time throughout the area. They bought an electric clock, mounted it at the University, and connected it to other clocks at local banks, hotels, and retailers; Rees, professor of mathematics and astronomy, kept them all properly regulated through his astronomical observations.

STAR-GAZING AND CLOCK-SETTING

Ever since William Chauvenet first came to Washington University, it had been a focal point of astronomical interest. The U.S. Coastal Service had even sent instruments to campus that, in 1870, helped determine the latitude and longitude of the University grounds. "The most accurate methods were employed in obtaining the results, so that the latitude and longitude of the University is known probably with a degree of accuracy greater than that of any other point in the Mississippi Valley," wrote Woodward. William

The Washington University Observatory.
This building was constructed in 1878 on the corner of St. Charles and 18th Street. Its six-inch telescope is still in service in Crow Hall.
WU Archives

Eimbeck, who helped with this survey, joined the faculty in 1871 as professor of practical astronomy primarily to plan a new observatory, since the old rooftop observatory had been dismantled during the renovation of University Hall.

This new structure opened in 1878, though the money shortage meant that it was small and cheaply constructed — like "a bake-oven with a revolving top," grumbled Eliot. Henry Pritchett, a new faculty member in mathematics and astronomy, called it "a little shanty." *Student Life* disagreed, gushing that "the construction of the revolving roof of the Equatorial Dome is superior to that of many of the best observatories, in its arrangements for opening and closing the skylights." Whatever its shortcomings, the observatory was the hub of significant work by "two enthusiastic young professors," said Eliot later, "who know how to make much of little."

The first was Pritchett, who went on to become president of the Massachusetts Institute of Technology and president of the Carnegie Foundation for the Advancement of Teaching. The second was Edmund Engler, a University graduate who was a faculty member in mathematics and descriptive geometry. Altogether, he received five degrees from Washington University and served as dean of engineering before leaving to become president of Worcester Polytechnic Institute.

In cooperation with the U.S. Coast and Geodetic Survey, Pritchett and Engler took the work of Chauvenet and Rees another giant step forward, sending time signals to towns and rail lines from the Appalachians to the Rocky Mountains. Other U.S. observatories carried this effort still further; on the far side of the Rockies, Edward S. Holden, B.S. '66, supplied time signals to the West from the Lick Observatory. By June

Francis Nipher (1847-1926).
The Wayman Crow Professor of Physics for nearly 40 years, Nipher directed the first statewide weather service. When he died, a colleague praised him as a "resourceful scientist, prolific in research production…and tireless enemy of bigotry and chicanery." Washington University gave him an honorary LL.D. in 1915.
WU Archives

Crow chair.
After Francis Nipher, other faculty members to hold the Crow chair were: Nobel Laureate Arthur Holly Compton, from 1920-23; Arthur L. Hughes, from 1923-55; Edward U. Condon, from 1958-64; Eugene Feenberg, from 1964-75; Edwin T. Jaynes, from 1975-98; and **John W. Clark** (above), installed in January 2000.
WU Photographic Services

49

The "largest time service in the world" comes from the small, original observatory downtown

John K. Rees, a Columbia University graduate, was professor of astronomy and mathematics at Washington University from 1876-81 before returning to Columbia to build an observatory there. He supervised the building of the small observatory on the original Washington University campus and developed a small time service; his assistant in these efforts was Edmund Engler, A.B. '76, Ph.B. '77, A.M. '79, and LL.D. (honorary) '01. In 1892, Engler became the first faculty member awarded a Ph.D. by Washington University.

In 1881, Henry S. Pritchett and Engler were both appointed assistant professors — Pritchett in mathematics and astronomy; Engler in mathematics and descriptive geometry — and both were named full professors after only one year. Their time service became nationally known, but a bitter rivalry developed with the U.S. Naval Observatory superintendent over which one would supply time signals via Western Union. One astronomical magazine sided with Pritchett, outraged "at the language of the slum and the brothel which the superintendent relishes so well." However, Washington University lost the argument and with it the income for these services. Soon it lost its astronomical prominence, too.

Pritchett left to head the U.S. Coast and Geodetic Survey, then became president of the Massachusetts Institute of Technology; Engler left to become president of Worcester Polytechnic Institute from 1901-11, before returning to the University as treasurer and secretary to the board of trustees.

Henry S. Pritchett (1857-1939).
WU Gallery of Art

John K. Rees (1851-1907).
WU Archives

Edmund Engler (1856-1918).
WU Gallery of Art

1882, Pritchett could declare that the University's tiny observatory had become "the center of the largest time service in the world."

The geodetic service that Pritchett and Engler established was at least as important as the time service. In 1883, they acquired an excellent transit instrument, used to determine longitude, and with it did more of this work than anyone else in the United States. Their measurements became the basis for topographic maps drawn by the U.S. Geological Survey, and they were used to calculate the boundaries of several states, including Arkansas, Kansas, Colorado, and New Mexico.

THE LAW SCHOOL REORGANIZES

Meanwhile, the sciences were not alone in making progress. The St. Louis Law School had more than tripled its enrollment between 1867 and 1878. Economically and geographically, its student body was diverse, thanks to scholarship aid and aggressive regional advertising. Since its founding, the school had attracted students from 20 states, one territory, and the District of Columbia. In 1877-78, more than half of its 76 students came from out of town.

There were serious problems, however. Faculty members, all well-known local lawyers and judges,

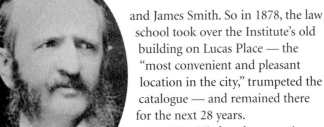

were paid only $500 a year, and the two-year program offered a limited curriculum. In 1870, an ailing Henry Hitchcock, the school's distinguished founder, had given up the deanship to George Stewart but stayed on as provost. Now, eight years later, Hitchcock abruptly resigned that job and convinced the entire faculty to follow suit until the University's board authorized certain changes.

Stunned, the directors acquiesced. They appointed Hitchcock as part-time dean, adopted a $1,200 annual salary for faculty members, broadened the curriculum, and lengthened the school term from six to seven months. Amid its own financial worries, the board could not yet act on two other Hitchcock proposals: recruiting a full-time dean and establishing a sufficient endowment.

There was also the question of space. The law school was still located in University Hall, which it shared with the Polytechnic Department. Luckily, Mary Institute had outgrown its old building and was moving to a spacious new structure at Locust and 27th streets, built on a lot bought with funds given by George Partridge

and James Smith. So in 1878, the law school took over the Institute's old building on Lucas Place — the "most convenient and pleasant location in the city," trumpeted the catalogue — and remained there for the next 28 years.

By 1880, Hitchcock was again ready to step down as dean, but the University was slow to find a replacement. In November, he resigned again, and the board finally acted, appointing a committee to name a successor. They settled on William Gardiner Hammond, a noted constitutional law scholar and chancellor of the law department of the State University of Iowa, who took office in 1881 at a salary of $4,000 a year. Hitchcock stayed on briefly as a faculty member but resigned for the third time in 1884.

MANUAL TRAINING BEGINS

Just as the law school was reorganizing, another University department was getting underway. By 1879, Calvin Woodward had already spearheaded a period of activity in the Polytechnic Department, lengthening the three-year course of study to four and briefly adding a program in science and literature for students not intending to become engineers. Under his leadership, a well-equipped mining and metallurgy laboratory was set up, even a commercial-level mill for the sampling and testing of ores. In 1883, he recruited John B. Johnson to fill a recently endowed chair and become William Palm Professor of Civil Engineering as well as head of that department; Johnson produced a series of classic textbooks and a prominent engineering index.

Several years earlier, in 1871, Woodward had made a startling discovery. When he asked his applied mechanics students to build some models for the class, they demurred — they did not know how to use the necessary tools. So Woodward asked Noah Dean, the University carpenter and mechanic, to outfit a shop where students could learn basic skills such as carpentry, wood turning, blacksmithing, and light machine work. Soon shop work was a required course in the Polytechnic Department, and the Academy boys were clamoring for their turn with the tools.

William Gardiner Hammond (1829-1894).
A Rhode Island native and Amherst College graduate, Hammond was a co-founder and first chancellor of the law department of the University of Iowa. He became Washington University's law dean in 1881. He was a noted common law scholar; in 1890, he published an annotated edition of *Blackstone's Commentaries*.

John Butler Johnson (1850-1902).
In 1884, Johnson was named the second William Palm Professor of Engineering, a chair established by an 1880 bequest of William Palm who desired to contribute "to the cultivation and dissemination of the mathematical and other exact sciences." He held the chair until 1899, and it has since been occupied by four others: John L. Van Ornum, Ernest O. Sweetser, Andrew D. Dimarogonas, and Ramesh Agarwal.

St. Louis School of Law building.
Formerly the home of Mary Institute, Washington University's law school held classes in this building from 1879 to 1905.

All images, WU Archives

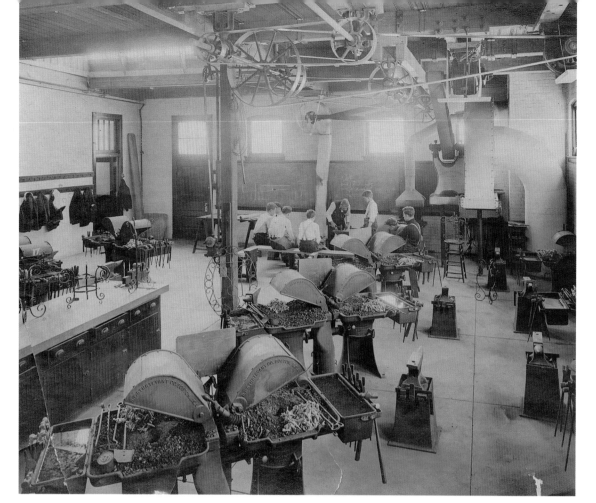

Manual Training School interior. Students work in the forging shop.

Samuel Cupples (1831-1925). Cupples, president of the Cupples Woodenware Company, was intrigued by the idea of manual training. He helped fund the construction of the University's first manual training building, then endowed the school with a gift of $115,000 in 1884.

The unexpected appeal of this program changed Woodward's future, transforming him into a staunch advocate of vocational education and a crusader for secondary education reform. By 1878 he was recommending that instruction in basic skills be offered to males and females alike from kindergarten through college. He gave this new educational concept a name: "manual training."

Soon Woodward's program blossomed, outgrowing its first small shop and graduating to three floors of an old mansion near campus. In 1879, woodenware manufacturer Samuel Cupples heard about its success and was intrigued by the concept; with manufacturers Edwin Harrison, a University board member, and Gottlieb Conzelman, he approached the board, offering funds to construct and equip a manual training school that would operate under the auspices of the Polytechnic Department. That new school — the University's third secondary department, after the Academy and Mary Institute — opened in 1880 at the corner of 18th and Washington.

It was an instant success. The three-year program taught high school-age boys strong vocational skills, along with some mathematics, science, and humanities, but it also fostered "a higher appreciation of THE VALUE AND DIGNITY OF INTELLIGENT LABOR, and the worth and respectability of laboring men," declared the prospectus. In the first year, 67 boys enrolled; by the third year, 176. Two years after it opened, the Manual Training School building had to double in size, and within a decade it was the most popular secondary school in St. Louis.

Delegations from around the U.S. and abroad began arriving to see the school for themselves. Soon other cities — Chicago, Philadelphia, Cleveland, Baltimore, and New York, among others — had adopted Woodward's concept,

Calvin Woodward (1837-1914). Woodward's innovations as developer of the Manual Training School made him a leader in vocational education.

establishing their own manual training programs. Woodward himself became an educational leader, lecturing widely on the value of progressive education.

FINE ARTS BECOMES A FULL DEPARTMENT

In 1857, Eliot expressed his first wistful hopes for a school of art. The O'Fallon Polytechnic Institute had made a modest beginning with its small School of Design. When O'Fallon was sold, this program became part of the University's Polytechnic Department, and was renamed the "School of Art and Design" in 1871. On the top floor of University Hall, amid reproductions of famous statues, instructor J. William Pattison taught drawing to a few undergraduates and a larger group of pay-as-you-go, part-time students. By 1872, he was teaching 38 women at 50 cents a lesson.

In November 1874, the University hired a new drawing instructor, Halsey C. Ives, a lightly educated itinerant painter who went on to earn a giant reputation. After a year on the faculty, he took a leave of absence, traveling to Europe to visit museums and expand his cultural horizons. Upon his return, he was promoted to full professor and began applying the lessons he had learned abroad to art education at the University. He added painting, sculpture, and decorative arts to the curriculum and convinced some undergraduates to study art full-time. In the community, he wheedled art collectors into opening their homes for public showings and booked traveling exhibits.

St. Louis Museum of Fine Arts.
From 1881 to 1904, the University's most important functions, including Commencement exercises, were held in the museum's grand Memorial Hall.
WU Gallery of Art

One local art lover was Wayman Crow's only son, Wayman Crow, Jr., who died suddenly in 1878. As a memorial to him, his grieving father decided to give the University a grand new museum — the St. Louis Museum of Fine Arts, dedicated in May 1881 at the corner of 19th and Locust. With this building in the offing, the board agreed in 1879 to create a School of Fine Arts, independent from the Polytechnic and under Ives' direction. The 1885-86 catalogue exclaimed: "this is the first University in the United States that has established a School of Fine Arts as a full department, in equal rank with the rest." However, the school offered no degree as yet and continued to cater mostly to part-time students, especially women and local artisans.

THE FACULTY ACTS TO IMPROVE THE COLLEGE

Such progress could not mask the fact that the College, the University's liberal arts division, was not thriving. Amid the hodgepodge of academic institutions that made up Washington University — three secondary schools, the Polytechnic Department, the St. Louis Law School, the School of Fine Arts — the College routinely had the lowest enrollment of all. In 1871, it had 27 students across all four classes; by 1887, the College and Polytechnic combined had an enrollment of only 100.

Daunting entrance exams, adopted in 1875 as a requirement for admission, were part of the problem; so were classes that relied on recitation and strict discipline. The school's location, in the smoky heart of downtown with no green space and little room for athletics, was also a disadvantage. Even in a good year, only a handful of students graduated, and in 1876-77, there was no senior class at all. The *Irving Union* teased in 1872 that the College had only seven sophomores and seven juniors, though rumors were flying in each class that one more was coming. "On the whole," the writer said wryly, "we think that the one more coming had better hurry up."

In 1880, the faculty took action to improve matters. They decided to forego the entrance test for graduates of the University's secondary schools and St. Louis Central High School. They authorized the College to offer, along with the bachelor of arts degree, a bachelor of philosophy (Ph.B.) degree for students who did not wish to study

Edward Fisher Jackson, A.B. '81, A.M. '00 (1861-?). The first summa cum laude graduate of the University. Jackson went on to become an instructor, Latin master, and assistant principal at Smith Academy from 1884 to 1901.
WU Archives

Jennie R. Lippman, A.B. '83, A.M. '93 (?-1917). Lippman, the first female summa cum laude graduate, later became a Latin teacher and head of college preparatory work at Mary Institute, where she received the Danforth Faculty Service Award for more than 25 years of service.
WU Archives

Wayman Crow (1808-1885).
Oil on canvas by Frederick Porter Vinson
WU Gallery of Art

Wayman Crow, Jr. (?-1878).
Oil on canvas by Rose Lamb
WU Gallery of Art

William Trelease (1857-1945).
First Engelmann Professor of Botany and director of the Missouri Botanical Garden after Henry Shaw's death in 1889, Trelease was a Ph.D. botanist who was committed to graduate training and research.
WU Archives

Henry Shaw (1800-1889).
Shaw, a wealthy cutlery maker, began the Missouri Botanical Garden in 1858 and deeded it to the city of St. Louis at his death in 1889.
Missouri Historical Society, St. Louis

Shaw medallion.
This medallion was likely created by Victor S. Holm in 1904 as a prize awarded by the Missouri Botanical Garden to a World's Fair participant. As a part of the John Max Wulfing Collection, the medallion is housed at the West Campus.
WU Wulfing Collection

Greek but wanted more math and science, as well as more electives. They combined the College and the Polytechnic into a single Undergraduate Department. Gradually, they began to relax their classroom practice, relying more on lectures than on rote-learning.

Later that same year, they went further, adopting a plan for conferring degrees with distinction: a 90 percent average meant summa cum laude, 85 percent magna cum laude, and 75 percent cum laude. In 1881, Alfred Greve and Edward F. Jackson were the first two graduates awarded degrees with honors; in 1882, Edith Smith Kellenberger became the first woman to graduate magna cum laude and in 1883, Jennie Rebecca Lippman earned special distinction, as the first woman to graduate summa cum laude.

"City Set upon a Hill"

In 1882, the University marked the 25th anniversary of its inauguration. At a gala event, held in the grand hall of the new museum, Eliot once again talked about the University's past and future. He described its progress, despite the "many vicissitudes of social, political, financial, national convulsions. We have met and measurably overcome all manner of discouragements, singly and by battalions, which naturally encounter those who undertake a great work with insufficient means."

Altogether, the University had 1,486 students, counting the popular evening division, and 87 professors with "not an idler among us. Scarcely one who does not bring energy and enthusiasm to the performance of every daily task," he said proudly. The alumni were fully the equals of Harvard and Yale graduates. "Think over the list of them, as lawyers, or doctors, or clergymen, or teachers, or journalists, or merchants, or mechanics, or engineers — for the record contains all these — and you will see that I speak the truth."

Still, the University had great needs, as he well knew. He ticked them off: works of art for the museum, a home for the art school, more income for the law school, more space for the secondary schools, student rooms and a dining hall for the Undergraduate Department, housing for the scientific collections, and a vastly increased endowment. Despite an annual income of $100,000, he said sadly, "I regret to say our expenditures are still considerably in excess. Ah, how I wish the balance were on the other side!"

He surveyed his audience with his familiar, hopeful gaze, and the faces he had once seen — those old friends in this enterprise, who had provided for it in the past — were largely missing.

Hudson Bridge had died in 1875; Seth Ranlett in 1881. James Smith, perhaps the most generous donor of all, had died in 1877 leaving Eliot half of his estate, more than $150,000 altogether, "as a testimony of sincere and long continued friendship and regard." He trusted Eliot, he said, to use this money "for the good of others." Eliot had done so, funding various University projects. Among them was a $60,000 gift to the Academy, now renamed "Smith Academy," which had made possible a much-needed new building at 19th and Washington in 1879.

These loyal colleagues were disappearing from the scene and Eliot, 71 and frailer than ever, was nearing the end of his own life. Although he had worked faithfully for Washington University, he would never succeed in securing its financial future. Others, he urged the audience, should step forward to take on this important task. Not only would this work benefit the University, he said, but it would also bring credit to St. Louis as "'a city set upon a hill,' of which the whole nation will be proud."

The Eliot Era Ends

Over the next five years, Eliot slowed down perceptibly, but he still recorded some accomplishments. Prodded by a letter from Sylvester Waterhouse, Missouri Botanical Garden founder Henry Shaw agreed in 1885 to endow the Henry Shaw School of Botany as a department of the University, with a mission of encouraging botanical research. At the same time, Shaw endowed a professorship named for George Engelmann, a physician, noted botanist, and Shaw's close adviser; its first occupant was William Trelease, an active

researcher with a commitment to graduate training, who became Garden director after Shaw's death. Shaw's will established another connection with the University, giving the chancellor an *ex-officio* seat on the Garden's board.

By fall 1886, Eliot felt increasingly unwell, though he valiantly tried to teach his usual class in political economy. In November he finally had to give up and take to his bed. Marshall Snow visited him daily. "The very last hour which I spent by his bedside," he said later, "was occupied chiefly in talking about the future of the University which he loved so well." Hoping to recover in a warmer climate, Eliot traveled to Pass Christian, Mississippi, where he died on January 23, 1887.

At his funeral, held four days later, the Church of the Messiah was overflowing with guests, among them the entire faculty of Washington University. As Eliot had requested, there were no flowers and only a brief service, "but these tributes were not needed to testify to the affection of those present," said one obituary. Every one of Eliot's eight pallbearers had been named for him, including Hudson Eliot Bridge and William Eliot Smith. He was buried in Bellefontaine Cemetery, where his marker bore a simple epitaph: "Looking Unto Jesus."

Samuel Treat, one of only two surviving members of the original board, was deeply grieved, adjourning U.S. District Court so that he could "pay his last respects to a lifelong friend, with whom [I have] been closely associated in many of his grand works for more than forty years." In the official court record he placed a moving tribute to Eliot, a man "worthy of all the love, gratitude,

and honor which should cling to the memory of a pure, unselfish, and exalted life, the fruits of whose labors appear everywhere, blessing and blessed now and for the indefinite future."

Faculty and alumni expressed their sorrow, and University board members included a "testimony of love" in their minutes. "Turn backward these pages for the record of his daily life, and look around you for his monument," they wrote. "His prayers and hopes, his ideals of manly and womanly duty, of sacred devotion to a life of usefulness to his fellow-men, have been wrought into the very fiber of the University; and whatever place it has filled in the culture and advancement of the city and of the west, is due in the largest measure to his clear foresight." They concluded:

"His rich sympathy in trial, his cheerful encouragement in trouble, his earnest words, which called to duty, remain to us as a precious memory of one whom it was a blessed privilege to know. In parting with him as president of this board — as chancellor, as co-worker, and friend — in humble submission to a wisdom greater than ours, in profound sadness we enter upon these pages the word —

'Farewell!'"

NUNC DIMITTIS.

W. G. ELIOT, AUGUST 5, 1886.

Fain would I breathe that glorious word,
" Now lettest Thou thy servant, Lord,
  Depart in peace."
When may I humbly claim that kind award,
  And cares and labor cease ?

With anxious heart, I watch at Heaven's
    gate,
  Answer to hear ;
With failing strength, I feel the increasing
    weight
  Of every passing year ;
Hath not the time yet fully come, dear
    Lord,
  Thy servant to release ?

Be still, my heart ! In silence God doth
    speak,
  Here is thy place ; here—not at Heaven's
    gate ;
Thy task is not yet finished ; frail and
    weak,
  Doing or suffering steadfast in thy faith,
Thy service is accepted, small or great.
  His time is thine—or soon or late ;
If daylight fades, work while the twilight
    lasts,
  Then stand and wait.

George Engelmann, M.D. (1809-1884).
A faculty member and sometime lecturer at Washington University, Engelmann came to St. Louis in 1835. With Eliot, he founded the Academy of Science of St. Louis and served for many years as its president. His son, George, A.B. '67, became a well-known St. Louis physician.
Missouri Historical Society, St. Louis

Engelmann medallion.
This medallion was created by Max Slilel in 1906 to commemorate the 50th anniversary of the founding of the Academy of Science of St. Louis.
WU Wulfing Collection

Nunc Dimittis.
This poem by William Greenleaf Eliot was reproduced in *Student Life* just before Eliot's death.
WU Archives

THE DOWNTOWN CAMPUS

No trace of the first Washington University campus remains today, but in the 1880s and '90s, it occupied most of three city blocks in downtown St. Louis. Two other buildings — Mary Institute and the St. Louis Law School — were just a short distance away.

In those days, the University was largely a commuter school. While a few out-of-town students roomed in nearby boarding houses, most lived at home and arrived each morning by train or streetcar. They began the day — some of them grumbling — with nondenominational chapel exercises. Then the College students had classes until early afternoon, while the Polytechnic undergraduates had classes and labs until 5 p.m. or later. Until 1880, rote learning was the norm, and there were few electives.

In this distinctly urban environment, students found little green space. On hot days, they sweltered in the solid brick buildings, choking on the dust that rose from the unpaved streets and blew through the open windows. They longed for room to run, play handball, work out. A succession of gymnasiums — though small and inexpensively built — were among the most popular spots on campus.

Here is a look at Washington University's downtown campus, as it appeared in the late 19th century.

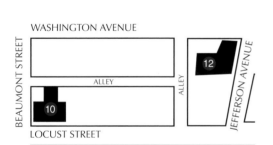

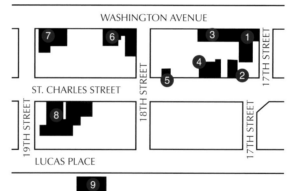

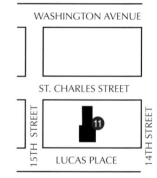

1 Academic Hall. It was completed in 1856, the first building of Washington University and the first home of the Academic Department, later known as Smith Academy.

2 Chemistry Laboratory. The University's second building was constructed at William G. Eliot's own financial risk in 1856.

3 University Hall. Built as Collegiate Hall in 1861, it was enlarged and renamed in 1871 when it also became the home of the Polytechnic Department and Law.

4 Gymnasium. Several small, inexpensive gymnasiums were built over the years at the rear of the college complex. One had a bowling alley in the basement.

5 Observatory. A telescope, given by James Yeatman, was first mounted in a tower on top of Collegiate Hall. During the transformation of this building into University Hall, the tower was dismantled. In 1878, a small observatory opened on campus.

6 Manual Training School. The University's third secondary department after the Smith Academy and Mary Institute, it was completed in 1880. Classes previously met in the basement of Noah Dean, university carpenter.

7 Smith Academy. The Academy began life in Academic Hall, but in 1879 moved to a large new building at the corner of 19th and Washington.

8 St. Louis Museum of Fine Arts and School of Fine Arts. The school was founded in 1879, and the grand new museum building was dedicated in May 1881.

9 St. Louis Medical College. This new building was constructed at 1806 Locust in 1892. Eames and Young were the architects; William S. Eames, A.B. '78, was a Washington University graduate.

10 Mary Institute. From 1859-78 it was located at 1417 Locust, then it moved to this new building at the northeast corner of Locust and 27th streets.

11 St. Louis Law School. It began life in 1867 in the ill-suited Polytechnic Institute building at 7th and Chestnut. In 1878, after seven years in University Hall, Washington University's law department moved to Mary Institute's old building at 1417 Locust.

12 Missouri Medical College and Polyclinic later became Washington University Hospital.

1 **Academic Hall.**
Missouri Historical
Society, St. Louis

"In view of the disparity between the size of the new building and the number of students who are to inhabit it, it is suggested that each [student] be required to wear a bell round his neck, that he may be readily found when wanted."

—*Irving Union*, October 1871

 **3** **University Hall.**
WU Archives

Library.
The library consisted of a single room, located in University Hall. Prior to the 1880s, students used public library collections and the Mercantile Library for their studies.
WU Archives

Chapel.
Morning chapel services of Bible readings and singing were held in this room in University Hall. *Irving Union* described the musical portion of services as "an old and nearly worn-out melodeon…accompanied by a faint chorus of students who sang in every key of the circle."
WU Archives

Sellew Medal.
Named for Manual Training School benefactor and board member Ralph Sellew, this medal was awarded annually to the student with the highest grade point average in the graduating class.
WU Wulfing Collection

"Remember! We are graduates from the M.T.S. Long may she live! Shall we stop here? No! Let us take for our motto: 'Even higher.'"

—*Student Life*, June 1890

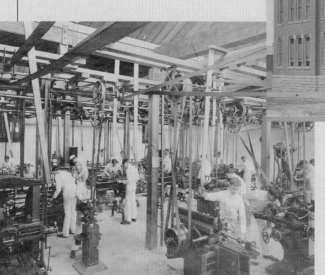

6 **Manual Training School.**
The exterior is pictured above. At left, students work in the machine shop.
WU Archives

7 **Smith Academy.**
WU Archives

Smith Academy football team.
This photograph of the 1897 football team appeared in the *Smith Academy Record*.
WU Archives

"We are glad to see that the St. Louis Medical College contemplates moving from its downtown location into our neighborhood. Nothing is better for the promotion of college spirit and fellowship than the grouping together of the various departments, which this move will accomplish."

—*Student Life*, February 1892

9 **St. Louis Medical College.**
The exterior is pictured above; at left, students work in the dissecting room in 1909. In 1891, St. Louis Medical College became the Medical Department of Washington University.

WU Becker Medical Library

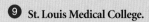

10 **Mary Institute.**
The exterior is pictured above. At right, members of the class of 1895 identify themselves in French on the chalkboard. At far right, the class of 1907 is pictured in the primary room.

All images courtesy of MICDS Archives

"YEARS OF TRIAL"

1887-1899

St. Louis from the Eads Bridge above the Mississippi River.
Views of St. Louis in 1888, drawn by Charles Graham and published in New York by *Harper's Weekly.*
Collection of A.G. Edwards and Sons, Inc., St. Louis, Missouri

"Years of Trial"

Following the death of William Greenleaf Eliot, a cloud of gloom settled over Washington University. At one blow, the young school had lost its co-founder, third chancellor, and the only board president it had ever known. More fundamentally, it had lost the moral leader who had shaped its generous social and educational policies: its liberal scholarship assistance, its hospitality to students of varied religious and ethnic backgrounds, its early admission of women, its accommodation of students who wanted to pursue nonprofessional careers, and its belief in allowing faculty members to teach and publish as they wished.

View of the levee, from the br[...]

1887 1899

1889 Walter Moran Farmer, the first African-American student to graduate from Washington University, received his law degree cum laude.

1891 On April 14, the board approved the creation of a new Medical Department, which was still called the St. Louis Medical College.

1892 Winfield Scott Chaplin was inaugurated as the University's fourth chancellor on January 11.

1894 A real estate subcommittee of the board selected a hilly site west of Skinker Road for the University's new campus — the site of today's Hilltop Campus.

1895 Robert S. Brookings was named president of the board of directors.

Col. George Leighton (1835-1902).
An ardent Unionist during the Civil War, who had served as colonel of the 7th Missouri Regiment and as provost marshal of St. Louis, Leighton was general counsel of the Missouri Pacific Railway. Longtime board member and president from 1887-95, he received an honorary LL.D. in 1901.
WU Archives

His death exposed, with stark clarity, a serious institutional weakness: the lack of an academic vision for the University. Eliot and his entrepreneurial board, none of them educators by profession, had created a hodgepodge of poorly integrated programs: three secondary schools (Mary Institute, Smith Academy, the Manual Training School); the Undergraduate Department, composed of the College (or liberal arts program) and Polytechnic (or science and engineering program); the St. Louis Law School, which was the University's law department; the fledgling St. Louis School of Fine Arts and art museum; and the new Henry Shaw School of Botany.

Worse still, this miscellaneous enterprise was in financial trouble. That fact should not have surprised anyone, since Eliot had warned of fiscal problems in every speech he ever gave. But older members of the board, such as James Yeatman, were inured to financial crises by years of watching Eliot come up with key donations, often at the very last minute, while younger members likely were awed by Eliot's commanding presence. A few must have seen him as a father figure; in fact, the board now included Eliot's own son, Henry W. Eliot, and Col. George Leighton, the son-in-law of Eliot's old friend and fellow charter board member, Hudson Bridge.

Leaderless now, the board had to grapple with a deficit of nearly $40,000 per year and with the University's unsustainable pattern of spending unrestricted endowment, just to make ends meet. The underlying dilemma was simple: Most programs had sprung up without adequate endowment to

James K. Hosmer.
A Harvard graduate, Hosmer came to the University in 1874 as professor of English and German literature, then took on other courses. He left in 1892 when "the outlook was not a cheerful one. With the death of Dr. Eliot disappeared the dynamo that had driven it through its inception. Its funds suffered loss, its old friends were largely dead or weary in their striving, and new friends did not at once come forward." He received an honorary LL.D. in 1897.

Carte de viste photo by Robert Benecke, c. 1880.
WU Archives

support them. The tiny Undergraduate Department, with its high faculty costs and small tuition income, posed the biggest problem of all. Much later, onetime faculty member James Hosmer recalled that, during these "years of trial," the University's income came largely from its prosperous secondary schools, which shored up the undergraduate program. "Dr. Eliot…used to compare the struggling university to a small dog with an inordinate tail," he said. "The dog did not wag the tail, but the tail wagged the dog."

THE BOARD TAKES DRASTIC COST-CUTTING MEASURES

Clearly, no one with any sense would serve as chancellor of such a financially strapped institution, so the board again asked the University's loyal dean, Marshall Snow, to become acting chancellor until the situation improved. Meanwhile, it needed a new board president to deal with these difficult times, and chose the vice president, Leighton, for the job. A prominent attorney, he had given up his legal practice to head his father-in-law's iron manufacturing business, and now he took Bridge's place as University board member and donor. In private life, Leighton was a cultured man, a collector of literary and artistic treasures, with a private library of western Americana that was the largest in St. Louis and possibly in the United States.

Marshall Snow (1842-1916).
He served as acting chancellor after Eliot's death, until Winfield S. Chaplin took his place.
WU Archives

Not a reformer at heart, Leighton still did his job honorably, taking stock of the University's finances and recommending stringent austerity measures: trying to make the University's holdings more profitable, raising tuition, increasing the endowment, and reducing operating expenses. The founders themselves, he said once with feeling, "had seen many dark days; many when the burden seemed too great….But theirs were hearts not given to failure, and they came at last out of the valley of gloom." Plainly, he was hoping for the same result.

Between 1887 and 1889, his rigid economies made some difference, as the deficit shrank by two-thirds. At the same time, the endowment grew by more than $240,000 — though, in the board's time-honored fashion, its members gave most of the total themselves. Yet this increase had to offset new expenses, such as a recently introduced fifth year in the engineering program — and the faculty, which suffered most in this belt-tightening, finally became restive.

In June 1889, 17 professors signed a stunning critique of the University's instruction, academic standards, and resources. They described vast deficits in books and equipment that they routinely filled from their own collections. Admission standards were comparable to those at leading colleges, they said, and they themselves were highly productive; some departments, notably astronomy, were among the best in the nation. The facilities, however, were outdated, dismal. To rectify matters, they needed a well-equipped library, better apparatus, bright new buildings, and greatly increased salaries:

> "We have given our best years and even of our means that the work might go forward, and through our devotion and labor it has been brought to a creditable standard. Sacrifices have been made through these years, but not for the small money compensation received; it is the interest felt in the work, the faith in its ultimate success, and the hope that provision would be made for its maintenance that have given us courage to wait and to labor. But now a limit has been reached."

Six months later, Colonel Leighton responded in another report, which "will not be read with pleasure by the people of St. Louis," predicted one newspaper, because it was even bleaker than his first. A limit *had* been reached, he agreed. The deficit was down to around $11,000, but there was no new way to cover it. While emergency measures might hold the line for two years, he said, it would then be necessary to trim the educational program, "however humiliating to us and to this city it may be." Reluctantly, he named five candidates for elimination, and at the top of the list were the two programs — the A.B. and Ph.B. courses, leading to degrees in arts and philosophy — that made up the liberal arts portion of the Undergraduate Department. And yes, he admitted candidly, the faculty was right: Their salaries were indeed too low, and cuts made during the economic panic of the 1870s had never been restored. "We have no right to ask their continued loyalty under conditions now prevailing," he concluded grimly.

Amid these lean times, key faculty members began to depart. "I could not support my family on my salary," recalled James Hosmer, professor of English and German, who left in 1892 to become librarian of the new Minneapolis Public Library. William B. Potter resigned in 1893, thus ending the successful, 22-year life of the Department of Mining and Metallurgy — ironically, the program

Alexander Langsdorf (1877-1973).
WU Archives

that ranked at the top of Colonel Leighton's list to preserve. Henry Pritchett, the distinguished astronomer, became director of the U.S. Coast and Geodetic Survey in 1897, and soon after president of the Massachusetts Institute of Technology. John B. Johnson, a civil engineering giant, resigned in 1899 to become dean at the University of Wisconsin.

However, many other faculty *did* wait and labor — and it was their loyalty, above all else, that sustained the troubled University. Alexander Langsdorf, B.S. '98, who later became dean of the Schools of Engineering and Architecture, recalled that he "had the great privilege of knowing twelve of them…and can testify that as a whole no finer men could have been found anywhere." He added gratefully: "They may be said to have been the brains, bone, and sinew of the institution through all the lean years."

SEARCH COMMITTEE NAMES A NEW CHANCELLOR

Before Leighton was forced to make his threatened cuts, an extraordinary gift came from a familiar source: the Eliot family. Just as William G. Eliot had so often reached into his own thinly lined pocket for funds to support University ventures, his widow now did the same. In May 1891, Abby Eliot pledged $100,000 in stock from Henry W. Eliot's company, Hydraulic Press Brick, to be given to the University as soon as it named a new chancellor. The effect on the weary board members was immediate and dramatic. They formed a committee and by October had selected their candidate: Winfield Scott Chaplin, most recently dean of the Lawrence Scientific School at Harvard.

A Maine native and an 1870 West Point graduate, Chaplin was a civil engineer who had served two years in the military, then taught at Maine State College, the Imperial University in Tokyo,

Winfield Scott Chaplin (1847-1918).
He was inaugurated the fourth chancellor of Washington University in January 1892. A West Point classmate said Chaplin had four educational dogmas: "1, a certain amount of knowledge; 2, a certain mental training; 3, fixed moral standards; 4, a set purpose." Privately, he was an "indefatigable smoker of cigars" and an "incomparable spinner of yarns."

Oil on masonite by Gustav von Schlegell
WU Gallery of Art

George Herbert Walker

George Herbert Walker, LL.B. '97, founded the G.H. Walker Investment Co. in St. Louis in 1900. As president of the U.S. Golf Association in 1920, he promoted amateur competition between British and American teams. The first match occurred in 1922, with a cup he had donated — still known as the Walker Cup — as the prize.

His daughter, Dorothy, who had attended Mary Institute, married Prescott Bush in 1921. Their second son, George Herbert Walker Bush, became U.S. president, as did their grandson, George W. Bush.

George Herbert Walker (1875-1953).
WU Archives

and Union College, before migrating to Lawrence. Physically, he was more imposing than the diminutive Eliot. A Union student remembered him as "over six feet in height, broad-shouldered and erect, a typical West Pointer, with a mop of reddish hair, a big mustache and eyes that twinkled with humor and kindness." He could also "roar when angry," said Langsdorf, "woe betide anyone who roused his wrath!"

On January 11, 1892, Chaplin was inaugurated as the University's fourth chancellor in an event that reflected the school's pecuniary problems. The *Post-Dispatch* described it tactfully as "a simple ceremony." *Student Life* was more blunt, calling it "miserably managed, miserably attended....What a stage! There were absolutely no attempts made to decorate it. It looked, as someone remarked, like the roof of a freight car. And the sumptuous decorations...consisted of a few flags, scattered mournfully about, as if to bury the Chancellor."

Undeterred, Chaplin gave an address in which he described his educational philosophy. A born pragmatist, he believed that higher education was simply "stimulated mental growth," intended to refine inborn tastes and aptitudes. Since these aptitudes differ from one student to another, he said, a university should offer a wide range of educational choices. Ideally, "it neither prescribes nor proscribes any subjects" for its students; rather, "it leads them to study by a splendid display of opportunities, and by satisfying the interest and desires of each." This address would not have surprised one West Point classmate who described Chaplin as "an educational officer in chief command," with "an attitude of unyielding independence before the 'latest cries' of educational faddists, sensationalists, and humbugs."

Whatever Chaplin lacked in theory, he made up for in determination. He went on to admit frankly — without naming names — that *some* colleges had unwisely added programs before fully endowing existing ones. He conceded that Washington University was not doing as well as other institutions, despite its strong academic record. "Why this

Nationally prominent architects who attended the University design Medical Department building

William S. Eames (1857-1915).
WU Archives

Thomas C. Young (1858-1934).
Missouri Historical Society, St. Louis

William S. Eames graduated from the University in 1878 and in 1885 launched a partnership, Eames and Young, with fellow architect Thomas Crane Young, who had attended the University from 1878-79. Together, they designed a number of buildings connected to the University or its staff: an office building for John Green, a house for Halsey C. Ives, a house for Robert S. Brookings, and his Cupples Station Warehouses. Additionally, the firm was asked to design a building on Locust Street for the St. Louis Medical College, which had become the new Medical Department of Washington University in 1891. The College moved into this building in 1892.

St. Louis Medical College.
Eames and Young designed this building on Locust Street for the new Medical Department of Washington University.
WU Archives

is so I leave you to decide," he said. "I am more concerned with its future course." At last he came to the bottom line: The University needed money, he would be looking for it soon, and he expected "a hearty response" from the St. Louis community.

A New Medical Department Joins the University

Yet another program had been added to the University shortly before Chaplin's arrival — the St. Louis Medical College, founded in 1841, which had long-standing, informal ties to the University. William G. Eliot and Col. John O'Fallon had served as its trustees, and Henry Hitchcock was its legal adviser; two University professors, Abram Litton and Charles A. Pope, had been members of its faculty. Pope, who was O'Fallon's son-in-law, had become dean of the Medical College in 1849, and in 1855 O'Fallon financed construction of a new building for the school at 7th and Clark. After Pope died in 1870, John Hodgen took over as dean. He had ties to the University, too, serving as a "University Professor," or occasional lecturer, beginning in 1875.

By 1890, the Medical College's building was old and small, and the Medical Fund Society — a consortium of senior medical faculty members who had bought the building after Pope's death — sold it and began scouting for a new site. At the same time, eminent faculty member William Townsend Porter returned from study in Berlin ready to establish a German-style physiology lab-

oratory in St. Louis. Using Hitchcock as an intermediary, the Medical College approached the University board about setting up this program jointly and sharing the expense.

Given their financial headaches, the board members must have felt some dismay at this proposed new source of expenditure. Hitchcock reported back that they had to refuse the offer because of the University's "present financial embarrassment." Unexpectedly, the Medical College did not quit there. John Green, an ophthalmology professor — "a Harvard graduate who could quote Latin by the yard, and who had been [Eliot's] longtime friend and next-door neighbor," said Langsdorf — proposed a full-scale union. The board authorized the current Medical College dean, Henry Hodgen Mudd, nephew of John Hodgen, to form a committee and begin negotiations.

In pleading their case, they had a secret weapon: James Yeatman, their own secretary as well as a respected University board member, who offered to facilitate a merger. They were tapping a long history of interest in such a union. In his 1859 inaugural address, Chancellor Joseph Hoyt had dreamed of a medical department for the University, and in 1872, Eliot had done the same: "Nor am I without hope that a medical department may, by-and-by, be added," he had said, "somewhat after the Harvard plan, which…insists upon a thorough three years' curriculum of study." The Medical College fit this description exactly. In 1880, it was well ahead of its time in stipulating a three-year course of study, and by 1890, Porter and others were arguing for a fourth year, which they finally added in 1897.

On April 14, 1891, the University's board unanimously approved the creation of this new Medical Department, which would still be called the St. Louis Medical College. One newspaper called it "an educational event," and said that this union "contemplates greatly enlarged provisions for thorough medical education." Certainly, the Medical Fund Society moved ahead quickly with its plans for a new building, buying a lot at 1806-14 Locust Street opposite the museum and close to other University buildings. For their architects, they hired the firm of Eames and Young, whose principal, William S. Eames, was an 1878 University graduate and son of William H. Eames of the Missouri Dental College faculty.

Joseph Nash McDowell (1805-1868).
In 1840, McDowell founded Kemper College, the forerunner of Missouri Medical College. That school merged in 1899 with the St. Louis Medical College to become the Medical Department of Washington University.

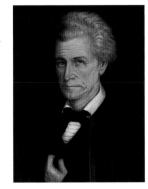

John Hodgen (1826-1882).
A graduate of Missouri Medical College, Hodgen was professor of anatomy and physiology at St. Louis Medical College and the school's dean from 1875-82, as well as president of the American Medical Association in 1880. He developed the Hodgen splint for hip fractures.

William Townsend Porter (1862-1949).
A St. Louis Medical College faculty member, Porter made the first overtures for the college to merge with Washington University.

John Green (1835-1913).
A brilliant ophthalmologist, Green was broadly educated with a special interest in the classics. The University awarded him an honorary LL.D. in 1905. Chancellor Frederic A. Hall, himself a Greek scholar, recalled of his first meeting with Green, "I found him able to make suggestions with reference to Greek tragedy which had never occurred to me."

All images, WU Becker Medical Library

Mary Institute.
Members of the class of 1899 line up in their starched white linen graduation gowns.
Courtesy of MICDS Archives

The Dental College was involved in these events, too. It had been founded in 1866 as the first dental school in Missouri and the first in the world allied with a medical college — in this case, the St. Louis Medical College. Ever since, the two programs had been closely related. Now they shared the same building and the same dean, held joint commencements, and taught the same first-year curriculum, with some of the same faculty members. Not surprisingly, the Missouri Dental College decided in February 1892 to join with the University and to continue to share space in the new building: an ornate, four-story structure that was ready for use in fall 1892.

The rest of the University was delighted to welcome the Medical College, which will be "the best equipped in the West," enthused *Student Life.* "It will have many conveniences for the students beside the necessary operating and recitation rooms, such as reading and smoking rooms, club room, etc…[and] should graduate men eminently fitted for practicing the profession of medicine."

OTHER UNIVERSITY DEPARTMENTS FLOURISH

Meanwhile, the University's three secondary departments were burgeoning. Mary Institute's new building at Locust and 27th streets had reached capacity by 1891. In that same year, the school acquired its fourth principal, Edmund Sears; its second principal, Calvin Pennell, had resigned in 1887 after a 25-year tenure and was briefly replaced by James Dillard, who began to update the curriculum. Sears — "a man of literary ability, high character and good taste," said *Student Life* approvingly — continued this effort, adding a college preparatory program as well as a non-college track, which emphasized art and a course in domestic science.

Smith Academy, too, was bursting at the seams. In 1893, there was such heavy enrollment that 60 desks had to be placed inside the chapel. That year, all the graduates went on to college: one each to Harvard and MIT, two to Williams, three to Yale, and ten to Washington University. Through these years, Smith regularly sent a few more students to the University than to out-of-town schools. Of 462 Smith alumni from 1884 to 1903, 196 went to other colleges and universities and 230 to the University.

The Manual Training School — which described itself as "a three years' course, including

Condé Nast earns fame as magazine publisher after graduating from Washington University

Condé Nast (1874-1942).
WU Archives

Condé Montrose Nast received his LL.B. from the University in 1897, then from 1909-14 began building his publishing empire with the purchase of several magazines: *Vogue, House and Garden, Vanity Fair.* He pioneered the technique of targeting groups of readers by interest group or income level. Today, his company, Condé Nast Publications, is an industry giant that publishes the original three magazines and others, including: *The New Yorker, GQ, Bon Appétit, Condé Nast Traveler, Glamour, Self, Bride's,* and *Architectural Digest.*

William Samuel Curtis (1850-1916).
Curtis, himself an 1873 graduate of the College and an 1876 alumnus of the law school, was practicing law in Omaha when he was named the school's new dean.
WU School of Law

Daisy Seidel receives law degree

Daisy Barbee Seidel LL.B. '96 cum laude, was the second woman, after Phoebe Couzins, to graduate from the law school. She used her $50 senior thesis prize to set up her first St. Louis law practice. In 1897, she defended a woman charged with grand larceny and became the first female attorney to try — and win, by a unanimous verdict — a criminal case in the city; newspapers called her the "Portia of St. Louis." Later, she practiced with another woman attorney, Gratia E. Woodside, and still later, married and moved to Goldfield, Nevada, where she became the first woman attorney in the state.

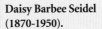

Daisy Barbee Seidel (1870-1950).
Western Historical Manuscript Collection, University of Missouri-St. Louis

Otto Heller (1863-1941).
When Heller joined the faculty as professor of German in 1891, he was said to be the youngest professor in any accredited university in the country. He remained for 46 years, becoming professor of modern European literature and eventually dean of the School of Graduate Studies.
WU Archives

English studies, Drawing, Carpentry, Pattern-Making, Blacksmithing, Machine Work and the Management of the Engine" — sent some graduates on to business and manufacturing jobs, but many others to the University's Polytechnic Department. During these years, the school's fame was spreading: It was selected as an exhibitor at the Paris Exposition of 1889, where its display of tool work won the gold medal, and at the 1893 World's Columbian Exposition in Chicago. In 1891, Manual Training, Smith, and undergraduate division students could all take a new course in military science taught by John Stafford, First Lieutenant in the Eighth U.S. Infantry.

Within the Undergraduate Department, times were changing. As he had hinted earlier, Chaplin did eliminate the Ph.B. degree, along with most required courses, and introduced a largely elective system. "Three years ago," he told some businessmen, "the college said to the student, 'here are two courses of study, take one of them as it is arranged or do not come to us at all.' Now the college says, 'come to us and take what you…choose. Do so much work in any of these subjects…and we give you a degree.'" In 1893, Calvin Woodward took another step toward simplification, changing the name of the Polytechnic to the "School of

Engineering," and the school returned to a four-year curriculum. At age 78, the beloved chemistry professor Abram Litton retired; new faculty members arrived, notably Otto Heller, professor of German, whose salary was underwritten by Adolphus Busch, the founder of Anheuser-Busch Brewing Company who became a University board member in 1895.

In the late 1880s, the Law Department was basking in the glow of a successful fund drive that produced a $77,500 endowment and made it nearly self-sustaining. Then in 1894, Dean William Hammond, an authority on the history of common law, died unexpectedly, and the board asked William Samuel Curtis, A.B. '73, LL.B. '76, who was practicing law in Omaha, to take his place. Longtime faculty members retired, especially George Madill and Henry Hitchcock, who had returned to the faculty in 1888 but left for the fourth and last time in 1894. New faces appeared, among them Isaac Lionberger to lecture on

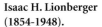

Isaac H. Lionberger (1854-1948).
Lionberger attended the University, graduated from Princeton, and became lecturer in the law school from 1892 to 1910, serving as University board member from 1894 to 1919. From 1896-97, he served as assistant U.S. attorney general by appointment of President Cleveland. His wife, Mary Shepley, was the daughter of John R. Shepley, a longtime University board member.
WU Archives

Fine Arts appoints first woman faculty member

The first woman to become a faculty member in a non-secondary department of Washington University was Mary L. Fairchild (1858-1946), a student in the School of Fine Arts from 1879-83, who became an "assistant in elementary work" from 1882-85. While there, she chafed at the rule that women could not draw nude models and persuaded the school to change its policy. Later she studied in Paris on a Washington University scholarship specially cre-

ated for her by Halsey Ives, had her work accepted by the Salon, and won a bronze medal at the Paris Exposition Universelle. She also exhibited at the 1893 World's Columbian Exposition. Twice married, she eventually settled in Bronxville, New York. Today, her work is in the collections of major museums.

The Breeze, **1895.**
Oil on canvas, 69 x 72 inches,
by Mary Fairchild MacMonnies,
Terra Foundation for the Arts,
Daniel J. Terra Collection, 1987.23.
Photograph courtesy of Terra Foundation for the Arts

George A. Madill (1838-1901). A law faculty member from 1869-94, Madill received an honorary LL.D. in 1892. He served as Judge of the Circuit Court, then formed a law partnership — Hitchcock, Madill & Finkelnburg — with colleagues in the School of Law. A generous donor to the school, he endowed two chairs: the Madill Professorship of Contracts and Commercial Law, which is not currently filled, and the Madill Professorship in Law, held today by John Drobak.
WU Archives

statutes of limitations and of fraud; James O. Broadhead, former Congressman and minister to Switzerland, to teach international law; and Roderick Rombauer, respected St. Louis Court of Appeals judge, as professor of real property and equity jurisprudence.

Under the direction of Halsey C. Ives, the St. Louis School of Fine Arts was expanding its day and evening sessions. In 1891, it acquired part of a new facility, an eastward extension to the art museum, which was completed eight years later. By 1894, said a faculty member, the school had become "one of the best equipped, and most thorough, art schools in America." At the Columbian Exposition, the school won first prize for its exhibit of students'

Holmes Smith (1863-1937). A longtime faculty member, Smith came to the University in 1884 as a drawing instructor and became professor of drawing and history of art in 1907.
WU Archives

work. Holmes Smith, who married William G. Eliot's daughter, Rose, joined the faculty in 1884; a decade later, Edmund Wuerpel — a Manual Training School graduate, and onetime Fine Arts student — came on board as a painting instructor. In 1883, Fine Arts became the first of the University's non-secondary schools to employ a woman, Mary L. Fairchild, as an "assistant" on the faculty. As a student in the school, she had won the Wayman Crow medal, a student art prize, and later she developed a successful painting career in Paris. Famed western artist Oscar Berninghaus (1874-1952) received his only fine arts training in night classes at the School, which he attended for three terms during the 1890s.

Visitors were discovering the art museum — more than 13,000 in 1888-89. The museum was filling up with donations, such as Carl Wimar's 1860 oil, *The Buffalo Hunt,* given in 1886. As chief of the Department of Fine Arts at the Columbian Exposition, Ives used his travels to acquire masterpieces for the museum; by 1894, he had bought paintings and art objects worth $25,000. Some friends, such as Adolphus Busch and law professor Charles Nagel, purchased art at the Exposition and donated it to the museum.

Under William Trelease, the Henry Shaw School of Botany acquired a library, nascent herbarium, and small laboratory — temporarily located at 1724 Washington Avenue — for undergraduates and nondegree students. Advanced students used the superior facilities at the Missouri Botanical Garden. For years, Trelease remained one of the few faculty members at the University to have earned a Ph.D., and he was committed to graduate education. In 1895, his program produced the first Ph.D. going to a student — the second doctoral degree awarded by the University — in Anna Isabel Mulford, an 1886 Vassar graduate, whose dissertation examined *Agaves* in the United States.

The Buffalo Hunt.
Carl Wimar's 1860 oil painting was given to the University in 1886 by William Van Zandt.
WU Gallery of Art

CAMPUS LIFE IN THE 1890S

Despite the financial woes, students managed to enjoy some extracurricular activities: a banjo club, glee club, outing club, a small orchestra, a new literary society. After dropping its early fraternities, including the Ugly Club, the University gained new ones, such as Kappa Gamma Upsilon for undergraduates and Phi Delta Phi for law students. Another group was the Texta Club, appreciated for its annual hop. In 1894, the Myrtle and Maroon Dramatic Club formed; now "the latent dramatic talents in the University will no longer 'blush unseen,'" said *Student Life*. Students competed for prizes in the annual oratorical contest.

Athletics was gaining strength, too, with a new football team that played its first intercollegiate game in 1890, and the Washington University Athletic Association, founded in 1884, which reported 50 members only three years later. Field Day, established in 1887, was a springtime event, handball remained popular, and students could take gymnastic instruction in the small gymnasium. Still, grumbled one student, "it is sometimes a matter of comment among the students that the University is not better provided with facilities for athletics."

Students and visitors alike attended a lecture series, endowed several years earlier by Mary Tileston Hemenway, and regularly offered until 1900 by Harvard University history professor John Fiske. Said a student, "The lectures are composed almost entirely of new material, fresh and racy, as Prof. Fiske himself expresses it." In a sign of hard times, the lecture series endowed earlier by William H. Smith disappeared, probably because the board could not afford to continue it.

Myrtle and Maroon program.
This new dramatic group formed in 1894. The play advertised here was written by French professor Henri Dumay.
WU Archives

Campus Life.
These three College juniors are having fun outside the downtown buildings in 1898.
Missouri Historical Society, St. Louis

71

Walter Moran Farmer
(1867-1943).
The first African-American graduate of the law school, Farmer went on to have a remarkable legal career and to become a leader in the black community. During a "Day of Lamentation" meeting in May 1892, which drew 15,000 black citizens to a St. Louis hall, he and others spoke out against crimes of violence against blacks, especially lynchings.

The *St. Louis American*

"No Distinction Is Made...on Account of Color"

Women were a well-established presence at the University, though the men still registered occasional complaints. In 1892, one *Student Life* writer muttered that "the Freshman class seems to be adorned with an unusually large number of co-eds. Gallantry requires that we welcome their coming; yet is it not with feelings of apprehension, at the increasing number of young ladies at our university? Let us be thankful that at least the engineering courses are safe from their incursions."

The University awards its first student Ph.D.

I n 1895, Anna Isabel Mulford, a graduate student in the botany program, was the first student to earn a doctoral degree from the University. Her dissertation examined *Agaves* in the United States and, as part of her research, she discovered several species that were subsequently named for her, including "Mulford's milkvetch" *(astragalus mulfordiae)*, which she discovered in 1892 near Boise, Idaho.

Anna Isabel Mulford (1848-1943).
Courtesy of St. Louis Public Schools Records Center/Archives

Black students had not achieved even this grudging acceptance. After Hale Parker, the next African American to inquire about admission to the law school was Walter Moran Farmer, an 1884 graduate of Lincoln Institute in Jefferson City. On September 22, 1887, Dean Hammond replied graciously: "I write at once to say that you will be welcome. No distinction is made here on account of color, and one young man of color has gone thro' our session since I came here six years ago."

Farmer matriculated that fall, and in November *Student Life* commented: "The junior class has one colored member, Farmer. He seems a level-headed man and is well liked by the other students." He graduated in 1889 and, as the *St. Louis American* reported in 1946: "on the call for the 'cum laude' student to stand, and a Negro arose, there came the loudest applause of the whole commencement." Farmer had a distinguished career as the first African-American lawyer to argue before the Missouri Supreme Court and one of the first to argue before the U.S. Supreme Court.

After Farmer, two other black students attended the law school — Eli Hamilton Taylor from 1891-93 and Crittenden Clark from 1895-97 — but it is not clear that either received a degree. Clark became an associate city counselor and Justice of the Peace for the Fourth District, the first African American to hold this office.

On the undergraduate side, the board reported in 1888 that it had received an inquiry "stating that Mr. J.H. Jones, a colored man, wished to make application in September for admission to the Freshman Class, and asking if his color would be any bar to his entrance." By the board's June meeting, the faculty had decided unanimously "after careful consideration, that every facility should be given to Mr. J.H. Jones." Their motives

Eli Hamilton Taylor.
The *St. Louis American*

may have been financial as well as moral, since they added: "the Faculty are clear that they can better afford to admit than to reject such applications." However, there is no record of Jones enrolling as a student.

Several black students attended the Manual Training School and two, Eugene Hutt and Augustus O. Thornton, were seniors in 1892

St. Louis alumni families, the Martins and the Davises, make names for themselves in public service and in tennis

William McChesney Martin, Sr., LL.B. '00, became a prominent St. Louis banker and chairman of the board of the Federal Reserve Bank of St. Louis; he helped President Woodrow Wilson draft the Federal Reserve Act, which created the central bank in 1913. His son, William McChesney Martin, Jr. (1906-1998), the longest-serving U.S. Federal Reserve chairman in history, married a St. Louisan, Cynthia Davis.

Her father, Dwight F. Davis, was a Smith Academy alumnus who graduated from the University's law school in 1903. Parks commissioner in St. Louis, he built some of the nation's first municipal tennis courts. He later served as Secretary of War under President Calvin Coolidge, governor general of the Philippines, and chairman of the board of the Brookings Institution. A national amateur tennis champion, Davis was named to the Hall of Fame in 1956. In 1900 he established the Davis Cup, the premier annual award in international tennis competition.

Dwight's father, John T. Davis, A.B. '63, was one of the earliest graduates of the young University. Afterwards, he built his father's wholesale dry goods business into a commercial giant and became one of the city's wealthiest men. He remained loyal to his alma mater, serving on the board from 1871-94.

William McChesney Martin, Sr.
Missouri Historical Society, St. Louis

Dwight F. Davis (1879-1945).
WU Archives

John T. Davis (1844-1894).
WU Archives

---

when Calvin Woodward invited them on a student trip to the glass works in Crystal City. They were, he said, "exemplary scholars." However, some white students protested and, in the bitter aftermath of this dispute, Manual Training stopped admitting blacks; as waves of late-19th-century racism swept the country, other departments followed suit. Woodward told a reporter that, when Hutt and Thornton came, "there was no manual training school for negroes….[But] there is now a colored manual training school at Jefferson City and that those who apply…hereafter will be referred to that institution." Rufus

Stokes, the last African-American student at Manual Training, graduated in 1894.

Soon the University did not even acknowledge that black students had ever been admitted. In August 1906, a young black man, Edward R. Richardson, wrote to Chaplin saying that he had studied mechanical engineering at Purdue for two years and "it would be a great thing for me if I could continue my studies at Washington University." Chaplin replied: "I am obliged to state to you that

Augustus O. Thornton.
The *St. Louis American*

St. Louis' Union Station takes shape

When St. Louis' Union Station was dedicated in September 1894, several St. Louisans with ties to Washington University had played a part in its construction. Edward A. Cameron, a young St. Louis architect who had studied at Washington University, may have helped architect Theodore Link at key points in the design process. The enormous train shed — the world's largest, at 700 by 606 feet — was designed by George H. Pegram, B.S.C.E. '77, described in a 1927 *Washingtonian* as "one of the most distinguished engineers in America." Robert Bringhurst, a School of Fine Arts student who taught sculpture there from 1884 to 1903, modeled the female figures that decorate the Great Hall; Sylvester Annan, another former Fine Arts student, designed the allegorical window over the stair landing.

George H. Pegram (1855-1937).
WU Archives

Union Station window.
Sylvester Annan's stained glass window still adorns the wall over the grand staircase inside Union Station.
David Kilper, WU Photographic Services

---

negroes have never been admitted to Washington University, and it would therefore be useless for you to try to make any arrangement to continue your studies here." The University did not begin admitting African Americans again until 1947.

GRAND STRUCTURES AND BEAUTIFUL SURROUNDINGS

The April 14, 1891, board meeting that ushered in the new Medical Department was the scene of a second epochal event: the appointment of Robert S. Brookings as a new member. His friend and colleague, Samuel Cupples, longtime donor and board member for a decade, had nominated him. Brookings, then 41, had worked for 24 years in Cupples' firm, the Samuel Cupples Woodenware Co., rising from clerk to leading salesman, then to partner and head. A bachelor with a fortune of some $5 or $6 million, he was now scanning the community for new civic and charitable challenges. He was not the only St. Louisan in such a position.

Through these last years of the 19th century, St. Louis was continuing its explosive growth; between 1850 and 1890, the population rose from nearly 78,000 to almost 458,000 — a sixfold increase. And despite a temporary economic downturn caused by the financial panic of 1893, the city's wealth was increasing as well. A new class of millionaires had sprung up: successful business leaders, like Brookings, with money and a social conscience. Brookings knew them socially as well as professionally and eventually would tap their wealth on behalf of the University. Quietly, he saw to it that some filled vacancies on the board. In 1894, Isaac Lionberger was voted a new member, A.L. Shapleigh joined the next year, and Brookings himself nominated Adolphus Busch, who took office in 1895.

For the most part, Brookings maintained a low-key presence on the board, still focusing most of his energy on building up his large, innovative Cupples Station warehouse complex in downtown St. Louis. Then in spring 1892, he and three other members — Edward Rowse, Henry W. Eliot, and William Huse — were appointed to a special real estate subcommittee charged with finding a new site for the University.

This idea had been simmering for years. In William G. Eliot's inaugural address, he had mentioned the "desirableness of having some departments of the University in the suburbs, a few miles from the city's center, where we could enjoy the larger space of fifty or a hundred acres of ground." Students, too, had been murmuring about a real campus, some green space — "an abundance of pure air and a supply of unimpaired daylight," said *Student Life* in 1888 — and their protests were getting louder. Even Chancellor Chaplin sounded wistful at his inauguration when he described his vision of a great university: "Its structures are grand," he said, "and its surroundings beautiful."

Who could blame them for such longings? By the 1890s, the city was pushing westward, and fashionable St. Louisans left nearby residential areas that had once supplied most University students. Surrounding the campus was a dingy commercial district, with a seedy sprinkling of saloons and brothels. Steel-tired dray wagons chattered noisily over the granite cobblestones of Washington Avenue, while a new streetcar line on 18th Street

shook the physics laboratories and observatory, making research almost impossible. Smoke was an ever-present feature of this landscape, casting a grimy pall on the University's already-aged and depressing buildings. As a student, Langsdorf knew their dim interiors, with "lighting fixtures so inadequate by modern standards as merely to punctuate the gloom on dark winter afternoons."

In his 1893 "Chancellor's Report," Chaplin took for granted that a move was needed, especially for the struggling undergraduate program — but where? Buying land somewhere in the city

Alfred Lee Shapleigh (1862-1945). Shapleigh, who attended Smith Academy and Washington University, became a board member in 1895 and served for 50 years; his son, A. Wessel Shapleigh, another Smith graduate, served on the board from 1946-66.
WU Archives

Graduates take "most astonishing" bicycle journey around the world

William Lewis Sachtleben and Thomas Gaskell Allen, Jr., both A.B. '90, were adventurous young men, who left St. Louis the day after graduation to embark on a 15,000-mile journey by bicycle around the globe. Their goal, they said, was to "get a practical finish to a theoretical education" — and they succeeded, crossing Europe, Asia, and finally the United States in a trip that took nearly three years. In

rural China, villagers were stunned by their first sight of a westerner and the newly invented safety bicycle; the Chinese prime minister met with the pair and expressed his surprise at the trip. The *London Chronicle* described it as "the most astonishing journey of modern times."

William Sachtleben (left) and Thomas Allen in China, 1892. The flags on their handlebars, calling them "The Traveling Students," were given to them at Lan-Chou-Foo.
Allen and Sachtleben, *Across Asia on a Bicycle,* The Century Company: 1894

William Lewis Sachtleben (1866-1953).
WU Archives

Thomas Gaskell Allen, Jr. (1868-?).
WU Archives

The University shield, 1896.
The first University shield, officially adopted by the board in 1896, consisted of a silver shield with two red bands and three green stars (above). This part was modeled after George Washington's coat of arms. In the center was an open book, symbolizing knowledge; below were three green fleurs-de-lis, the symbol of Louis IX, for whom St. Louis is named.
WU Archives

was possible, he said, though it would mean small buildings and a local student body. But if "it is decided to go further out and purchase a large tract of land," he said, "the probability is that around the college there will be a group of dormitories which can accommodate students from a distance, fields for athletic sports, and other attractive and beneficial features." A month later, the board chose this second scenario: deciding to secure land, engage a landscape firm and an architect to look it over, and finally show this plan to "gentlemen" who would pay for it.

PLANNING FOR AN ACROPOLIS ON THE HILLTOP

By the following June, the committee could report its success at finding a location: a 103-acre tract on the western limits of the city, which would cost $185,000. Yet "the choice of this site, as the best for the purpose, was not so simple as it may seem today," said architect James Jamieson at a later time. The area was still unimproved countryside. Skinker Road, not yet paved, turned into clay muck when it rained; the untamed western end of Forest Park, which abutted the campus, was known as "The Wilderness." But the hilltop vantage point and sweeping front vista made this site ideal, said Jamieson, adding: "Its selection was nothing short of a stroke of genius."

Polyclinic Hospital.
This hospital, located at 611 N. Jefferson, had belonged to the Missouri Medical College. After the merger it became, along with the adjoining building to the left, the teaching hospital of the new Medical Department of Washington University.
WU Archives

Olmsted, Olmsted, and Eliot — the nationally prominent landscape architects and designers of Central Park in New York City, who had been employed by the board in 1895 to develop a preliminary plan for the site — were charmed by its "commanding monumental aspect," as they called it. "The site is suggestive of the Acropolis of Athens, and of other Greek cities, upon which the public buildings were erected," they said, with enthusiasm. However, they strongly urged the board to fill out the campus with more acreage at its southern edge, and four years later the board complied, purchasing a 50-acre addition that shifted the University's boundary south to Forsyth and west to Big Bend.

By then a critical change had taken place in board leadership. Early in 1895, Leighton announced that he would step down from the presidency that fall; in his place, he said, the board might wish to create the same dual role for Chaplin that Eliot had once filled, as president and chancellor. However, the board declined to do so, and in November named Robert Brookings as its new president. Chaplin said he was so elated by this news that "he walked on air." Everywhere there was now the sense that the tide had finally turned. Brookings "has the reputation of making a success in all things which he attempts — a reputation which is of promise to the University," said *Student Life* joyfully. A local newspaper announced heartily, if a little prematurely, that "work on the new university will be commenced at once."

In fact, there were more dreary days before this work commenced or the University had fully made a new beginning. While the promise of a new campus improved morale, it did not raise faculty salaries or offset the persistent annual deficit. In 1897, board vice president Henry Hitchcock wrote two scathing financial appraisals that echoed both the worries and solutions of Colonel Leighton's earlier reports. He called for new reductions in operating expenses, and Chaplin responded by cutting instructors in engineering and chemistry. To save still more money, Chaplin added the role of University treasurer to his own duties. There seemed little hope, though, that Hitchcock's additional appeal — for a $500,000 endowment — had any prospect of fulfillment.

A few bright spots lit up these hard times. In 1896, after prolonged litigation, the University was finally awarded the proceeds of a trust — around $118,000 in all — established in 1855 by William Russell. Another nest egg was growing, too. In 1889, Stephen Ridgley had given the University property worth $66,000 for eventual use towards a new library, and by 1899 its value had reached $100,000.

In this same year, the University's young medical department, the St. Louis Medical College, merged with an old rival: Missouri Medical

College, founded by Joseph Nash McDowell in 1840. While St. Louis Medical was the state's second oldest medical school, Missouri Medical was the oldest, and now the two joined forces as the Medical Department of Washington University. Both faculties resigned and a committee, representing both institutions, selected a new joint faculty, with Henry H. Mudd elected as dean. All at once, the new school had the use of three buildings: 1806-14 Locust for teaching and laboratory work and two adjoining medical buildings on north Jefferson at Lucas.

For the first few years after becoming board president, Brookings did nothing dramatic. In June 1896 he spread the welcome word that $200,000 was in hand for the purchase of the new campus, but then he took time to study the University's finances and faculty, its curriculum and facilities. Behind the scenes, he and fellow board members began soliciting help from key donors. Finally, in spring 1899 this quiet time was past: Brookings announced that a $500,000 endowment was in place — and that, following in Eliot's worthy footsteps, he had given the first $100,000 himself. More astonishing still, a parade of wealthy St. Louisans had lined up to endow a cluster of new buildings. Olmsted, Olmsted, and Eliot came back to revise their earlier plan, adding the newly acquired acreage, and an architectural competition was in the offing.

A deep sigh of relief came from *Student Life*, which called this proposed move "an event second in importance only to [the University's] founding in 1853." The years of trial were nearly past, and a magnificent new campus was on the western horizon. (Ⓦ)

Students, faculty serve in Spanish-American war

"'On to Havana' is the cry heard all over the country," said *Student Life* in June 1898. During the Spanish-American war, University students enlisted, and the University's first military science instructor, Major John Stafford, U.S. Army, served in the war. At Fort LaPunta, the south entrance to Havana Bay, he and other soldiers had to demolish a section of the fortification, and Stafford managed to rescue the keystone anchoring the archway. He sent it to the University as a souvenir of the war (below), and it was mounted in a wall of the new campus, on south Brookings Hall. On a visit to the University in 1927, Stafford saw the stone and said he still treasured the "handsome and costly sword given me by the Washington University Corps of Cadets."

Major John Stafford.
WU Archives

The Keystone from Fort La Punta at Havana Bay.
WU Photographic Services

Tornado of 1896.
The city of St. Louis looking toward the Eads Bridge shows the area devastated by the tornado of May 27, 1896. Drawn by G.W. Peters and published in New York by *Harper's Weekly*.
Collection of A.G. Edwards and Sons, Inc., St. Louis, Missouri

Casting a "Lengthened Shadow": Robert Somers Brookings

Robert S. Brookings (1850-1932).
"He was a strikingly handsome man, tall and well proportioned, with black hair and beard beginning to show the white later attained, and with a pair of dark eyes that one could feel piercing straight through to the back of one's head," said Alexander Langsdorf of Brookings in the late 1890s.

Oil on canvas by Anders Leonard Zorn
WU Gallery of Art

Mary Carter Brookings Reynolds (1828-1867).
The mother of Robert Brookings, Mary Reynolds was a descendant of Abraham Carter, a Quaker, who came to the United States with William Penn and settled in Pennsylvania, then Maryland.

Brookings Institution Archives

I n 1895, Robert S. Brookings had just concluded the biggest business deal of his life. Thanks to his earlier efforts, the firm he had served faithfully for 28 years — the Samuel Cupples Woodenware Co. — was already the largest of its kind in the United States. "I chased fortune and knifed my competitors," he once admitted. Now he had completed an innovative new project that was soon duplicated around the nation. In downtown St. Louis, he had built a giant warehouse complex, strategically located near major rail lines, that had space for 40 companies doing $100 million of business a year.

He had even managed to keep this "Cupples Station" project afloat during the 1893 business depression. When American banks refused to loan Brookings the money he needed to finish construction and stave off bankruptcy, he sailed for London. There he persuaded Seligman Brothers to give him a $3 million loan — "a personal triumph," said his biographer, Hermann Hagedorn, "that marked the peak of Brookings' business career."

Wealthy, single, energetic, Brookings was ready for a new challenge. In 1891, his business partner, Samuel Cupples, had convinced him to become a member of the Washington University board, and he had already played a key role in choosing the site for a new campus. "The saddle being my favorite exercise, I had galloped my horse over every foot of the surrounding country, and I lost no time in selecting a hill adjoining and overlooking Forest Park on the west as an ideal site," he later recalled.

With Cupples Station now secure, he was seeking something more than mere board membership: He longed for a sense of purpose, a way to do good in the world. Intrigued by Andrew Carnegie's notion that the rich are merely stewards of their wealth, he consulted Cupples, his

mentor and friend, on various forms of benevolence. A charitable gift, said Cupples, had to involve some effort on the recipient's part or it would only confer "the palsy of pauperism." On the other hand, he added, "education — the higher education which trains for leadership... is at least free from this defect."

So education it would be. Accepting the board presidency, Brookings devoted himself to Washington University, which he admired for its strong charter and able faculty. For 33 years he remained in this role, giving nearly all of his time and at least $5 million of his fortune, including Cupples Station and his own home on Ellenwood Avenue, to revitalize the University and its medical school. Much later, Alexander Langsdorf, then dean emeritus of the School of Engineering, said of him: "If it is true, as Emerson said, that an institution is the lengthening shadow of a man, it can be said with complete certainty that Washington University, in the form it now has, is the lengthened shadow of Robert Brookings."

University-building was an odd fate for a man who had little formal education. Born in 1850 in Cecil County, Maryland, he was just two when his father, a country physician, died suddenly. His mother remarried and Brookings, along with older brother Harry and young sister Mary, grew up on a farm near Baltimore. He spent part of each summer making rounds with a physician uncle, acquiring a nickname: "little doctor."

His school was basic and crowded, and Brookings was restless. Harry sent back glowing letters from St. Louis, where he was now working for a young firm, Cupples & Marston. Eager to get ahead, Brookings persuaded his mother to let him quit school at age 16, take a quick book-keeping course, and join Harry in the West. He arrived on January 1, 1867, crossing the ice on the frozen Mississippi River. Within weeks, his mother had died of a stroke; within a year, Mary had joined Robert and Harry in St. Louis.

He took a job as receiving clerk at Cupples & Marston for $25 per month and supplemented his income by doing evening bookkeeping for the firm, which had been founded in 1851 by Cupples, then a 19-year-old from Ohio. They were wholesale dealers for an eclectic list of items: "Cordage, Twines, Wicking,

Batting, Paper, Brooms, Brushes and Cigars, Wood and Willow Ware, Mats, Matches, Blacking, Sieves, Bird Cages, and French, English and German Fancy Goods," said their advertising. Brookings took to the business, coming in early each morning to gain sales experience with customers who turned up before regular selling hours began.

Promoted to "fiddling drummer" in 1868, he peddled his company's wares throughout a vast territory that extended from the Mississippi to the Pacific. By train and stagecoach, he traveled 300 days a year, pleasing his German customers by learning a little of their language, playing his violin on lonely evenings, making friends wherever he went. "He had the glittering gifts of the successful salesman," wrote Hagedorn — and orders poured in. In 1872, Cupples made Robert and Harry, his leading buyer, partners in the firm; another principal was Asa Wallace, who married Mary Brookings.

Selma Hall.
At this 5,000-acre estate on the Mississippi River 35 miles south of St. Louis, Brookings entertained weekend guests and blazed trails along the river banks on horseback.
Missouri Historical Society, St. Louis

Brookings' home, "Cecilwood," 6510 Ellenwood.
Just after former Gov. Herbert S. Hadley was named chancellor, he and his wife stayed with Robert Brookings, while they looked for a residence. They remarked on how lovely Brookings' home was. "I am glad you like it," he said. "It is yours." He left with only his hat and overcoat; the next day, he deeded the property to the University as a permanent home for the chancellor. Today it is called "Alumni House."
WU Archives

January Hall.
Completed in 1923
with a gift from
Isabel January, the
building initially
housed the School
of Law. Today it
provides space for
University College
and the East Asian
Library, both in
Arts & Sciences.

David Kilper,
WU Photographic
Services

By 1878, Brookings had groomed replacements and gotten off the road himself. With Samuel Cupples ill from asthma and often out of town, he and Harry ran the business, positioning it to break into manufacturing. He remained close to Cupples, who had embraced philanthropy. "There was an attractive father-and-son relationship between himself and this young man…they reacted on each other, stimulating each other to think beyond their bank accounts," said Hagedorn.

Brookings reached out to the community, becoming president of the Mercantile Library Association and helping to found the new St. Louis Choral Society. He wanted more polish so that he could move in elite social circles, so he learned manners while renting a room from local dowager Sarah Beaumont Keim, daughter of pioneer physician William Beaumont. University faculty member Marshall Snow came occasionally to provide academic lessons.

In 1885, Brookings took a year off business and traveled abroad to live in Berlin, practice his beloved violin, and hike in Switzerland and Bavaria. On one of these hikes he got word that his company — now the Samuel Cupples Woodenware Co. — had lost a large manufac-

turing plant in a fire. That news brought him home, and this time he settled down, buying a series of St. Louis houses and a country castle, Selma Hall.

Once he became Washington University board president in 1895, he threw himself into that work, making an in-depth study of the University and its needs. Board meetings turned into a kind of monologue in which Brookings detailed his findings. His knowledge "was nothing short of amazing, and could have been accomplished only by a man of active and versatile mind, who had withdrawn from practically every other pursuit," said board member Charles Nagel. In 1905, Brookings wrote to Chancellor Chaplin, "I feel so intensely about the University that anything which concerns it strikes at my very vitals." Offered a chance to run for the U.S. Senate in 1909, Brookings, a Republican, sacrificed it in favor of rebuilding the University's medical school.

In 1917, he was camping in Glacier National Park when he was called to Washington, D.C., by President Woodrow Wilson, who asked him first to serve on the War Industries Board and a year later to chair the Price Fixing Committee. These experiences revealed to him the inefficiency of government and awakened his interest in reform. He reorganized an existing Institute for Government Research, convinced the Carnegie Foundation to finance a new Institute of Economics, and — with major funding from an old friend, Isabel Vallé January — founded the Robert Brookings Graduate School of Economics and Government, which was at first part of Washington University, then independent. In 1927 he merged the institutes and school into the new Brookings Institution, still a prominent think tank in Washington, D.C.

He had never married, and at age 77, after two heart attacks, he finally decided to act. He proposed to Isabel January, 51, whom he had first met in St. Louis as a pigtailed 8-year-

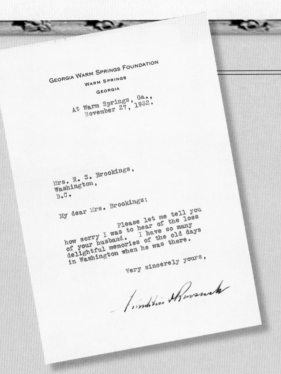

old. She had Washington University roots as well, since her grandfather, Derrick January, had been an early board member. As a young widow, Isabel's mother, Grace, had become a dear friend of Brookings — she and Isabel called him "Bobberts" — and he visited them often after they moved to San Remo, Italy. Grace died in 1919, but Isabel and Brookings remained close. On June 19, 1927, they eloped, marrying in the rectory of St. Paul's Episcopal Church in Baltimore. "I am very happy," was Brookings' only public comment.

The next year he resigned as University board president, amid a flood of tributes; the building he had donated, University Hall, was renamed "Brookings Hall" in his honor. Already the recipient of honorary degrees from Yale, the University of Missouri, and Harvard, Brookings was awarded Washington University's LL.D. and M.D. degrees at the 1929 Commencement. Ailing and weak, he spoke only briefly, saying that the University owed him nothing, that he had always received more than he had given. "As he undertook to express his 'overwhelming gratitude,'" said the *Washingtonian* later, "his voice broke and he resumed his seat."

Brookings died in 1932, Isabel in 1965; they are buried side-by-side in Bellefontaine Cemetery in St. Louis. Like founder William Greenleaf Eliot, said the *Washingtonian*, Robert Brookings left an extraordinary legacy:

> "Washington University is the product principally of two successive leaders, each in his time with a heart and mind singularly like that of the other, each devoted idealistically to the cause of education, each offering his effort, his life and his means unstintingly to the work of his heart. What secular institution anywhere can point to two such inspired founders of such singleness of purpose as William Greenleaf Eliot and Robert Somers Brookings?" Ⓦ

The Brookings' monument in Bellefontaine Cemetery.
Under the inscription on their headstone is a miniature replica of the archway and towers of Brookings Hall.
David Kilper, WU Photographic Services

Isabel Vallé January Brookings (1876-1965).
Isabel married Robert Brookings in 1927, when she was 51 and he was 77. This 1914 photo shows her as a longtime family friend of Brookings.
Brookings Institution Archives

Grace Vallé January (?-1919).
Widow of Jesse January and the mother of Isabel, Grace January was a close friend of Robert Brookings.
WU Archives

Derrick January (1814-1879).
Born in Kentucky, January moved to St. Louis in 1837 and opened a successful wholesale grocery house on the levee; he was actively involved, too, in insurance and real estate. He joined the Washington University board in 1860.
WU Archives

CHAPTER FIVE

"THE PEARLY GATES OF PARADISE":

A New Campus for the University

1900-1908

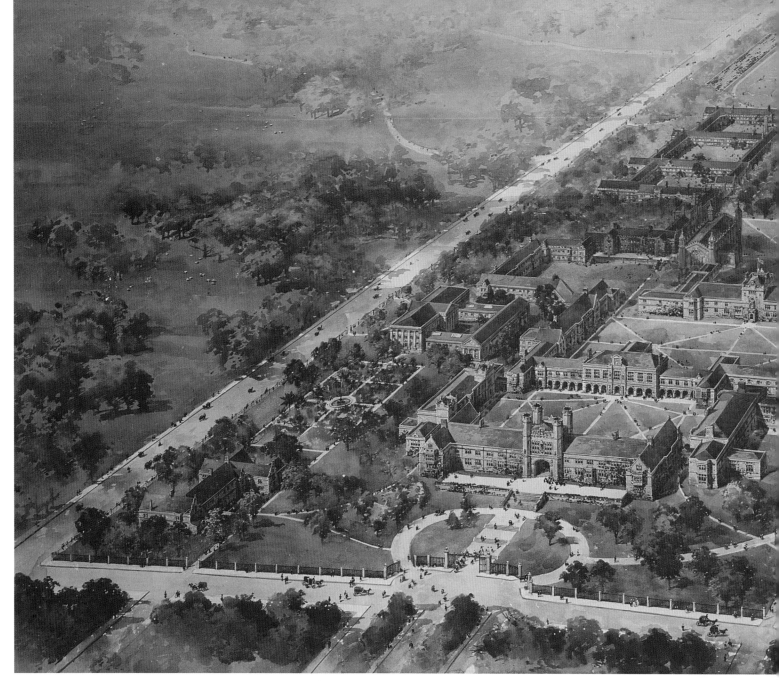

Envisioning a campus. This rendering of the proposed Hilltop Campus was done by Hughson Hawley in 1899.
WU Archives

A New Campus for the University

Washington University had its splendid new location — and by mid-1899 it even had money. Along with the 157 donors who had contributed $100 or more to the recently concluded endowment campaign, five people had pledged to sponsor the first six buildings on campus. Robert Brookings, the dynamic board president, had promised $200,000 for an administration building; and $100,000 each had come from Adolphus Busch for a chemistry building, Elizabeth Liggett for a men's dormitory, and Stephen Ridgley's fund for a new library. Samuel Cupples had been generous, too, giving $250,000 for two engineering buildings, plus a laboratory annex.

1900 — 1908

1900   *The cornerstone was laid for Busch Hall, the first building on the new Hilltop Campus, on October 20.*

1901   *Board President Robert S. Brookings leased the new buildings on the Hilltop Campus to the Louisiana Purchase Exposition Company to serve as headquarters for the World's Fair.*

1904   *The World's Fair took place from April 30 to December 1.*

1905   *A chapel service on January 30 marked the start of classes on the new campus.*

1908   *David F. Houston was named the University's fifth chancellor.*

Thomas K. Skinker (1845-1924).
Skinker, A.B. '63, a lawyer, owned a large tract of land near the University's new site, which was said to be "just beyond Tom Skinker's road." He owned the Clayton and Forest Park Electric Railway, as well, which skirted the edge of the new campus.

Undeveloped site.
Robert Brookings found the hilltop site for the University's new campus while riding on horseback west of the city.

But what would this new campus look like? Olmsted, Olmsted and Eliot, the premier landscape architects in the country, had recommended a monumental main building, facing eastward from the hilltop toward Forest Park, with a series of quadrangles behind it. Now the board needed the right architect to carry this vision forward. Confidently, Brookings approached leading firms and asked them to enter a design competition — but they declined. They had been singed too often by amateur-run contests, Brookings said later, "when the judgment of a lay jury, influenced by the embellishment of a drawing, had at times discredited them."

Brookings, an old hand at driving a bargain, proposed a more attractive scheme: Each firm would submit drawings under an assumed name and receive $750 for its trouble; the University

jury making the selection would be advised by a panel of three prominent architects, unconnected with the competition. Mollified, six prominent firms accepted his invitation. By October 15, 1899, they were to submit detailed block plans and elevations, providing for buildings likely to be needed in the future. Their instructions hinted that a plan involving quadrangles would be most acceptable.

For all his talk of anonymity, Brookings must have known there would be small doubt as to the origin of each plan, since the firms he had asked to participate — some of the nation's most outstanding institutional architects — had diverse but well-known stylistic leanings. Carrere and Hastings, who had recently designed the New York Public Library, would surely provide a Classical

University, they strongly favored the Collegiate Gothic style. Both Brookings and Chancellor Winfield Chaplin had already visited Bryn Mawr and liked their work.

On schedule, six unmarked envelopes were delivered to the University jury, which included Brookings and Chaplin, four board members, and the three outside architects — Robert Andrews and R. Clipston Sturgis of Boston, and Walter Cook of New York. For four days, they pondered the submissions, then announced their decision: They had unanimously selected the Cope and Stewardson plan, with its Collegiate Gothic-style buildings, cloistered quadrangles, and flexible spaces. Several years later, Sturgis explained that this design had intrigued the jury with its "evidence of thought and study" and its "intelligent understanding of the needs of each group of buildings." Apparently, the other firms were gracious in defeat. Brookings reported that they all wired Cope and Stewardson their congratulations, saying "this was the fairest and most satisfactory competition they ha[d] ever known."

or Renaissance design; so would McKim, Mead and White, architects of Columbia University, and Cass Gilbert, designer of the Minnesota State Capitol. Two others — Shepley, Rutan and Coolidge, architects of the Stanford University campus, and St. Louis-based Eames and Young — would likely supply Colonial Revival designs. The sixth firm, Cope and Stewardson, was the least mysterious of all. Architects of key buildings at Bryn Mawr, the University of Pennsylvania, and Princeton

EAST FRONT BROOKINGS BUILDING

Cope and Stewardson elevation. "It was architectural genius," says architectural historian and former architecture dean Buford Pickens, "that based the plan of spaces and buildings upon the medieval courtyard tradition of Oxford and Cambridge Colleges, a tradition that has evolved successfully from the fortress-like gateway tower (Brookings) to the open round-arch, Renaissance loggia (Ridgley)." Unlike the other plans, he said, this one "was conceived in such a manner that it would appear complete at any time after the erection of the initial buildings."
WU Archives

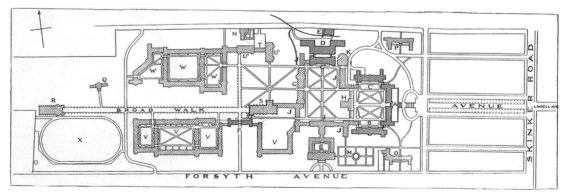

Cope and Stewardson block plan. "It is worthwhile to plan for many quadrangles," explained Walter Cope in November 1899, "for each will develop a character of its own. These are the out-door rooms, with the sky for the ceiling, which, when the sides are once completed, can never be disfigured by later additions."
WU Archives

In November, Walter Cope came to town to elaborate on his plan at a special board meeting. At the time he was just 39; he and John Stewardson, childhood friends, had founded their firm in 1885 and achieved almost instant success. But Stewardson had died tragically in an 1896 ice-skating accident, and even though his brother, Emlyn, had taken his place, Cope — "an indefatigable worker, and almost entirely absorbed in his profession," said his obituary — was greatly over-taxed. Only three years after this meeting, he died of a stroke.

His presentation to the University board was a ringing defense of the Collegiate Gothic style. "The site may at first suggest a monumental group of Classic buildings on a central axis; but we have rejected that idea," he said, taking a gentle swipe at his fellow contestants. "It is not a State Capitol nor a World's Fair which is to be built — but a great University." Overall, he added, the Gothic style would harmonize best with the site, prove flexible enough to provide for future growth, and "satisfy the aesthetic ideal of a University":

"Classic Architecture expresses completion, finality, perfection: Gothic Architecture expresses aspiration, growth, development. To the beholder the Classic says: This is the sum — Here is perfection — Do not aspire further. The Gothic says to him: Reach higher — Spread outward and upward — There are no limitations. Now, when we consider what a University is, can there be any doubt which of these two styles best answers to its idea?"

In preparation for the construction to come, grading had already begun on campus — the biggest project of its kind yet undertaken in St. Louis. Using a narrow-gauge railway for transport, workers moved a million cubic yards of soil, adding 12 feet to the main quadrangle alone to raise it to its intended height. On the northern edge of the property, they created a huge mound of topsoil, planning to spread it after buildings were in place. Then in spring 1900, newly arrived Cope and Stewardson architect James Jamieson was horrified to discover that this dirt was fast disappearing. "A calamity for the University was narrowly averted," he later wrote, "when it was discovered that men were filling sacks with this precious black earth, and carrying them off to raise the river banks, as the 'June rise' threatened damage to the low lands."

Soon the board, the architects, and Chancellor Chaplin — who became a nearly full-time coordinator of this building effort — began making detailed decisions about the buildings to come. Cope had suggested light gray limestone for the walls, accented by Indiana buff limestone

Cass Gilbert elevation. Gilbert's plan, says Buford Pickens, was "unquestionably the most skillful reworking of Olmsted's site plan in the competition." But he may not have been as keen for the job as others, since he had won a hard-fought competition to design the New York Customs House in October 1899.

Carrere and Hastings elevation. Their proposed design, in the French Renaissance style, called for a domed, classical administration building.

McKim, Mead and White elevation. This plan, featuring a colonnaded east front on the administration building, was different from their Columbia University design.

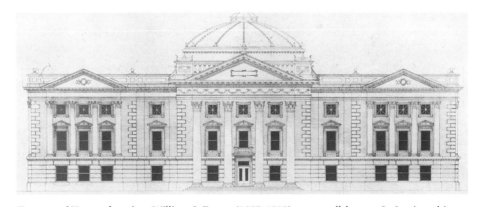

Eames and Young elevation. William S. Eames (1857-1915) was a well-known St. Louis architect and 1878 University graduate. His firm's plan featured Colonial Revival buildings and an interior drive around the quadrangle.

Shepley, Rutan and Coolidge elevation. This firm must have been a popular local choice for the job. George Foster Shepley (1858-1903) was a St. Louis native and 1880 University graduate; his brother-in-law, Isaac Lionberger, was a board member; and his firm had established a St. Louis office in 1891. They proposed alternative elevations in the Colonial Revival and Collegiate Gothic styles.

All images, WU Archives

moldings, but added that the Gothic style could be successfully expressed through a range of building materials. Uncertain which to choose, the entire board trooped down to the Pickel Stone Company yards on South Vandeventer Avenue to inspect sample walls of brick and Missouri red granite — and granite was the group's unanimous choice. Robert Brookings boasted to Cope that "we will have a better job of stonework than either Princeton or Bryn Mawr."

Meanwhile, students — still attending classes in the shabby downtown buildings — were wild with anticipation for the new campus. As construction progressed, *Student Life* buzzed with comments. "Those who are addicted to the use of the wheel

William Ewing Shahan (1877-1958). Shahan, A.B. '01, M.D. '04, became a distinguished ophthalmologist, member of the University's medical faculty, and inventor of various instruments, including the "thermophore," a heating device used to treat corneal infections.
WU Archives

would do well to ride out on Lindell Boulevard and take a look at the University grounds during the spring weather," one student wrote in May 1899. Another undergraduate, William E. Shahan, A.B. '01, was even moved to verse:

Busch Hall is the first building on the Hilltop Campus

Adolphus Busch (1839-1913).

Born in Germany, Adolphus Busch emigrated to the United States in 1857 and built the Anheuser-Busch Brewing Company into the world's largest brewery. He served on the University's board from 1895 to 1913 and gave generously: funding Busch Hall, donating works of art, sponsoring Otto Heller as professor of German, and creating the Adolphus Busch Professorship in Medicine, held today by Kenneth S. Polonsky.

Busch Hall, which had its gala cornerstone-laying in October 1900, was designed with laboratories for general chemistry on the first floor and specialized labs on the second. "It will be unique among buildings of its kind, in that no student while making his experiments

can possibly be more than 12 feet from a window," bragged one newspaper.

Edward H. Keiser, appointed Eliot Professor of Chemistry in 1899, was excited by the prospect of a fine new chemistry building. "Three or four times a week he makes the trip out to the new site, to watch the progress," said *Student Life*.

Busch Hall opened for classes in 1905 after being leased to the Louisiana Purchase Exposition Company for the World's Fair.

Edward H. Keiser (1861-1949).

Interior of Busch Hall.
All photos, WU Archives

"Come, O friends, in great delight,
And join us in a song of glee,
We're soon to leave our crowded site
And be once more most gladly free.

"The thund'ring noise of passing cars,
The soot that sprinkles us all o'er,
The smoke that all our pleasure mars,
Shall vanish then forever more."

The hotly debated question was precisely *when* this vanishing would take place. In 1899, *Student Life* predicted with confidence that "the class of 1902 will graduate from the new halls" — but events were coming to postpone those plans, disappointing students, while securing the University's future. It would be several years before, as one wistful undergraduate put it, "we enter 'the pearly gates of Paradise' out on the Skinker Road."

"A PIONEER GROUP" OF BUILDINGS EMERGES

On the afternoon of October 20, 1900, dozens of fashionable carriages made their way toward campus for the gala ceremony that marked the cornerstone-laying of the first new building, Busch Hall. The large crowd included prominent citizens: former governor David R. Francis, now negotiating for a St. Louis-based world's fair; local judges, physicians, and business leaders; board members; the entire faculty and many students. Since Adolphus Busch, the building's donor, could not be present, his son August brought a large party out in his tally-ho, drawn by a four-in-hand team. Impressed by this sea of vehicles, one reporter said: "The collection of fine turnouts in the university quadrangle, now littered with granite blocks and building material generally, was in itself a gallant sight."

Guests sat on raised platforms, glanced over plans for the campus, and listened to board member Charles Nagel, who gave an eloquent address full of hope for the University. "We trust that these granite blocks may be symbolic of its strength, and we have faith that the cause to which it is to be devoted can never die," he said. One cause, he said, was educational opportunity — "that the artisan here employed may be laying the steps by which his child shall climb to distinction and to fame." Yet, he added "the chief significance of this gift lies in the fact that this building is but one of a pioneer group; the first tangible proof that the hope and the promises so long held out are to be realized."

Over the next several years, this kind of occasion became routine, as the "pioneer group" grew to nine buildings in all. On November 3, 1900, just two weeks after the Busch gala, well-wishers gathered again to lay the cornerstone of the new adminis-

Law professorship honors Charles Nagel

Charles Nagel (1849-1940).
WU Archives

The speaker at the dedication of Busch Hall was Charles Nagel, LL.B. '75, who came to St. Louis in 1865 and became a noted attorney, member of the Missouri House of Representatives (1881-83), and in 1909, Secretary of Commerce and Labor under President William H. Taft. In addition, he was a founder of the U.S. Chamber of Commerce. At the University, he served for nearly 50 years as board member and was a law faculty member.

The Charles Nagel Professorship in Jurisprudence and International Law, held today by Stephen H. Legomsky, was endowed in Nagel's honor by Daniel K. Noyes in 1945.

Stephen H. Legomsky in 1987.
WU Photographic Services

tration building, University Hall; its sponsor, Robert Brookings — the University's tireless fundraiser — had refused to give his name to it for fear people would accuse him of seeking money for memorials to himself. On this afternoon, there were seats for a thousand, yet many had to stand; all the ladies in attendance received myrtle and maroon bows. The speaker, former board president Col. George Leighton, stirred the crowd with his grandiloquent rhetoric: "Lift up your heads, O towers, to greet the morning light of the new century," he said. Before the day was over, reported one newspaper, "all the staid members of the alumni, professors and business and professional men were giving the college yell."

Sundial on Cupples I.
The class of 1908 donated an embellishment to Cupples I: a vertical sundial that bears the motto: "I am a shadow/So art thou; I mark time/Dost thou?"

David Kilper, WU Photographic Services

Cupples I progresses.
The construction of the first Cupples building was among a flurry of projects on the new campus that marked the turn of the century.

Construction photos, WU Archives

Next came the two Cupples building cornerstones on May 11 and 25, 1901. Once Cupples I was finished, its first floor housed a new architecture program, part of a revamped School of Engineering and Architecture, and its second floor, civil engineering. Cupples II would be the new home of mechanical and electrical engineering. At each Cupples Hall ceremony, the keynote speaker was an engineer: first Calvin Woodward, who foresaw a growing need for technical graduates; then civil engineer Robert Moore, who talked about the "striking lessons of the value of truth and probity" within his profession. "A false theory in economics or politics may survive for hundreds of years," he said, "but for the engineer the judgment is immediate and without appeal. The false structure falls and buries its author in the ruins."

On June 15, 1901, the last building launched in this flurry of ceremonies was Liggett Hall (later renamed Prince Hall), a new dormitory that could accommodate 75 men. It was the gift of Elizabeth J. Liggett in memory of her husband, tobacco magnate John E. Liggett. She was not the last widow to donate a building; fully four of the early buildings honored late spouses. Some said that Brookings, handsome and single, attracted this generosity. His "imperial charm had its utilitarian value," admitted his biographer slyly.

The University still needed a physics building, athletic grounds, and a gymnasium; the Ridgley fund fell short of the total needed to build a new library. There were other financial worries, too. Building costs were rising rapidly, particularly with talk of a world's fair — and soon those first five donors were asked to supplement what they had promised. With the costly grading project and the need for some unforeseen land acquisition to the south, the University had had to incur troubling new debt.

In May 1900, Robert Brookings and Samuel Cupples had joined in a gesture that stunned the University and rippled across the nation. After his hard work on their giant downtown warehouse project, Brookings later recalled, "I said to Mr. Cupples one day that I could never justify to myself the blood I had sweat over Cupples Station unless it accomplished some great good in the world, and if he had no objection to the University as a partner, I would like to give my half interest in the property to the University's general endowment fund. Without a moment's hesitation he replied: 'Robert, that is a good scheme, and if you have no objection, I would like to join you in giving my half to the University for the same purpose.'" That gift — worth $3 million on paper, though it carried a heavy indebtedness — was a tonic to the struggling school and a lesson in generosity to the community.

A NEW LEASE ON LIFE FOR THE UNIVERSITY

Still, it was not enough. In 1901, the University had an immediate need for $600,000 — and the old campus on Washington Avenue, sold that spring, only realized $100,000. Brookings, ever resourceful, had to find a new solution. The answer arose from the world's fair project, which was quickly gathering momentum. In June 1901, the company planning the exposition to mark the 100th anniversary of the 1803 Louisiana Purchase decided to place the major buildings of the fair in the western half of Forest Park. Yet even that expanse of ground — 657 acres in all — was insufficient. Later that summer, they instructed their president, David Francis, to ask the University about leasing its campus and new buildings.

Word of this offer soon filtered down to students, who were counting the days until the move. In October, *Student Life* bristled: "This would mean that the removal to the new University would not take place for four or five years to come. Thus the present students would never receive the benefit." By November, its tone was even more hostile. "We desire to enter a protest against the consideration of the proposal. To divert the buildings to uses entirely foreign to university work…we feel would be eminently improper."

By December, however, the deed was done. Brookings had signed a contract that gave the University $650,000 in rent, $500,000 of which would support the construction of three more buildings, also to be leased by the exposition company. If the fair should be postponed a year from its intended start date of 1903, the company would add $100,000 more, which would pay for a fourth building. *Student Life* accepted the news with resignation: "They say every cloud has a silver lining and probably we shall find it in time, even though it is rather hard to see now."

Brookings faced another dilemma: where to put the undergraduates after the old campus was turned over to its new owners in summer 1902? Fortuitously, Mary Institute had been planning for a new building since 1899 when William McMillan donated $100,000 toward its construction. Now it was on the verge of moving to its new West End location at Lake and Waterman — leaving vacant its old home at Locust and Beaumont. Brookings pounced, securing the building for the College; behind it he threw up a flimsy, four-story structure that housed physics, chemistry, engineering, a new department of zoology, and even

University Hall rises on the Hilltop

L ater renamed for board president Robert Brookings, University Hall was built in 1901 to accommodate offices of the chancellor, other administrators, and faculty, as well as lecture rooms for courses in the humanities. Its four, 85-foot-high towers are nearly octagonal, but are nine inches narrower in their north-south faces.

University Hall takes shape. Construction began in 1900 on a new administration building, now known as Brookings Hall.
All photos, WU Archives

Holmes Lounge, Ridgley Hall.
With its cloister arcade, Ridgley is the only building of the first five in the English Renaissance style. Later it would successively be the home of the law school, psychology department, and Romance languages. Its main reading room today is the Mary Brooks Holmes Lounge, which was fully renovated in 1997.
David Kilper, WU Photographic Services

Stephen Ridgley (1806-1892).
The British-born Ridgley, who made a fortune in lamp manufacturing, bequeathed $66,000 to the University. This fund matured until it allowed construction of a library in 1902, with additions from the World's Fair income.
WU Archives

John Van Ornum (c. 1864-1943).
Ornum first came to the University as an assistant to Professor John B. Johnson; from 1892-94, he left to become chief topographer of the international boundary survey between the U.S. and Mexico. He returned in 1900 as William Palm Professor of Civil Engineering.
WU Archives

part of the dental program, displaced after the 1899 merger. "Who would have thought, on entering Washington University, that he would graduate from a female seminary?" sniffed *Student Life*. To placate the students, Brookings bought the elegant old St. Louis Club, which became their dining and social center until the new campus was ready.

On the new campus, buildings were taking shape as stonemasons hand-chiseled blocks of granite hauled from quarries 100 miles south. Site superintendent James Jamieson provoked a series of minor squalls, first when he tried to give pointers to the masons. "Some took it pleasantly, others could not stand the criticism, threw down their tools and quit in a huff," he later recalled. He caused another outcry when he insisted upon using Portland cement instead of a cheaper but less reliable brand of "natural" cement. He laid down 10 work rules, soon known as the "Ten Commandments" — which "were quite as frequently broken, as the Biblical originals," he said, though they led to good results.

With the lease income from the Fair, construction surged forward. Ridgley Library, with its elegant cloister arcade, went up in 1902. That fall, two more cornerstones were laid: Tower Hall

dormitory, later renamed for board member John F. Lee and again for Karl Umrath, who gave $1.5 million to the University from 1958-63; and the gymnasium which, like the athletic fields, was named for David Francis. In 1901, Eliza Eads How — daughter-in-law of charter board member John How — had donated the money for a memorial to her late father, Capt. James B. Eads. Now the lease freed that money to finance a new physics building, Eads Hall, at the rear of Ridgley.

FACULTY ADDITIONS ENRICH CAMPUS LIFE

The exodus of key faculty members over the previous decade, plus the recent upsurge in income, meant that the time had come to replenish the teaching staff. In 1900, the first wave of new faculty members arrived, among them John L. Van Ornum, a replacement for John B. Johnson as William Palm Professor of Civil Engineering, who immediately jumped in to supervise the soil-grading effort. By fall 1901, Frederic Aldin Hall had arrived to teach Greek and stayed on to eventually become chancellor. He replaced

Elizabeth J. Liggett (1827-1909).
WU Archives

Liggett Hall. Named for John E. Liggett (1826-1897), who built a fortune as president of Liggett & Myers tobacco company, it was a men's dormitory, then remodeled for other uses and renamed Prince Hall. Today, the Liggett name is preserved on the Liggett/Koenig Residential College.
WU Archives

Tower Hall. The cornerstone of this dormitory, designed to accommodate 150 students, was laid in October 1902. It was later renamed for John F. Lee, a lawyer and board member who served from 1902 until his death, and still later for donor Karl Umrath (1884-1968). Today, the Lee name continues through the Beaumont/Lee Residential College.
WU Archives

John F. Lee (1828-1926).
WU Archives

Sylvester Waterhouse, now retired, who had become an institution during his 43 years on the faculty; at his death in 1902, a faculty resolution warmly praised his "character, intellect and life."

Others came in 1901: Frederick M. Mann, the first professor of architecture in this new program, officially established as part of the School of Engineering and Architecture in 1902; Robert H. Fernald, who took John Kinealy's place as professor of mechanical engineering. A new mathematics professor, Russian-born Alexander Chessin, replaced Edmund Engler, who left to

assume the presidency of Worcester Polytechnic Institute. Students were grieved to see Engler go, and one took a stab at poetry to mark his leaving: "Our bestest Prof. will soon be gone/And Math. for us will be hard chawin.'" Outside of class, Chessin proved popular with students because he attended athletic events and promoted school spirit. In class, recalled Alexander Langsdorf, who himself became head of electrical engineering in 1901, Chessin "was impatient with the shortcomings of undergraduates, and his caustic comments, written in red ink all over his students'

Eads Hall honors James B. Eads

Eliza Eads How was the daughter-in-law of charter board member John How, the controversial founder of the O'Fallon Polytechnic Institute. She was also the daughter of Capt. James Buchanan Eads, engineer, bridge-builder, and inventor, whose memory she honored through this building. For many years, Eads Hall was the home of the physics department, where Arthur Holly Compton did his Nobel Prize-winning research in the 1920s. It was then home to the psy-

chology and education departments in Arts & Sciences. Since its renovation, completed in August 1998, Eads has classroom space, the Teaching Center, the Writing Center, and the Arts & Sciences Computing Center, which includes a Language and Instructional Media Center.

James Buchanan Eads (1820-1887).
WU Archives

Eliza Eads How (1847-?).
WU Archives

Eads Hall.
David Kilper, WU Photographic Services

**Robert H. Fernald
(c. 1872-1931).**
Fernald, who had a Ph.D.
from Columbia University,
was professor, then chair,
of mechanical engineering.

**1908 Sigma Nu
scrapbook.**
A student, Paul H.
Hawkins, created this
leather-bound scrap-
book detailing his
time at Washington
University from
1905-08.

Naokazu Fujimori, M.D. '04.
Said *Student Life*: "We may rea-
sonably hope that he is only the
fore-runner of a host of his
countrymen who will be thoroughly welcome and will add a
cosmopolitan tinge to the fabric
of which our student body is
made."

All images, WU Archives

papers, gave him the reputation
of being a holy terror."

By and large, they were a
young group — Mann called
them a "boy faculty" — and
increasingly, they had Ph.D.
degrees. Edgar James Swift,
new chair of psychology and
education, earned his from
Clark University; George O.
James, instructor in mathematics and applied mechanics, and
later dean of the College, got
his from Johns Hopkins.
Noting this trend, other faculty
members felt pressure to
acquire a doctorate, too. In
1900, German professor Otto Heller took time off
to complete his at the University of Chicago. At
the 1903 Commencement, faculty members
appeared for the first time in gowns and hoods,
their colors denoting the university they had attended
and degree they had received.

Gradually, school spirit among the students
began to improve, as clubs appeared for music,
literature, and German. Fraternities prolifer-
ated: Phi Delta Theta,
Sigma Alpha Epsilon,
Kappa Sigma, and Sigma
Nu for undergraduates;
Nu Sigma Nu for
medical students; Phi
Delta Phi for law stu-
dents; and Xi Psi Phi for
dental students. A few sorori-
ties — Theta Sigma, Eta Epsilon Tau, and WAG —
also came to life. In 1903, the first student yearbook
appeared: the *Hatchet*, named tongue-in-cheek for
the tool George Washington was said to have used
in cutting down the cherry tree.

The campus was becoming more diverse, though
no longer in racial terms. Women were a vital part of
University life, despite occasional jabs by male
students in the pages of *Student Life*. For the first
time, there were international students in University departments, especially the medical school, as
Egyptian, Syrian, and one Japanese student matriculated. Jewish students, welcome from the early
days of the school, were also a growing presence.
When chapel services were revamped in 1902, with
area clergy taking turns at leading them, rabbis
such as Rabbi Samuel Sale from Shaare Emeth
Congregation had a place in the rotation; and
Rabbi Leon Harrison, senior rabbi of Temple Israel,
was the University's Commencement speaker in
1909. In 1906, Temple Israel asked the Dramatic
Club, formed in 1904, to perform Smith Academy

Fannie Hurst (1889-1969).
Hurst, A.B. '09, later became a
prominent novelist. Her bequest
endowed the Hurst Professorship
for visiting writers, and Hurst
Lounge in Duncker Hall is
named for her.

graduate and novelist Winston
Churchill's *The Title Mart* as a benefit
for the organ fund at its new syna-
gogue. The club did, and its performance was a great success; a star of the
show was Fannie Hurst, A.B. '09.

The school was turning out academic stars as well, such as Samuel Ely Eliot,
A.B. '05 — son of Thomas L. Eliot and
grandson of Rev. William G. Eliot —
who became the first University student
to win a coveted Rhodes Scholarship in
1905. But in 1904, even he worried aloud
about "a lack of unity, both among the
several departments, and among the
classes of a single department." The
University, with its disparate parts —
soon to become more isolated from one another
when the College and Engineering left behind the

The 1902 Varsity Track Team.
Track was among the sports in the growing athletic depart-
ment. The team beat Missouri State University, based in
Columbia, 37-28 at its first dual meet in May 1903.

downtown departments of law, medicine, art,
botany — did not yet have a cohesive sense of
identity. The three secondary schools were distant,
too. Mary Institute was at its new location, while
Smith Academy and the Manual Training School,
forced to leave downtown by a noisy stove factory
nearby, were housed in new buildings, completed in
1905, on a nine-acre parcel near Union Boulevard.

The mediocre athletic program, hampered by
inadequate facilities downtown, posed another

Women's art class.
The presence of women on campus became more common in the early 1900s, as evidenced by this women's sketching class at the art school.

problem. At a nearby rink, a brand-new University hockey team played its first game against a Canadian team in 1899; baseball and a new basketball team competed too. Football, however, caused continuing disputes. Coaches, driven to despair by the small pool of University athletes, brought in outside players, or ringers, to fill out their teams — and won a few games. In 1900, the board ruled that athletes must be degree candidates, with the deans supervising the teams. Students protested immediately, saying they did not want to be "nursed by

Phi Delta Theta fraternity.
Fraternities and sororities were an important part of campus social life in 1901.

our dear Auntie Dean." In 1908, this tension erupted into a two-week strike after the *Student Life* editor was suspended for calling the faculty, which had declared the basketball captain ineligible just before an important game, "a bunch of asses."

Student honesty — and how to enforce it — was another hotly debated issue. In March 1901 a *Student Life* editorial declared: "It is perfectly safe to say that there was not a single examination, at least in the lower grades, in which someone did not receive illegitimate aid." Behind the cheating was the students' desire to raise their averages and graduate with honors. By May, the faculty had voted to abandon honors, but the cheating continued. In 1903, the University suspended some students and two years later established an official honor system, which was dropped in 1907 when a student board failed to convict a classmate who was clearly guilty of an infraction.

School for Scandal.
Thyrsus, a campus theater group, performed the play at the Odeon Theatre in 1906.

Meanwhile, the spectacular 1904 World's Fair began at the end of April with the help of University board members to plan it, the University's campus to stage it, and some students and even faculty to run it. As the months wore on toward the Fair's December 1 closing, undergraduate morale began to soar as the new campus came closer to reality. Packing now began in earnest for what one student called, "the long-expected exodus to the new buildings."

"A DREAM COME TRUE"

In a decade rich with ceremonies, the quiet event held on the morning of January 30, 1905, was perhaps the most satisfying and, for longtime faculty members, the most poignant. Here, finally, was the realization of all their hopes; "here at long last," said Langsdorf, "was the living realization of a dream come true." The chapel services that morning, held in the

Samuel Ely Eliot (1882-1976).
Eliot, A.B. '05, grandson of William G. Eliot, was the University's first winner of a prestigious Rhodes Scholarship, created in 1902 by a bequest of Cecil Rhodes, a British philanthropist and colonial pioneer, for study at Oxford University. Altogether, the University has had 21 recipients of the award from 1905 to 2001.

All photos, WU Archives

McMillan Hall: First women's dormitory

Eliza McMillan (1845-1915).
WU Archives

William McMillan was chairman of the board of American Car and Foundry, one of the largest car-building companies in the world. After his death, his widow, Eliza McMillan, gave funds to build McMillan Hall, originally a women's dormitory and then remodeled in the 1960s for other uses. She also donated $1.5 million to build the McMillan

Eye, Ear, Nose, and Throat Hospital on the medical school campus.

Fannie Hurst, A.B. '09, was among the first group of 16 women who inhabited the cavernous McMillan, built to house 125. Many were local students who wanted a taste of freedom, but liked to go home on the weekend. At the sight of them leaving, faculty nicknamed the hall "Suitcase U."

Left and above:
McMillan Hall interiors.
WU Archives

William McMillan (1841-1899).
Oil on canvas by Carl Gustav Waldeck
WU Gallery of Art

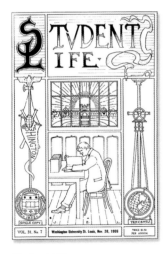

Student Life.
The student newspaper minced no words in its editorials about the university administration, student cheating, and other issues.
WU Archives

beautiful, oak-paneled room over the University Hall arch (now called the Chancellors Room, lined with portraits of all past chancellors), inaugurated the academic use of the new campus. Two deans with more than seven decades of service between them — Calvin Woodward and Marshall Snow — spoke in quavering voices about the early struggles of the University; Chancellor Chaplin was deeply moved, declaring that the vision he had described in his inaugural address had finally been realized.

The University's problems were not over, however. For one thing, the entire campus was littered with debris from the Fair. More than 20 buildings awaited removal, among them a shabby Hires Root Beer booth; there was no grass at all and only a few trees. Inside the buildings was similar desolation. Next door to David Francis' office in 200 University Hall was a room, used as a barroom for prominent Fair visitors, that reeked of champagne for the entire year to follow. "When our class entered

Washington University in the fall of 1906," recalled Arthur Proetz, A.B. '10, M.D. '12, "any lecture room window afforded a full view of the mopping up."

Certain economies in the construction of these buildings became quickly apparent. There was only one overworked telephone for the whole campus. Professor Kinealy supervised a primitive heating system, operating from the school's new power-house, that created "overheated rooms on one side, underheated on another," with "all of the occupants, from the under janitor to the gray haired Ph.D., condemning conditions," wrote James Jamieson. Gradually things began to improve, as the trash disappeared, grass was planted, and Calvin Woodward rallied the school for a tree-planting day in late April.

By the first Commencement on June 15, 1905 — a day of festivities that included the official dedication of the new buildings — the "grounds had never looked so well, with their spread of green lawn and newly made walks," said one

University publication. On behalf of the women students and alumnae, Lillie Rose Ernst, Ph.B. '92, presented Chancellor Chaplin with a silk myrtle-and-maroon flag, saying: "Wave over our beloved School in benediction and proclaim to the wide world her message: *Per Veritatem Vis,*" which translates as "strength through truth." The speaker for the day, David R. Francis, marveled that "when we contemplate the changes that have taken place within a third of a century it is almost impossible to believe that so much has been accomplished in so short a time." To cap off the day, the University awarded honorary degrees to such alumni and faculty members as Francis himself, Samuel Cupples, Minard Holman, Calvin Woodward, Marshall Snow, Francis Nipher, Halsey Ives, and John Green.

The campus was not only improving but growing. A small observatory went up to house the University's venerable telescope. Eliza McMillan donated a women's dormitory, completed in 1907, in memory of her late husband, William; Christine Blair Graham paid tribute to her late husband, Benjamin Brown Graham, by donating Graham Chapel, finished in 1909, which was modeled after King's College Chapel at Cambridge University. At the same time, some departments shifted location. In 1905, the Dental Department took possession of the onetime Mary Institute building, vacated by the College, while the law school moved into the old St. Louis Club two blocks west.

School spirit blossomed, bringing with it an official alma mater and a flood of new clubs: a political science club, the Blackstone Debating Society, an Esperanto Club, the Kakodyl Club, Architectural Society, Civil Engineering Club, a bowling group. Four new honoraries appeared in 1904: Obelisk for freshmen, Lock and Chain for sophomores, Thurtene for juniors, and Pralma for seniors. The *Washington University Record* was founded in 1905 with Otto Heller as editor. In 1907, the Dramatic Club acquired a new name, Thyrsus, signifying a staff carried by Dionysus, later associated with drama, and sometimes topped with a pinecone.

More new faculty arrived on campus, including George Throop, instructor in Latin and Greek and later chancellor; Walter E. McCourt, assistant professor of geology — later dean of engineering and finally assistant chancellor; and Roger Baldwin, hired in 1906 as an instructor in sociology. Baldwin spearheaded an affiliation with a graduate program, the School of Social Economy, previously associated with the University of Missouri. The School offered a year's program leading to a master's degree in social work and, with a grant from the Russell Sage Foundation, took on a broad program of research.

The Hatchet.
Named for the implement George Washington supposedly used to chop down a cherry tree, the *Hatchet* was introduced in 1903 as the student yearbook.

An alma mater for the University

For years, students had been proposing school songs in the pages of *Student Life,* such as Alexander R. Skinker's 1905 "A Hymn of Washington." In February 1906, a special supplement excitedly suggested a new alma mater, written by William Schuyler, A.B. '74. But in 1907 two other students — George B. Logan and Milton B. Rosenheim, both undergraduates in the class of 1908 and law graduates in 1910 — gave new lyrics to the tune "How Can I Leave Thee?" and this version stuck, quickly becoming accepted as the University's alma mater.

George B. Logan.
(1886-1950).

All images, WU Archives

THE ALMA MATER

Dear Al-ma Ma-ter, Thy name is sweet to me.
Those days of youth which All of us spent with thee

Our hearts are all for thee Fair Wash-ing-ton.
Form a dear his-to-ry, Fair Wash-ing-ton.

Thy halls shall hon-ored be Through-out this great coun-try
Could they re-new-ed be, We'd live our days with thee

For all e-ter-ni-ty, Our Wash-ing-ton.
For all e-ter-ni-ty, Our Wash-ing-ton.

Words by
M. B. Rosenheim '08
George B. Logan '08

University leaders.
Celebrating Arbor Day April 22, 1905, are, from left to right, Marshall S. Snow, Edward Mallinckrodt, Sr., Isaac H. Lionberger, Robert S. Brookings, Winfield Scott Chaplin, Calvin M. Woodward, Alfred L. Shapleigh, William K. Bixby, Charles Parson, and Henry Ware Eliot.
WU Archives

Parsons leaves art collection to University museum

A t his death, Charles Parsons left the University's St. Louis Museum of Fine Arts his large art collection, which he had amassed during 40 years of world travel. The University added other works of art through a fund established in his name.

The collection includes American, British, and French paintings by Jean Baptiste Camille Corot, Frederic E. Church, Aelbert Cuyp, Asher Durand, Léon Bonnat, El Greco, William Hogarth, George Inness, and Honoré Daumier, among many others.

**Charles Parsons
(1824-1905).**
WU Archives

Mummy and coffin.
The sarcophogus of Henut-wedjebu, c. 1391-1350 B.C., made of wood, bitumen, and gold, was given to the museum by Charles Parsons in 1896.
WU Gallery of Art

NEW LEADERSHIP FOR THE UNIVERSITY

Worn down by his work in planning the move, Chaplin gave up his added role as University treasurer in 1906, and a year later said he would leave the chancellorship itself. At the June 1907 Commencement, which also marked the 50th anniversary celebration of the University's 1857 inauguration, Chaplin — whose quiet role in building the school had been largely overshadowed by Brookings' more public efforts — expressed the simple wish that the University would always contribute "the essential element of democratic government, the moral and intellectual development of the people." Adding distinction to the occasion was the Hon. James Bryce, then British ambassador to the United States, who was the principal speaker for the day.

Within days of Chaplin's announcement, Brookings jumped in to pick a successor. A year dragged by, with the saintly Marshall Snow once again serving as interim chancellor and Frederic Hall as acting dean of the College, while Brookings tried to attract Edwin Alderman, president of the University of Virginia. When Alderman finally turned him down, Brookings asked an old friend, Charles W. Eliot, president of Harvard, for a recommendation — and Eliot strongly endorsed David Franklin Houston, president of the University of Texas. Brookings approached him, and three months later Houston, only 42 years old, agreed to become Washington University's next chancellor.

A North Carolina native, Houston had graduated with honors from the University of South Carolina, then worked as Spartanburg schools superintendent. After receiving a master's degree in political economy from Harvard, he became an adjunct faculty member at the University of Texas in 1894, moving up to serve as professor, head of political science, and the first dean of the faculty. His career there was interrupted by a brief stint as president of Texas A & M, but he was soon back to become the University of Texas president.

A self-effacing man, he refused inaugural ceremonies at Washington University and plunged in to tackle the educational issues that Chaplin had been forced to neglect. In this effort, he had the full support of the faculty, who admired him, and of Brookings, who was a little afraid of him. Houston was, as Brookings told Adolphus Busch, "the great Chancellor whom you always have been talking about." Yet these two leaders were polar opposites: Houston was as taciturn — even austere — as Brookings was verbose, and as realistic as Brookings was enthusiastic. A magazine article once gave Houston, whose office was sometimes referred to as "the refrigerator," credit for being able to keep silent in seven languages.

Yet both men were united in their commitment to the University. Over the next five years, Houston's vision — buoyed by Brookings' strenuous efforts — shaped and extended the University's mission. Brookings, more than Houston, soon confronted another, unexpected challenge: After revitalizing the College, he now had to take on a complete rebuilding of the medical school. Ⓦ

WU Photographic Services
Christine Blair Graham (?-1915).
WU Archives

Christine Blair Graham builds chapel to honor her husband

I n 1905, Christine Blair Graham, widow of paper distributor Benjamin Brown Graham (1840-1904), told her former next-door neighbor Robert Brookings that she would like to build a chapel on campus to honor her late husband. The cornerstone for Graham Chapel was laid on November 23, 1907. The building is festooned with decorative grotesques; its limestone interior features a trussed Tudor-style ceiling, marble floors, and lavish stained-glass windows, notably the "Dedication of Solomon's Temple" at the east end of the chapel.

Over the years, there have been changes. The balcony above the entrance to the nave was added in 1947 and modified again in 2002, and four organs have been installed, the most recent one in 1986. Its elaborate carved case, dating from 1948, is an exact copy of the original case.

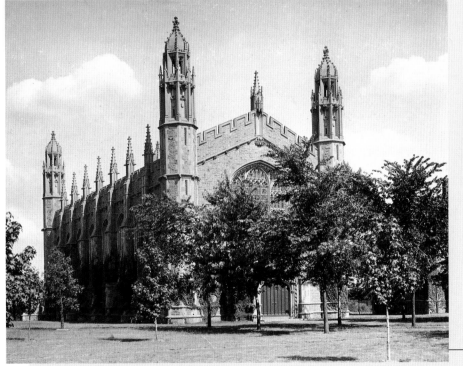

Graham Chapel.
The lavish interior of the chapel (above) is the site of many lectures, performances, and special events, while the exterior (left) is a focal point at the center of the Hilltop Campus.
WU Archives

"A VICTORY OF PEACE": THE 1904 WORLD'S FAIR, THE OLYMPICS, AND WASHINGTON UNIVERSITY

David Rowland Francis (1850-1927).
Francis, A.B. '70, LL.D. '05, was St. Louis mayor, 1885-89; Missouri governor, 1889-93; U.S. Secretary of the Interior, 1896-97; and Ambassador to Russia, 1916-17.
WU Archives

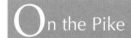n the Pike

I stood on the Pike at half-past eight;
I was broke as broke could be;
And I looked for some kind-hearted manager
To hand out a pass to me...

Student Life, **October 1904**

At the University's 1905 Commencement, the first held on the new Hilltop Campus, David R. Francis, A.B. '70, LL.D. '05, asked the crowd to recall the spectacular St. Louis World's Fair — the Louisiana Purchase Exposition (LPE), as it was officially known — that had ended just six months earlier. "Come and stand with me in the great archway of the Administration Building and cast your eye...beyond," he said nostalgically, looking eastward toward Forest Park. For most of his listeners, conjuring up the Fair could not have required much of an imaginative leap.

After all, remnants were all around them that day, and nearly everyone present must have known the Fair well during its short, sparkling life from April 30 to December 1, 1904. Alumni and board members were among the 118 directors who had organized and backed it under Francis' energetic leadership. Faculty members had designed parts of it and won prizes in its competitions, while students had staffed the booths and reveled in its wonders, especially "the Pike," its seductive entertainment strip.

Thanks to an agreement negotiated by board president Robert Brookings — to lease the new campus to the LPE directors for a fee that made possible much-needed campus construction — every University building, old and new, held Fair-related memories. For example, Room 200 of the Administration Building (now Brookings Hall) had been Francis' own office,

Louisiana Purchase monument. Sculptor Karl Bitter created "The World's Work" on a design by E. L. Masqueray.
Missouri Historical Society, St. Louis

Palace of Education and Social Economy. The building, designed by Eames and Young, fulfilled the Fair's educational mission with exhibits of teaching methods and live students at work in model classrooms. The social economy section included exhibits on health and hygiene as well as a Model Street outside the building depicting ideal solutions to urban problems.
Missouri Historical Society, St. Louis

and on the walls of the adjoining barroom (now Room 220) were dirty streaks — scratches left by smokers impatient to light their matches.

At this Commencement, Francis invited his audience first to recall the Fair's Louisiana Purchase monument, topped by the splendid "Peace" statue, and then the majestic Festival Hall, with the goddess of "Victory" on its dome. "Those are the figures that symbolize the scope and the achievements of man," he said. "Peace and Victory. A Victory of Peace...Let us transfer, in our imagination at least, Victory and Peace to the [Brookings Hall] towers that mark the grand entrance to the University Quadrangle, there to remain for another hundred years."

THE FAIR TRANSFORMS ST. LOUIS

The Fair that excited these happy memories had its roots in a failed attempt to secure the 1893 exposition, captured by Chicago. St. Louis boosters regrouped, gathering $5 million each from the city, local backers, and the federal government. All the while, staunch support came from the

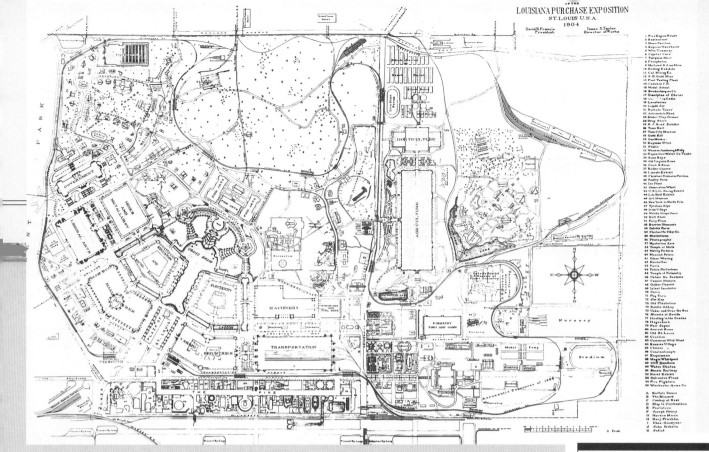

LOUISIANA PURCHASE EXPOSITION
ST.LOUIS U.S.A.
1904

David R. Francis   Isaac S. Taylor
President   Director of Works

World's Fair map. The Hilltop Campus is located in the lower right corner. This map is oriented with south at the top.
WU Archives

University, particularly faculty member Sylvester Waterhouse. Not only did this fair commemorate the 1803 Louisiana Purchase, albeit a year late, it would "cause the city to cleanse, beautify and better pave its streets," Waterhouse said in *Student Life*. And it broadened "the mental horizon of our people by the sight of all that is grandest in human progress."

He was right. In preparation for the Fair, hotels were built, streets were paved, and officials tackled the city's muddy water supply — one cause of the frequent typhoid outbreaks. They asked engineers in the city water department, all University graduates, to get involved, and their efforts were successful. By the time the Fair

opened, clear water flowed from St. Louis taps, thanks largely to Edward Flad, B.S. '81, longtime water commissioner; Silas Bent Russell, B.S. '81; and John Wixford, B.Ph. '85, B.Chem. '87.

Meanwhile, crews of workmen were transforming Forest Park, creating lagoons and pools, fountains and cascades. They cut down 40,000 trees, temporarily leaving a wasteland of stumps. "It was a pity…to see giant monarchs of the forest fall before the woodman's ax to make room for the exhibit palaces," wrote Edward V.P. Schneiderhahn, LL.B. '96, in a Fair reminiscence.

On campus, four new buildings went up: the David R. Francis gymnasium, outfitted as a model gym by the Spalding Company; Tower Hall, a dormitory for out-of-town students and teachers; and Eads Hall, headquarters for women's organizations. The fourth, Ridgley Library, was especially grand. Its reading room (now Holmes Lounge) became the focal point for social events, such as a gala ball given by West Point cadets; on its second floor was a glittering display of Queen Victoria's Diamond Jubilee gifts. Existing buildings were put to use, too. The Administration Building held staff offices; Busch, architects and engineers; and Liggett, Fair guests. Cupples I had American

University Hall (right) served as Fair headquarters. The Italian Pavilion is in the foreground.
Missouri Historical Society, St. Louis

Alumni clean up city water

Engineering graduates Edward Flad and Silas Bent Russell, both '81 — and chemistry graduate John Wixford, '87, worked to clean up the city's sediment-laden water supply. They had help from other alumni: Ben C. Adkins, '86;

John Wixford (1861-1935).

John A. Laird, '87; William E. Rolfe, '95; Arthur Jacobs, '97; and Gurdon G. Black, '01.

At the 1905 Commencement, one speaker said: "To the modest and retiring Wixford the city of St. Louis should erect a statue of crystal to typify the bright water which he has evolved from the turbid stream that flows by us."

Edward Flad (1860-1952).

Photos courtesy of Missouri Historical Society, St. Louis

Congress of Arts and Sciences.
In September 1904, scholars from many countries discussed human knowledge and progress.
Missouri Historical Society, St. Louis

Louis Clemens Spiering (1875-1912).
Gardens, bridges, restaurants, the Palais de Costume, and the Horticulture Building were all designed by Spiering, a member of the board, instructor in architecture from 1903-10, and assistant professor from 1910-11.
St. Louis Republic
WU Archives

James D. Lightbody.
Lightbody received the trophy for winning the 800-meter run at the 1904 Olympics.
Missouri Historical Society, St. Louis

ethnological exhibits, and Cupples II the Jefferson Guards, the Fair's private police force.

At the eastern edge of campus were the showcase buildings of 13 foreign nations. Among them was Great Britain's replica of Queen Anne's Orangery at Kensington Gardens, with an ornate interior and elegant formal garden. Until Bixby Hall was built, it housed the School of Fine Arts. China's pavilion, copied from the summer palace of Prince Pu Lun, was a wonder, created from more than 6,000 pieces of wood and decorative elements, including ivory-inlaid panels. The prince himself arrived for the Fair's opening ceremony — and had such fun that he stayed for two months, then gave Francis the pavilion at the close of the Fair.

At the western end of campus, just in front of the gymnasium, was a fenced Aeronautics Concourse where hot-air balloons took off on races, and aeronauts from Brazil, France, and the United States displayed primitive airships. To the south were the parade grounds for Army, West Point, and National Guard troops who held daily drills. The Fair's greenhouses were located on what is today the South 40.

Some faculty members played a role at the Fair, including architect Louis C. Spiering, who designed bridges, colonnades, and buildings.

Physics professor Francis Nipher received a gold medal for experimental work on the effect of wind pressure on buildings. And Halsey C. Ives, director of the School of Fine Arts and fine arts chief at the 1893 Chicago exposition, filled the same role this time. In 1903, he hired George Julian Zolnay, later an art faculty member, for the Fair's sculpture division.

Also involved were alumni like Capt. Llewellyn P. Williamson, M.D. '87, a member of the Philippine Exposition Board that brought in native soldiers and tribal peoples; George D. Markham, LL.B. '91, head of the Bureau of Music, which promoted concert bands; and architect William S. Eames, A.B. '78, designer of the much-acclaimed Education Palace. On June 16, 1904 — the official "Alumni Day at the Fair" — exercises were held in the 3,500-seat Festival Hall auditorium; the official organist was Charles Galloway, later the University's longtime organist, who played the Fair's 10,000-pipe organ, the largest in the world.

Enraptured students paid frequent visits to the Fair and made sly jokes about it in student publications. "Where is the best place to hold the World's fair?" asked one. "Around the waist," came the answer. They worked at attractions on the Pike, a one-mile entertainment strip along the Fair's northern edge that gave its name to the University's athletic teams, the "Pikers," and much later to a male *a cappella* group. After the Fair, Brookings formed a syndicate to buy this land, once owned by tobacco magnate and board member Daniel Catlin.

THE OLYMPICS COME TO CAMPUS

From August 29 to September 3, the University's new gymnasium and athletic fields were the site of an event that Francis had stolen away from Chicago: the 1904 Olympic Games, the 3rd Olympiad of the modern era and the first held in the western

hemisphere. The athletes, most of them American, competed in 26 events, largely track and field, but also weightlifting and tug-of-war. Overall, 13 Olympic and four world's records were broken.

The oddest event was the 24.8-mile marathon. On a blistering hot day, 31 runners, including two South Africans who happened to be taking part in the Boer War exhibit, left the University's cinder track, running west out Forsyth to Manchester then back again. Along the way, one contestant hitched a ride on a truck and was disqualified; one of the South Africans was chased off the road by dogs. In the end, 14 runners finished; the exhausted winner, dosed with strychnine by his handlers to keep him going, was Thomas J. Hicks of Boston, with a time of 3:28:53.

A CONGRESS OF SCHOLARS

On September 19, another major event opened: the Congress of Arts and Sciences, in which 500 scholars gathered for a week to discuss human knowledge and progress, often meeting in the Ridgley reading room. Many smaller congresses were held at the Fair, but this one, with its broad scope and distinguished participants, was extraordinary. An organizer, Harvard professor Hugo Münsterberg, had traveled to Europe to invite key academics, including Henri Poincaré, French mathematician and physicist, who described relativity in a landmark address.

At midnight on December 1, the Fair ended. University students thronged the Pike, overindulging in food and drink. That led to "R-E-M-O-R-S-E" groaned *Student Life*. At the suggestion of President Theodore Roosevelt, the last day was dedicated to Francis, who called the Fair "the work of my life." The closing fireworks featured his profile in lights.

The Fair had a beneficial effect on the University, argued Francis in the 1905 *Hatchet*. For one thing, the campus had appreciated in value, and improvements made during the Fair would remain. More important, he said, the University was now "permanently photographed on the memories of many millions of World's Fair visitors from all parts of the Union and from all parts of the world."

Most people, like Schneiderhahn, felt bereft by its loss. At the end of his reminiscence, he recalled feeling mingled delight and sorrow during the final, brilliant illumination of Fair buildings, just before Francis turned off the lights. "Words fail. Magic picture....Never expect to see anything so grand again."

"Beautiful Fair," he continued sadly.

"Goodbye." (WU)

George Zolnay oversees the Fair's sculpture exhibits

A Hungarian-born graduate of the Imperial Academy of Fine Arts of Vienna, George Julian Zolnay came to St. Louis in 1903, one of the artists attracted by the Fair. Halsey Ives put him in charge of sculpture exhibits; afterwards, he became an instructor in modeling and a sculptor in the School of Fine Arts. In 1909, he was commissioned by E.G. Lewis, founder of University City, to sculpt two lions for his city's new entrance gates. He also sculpted a bust of David Francis, now in the Missouri Historical Society collection.

David Francis and George Julian Zolnay (1863-1949).
Missouri Historical Society, St. Louis

Lion gates.
George Zolnay's sculptures of a lion and lioness sit atop the "Gates of Opportunity" designed by architects Eames and Young and built in 1909. In this 1911 photograph, the lions look east on Delmar Boulevard.
Archives of the University City Public Library

Chinese Pavilion.
China's exhibit was a reproduction of Prince Pu Lun's summer residence. The imperial family's prince attended the Fair's opening day ceremonies.
Missouri Historical Society, St. Louis

CHAPTER SIX

AN "AMERICAN IDEAL":

A New Medical School for the University

1908-1919

Barnes Hospital, which affiliated with the School of Medicine in 1911.
Barnes Hospital as it appeared in 1915 immediately after its completion. The two smaller buildings in the right foreground were originally segregated wards.

A NEW MEDICAL SCHOOL FOR THE UNIVERSITY

*D*avid F. Houston, the University's able but reserved new chancellor, chose to forego the pageantry of a formal inauguration and immediately set to work. By early fall 1908, a major campaign was in the offing. The General Education Fund, a charitable foundation created by John D. Rockefeller, had promised the University $200,000 if it could find $800,000 in matching funds. As Houston realized, the moment was ripe for a rhetorical triumph — a compelling message to inspire wealthy St. Louisans and prod them to new heights of generosity.

Previous pages:
The School of Medicine and the Medical Campus.
The school and its affiliated hospitals make up one of the most respected academic medical centers in the nation.

1908 *On October 31, Chancellor David F. Houston outlined his vision for Washington University in a talk before the Commercial Club titled "A University for the Southwest."*

1910 *Abraham Flexner's report,* Medical Education in the United States and Canada, *found Washington University's Medical Department "inadequate in every essential respect."*

1911 *The University forged agreements linking the medical school and its faculty with Children's Hospital and Barnes Hospital.*

1913 *David Houston took a leave of absence to serve as U.S. Secretary of Agriculture. Frederic Aldin Hall became the acting chancellor.*

David F. Houston (1866-1940). Houston was chancellor from 1908-13. He later served as U.S. Secretary of Agriculture, then U.S. Secretary of the Treasury under President Woodrow Wilson.

Oil on canvas by J.W. DeRehling Quistgaard
WU Gallery of Art

When an invitation arrived from the Commercial Club, a group of prominent business leaders, Houston agreed to appear on October 31 and give a talk, "A University for the Southwest." He shared the podium with the man who had hired him: Board President Robert Brookings, himself a successful businessman with strong practical sense but little formal education, who stood in awe of Houston's formidable intellect. On this occasion, Brookings delighted in Houston's every word; like a doting parent, he later had the talk printed — and sent to prospective donors.

This speech, the most important of Houston's career, sketched a vision for Washington University — still largely a regional school — as a great national institution, with special ties to the underserved South and West. Realizing this dream, however, would require an array of new programs and expenses, among them an improved medical school, bolstered by more basic science research. Such growth, he said, would benefit everyone, solving "problems of community health and living."

With Houston's lofty eloquence still echoing in the air, Brookings, the consummate salesman,

Commercial Club program. Houston's landmark speech set forth his vision that the University would serve more than just the young people of St. Louis.

WU Archives

Gustav Baumgarten (1837-1910).
Baumgarten, St. Louis Medical College M.D. '56, became professor of physiology in 1873, held a chair in pathology from 1887-93, then was professor of medicine and briefly dean. In 1899, he was president of the Association of American Physicians.
Oil on canvas painting by Richard Miller.
WU Gallery of Art

John B. Shapleigh (1857-1925).
Dean W. McKim Marriott called Shapleigh, A.B. '78, St. Louis Medical College M.D. '81, professor of otology from 1895 to 1922, and dean, 1901-02, "one of the great group of medical men in St. Louis in the '80s." A memorial tablet in McMillan Hospital was dedicated to Shapleigh; and his family endowed the Shapleigh Ward for Ear Patients on the fifth floor in his honor.
WU Becker Medical Library

Missouri Medical College.
After the oldest medical college in Missouri became part of the Medical Department of Washington University in 1899, its former building served as Washington University Hospital.
WU Becker Medical Library

got up to close the deal, praising the University's programs and offering a few hints about money. For example, its Medical Department — formed through the 1891 acquisition of St. Louis Medical College, which merged in 1899 with Missouri Medical College — had an illustrious corps of alumni, he said. "Practically every physician and surgeon of any prominence in this city, is a graduate of one or the other of these schools, and you will find their graduates in every state in the union." Further, the school's entrance requirements had been raised and its instruction broadened. The University hospital, too, gave "splendid service," he added, guaranteeing patients "the best possible treatment."

Here Brookings, a tireless University booster, hesitated just a little. A few weeks earlier, he had met with the president of Johns Hopkins University, widely known to have the nation's most progressive medical school and hospital — and even Brookings at his most optimistic could not claim that Washington University rivaled Hopkins' success. However, the only thing lacking was money, he stressed, and the transformation could easily occur. "How long will it be," he asked hopefully, "before some wise philanthropist gives to St. Louis…a hospital to be affiliated with our

Medical School, universally recognized as having the strongest clinical faculty in the West?"

"THE GRIME AND SOOT OF YEARS"

For the Medical Department and the hospital, help was sorely needed, and more urgently than Brookings knew. Though nominally affiliated with the University, the school was actually owned by its faculty and supported by tuition fees — $122 a year in 1908-09 — with no financial support from the University and little oversight. A series of deans — Gustav Baumgarten, John B. Shapleigh, and Robert Luedeking — were skilled physicians, committed to the school's welfare, but they headed a sprawling, part-time staff that lacked cohesive purpose. In 1908-09, for example, nearly all 150 instructors who taught the 185 medical students had demanding clinical practices of their own. The result was a hit-or-miss curriculum and poorly coordinated instruction, with some topics covered in a number of courses and others not at all.

Despite the school's annual attempts to make improvements, the little more than decade-old facilities were already obsolete. As one medical student complained in 1903: "Inside the building one can never tell whether it is raining or not — all days seem to be cloudy and dismal. The floors are dirty; tables, chairs, everything covered with the grime and soot of years. This in a school whose professors are trying to teach methods of strictest cleanliness."

Up-to-date hospital facilities were an additional problem. Five years before Houston's Commercial Club speech, a faculty committee had stressed the need for a new hospital, but the $250,000 sum was out of reach; instead, the school had spent $50,000 to renovate the former Missouri Medical College building at Jefferson and Lucas as the 125-bed Washington University Hospital. Next door, in the Polyclinic, they created a dispensary with laboratory space, X-ray equipment, and a surgical amphitheater.

The revamped hospital was far from lavish and, like the school itself, operated at a deficit. In 1905, Brookings and Adolphus Busch each donated $25,000 to wipe out the department's existing debt — then Brookings decided it was time for greater control. With thanks for the bailout, the faculty agreed, asking for a "complete union" that would make "the Medical

Department an integral part of the University." The result was a 1906 ordinance that established it as a true University department and gave the board control over its budget, faculty appointments, and policies.

A few reforms took place as the faculty added several full-time members and chose a new dean, William H. Warren, professor of chemistry and toxicology. The faculty voted to upgrade admission standards and require students, who formerly needed only a high school education, to have a year's worth of college preparation beginning in 1910. Yet teaching was still uneven — Warren complained about "lectures extemporized in the automobile" — and clinical training inadequate.

ABOLISH OR REORGANIZE

Then in 1906, an old friend of Washington University — Henry S. Pritchett, professor of astronomy from 1883-87 — took an important, newly created job: president of the Carnegie Foundation for the Advancement of Teaching, a fund established by industrialist Andrew Carnegie for the benefit of teachers. Throughout his distinguished career, most recently as president of the Massachusetts Institute of Technology, Pritchett had maintained his warm friendship with Robert Brookings. In a eulogy to Brookings, delivered in 1933, Pritchett called him "a very gallant gentleman," adding that "he dreamed noble dreams and to a remarkable extent he made them come true; he never ceased striving."

The Council on Medical Education, an American Medical Association-sponsored group dedicated to reforming medical education, approached Pritchett in 1906 with an intriguing suggestion. What if the foundation undertook an independent survey of medical schools to assess their quality? Pritchett agreed, but determined to find a layman, not a physician, to do the investigation. Fortuitously, just such a

Henry S. Pritchett (1857-1939). Later he wrote of the Flexner report and its impact on Washington University: "This report while it made clear the fact that the medical school at Washington University was amongst the better schools of the region, nevertheless pointed out the weaknesses which are sure to ensue when the medical practitioner is the only professional teacher in the medical school."
WU Archives

The University begins training nurses

Nurses' training was critically important to the revamped medical school. A Washington University Training School for Nurses opened in 1907-08, and a school for pediatric nurses was also established. The two merged in 1910. In 1913 the admission requirements were: "a good common school education, good moral character, and a sound physique. Women of superior education and culture will be given preference in filling vacancies. The age of the applicant must be between 20 and 35 years old."

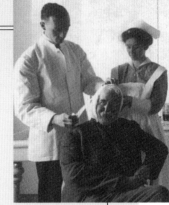

A doctor and nurse examine a patient, c. 1915.

No tuition was charged for the three-year program, and students received free board and lodging; the University built a nurses' residence for them on Kingshighway. In 1914, Julia Stimson, already director of social service at Children's Hospital, became nursing director. During World War I, some nurses from the school joined Stimson as part of the University's Base Hospital 21 unit in France.

The school reorganized in 1924 as the Washington University School of Nursing, with the addition of a program leading to a B.S. degree in nursing. From 1929-36, a program in public health nursing was offered. The school closed in 1969.

School of Nursing graduates, 1908.
The first class to graduate from the nursing school included (left to right) Miss Ruby Cady (Mrs. Riley); Mrs. Ora Wright; Miss Nettie Anderson (Mrs. Stanson); Miss Kathryn A. Weber; Miss Mary A. Lannigan (Mrs. Thorburg).
Photos, WU Becker Medical Library

William H. Welch (1850-1934).
The first dean of the Johns Hopkins School of Medicine and a well-known figure in academic medicine, Welch advised Abraham Flexner and offered guidance on the medical school's reorganization. He received an honorary degree at the 1915 dedication.

Alan Mason Chesney Medical Archives of the Johns Hopkins Medical Institutions

man arrived in his office, looking for a job: Abraham Flexner, a Louisville native and Johns Hopkins graduate, who had run his own secondary school for troubled boys. He was, as he wrote in his autobiography, "an unfettered lay mind."

To prepare for his new task, Flexner traveled to Johns Hopkins to talk with physicians, including that school's guiding spirit and first dean, William Welch, a nationally renowned professor of pathology. He even consulted his brother, Simon Flexner, another eminent pathologist and first director of the Rockefeller Institute for Medical Research, where Welch was chairman of the board. With the Hopkins model in mind as the ideal, Abraham Flexner set out in December 1908 to visit 155 U.S. and Canadian medical schools. "I had no fixed method of procedure," he recalled. "I never used a questionnaire. I invariably went and saw the schools and talked with teachers of medicine and the medical sciences and their students."

What he found in many places — filthy conditions, shoddy equipment, wholly inadequate facilities — shocked him profoundly. In 1910, he published his findings in a hard-hitting book, *Medical Education in the United States and Canada*,

which made headlines, contributed to the closing of more than 100 schools, and instigated widespread reform; Welch believed it "was one of the most remarkable and influential publications in educational literature." When Flexner's survey took him to St. Louis in April 1909, Pritchett reassured him that he finally had a treat in store: "Now you are going to see something better," he said, "for my friend Brookings has taken particular interest in developing the medical school."

A two-day visit, however, left Flexner unimpressed. As he wrote later, he "found the school a little better than the worst I had seen elsewhere, but absolutely inadequate in every essential respect." Dismayed but still supportive, Pritchett — who always "stood behind me like a stone wall," Flexner recalled appreciatively — mailed off this indictment to a surprised and angry Robert Brookings. "I was so indignant on receipt of this report that I protested to Dr. Pritchett…that it was inaccurate," wrote Brookings. He and Houston felt personally affronted, since Flexner had not contacted either during his visit. Soon the two rallied though and began considering Flexner's charges.

In late May, Houston called a meeting of the

The Flexners play a significant role in medicine and American medical education

A braham and Simon Flexner were children of German immigrants who settled in Louisville, Kentucky. Simon became a faculty member of the new Johns Hopkins University medical school, and later director of medical research at the Rockefeller Institute.

Abraham, a Johns Hopkins graduate, opened a Louisville school for problem boys in 1890. After it closed in 1905, he wrote *The American College*, a critique of higher education. Henry Pritchett of

Abraham Flexner (1866-1959).
WU Becker Medical Library

the Carnegie Foundation admired the book and hired Abraham Flexner to do his famous survey of medical schools. In 1913 Flexner joined the General Education Board and raised $600 million to further medical education.

In 1916, Morris Flexner, a nephew who earned an M.D. from Johns Hopkins, joined the Washington University faculty as an assistant in medicine, later becoming a Louisville physician.

Simon Flexner (1863-1946).
Alan Mason Chesney Medical Archives of the Johns Hopkins Medical Institutions

most active members of the medical faculty to solicit their feelings about reform. Whatever such an overhaul might mean for them personally, they were ready — even eager — to see it happen, since "it was impossible to improve the old system with minor changes," said Baumgarten. Shapleigh agreed, saying: "There must be re-organization and the Faculty cannot do it." Warren concluded: "It must therefore be left to the Chancellor and Board to bring about this change, otherwise nothing will be accomplished."

BROOKINGS TAKES ACTION

With this endorsement, Houston and Brookings moved forward quickly. In June, the board approved the faculty's request and in October named three of Brookings' closest friends — William K. Bixby, Robert McKittrick Jones, and Edward Mallinckrodt, Sr. — as a reorganization committee, charged with recommending appropriate action. Meanwhile, Flexner was planning a second visit to St. Louis, and this time the mild-mannered Pritchett instructed him, rather sharply, to meet with Brookings and Houston, both of whom were "considerably disappointed at not having seen you" last time. Flexner later described his campus visit:

Leaders of medical school reorganization.
Philip A. Shaffer, Abraham Flexner, and Robert Terry, meeting here on February 21, 1950, on the centennial of Robert Brookings' birth, together helped lay the intellectual foundation for the Washington University School of Medicine.
WU Becker Medical Library

"I said to Mr. Brookings, 'How shall we proceed — will you show me the school, or shall I show it to you?' He chose the latter method. We went to the dean's office, and I asked to see the credentials of the students of the school, for the school pretended to require a flat four-year high-school education of all entering students. It was quickly

apparent to Mr. Brookings that no such requirement was being enforced. We went through other departments, not one of which was found to be what the catalogue represented. Within less than two hours Mr. Brookings was completely satisfied."

Immediately, Brookings called a meeting of the reorganization committee and asked Flexner to speak. "When I had finished, Mr. Brookings said: 'What shall we do?'" Flexner remembered. So he offered unvarnished advice: "'Abolish the school….Form a new faculty, reorganize your clinical facilities from top to bottom, and raise an endowment which will enable you to repeat in St. Louis what President Gilman [of Johns Hopkins] accomplished in Baltimore.' It was then and there voted that this plan should be carried through."

In a follow-up report, Flexner got more specific. The Medical Department's clinical branches were, "to state the facts candidly, in wretched condition," its hospital facilities poor and underused, and the methods used in the hospital "decidedly slipshod." The fault did not lie with the faculty; "it is probable," he wrote, "that the gentlemen giving the present instruction are just as competent physicians as the country possesses; but they are not teachers, and teachers alone can create a modern school of medicine." In short, he said, "heroic measures" were necessary: primarily a new dean with a strong background in clinical medicine to revamp the department.

Pritchett, keenly aware of Brookings' and Houston's feelings, tried to take the sting out of this report with an apologetic letter: "Flexner is very able and accurate, but he has the quality of the very acute mind to sometimes put things in a more sharp way than is necessary." Yet Houston, at least, had decided that Flexner was right. "The report was what I wanted," he wrote Pritchett in late November. "The fact that he speaks out his mind sharply pleases me."

In the meantime, Flexner had hurried east to talk to Welch and his own brother about finding a "man of distinction" to help guide the reform and perhaps become dean — and they recommended David L. Edsall, a brilliant young professor of therapeutics and pharmacology at the University of Pennsylvania. Just before Christmas 1909, Edsall

The second Children's Hospital.
St. Louis Children's Hospital moved to this building on Jefferson Avenue in 1884 and stayed until 1915.

The first St. Louis Children's Hospital at 2834 Franklin Avanue.
The hospital occupied this building from 1879-84.

Robert A. Barnes (1808-1892).
A wealthy merchant and financier, Barnes left the bulk of his estate for the establishment of a hospital "for sick and injured persons, without distinction of creed."

came to St. Louis — and Brookings rolled out the red carpet, inviting him to stay at his home. From Edsall's eager imagination came a plan for a new faculty "free of the 'dead wood,'" and filled instead with "the best men available." An excited Brookings reported to Pritchett that it was "a scheme of organization that would make the strongest aggregation of medical talent

for school purposes ever gathered together in this or any other country." These men should be hired as a group, Edsall warned, at salaries of $5,000 each and with permission to conduct their own consulting practices. By combining these men with new hospital space, laboratory buildings, and enough endowment income — the University would have, Edsall said, "an ideal medical school."

Brookings adored great dreams, and now he was hooked, too. This plan, he told Pritchett, "appeals to me very strongly, and is so much the best worth doing of anything that I know educationally…that I would be willing to make sacrifices which I can ill afford to do at present to bring it about." It would be even better if Carnegie or Rockefeller contributed, he hinted, since no St. Louisan of large means had yet stepped forward. For the time being, they would begin on a smaller scale — even though, he said wistfully, "it seems a terrible pity not to be able at once to enter upon the large plan, which is clearly the right plan."

Children's Hospital, dedicated January 9, 1915, on the Kingshighway campus.
Pictured to the left is the Elizabeth J. Liggett Memorial Building; to the right, the University Pavilion, containing isolation wards.

All photos, WU Becker Medical Library

In late January 1910, days before embarking on a three-month trip to Egypt, a fired-up Brookings could resist no longer. Writing to board vice president William Bixby, he declared himself willing to provide $500,000 of the $850,000 needed for new grounds and facilities, as well as one quarter of the rebuilt school's operating costs; he authorized Houston to begin the search for the dynamic young scientists they needed. Then he wrote to Pritchett admitting, with clear-eyed realism, that he knew his generosity was "only the beginning."

AFFILIATING WITH TWO HOSPITALS

During these same months, the hospital portion of Edsall's grand scheme was already moving forward on two separate fronts. On the one hand, plans were under way for a new hospital in St. Louis, thanks to a bequest left by wholesale grocer and banker Robert Barnes, who had died in 1892. In his will, he asked the three trustees of his estate to use $100,000 to build and equip this hospital, then another $900,000 to endow it. He directed them to begin work within three years after his death, but they knew the amount he had left was not enough for the purpose, so they invested it and waited. Meanwhile, they purchased a site for this hospital on Kingshighway in 1905, and two years later hired architect Theodore Link to design it.

At the same time, St. Louis Children's Hospital was planning to relocate. It had opened in 1879 in a house on Franklin Avenue and moved to a 60-bed facility at Jefferson and Adams in 1884. By 1889, it had grown again into an adjoining three-story building with two floors for infants and one for children with contagious diseases. Now, the hospital needed more space, and the board of managers was scouting for a site.

Years before Flexner's visit, Robert Brookings had become aware of all these hospital plans,

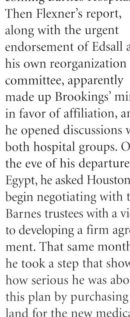

and they had begun to intrigue him. In 1908, he had already written to the Johns Hopkins president to ask his opinion about an affiliation between the Medical Department and the forthcoming Barnes Hospital. Then Flexner's report, along with the urgent endorsement of Edsall and his own reorganization committee, apparently made up Brookings' mind in favor of affiliation, and he opened discussions with both hospital groups. On the eve of his departure for Egypt, he asked Houston to begin negotiating with the Barnes trustees with a view to developing a firm agreement. That same month, he took a step that showed how serious he was about this plan by purchasing land for the new medical school buildings next to the Barnes tract.

In moving toward affiliation, Brookings had strong, well-placed allies. In 1905, his friend and business partner, Samuel Cupples, had become one of the Barnes trustees; like Brookings, Cupples served on the Children's Hospital advisory board. Heading that hospital's board of managers was Grace Richards Jones, the wife of Brookings' fellow University board member, Robert McKittrick Jones, who had already endorsed affiliation as a member of the reorganization committee.

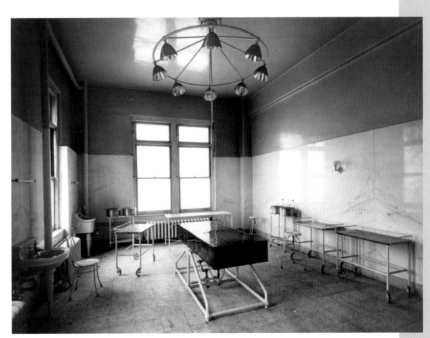

Early Barnes Hospital operating room, c. 1914-15.

Photos, WU Becker Medical Library

"A STUNNING GROUP OF MEN"

Fred T. Murphy (1872-1948). Head of surgery, Murphy later became the first director of Base Hospital No. 21 with the rank of major.

As 1910 wore on, Houston — with the avid support of Brookings, once he returned from abroad — pressed on energetically with the recruitment effort. In June, one of the rising young stars they had targeted, Joseph Erlanger of the University of Wisconsin, described the allure of those meetings in which Brookings and Houston spun visions of the future. "They were most interesting and inspiring," he wrote. "The enthusiasm that they awakened in me is dampened only by the weight of responsibility that rests upon our shoulders. The founders want to make a great school of the place and are willing to grant any reasonable request."

For the most part, this reorganization took place with the cooperation of the existing medical faculty, but once the scope of the change — and the need to displace some longtime faculty members — became apparent, a few emerged hurt and angry. Head of surgery, Herman Tuholske, kept Brookings up until midnight one August day with bitter complaints that he was being dismissed after 38 years of service, and that he had discovered this only by finding his name omitted from the fall course bulletin. A shaken Brookings wrote to Houston, "I do not care to spend many more such evenings."

In September, a remarkable corps of young faculty — known collectively as "the Wise Men from the East" — was in place: a fine clinical teacher, George Dock, as chair of medicine and soon dean, displacing Warren who left the University; Erlanger, a young Hopkins graduate, as head of physiology; John Howland of Columbia University as professor of pediatrics; Eugene Opie,

Eugene Opie (1873-1971). Opie was a distinguished researcher who wrote a well-regarded 1902 text on diseases of the pancreas. He was an able administrator, serving as dean from 1912-15; he was professor of pathology from 1910-23.

Robert J. Terry (1871-1966). Professor of anatomy from 1900-66 and head of the department for more than four decades, Terry was the only faculty member whom David Edsall recommended retaining after reorganization. He had a reputation as a tough teacher. "Being sadder and wiser," said one medical student in the 1915 *Hatchet*, "we did not 'Terry' long in Anatomy."

Philip A. Shaffer (1881-1960). When he came in 1910 as professor of biochemistry, Shaffer was the youngest member of the new group of faculty. He stayed for 50 years, serving as dean from 1915-19 and 1937-46; he did innovative research on insulin and developed an important test for blood sugar. Dean M. Kenton King once wrote of him: "No one stands above Philip Shaffer as the architect and builder of this School in its first quarter century."

another Hopkins graduate and Simon Flexner's colleague at the Rockefeller Institute, as professor of pathology; biochemist Philip A. Shaffer, a Harvard graduate and the only Ph.D. in the group.

In 1911, two others joined them: Fred T. Murphy, a Harvard graduate and faculty member, as head of surgery; and David Edsall himself, who had earlier refused the deanship but now became head of preventive medicine. Robert Terry, the sole holdover from the pre-reform faculty, stayed on in anatomy. As Henry Pritchett wrote Brookings approvingly, "You have certainly got a stunning group of men together. I do not think the like is to be found in America."

Following the lead of Hopkins, these department heads formed a governing group called the Executive Faculty — but its members, none of whom had prior experience with this model, interpreted their mandate differently. As dean, George Dock saw this group as existing to advise him, while the faculty thought Dock should be implementing the decisions they made. The resulting feud reached a flashpoint in 1912, when the Executive Faculty forced Dock out and convinced the board to require subsequent deans — Eugene Opie from 1912-15, Philip A. Shaffer from 1915-19, and G. Canby

Robinson from 1919-20 — to be appointed annually upon their nomination. As time went on, a beleaguered Houston parried attempts by this strong-willed group to take control of the reorganization effort, bypass him in their dealings with the board, and control the University hospital.

The new hospital, one of the glittering promises that had helped persuade these men to come to Missouri, had meanwhile run into trouble. In 1909, nephews of Robert Barnes filed suit to disallow his hospital bequest on the grounds that the trustees had ignored his three-year stipulation. For two years, this case wound through the courts until finally, in 1911, the Missouri Supreme Court decided to allow the Barnes bequest, by now worth more than $2 million, to be used for a new hospital. While this delay discouraged some new faculty members — Edsall left quickly for Harvard and Howland for an eventual berth at Johns Hopkins — the added time gave Brookings a chance to talk the Barnes trustees into an affiliation, plan and design an ideal new campus, and find money for its construction.

HOSPITAL AND MEDICAL BUILDINGS TAKE SHAPE

In 1911, Washington University forged two landmark agreements. That May, Brookings and Grace R. Jones signed a preliminary contract linking the University with Children's Hospital, which had bought property adjacent to the Barnes site. In October, he and the Barnes' trustees signed a similar document, in which the Barnes group agreed that, within the year, it would build "a first class hospital at a cost of not less than six hundred thousand dollars," while the University promised to construct "first class medical school buildings at a cost of not less than two hundred thousand dollars." Construction on the 220-bed Barnes Hospital and the three gray-brick medical school buildings — North, South, and Clinic — began in 1912; all were designed by architect Theodore Link, with frequent, expensive revisions from the faculty. Soon afterward, Children's Hospital got under way with its five-story, 120-bed main building. In each hospital, the staff was to consist exclusively of medical school faculty.

Herman Tuholske (1848-1922). Head of surgery, Tuholske, Missouri Medical College M.D. '70, was forced out during the reorganization. In 1890, he established his own hospital on Jefferson Avenue, which he closed in 1902 to become head of surgery and first president of the medical staff of Jewish Hospital. His old hospital building became the first home of the Barnard Free Skin and Cancer Hospital.

Robert S. Brookings at the May 17, 1913, cornerstone laying ceremony for the North Building.
Brookings (in academic gown) was the presiding genius behind the medical school reform. Henry Pritchett said: "The outcome of his effort was the establishment of one of the best medical schools of the country, and which is in some respects the most distinctive monument to his energy, his intelligence, and his generosity." The Rev. Lee James, pastor, St. John's Methodist Episcopal Church, South, is speaking. Seen between James and Brookings are Edward Mallinckrodt, Sr., and William H. Welch of Johns Hopkins University School of Medicine.

George Dock (1860-1951). In 1910, Dock came to the University as professor of medicine and quickly became dean, serving until 1912 when he was displaced in a clash with the Executive Faculty. He remained as a faculty member until 1922.

Children's Hospital opens a ward for "Negro Children"

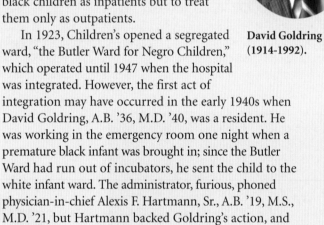

David Goldring (1914-1992).

Pediatrician John Howland, among the first faculty recruited to the newly reorganized medical school, left quickly and acrimoniously, in part because the promised new campus was slow to materialize. He had another reason: his disagreement with St. Louis Children's Hospital's policy not to admit black children as inpatients but to treat them only as outpatients.

In 1923, Children's opened a segregated ward, "the Butler Ward for Negro Children," which operated until 1947 when the hospital was integrated. However, the first act of integration may have occurred in the early 1940s when David Goldring, A.B. '36, M.D. '40, was a resident. He was working in the emergency room one night when a premature black infant was brought in; since the Butler Ward had run out of incubators, he sent the child to the white infant ward. The administrator, furious, phoned physician-in-chief Alexis F. Hartmann, Sr., A.B. '19, M.S., M.D. '21, but Hartmann backed Goldring's action, and the child was admitted.

In 1950, Goldring founded the Division of Pediatric Cardiology, served as its director for 35 years, and as physician-in-chief of St. Louis Children's Hospital from 1964-67. Hartmann (1898-1964) was head of pediatrics at the medical school from 1936-64; a lecture is named for him today. His son, Alexis F. Hartmann, Jr., M.D. '51, who joined the faculty in 1954, was a pediatric cardiologist at Children's.

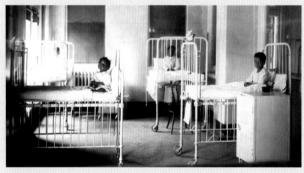

The Butler Ward for Negro Children at Children's Hospital.

Photos, WU Becker Medical Library

At one cornerstone-laying ceremony in October 1912, Brookings described these buildings in loving detail, then stressed the good he hoped they would do in facilitating teaching and research. Their cost was high, he said — and, as the crowd must have known, he had borne much of it himself. What lay behind this expense was an ideal, he added. "If we assume, either in teaching medicine or in administering a hospital, the responsibility for human life," he said, "how can we justify ourselves in giving anything less than the best that we know?"

Still, there was work to be done — primarily raising money. In 1912, Brookings had pledged another $1 million to the Medical Department, including $75,000 for a 40-bed contagious disease facility at Children's. While some of his old friends had been generous, his broad hints to Pritchett had so far proved futile. "I realize what a financial load you are assuming and wish devoutly I could do something for you with Mr. Carnegie," wrote Pritchett. "I fear it is hopeless to expect any help from his fortune in this direction, at least during his life."

In 1914, a much-depleted Brookings — who had been forced to undertake new land deals out West to replenish his fortune — finally flared up when the Barnes trustees asked the University to equip the new hospital. "I cannot refrain from calling attention to the fact," he wrote to them, "that though I have put as much money in buildings and furnishings and endowment in the medical group as the entire Barnes Trust Fund, my name is not attached in any way to any of the buildings…to the contrary, even the Chapel which I have built and paid for is the Barnes Hospital Chapel and will contain a bust of Mr. Barnes."

Early in 1914, Brookings did follow Johns Hopkins' lead in applying for a General Education Board grant — an opportune time to make such a request, since Abraham Flexner had joined the board's staff in 1913. Just days later, they awarded the University $750,000, later increased to $1 million, provided that the school raise a $500,000 match. This money, earmarked for the endowment fund, would allow the Medical Department to adopt a controversial new "full-time plan" — in which faculty members agreed not to take fees from private patients — within three departments: medicine, surgery, and pediatrics. The Executive Faculty, with the sole exception of surgery chairman Fred Murphy, enthusiastically supported this change, but to make this grant a reality, one more fund drive was in the offing.

Sadly, three partners from past campaigns would no longer be at Brookings' side. In 1912, Samuel Cupples had died, in 1913 so had Adolphus Busch, and in February 1913 came a different kind of departure: David Houston asked for a leave of absence, not

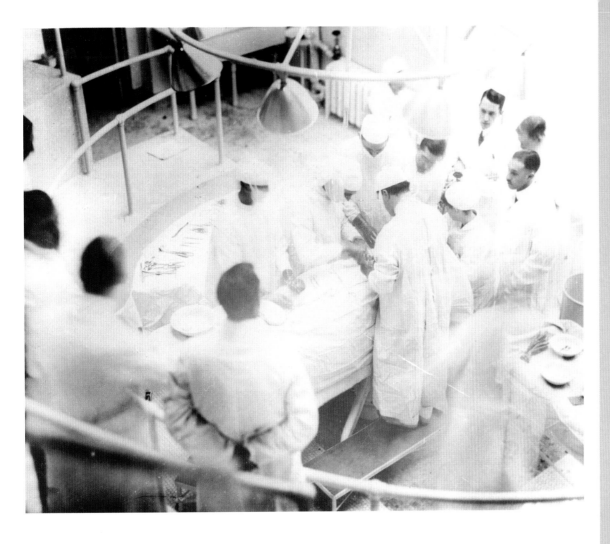

Barnes Hospital surgery, December 1914.
Fred Murphy, head of the Department of Surgery, performed the first surgery, an appendectomy, on a 24-year-old woman, Emma Bornefeld, in the new Barnes Hospital.

to exceed two years, so he could join President Woodrow Wilson's cabinet as Secretary of Agriculture. In the interim, the chancellor would be Frederic Aldin Hall, who had earlier replaced Sylvester Waterhouse as professor of Greek, then served as dean of the College after Marshall Snow's 1912 retirement; John Livingston Lowes, a talented young professor of English, became dean. Reluctantly, Brookings acquiesced, but "I could see that he was really considerably troubled at the thought of my possible absence," confided Houston to a friend.

MEDICAL COMPLEX IS DEDICATED

In late April 1915, Houston and Hall were both present for the gala, three-day dedication of the new medical complex. The festivities began on the morning of April 29 with a procession of luminaries — the mayor of St. Louis, guests from U.S. and foreign universities, the University's own officers and faculty — wending their way from the Barnes Hospital rotunda to the courtyard between the North and South Buildings, where the ceremony was held. There, Acting Chancellor Hall saluted Brookings as "the one man, pre-eminently, whose dream this day is realized" and called the grand occasion: "the second inauguration of the University."

Medical school dedication, 1915.
William H. Welch (left) of the Johns Hopkins School of Medicine and George E. Vincent, president of the University of Minnesota, attended the dedication of the new medical school.

The Fischels serve St. Louis and the School of Medicine

Washington E. Fischel (1850-1914), St. Louis Medical College M.D. '71, was a long-time professor of clinical medicine, as well as a founder and first president of the Barnard Free Skin and Cancer Hospital. In his eulogy, Chancellor Hall called Fischel "an eminent physician, a public-spirited citizen, a warm-hearted friend, a noble man." Washington Fischel's wife, Martha Ellis Fischel, directed the St. Louis School of Philanthropy, a predecessor of the George Warren Brown School of Social Work. Three of their children had strong ties to the medical school and the University.

One son, Walter Fischel, A.B. Harvard '02, M.D. '05, joined the faculty in 1914, rising to associate professor by 1949. His brother, Ellis Fischel, A.B. Harvard '04, M.D. '08, served on the clinical faculty, as well as the staffs of Jewish

Walter Fischel (1881-1950).
WU Becker Medical Library

and Barnard hospitals. A prominent surgical oncologist, Ellis worked for state funding to create a cancer hospital but died before it was completed. The Ellis Fischel Cancer Center of the University of Missouri–Columbia now bears his name.

Daughter Edna Fischel Gellhorn, a Mary Institute and Bryn Mawr graduate, became an active suffragist, civic leader, and first president of the Missouri League of Women Voters. Her husband, George Gellhorn (1870-1936), was on the clinical obstetrics and gynecology faculty from 1904-22 and 1932-36; he served Barnard Hospital as well. In 1964, Edna Gellhorn earned an honorary LL.D. from the University which, four years later, created the Edna Fischel Gellhorn Professorship of Public Affairs in her honor. Her papers are in the Washington University Archives.

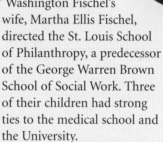

Ellis Fischel (1883-1938).
WU Becker Medical Library

Edna Fischel Gellhorn (1878-1970).
WU Archives

The medical class of 1915.
WU Becker Medical Library

Other speakers included William Welch, who complimented the school's well-equipped laboratories so convenient to its fine new hospital, and called its reorganization "a veritable renascence." Although Henry Pritchett could not attend, Lowes read his speech, laced with heartfelt congratulations: "To those to whom have been entrusted these splendid facilities we may well hope that there will come not only the spirit of work, but the courage to advance…that may result in contributions to the science of medicine which may be a honor to this city, to our country, and to our generation."

During an evening ceremony held in Graham Chapel on the brightly lit Hilltop Campus, the

University bestowed 16 honorary degrees, including those on Welch; Simon Flexner; former faculty member William T. Porter, now a noted physiologist at Harvard; Abbot Lawrence Lowell, president of Harvard; Professor Abraham Jacobi of Columbia University; and W.C. Gorgas, surgeon general of the U.S. Army. Visitors, said the *Washington University Record*, commented that they had never seen a "more dignified and impressive occasion." At a celebratory banquet, board member David Francis proposed, in his official toast, that the Medical Department take a new name: "The Brookings Medical School."

Brookings deflected this suggestion, but he was well pleased with the outcome of his labor. Late in life he would reflect with pleasure that this complex was "probably as complete and well-balanced a medical plant as exists in this or any other country." In fact, the whole splendid ensemble — buildings, hospitals, research facilities, and personnel — formed what was often called abroad, as he said with pardonable pride, "the American ideal."

MOVING TOWARD WAR

While this rebuilding took place, enrollment at the medical school was fluctuating. In 1909, 53 men were admitted; then in 1910-11, when the required one year of college preparation first took effect, that number dropped to 14, though it jumped back to 23 by the next year. In 1913, when a two-year requirement first took hold, only five men were admitted, and two promptly left after failing anatomy. Gradually enrollment began to rise — to 16 new students and 77 overall in 1914. Those medical students who had two undergraduate years at the University could now receive their bachelor's degree after two additional years of study at the medical school.

By 1916, Brookings had succeeded once again in a major fundraising effort. The General

Evarts A. Graham (1883-1957). A World War I veteran, Graham came to the medical school in 1919 as the first full-time head of surgery.
WU Archives

Barnes medical staff, 1916-17. Middle row, standing, second from left, G. Canby Robinson, dean, 1919-20; third from left, George Dock, dean, 1910-12. G. Canby Robinson became dean in 1919, but during the war years, he frequently filled in as acting dean for Philip Shaffer who, as a major in the U.S. Army Sanitary Corps, was in charge of food inspection for U.S. troops.
WU Becker Medical Library

Education Board grant was secure,
thanks to three new endowment
funds that created the Mary Culver
Department of Surgery, the John T.
Milliken Department of Medicine,
and the Edward Mallinckrodt
Department of Pediatrics.
Mallinckrodt proved generous again in
1919, when he endowed the Department
of Pharmacology.

Finally, after years of debate and foot-drag-
ging, the first women were admitted to the
Medical Department. For years, women had
inquired about admission, and a
handful had come as "special
students," notably Harriet
Stevens Cory, a student from
1906-09; when the faculty
refused to let her finish, she
completed her training at the
University of Chicago. In 1917,
Erlanger chaired a committee that
examined the question of admitting
women and made a positive recommendation to the Executive Faculty. In 1918,
Aphrodite Jannopoulo, M.D. '23, and Carol
Skinner Cole, M.D. '22, became the first two
women students, though Faye Cashatt Lewis,
M.D. '21, who transferred to the third-year
class in 1919, graduated before they did. In
1918 women were first accepted as house
officers in pediatrics.

The school changed its official name once
again in 1918, becoming the Washington
University School of Medicine. The faculty was
growing with young members who acquired
fame in years to come: Herbert Gasser came in
1916 to collaborate with Joseph Erlanger, his
former teacher, and won the Nobel Prize with
him in 1944; Nathaniel Allison, whose arrival
in 1919 signaled the beginning of an orthopaedic surgery department; W. McKim
Marriott, later dean, named professor of pediatrics in 1917; Ernest Sachs, first recruited
to the surgery department in 1910 and in 1919

**Students study in the Medical
School library.**
WU Becker Medical Library

Medical School c. 1917-18.
Future doctors learn their craft
in the anatomy department
dissection room under the
guidance of Robert J. Terry
(standing against the wall).
WU Becker Medical Library

Ernest Sachs (1879-1958). Professor of neurosurgery, Sachs helped found the Society of Neurological Surgeons in 1920.
WU Becker Medical Library

appointed the world's first professor of neurosurgery; Evarts A. Graham, the first full-time head of the surgery department in 1919, who achieved world renown for his groundbreaking lung research and pioneering surgical techniques.

World War I had interrupted this growth, however, drawing faculty and students from both campuses to the western front. At the 1915 dedi-

cation, William T. Porter, an 1885 St. Louis Medical College graduate and former faculty member, had noted the looming war clouds in his speech, but spoke of medicine's transcendent purpose as the reason why alumni rejoiced to see this new medical complex:

"In this world so cruelly scarred by war, so foolishly set on the pursuit of material success, it is noble to place on high the ideal of unselfish public service…to still the cry of suffering, to find, through reason, the remedies that conquer the ancient enemies of mankind, to discover laws by which generations still unborn may live, year after year, century after century, in greater happiness and peace….This is our heritage. It is for this that we return today with love and pride." Ⓦ

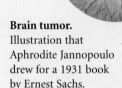

In 1918, the first women students enter the School of Medicine

Aphrodite Jannopoulo Hofsommer (1896-1976).

Brain tumor. Illustration that Aphrodite Jannopoulo drew for a 1931 book by Ernest Sachs.

When she registered at the School of Medicine in 1918, Aphrodite Jannopoulo worried that she and Carol Skinner Cole — the first women medical students at Washington University — would "face the storm alone," as she said in her diary. The next year they were joined by one more: Faye Cashatt, who became the only woman in her third-year class and the first woman to graduate in 1921.

Jannopoulo married Armin C. Hofsommer, Sr., M.D. '22, a pediatrician; for many years, she was a physician for the Webster Groves school district. Earlier, she used her artistic talent to illustrate a 1931 text by Ernest Sachs, *The Diagnosis and Treatment of Brain Tumors*, and do pen-and-ink sketches at the operating table for an eye text by Weiner and Alvis. Her daughter, Helen Hofsommer (1924-1999), B.S. '47, M.D. '47, a pediatri-

cian and child psychiatrist, married Robert J. Glaser, eventually dean of the medical schools at the University of Colorado and Stanford, who was an intern, assistant resident, and chief resident at Barnes Hospital, then faculty member and finally chief of immunology from 1949-57. He was a trustee from 1979-91 — now an emeritus trustee — and chaired the medical school's National Council.

Cashatt married a classmate, William B. Lewis, M.D. '21, her partner in outpatient neurology. They settled in Wilson City, Iowa, where he became a surgeon and she returned to medical practice after raising a family. Their son, Malcolm R. Lewis, graduated from the School of Medicine in 1952.

Faye Cashatt Lewis (1896-1982).

Carol Skinner Cole (1888-?).

"Over There": World War I and Washington University

Base Hospital No. 21. The unit arrived in France on June 12, 1917, and was demobilized on May 3, 1919. At first, it was mainly a tent hospital, but gradually wooden barracks went up.
WU Archives

"For the first time in this building since this world-wide trouble began, I use the word 'war,'" said Chancellor Frederic A. Hall to a hushed crowd in Graham Chapel less than a month after the United States declared war against Germany on April 6, 1917. "The war is on. No one knows how long it will last, nor what will be the experiences of individuals, families, or institutions while it continues."

It lasted 19 months, and during that time University life was utterly transformed by the war effort. First, students signed up by the dozens, leaving behind a smaller, largely female student body; then war-related programs came flooding onto campus, creating a space crisis and overtaxing the few remaining faculty. "In no other place in America did the outbreak of the war cause greater commotion than in the supposedly retired halls of learning," said Chancellor Hall.

In May 1917, the first undergraduates left for overseas service: 16 men, organized by English professor John Livingston Lowes, who volunteered for a six-month stint as ambulance and truck drivers in France. In letters to *Student Life*, some described their harrowing experiences: day-and-night ammunition deliveries for blistering artillery assaults on German trenches; dangerous trips to ferry the front-line wounded to nearby aid stations, with shells raining all around. The war, exclaimed former student Francis Douglas, "is all that it is cracked up to be, only more so."

John Livingston Lowes (1867-1945). Professor of English, then dean of Arts and Sciences, Lowes headed an American Field Service recruiting station, sending 50 men overseas for ambulance service.
WU Archives

That May, a group led by medical faculty and students — 28 officers, 141 enlisted men, 65 nurses — departed for Rouen, France, where they staffed Base Hospital No. 21, the second of some 50 military hospitals organized by the American Red Cross. The University had been planning this effort since 1916, so in April 1917, when surgeon and Base Hospital director Fred T. Murphy received a telegram from the Red Cross asking, "can your Unit go to Europe and how soon?" he answered exuberantly: "Yes — in one week." It took a few weeks longer, but the unit left amid great public fanfare.

The team Murphy had recruited — orthopaedic surgery chief Nathaniel Allison as adjutant; surgeon Borden S. Veeder as quartermaster; Walter Fischel as head of the medical service; Malvern B. Clopton as chief of surgery; Sidney I. Schwab as neurologist; Eugene Opie as

Arthur W. Proetz (1888-1966). Captain Proetz, B.S. '10, M.D. '12, an otolaryngologist, wrote while in France: "I miss a lot of things....Bell telephones, hot water taps, steam heat, barbers and FRIENDS.... On the other hand, I smoke all I can get, eat onions, snails and horsemeat, confront the rarest, oldest Camembert without fainting."
WU Becker Medical Library

pathologist; Lawrence F. Post as ophthalmologist; Arthur Proetz as otolaryngologist; Julia Stimson as chief of nurses — performed extraordinary service. By the end of the war, several had earned decorations for their work: Allison and Murphy the Distinguished Service Medal, Veeder the Order of St. Michael and St. George, and Stimson the Royal Red Cross.

Yet they were almost comically unprepared to become soldiers. They didn't know how to salute; their uniforms didn't fit. "I doubt if half of us knew the difference between a lieutenant and a lieutenant-colonel," wrote Proetz later. Before they embarked, two officers gave them physicals. "Two dozen of us in a little room, from the loftiest professors down, naked as frogs, hopping on the cold floor, being inspected, palpated and auscultated….It was a leveling experience, not the last; it broke down all barriers and taught us to live as one happy family, for the duration."

Once in France, they took over a British hospital with 1,350 beds — all but 70 of them in tents — located along a race track near the Rouen rail line. They were 80 miles from the closest units, 100 miles from the front lines. When a soldier was wounded, he was rushed to a "casualty clearing station" for rough dressing, then shipped to the base hospitals for surgery or medical care. "By the time they reached us," wrote Fischel in 1919, "most of these men were badly infected, many of them showing the horrible signs of gas gangrene." The effects of mustard gas were particularly shocking, he added. "It made every one of us feel that we wanted to…get a gun and go out and fight."

In the end, they treated 61,543 patients, mostly British soldiers: 31,837 medical cases and 29,706 wounded. Their peak time came during the Allied offensive of fall 1918, when their 50-75 patient-per-day load suddenly shot up to 500-600. The

World War I claims lives of prominent alumni

Capt. Alexander Skinker (1883-1918).

Three of the University's war dead were well-known members of the community.

- **Capt. Alexander Skinker, A.B. '05**, was the son of Thomas Skinker, A.B. '63. On the first day of the September 1918 battle for the Argonne Forest, when his company came under devastating machine gun fire, he ordered his men to take cover while he and a carrier charged the gun emplacement alone. "The carrier was killed instantly," said a citation, "but Capt. Skinker seized the ammunition and continued through an opening in the barbed wire, feeding the automatic until he, too, was killed." He was posthumously awarded the Congressional Medal of Honor.

Capt. Charles H. Duncker (1893-1918).

- **Capt. Charles H. Duncker, Jr., A.B. '14**, was class valedictorian, editor-in-chief of *Student Life* and the *Hatchet*. "It has been said by some of those who were in authority over him that…he was the most brilliant man who had ever sat in a Washington classroom," a friend said. In October 1918, he was promoted to captain of Battery A of the 340th Field Artillery, just ten days before he was killed by a German shell near Thiaucourt. The Duncker family paid tribute to him with the 1924 gift of Duncker Hall, the first home of the School of Commerce and Finance and now home of the Department of English in Arts & Sciences.

- **Lt. James H. Steedman, B.S. '89**, was one of the first St. Louisans to leave for military service. An expert on marine engines, Steedman — who had received his Naval commission in 1916 — was called up on the day war was declared and assigned to supervise the repair and maintenance of ships. An illness he contracted made him an invalid, and he died in 1921. In 1925, his widow and brother donated the "Steedman Fellowship" in his honor. This award, given every other year, provides nine months of study to the young architect who wins a nationwide competition sponsored by the School of Architecture.

Lt. James H. Steedman (1867-1921).

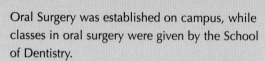

Putting on a show.
In their few free hours, Base Hospital No. 21 personnel tried to relax by giving teas, playing baseball, staging an open-air circus, and performing an original, two-act comedy, "C'est la Guerre."
WU Becker Medical Library

Julia Stimson (1881-1948).
When Base Hospital No. 21 embarked, Stimson, M.S. '17, was head nurse. Later the Red Cross promoted her to head its entire nursing service, and soon she became Chief Nurse of the American Expeditionary Forces, a signal honor. Stimson won a Royal Red Cross, first class, from the British government.
WU Becker Medical Library

Roland Greene Usher (1881-1957).
Usher, a history professor, predicted the war in his book, *Pan-Germanism*.
WU Becker Medical Library

result, wrote Veeder afterwards, "was that some of the juniors became competent to handle the most serious cases with rare ability and judgment." Thanks to such on-the-job training, fourth-year medical students were allowed to graduate in March 1918 while still serving — the only class ever to graduate away from St. Louis.

Overall, the death rate among the hospital's wounded was a remarkably low two percent — thanks in part to roentgenologist Edwin Ernst, who X-rayed every soldier before surgery. As time went on, the team's fine work won promotions for some: Murphy became head of the Medical and Surgical Service of the Red Cross; Allison took over front-line orthopaedic work for the American Expeditionary Forces (AEF); Schwab directed the first American hospital in France for war neuroses; and Stimson became the AEF's Chief Nurse, supervising 8,000 nurses.

Back home, other medical faculty were also serving. Medical Dean Philip Shaffer became the ranking officer of the Food and Nutrition Division of the U.S. Army's Sanitary Corp. As head of the Army's Oral and Plastic Surgery Unit, then the AEF's chief consultant in maxillo-facial surgery, Vilray P. Blair earned an international reputation for rebuilding shattered faces. An officer's school for Neurological, Plastic, and

Oral Surgery was established on campus, while classes in oral surgery were given by the School of Dentistry.

Across the University, people were leaving for war-time work. Twice David Houston extended his leave of absence, and in December 1916 he resigned from the University altogether; early in 1917, the board named Hall as his replacement. In that same year, President Woodrow Wilson appointed Board President Robert Brookings as a member of the War Industries Board, then chairman of the Price Fixing Committee, while David R. Francis was serving as ambassador to Russia. All told, more than 50 faculty members took leaves of absence or spent the bulk of their time on government work.

Amid the patriotic fervor that engulfed the campus, some faculty signed up to fight. In 1914, French instructor Maurice Fauré enlisted in the French army and in 1915 was awarded the Croix de guerre. Many students also enlisted, draining men from upper classes, graduate programs, and the law school. By the end of 1917, 200 faculty and students had signed up, and on December 19 a service flag with 200 stars was

Students' Army Training Corps.
"During the period of the S.A.T.C.," said the *Washington University Record*, "there was a noticeably less desirable standard of behavior maintained than is usual at this institution. Smoking and the use of profanity…was observable, whereas under ordinary conditions they are practically absent in those parts of the University frequented by the women students."
WU Archives

hoisted over University Hall. The next day an 83-star flag went up over the medical school. Eventually, 410 graduates and 93 undergraduates received commissions, and 22 students, staff, or alumni died while in service.

Meanwhile, faculty devised courses to meet war-related needs, such as Dean Alexander Langsdorf's engineering school course on radio communications, or did war-related laboratory work. In 1913, Roland Usher wrote a book, *Pan-Germanism*, that predicted the war with chilling accuracy and made him a popular speaker, but his anti-German sentiment brought angry demands from the community that he be silenced. In response, Hall made the University's first public statement supporting academic freedom.

Women of the University contributed, too, staffing one Red Cross unit that produced nearly 550,000 dressings in one six-month period; in 1918, Graham Chapel was dismantled to make room for this activity. A knitting unit was established, successful "Liberty Loan" drives took place, and *Student Life* spearheaded a cigarette drive for soldiers.

In spring 1917, the Fifth Missouri Regiment came to campus, using Francis Field as its drill ground, and the next January student soldiers arrived for woodworking, blacksmithing, and machine shop training. Perhaps the biggest disruption to University life, however, was the October 1918 arrival of hundreds of men in the Students' Army Training Corps (SATC), aimed at training recruits and developing potential officers. The SATC, said the *Hatchet*, "saved Washington from becoming a girls' college for the period of the war." Suddenly, enrollment skyrocketed; in

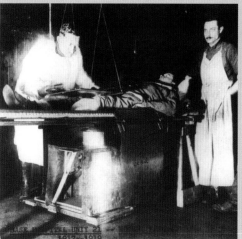

Edwin Ernst (1885-1969).
At Base Hospital No. 21, Major Ernst, M.D. '12, X-rayed every wounded soldier before surgery, using more X-ray plates than all other base hospitals combined.
WU Becker Medical Library

fall 1918, the University had 1,515 students — a 50 percent increase over the previous year.

All this activity, said Hall, turned the University into "an army post." Except for McMillan Hall, the women's dormitory, every building was used for government purposes. The SATC took over the fraternities and male residence halls, using one floor of Francis Gymnasium as sleeping quarters. Temporary buildings were thrown up along Forsyth: two barracks, a 1,200-man mess hall, and a YMCA canteen, which became the first student union before it was razed in 1920. A third barracks went up northeast of the gymnasium.

On November 11, the war was finally over. The SATC disbanded in December; "Demobilization of S.A.T.C. Unit Great Blow to Washington University Co-eds" read the *Student Life* headline. The Washington University Union, organized in 1915 to promote the University's social side, proposed a building to honor the war dead, but a memorial plaque went up instead on the wall of Ridgley. In January 1919, the University's first Reserve Officers' Training Corps (ROTC) unit was established under former SATC commandant Major Wallace M. Craigie.

During a March 1919 banquet, the Alumni Association honored the University's war heroes, and Hall welcomed home the triumphant veterans: "We have heard it said that the golden age of heroism and bravery was in the past, but let me say that the men now are just as brave and courageous as they ever were….We greet you in tears of gratitude." Ⓦ

Lloyd R. Boutwell (1889-1918).
Lloyd Boutwell, M.D. '16, and his wife had hoped to become medical missionaries in China, but when the war came he volunteered for service in France. Three days before the war ended, he was wounded when a shell landed near his front-line aid station, yet he worked to dress others until he lost consciousness. He died six days later.
WU Archives

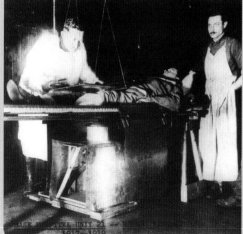

World War I plaque on Ridgley Hall.
This plaque honors alumni and students who died in the war.
WU Photographic Services

Classes And All Gatherings Suspended To Prevent Spanish Influenza Spread

The action of the University authorities in suspending all classes and gatherings after 12:30 last Wednesday was taken, according to Chancellor Hall, in deference to the wishes of the health authorities of St. Louis and of St. Louis County, who issued orders forbidding gatherings of any kind in the territory under their jurisdiction. It is hoped that the serious danger from

Influenza strikes.
The wartime activity was complicated by another deadly factor. By late 1918, the Spanish influenza epidemic was claiming many victims, especially young people. To minimize its impact on students, the University closed down completely for five weeks, from October 9 to November 18, 1918.
WU Archives

David Kilper, WU Photographic Services

CHAPTER SEVEN

"IN A WORD, 'EXPANSION'"

1908-1932

WASHINGTON UNIVERSITY
ST. LOUIS, MO.
SHOWING DEVELOPMENT
OF FORECOURT
JAMIESON AND SPEARL   ARCHITECTS

Hilltop Campus master plan. Jamieson and Spearl's 1929 master plan for the Hilltop Campus shows a fully developed east end of campus (the forecourt), much of which was never built.
WU Archives

"In a Word, 'Expansion'"

Chancellor David Houston had taken aim at more than the medical school in his seminal 1908 speech. The young Hilltop Campus, he declared, also needed sweeping change: a strong graduate program; an extensive library; a rich social environment; most of all, a broader geographic reach. "I have it in mind this evening to present two propositions," he said. "The first is that there is great need of an institution of real university rank in the southwest; and the second, that the greatest opportunity for development of such an institution presents itself in the city of St. Louis."

Previous pages:
Bixby Hall.
Completed in 1926 to house the art school, Bixby Hall was named for donor and longtime board member William K. Bixby.
Inset:
Maria Bain White, A.B. '16.
Courtesy of Katherine White Drescher

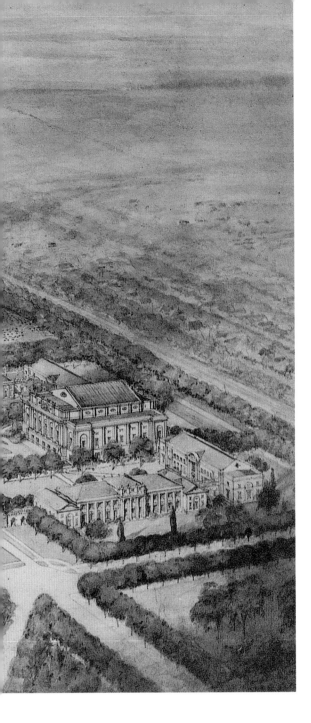

1909   *Chancellor Houston moved the law school and the School of Fine Arts from downtown to the Hilltop Campus.*

1913   *Frederic Aldin Hall became acting chancellor when David Houston took a leave of absence to become U.S. Secretary of Agriculture. Hall was named chancellor in 1917.*

1917   *The School of Commerce and Finance opened.*

1922   *The board approved a School of Graduate Studies.*

1923   *Herbert Spencer Hadley was inaugurated as chancellor on November 10.*

1927   *The George Warren Brown Department of Social Work was founded.*

1928   *Robert Brookings resigned as board president. In December, George Throop was named chancellor.*

Sorority field trip.
A member of Kappa Alpha Theta Sorority, c. 1916, explores a decorative urn; scaling the landscape was all the rage for students of that era.
Photo courtesy of
Katherine White Drescher

Houston was not the first chancellor to sketch a broad vision of the University. His predecessors had spun dreams of a Midwestern rival to the eastern Ivy League schools. William G. Eliot had talked grandly of a "Western American University," and Winfield S. Chaplin had once said that "we ought to have and, if we had the proper location and buildings, I believe we should have, a large number of students from outside of this city." But Houston was the first for whom such a vision had a glimmering of reality. With the glorious new Hilltop Campus and the rumbling of major reform at the medical school, the University seemed poised for national prominence. As the December 1908 *Washington University Record* described Houston's plan:

"The acts and statements of the new Chancellor during his first few months of office have made sufficiently clear the main outlines of the policy which is to mark the attitude of the administration....It is, in a word, expansion; its purpose, the training of leaders in the world of education and of affairs; its incentive, the vision of a great future and the splendor of a great achievement."

HILLTOP LIFE STRENGTHENS

Dreams are exciting — but they come with a price tag, as Houston and Board President Robert Brookings knew well. Bravely, the two began their improvement efforts on the Hilltop by shoring up the Arts and Sciences endowment, raising $800,000

Maypole dance.

In 1909, University women initiated a new tradition: McMillan Day, held each May. "The court of McMillan Hall was decorated in gala attire for this red-letter day," said the *Washington University Record*. Events included a play and a festive maypole dance, with "delightfully cooling ices" served to the audience.

to match the General Education Board's $200,000 grant. As always Brookings led the way, this time with a $250,000 gift from his diminishing personal fortune. In addition, in 1909, he gave the University a 50-acre tract of land south of Forsyth — much of it now the "South 40" — for use as a faculty residential park, though only two homes ever went up: the chancellor's residence, built in 1908 for Houston, which later became Blewett Hall, home of the music department; and Brookings' own home, Cecilwood, now Alumni House.

Early in Houston's tenure, many of the fine new buildings on campus — especially

the dormitories — were woefully underused, so he and Brookings tried the temporary expedient of renting rooms to faculty, particularly in McMillan, the women's residence hall, and renting space in the men's dormitories to the growing crop of fraternities. They worked to fill empty rooms by recruiting in regional high schools, liberalizing the entrance requirements, expanding scholarship aid, and enlisting alumni to help with public relations. Faculty pitched in, too; in 1913, 75-year-old Calvin Woodward made the University's first out-of-state student recruiting visit.

A onetime athlete and fraternity man himself, Houston encouraged the growth of student life, and by 1916-17, there were 60 student groups on the Hilltop Campus. A new student government, constituted in 1910, helped to regulate hazing and end the hazardous "color rush" tradition, in which freshmen set out to capture a flag mounted by sophomores in some hard-to-reach spot near campus. Architects staged a winter parade to mark the day of St. Fatima, their fictitious patron; engineers celebrated St. Patrick's Day, when the saint himself appeared to knight them; every May, the women held a maypole dance in the McMillan courtyard; and the whole campus enjoyed springtime Dandelion Day, when freshman men pulled dandelions from the Quadrangle and chose a Dandelion Queen. Meanwhile, faculty and their spouses forged closer ties with colleagues. In 1910, the Washington University Woman's Club was established, and in 1912 a Men's Club followed. In 1915, at the instigation of geology professor Walter McCourt, the Washington University Union

St. Patrick's Day pageant, spring 1920.

Each year, engineering students put on a celebration that featured St. Patrick coming to knight them.

Photos, WU Archives

sponsored its first events, aimed at expanding social interactions among alumni, faculty, and students.

Houston strengthened the academic experience as well, adding to the library collections, hiring such outstanding new faculty members as Stanford University economist Allyn A. Young, and tightening distribution requirements loosened by Chaplin. In 1911, he ended the tradition of daily chapel services in favor of a once-weekly lecture by lay speakers — which evolved into the Assembly Series during the University's centennial year. As one step in his promised enhancement of the graduate program, he affiliated with a community social work school, now retitled the School of Social Economy, which became a University department in 1913 but two years later disbanded due to financial constraints.

ACADEMIC PROGRAMS CONSOLIDATE AND GROW

To create a stronger sense of identity, Houston embarked on a program of consolidation on the Hilltop. In 1909 he moved the law school from the old St. Louis Club downtown to Ridgley, where it remained until January Hall went up in 1923. Shortly after its move, Law began requiring a year of college for admission, and in 1913 hired its first full-time faculty member, Tyrrell Williams, A.B. '98, LL.B. '00. Still, it was slow to give up its part-time faculty, which included local attorneys such as Arthur Shepley, LL.B. '97, appointed Madill Professor of Equity in 1910. Even after a new dean, former St. Louis Court of Appeals judge Richard Goode, arrived in 1915, it was reluctant to adopt the casebook method of teaching and discard its outdated custom of a pre-graduation examination by members of the St. Louis Bar.

In 1909, Houston moved the School of Fine Arts from 19th and Locust to the former British Pavilion, an elegant but temporary structure that Brookings had purchased for the University at the close of the World's Fair. By this time, the school

Tyrrell Williams (1876-1947).
Williams, A.B. '98, LL.B. '00, attended the University on the recommendation of Woodrow Wilson, then law professor at Princeton. In 1913, Williams became the first full-time member of the law faculty as Madill Professor of Contracts and Commercial Law, remaining until 1946 and serving several times as acting dean. He had "the bearing of an English judge," said the *Hatchet*.
WU Archives

Jewish students form Greek organizations

A mid the new fraternities and sororities were two that reflected the growing number of Jewish students on campus. On March 1, 1919, eight women students assembled to form a Jewish sorority, Chi Sigma Phi, under president Fannie Hoffman, A.B. '20, secretary Lilly Pattiz, A.B. '21, and treasurer Mollie Gubin, A.B. '25.

Chi Sigma Phi.
WU Archives

On Commencement night in 1919, Sigma Alpha Mu — the first Jewish fraternity at the University — was chartered with five members, one of them Hyman G. Stein, LL.B. '20. By the fall, ΣAM had no space yet on the crowded campus, so another fraternity kindly donated its own suite, while others helped with furnishings, member suggestions, even entertainment on party night —

which included campus football hero Jimmy Conzelman singing and playing his banjo. "When the party was over," wrote Stein, "there was not a rushee present who was not trusting that a bid would come his way."

Sigma Alpha Mu.
WU Archives

Edmund H. Wuerpel (1866-1958).
A longtime faculty member, Wuerpel replaced Halsey Ives as dean of the School of Fine Arts. As a Manual Training School student, Wuerpel had been the first recipient of the gold Sellew Medal, awarded annually to the top-ranked senior. A silver medal winner at the 1904 World's Fair, Wuerpel taught composition and artistic anatomy.
Oil on canvas by Ethel Grosskop Metelman
WU Gallery of Art

"On the Quad."
Hugh Ferriss (1889-1962), a 1911 architecture graduate, produced this charcoal drawing of Ridgley and Duncker halls for a 1930s alumni fund drive. Ferriss became a celebrated U.S. architectural artist whose dramatic renderings appear in his 1929 book, *The Metropolis of Tomorrow*. In 1928, the University awarded him an honorary Master of Architecture degree; the American Society of Architectural Illustrators still offers the Hugh Ferriss Prize annually for excellence in the graphic representation of architecture.
WU Archives

was no longer headed by its longtime dean, Halsey Ives, who had doubled as director of the University-owned St. Louis Museum of Fine Arts. A few years earlier, that museum had moved from its downtown location to a grand new Forest Park building, constructed as the Palace of Fine Arts for the 1904 World's Fair; however, the passage of a museum tax in 1907 to provide for its maintenance complicated matters. The city comptroller, supported by the Missouri Supreme Court, decided that the museum board, as an "agency" of the University, had no right to spend tax money, so the University and museum had to separate. Ives resigned as dean after 35 years to head the renamed City Art Museum, and Edmund H. Wuerpel, a faculty member since 1894, replaced him.

Other schools were changing dramatically, too. When Frederick Mann resigned in 1910 from the combined engineering and architecture school, Houston seized the chance to split the program. He hired John Beverly Robinson, chief architect for the New York City public schools, as the new architecture dean, and the brilliant Charles Abella, from the Ecole des Beaux Arts in Paris, as professor of design. Since Robinson — nicknamed "the Duke" — hated administrative work, that piece of his job was relegated to the engineering dean, who continued as the school's administrative head until 1948. A noted graduate from this period was Hugh Ferriss, B.S. '11, who became nationally known for his architectural renderings.

Meanwhile, Engineering lost its stalwart dean Calvin Woodward, who retired in 1910 after 45 years of service and was succeeded by Alexander Langsdorf, head of the Department of Electrical Engineering. In his resignation letter, Woodward wrote that Engineering was "so magnificently endowed and equipped that its permanent success is assured." Several young faculty members he had hired would help ensure this future: Ernest Sweetser, later William Palm Professor of Civil Engineering, who served until 1951; Franz A. Berger, professor of mechanical engineering, who retired in 1949; and Ernest Ohle, who headed the mechanical engineering department until his death in 1942.

Botany underwent a major change of leadership during Houston's tenure. In 1909, he and Brookings eagerly recruited George T. Moore, chief botanist at Woods Hole Research Center in Massachusetts, as professor of plant physiology and applied botany in the Shaw School of Botany. In 1912, when William Trelease left the University after

27 years, Moore replaced him as director. Undergraduate courses were held on campus, with graduate work at the Garden.

The University initiated efforts to reach out to the community. A 1906 attempt to start a Correspondence School, offering teacher training and college preparatory work, ended three years later. In 1908, however, a program of Saturday classes aimed at teachers was instantly successful. In 1914, Langsdorf talked the chancellor into giving him $100 so he could advertise evening classes in electrical engineering. Though he had only dared hope for 25 students, 104 enrolled; impressed, the College launched its own evening program. Some faculty were unhappy, but, as the *Record* said in 1915: "It is one of the opportunities of the urban university, as well as one of the obligations imposed upon it, to serve a public much larger than the body of its regular students."

At this point, the "public" living in the immediate vicinity of the University was starting to grow. Thanks to charismatic founder E.G. Lewis, University City was flourishing. East of the University, the Catlin tract had been subdivided and sold as large lots for upscale housing. The Parkview subdivision, developed by Julius Pitzman, was burgeoning to the north; so was Skinker-DeBaliviere to the north and east, with its mix of single and multi-family housing.

HALL SUCCEEDS HOUSTON AS CHANCELLOR

Houston, on leave since 1913 to serve as secretary of agriculture under U.S. President Woodrow Wilson, resigned from the University in 1917, and the board named Acting Chancellor Frederic Aldin Hall as his replacement. A Maine native and a graduate of Drury College in Springfield, Missouri, Hall had stayed on as classics professor and dean at Drury for more than 20 years, before joining the Washington University faculty in 1901 and rising to dean of Arts and Sciences. Temperamentally, he was unlike the cool, aloof Houston. According to Langsdorf, who knew him well, he was "not only an eminently fair minded man, ready to recognize merit when it appears, but also a most lovable man personally, plain in his manners and always approachable." In accepting the chancellorship, Hall said he wanted to strengthen graduate work and establish a business program.

In short order, he did both things. The board established 20 graduate fellowships in 1916, then six years later approved a new School of Graduate Studies, with German professor Otto Heller appointed its dean in 1924. Energetic faculty member William A. Gephart, who had succeeded Allyn Young as head of economics in 1913, quickly proposed a School of Commerce and Finance, though the board only gave lukewarm support to such a project — "as soon as the necessary funds would be provided," it said, dubiously. Unfazed, Gephart began visiting St. Louis business leaders and by 1917 had enough funds for the school to open with a two-year undergraduate program following two years of college preparation.

At this same time, two of the University's three secondary divisions were at last disbanding. Smith Academy and the Manual Training School, located at Windermere and Clemens in the city's smoky West End, had faced declining enrollment as the St. Louis public school system grew. Smith's 366 boys in 1905-06 had dwindled to 159 by 1916-17. In 1915, the University board merged the two schools to try to save them, but they closed anyway in June 1917, much to the horror of alumni. Some Smith Academy families helped found a successor school, St. Louis Country Day School, in that same year.

On nearby Lake Avenue, Mary Institute was thriving, with more applicants than it could handle and a budget surplus that Brookings routinely

treated as income and used for general expenses. Still, he was increasingly uncomfortable with the University's connection to Mary Institute and in 1928 tried to give the school its independence — an offer its alumnae did not accept. With many families no longer living near the school, and students taking crowded streetcars to get there, a new location, farther west, would be welcome in the future.

CAMPUS LIFE RESUMES AS WORLD WAR I ENDS

From 1917-18, World War I convulsed the University, as students and faculty left for the front and military trainees took their place on campus. Finally, in November 1918 the bloody struggle ended, and everyone rushed to return to normal life. "Reconstruction is on everybody's tongue," said *Student Life* briskly, only two months later. "Rehabilitate the soldiers, reconstruct the social organization, is the word of the day."

Activities, suspended during the war, quickly revived: Thyrsus, the student drama club, resumed its performances; *The Eliot Literary Magazine,* founded just before the war, now reappeared; the popular Univee Surkuss, forerunner of the Thurtene Carnival, again took place in May; and campus social life blossomed, with proms, parties, and

Frederic Aldin Hall (1854-1925). Hall was acting chancellor from 1913-17, then chancellor until 1923. A later chancellor, George Throop, said of Hall: "It is fortunate for the University that at the time of its greatest period of development it had at its head this kindly, level-headed gentleman, respected and loved both at Washington University and in the City, who guided all so sympathetically and so wisely."

Alexander Langsdorf (1877-1973). An 1898 mechanical engineering graduate, Langsdorf became full professor and head of the electrical engineering department in 1901. In 1910, he succeeded Calvin Woodward as engineering dean, serving until 1920 when he left to work in industry. He came back in 1926 as director of the newly created Department of Industrial Engineering and Research, an attempt to forge closer ties between the University and local industry. Langsdorf was appointed dean of engineering again in 1928 and served until 1948. He was the author of an important, though unpublished, history of Washington University.

Photos, WU Archives

Honoring Calvin Woodward's memory

WU Photographic Services

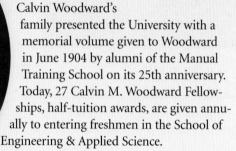

Calvin Woodward (1837-1914).
WU Archives

This bronze plaque (right), designed by Victor Holm and Gabriel Ferrand of the School of Fine Arts, was mounted on Brookings Hall in a 1923 tribute to Woodward that included the planting of 12 elm trees in the Quadrangle. In a eulogy, Alexander Langsdorf said: "Let us understand clearly that we have had to do with a big man, whose place in educational history is permanent." During the ceremony, Calvin Woodward's family presented the University with a memorial volume given to Woodward in June 1904 by alumni of the Manual Training School on its 25th anniversary. Today, 27 Calvin M. Woodward Fellowships, half-tuition awards, are given annually to entering freshmen in the School of Engineering & Applied Science.

While returning veterans played a part in this increase, other factors were at work. The end of the war heralded an era of prosperity in which a university education was within reach for more families. Further, the war had burnished the reputation of universities at the forefront of the struggle. "We feel justified in saying that before the war, Washington University was probably not widely known beyond the territory of the Middle West," mused *Student Life*. "We are told, in fact, that it was sometimes confused with George Washington University or the University of Washington. This state of affairs no longer endures, for Washington has made a name for herself in many fields of the service since the beginning of the war."

In fact, that declaration of victory proved premature. With the exception of the medical school, which drew students from around the United States, the University was still, for the most part, a regional school. However, its enrollment *was* rising along with its reputation, and this put a strain on faculty, academic buildings, dormitories, even parking spaces. Without delay, the University needed to embark on a hiring blitz and building program — a plan that seemed perfectly in step with this exciting, energetic age of progress. As one student wrote in October 1919:

"The golden hour of university life is now in this vigorous new world which has emerged from the war. The 'good old days' are gone....This is a new world — a new day everywhere — in the commercial and industrial sphere, and in the collegiate sphere, and particularly in the big little world of our own which we call Washington."

AN OVERCROWDED CAMPUS

With this influx of students, the Hilltop Campus was bursting at the seams — the College especially. Geology, with its fossil and mineral collections transferred from the downtown campus, needed its own building; so did zoology, a growing department in which new professor Caswell Grave was hiring a distinguished group of researchers. That meant Busch Hall, intended for chemistry, was housing several sciences, including the undergraduate botany program. Physics was crowded, too, and Hall had begun hinting about an addition to Eads Hall.

It was the same story in other schools. The law school was packed into Ridgley Library, which desperately needed more space for books; the new School of Commerce was holding classes wherever it could find a free room. In the art school, grumbling about the "temporary" British Pavilion home was growing louder each year, and by 1916

athletic events. Students, caught up for too long in cataclysmic world events, seemed to revel in the ordinary, grumbling cheerfully about a meal plan that was going to cost $3.75 a week, and campaigning to transform the old YMCA canteen into a student building.

And students kept coming. By fall 1919, university publications were marveling about the "phenomenal growth" that had swelled the enrollment to more than 3,000 students, an increase of some 700 over the year before. Law — which had been particularly hard hit by the war, losing 94 of its 148 students — surged back to 130, while Arts and Sciences, the biggest beneficiary of all, had an unprecedented 916 students. As the 1920s wore on, it increasingly came into its own as a school, with burgeoning numbers and even a new name: the "College of Liberal Arts."

admissions were affected because the porous structure was bitterly cold in wintertime. At the medical school, too, some programs were chafing for their own space, especially oto-laryngology and a young radiological laboratory, established as a division of the surgery department under R. Walter Mills.

Even the dormitories, once more than half-empty, were overflowing. "McMillan Hall, for the first time since it was built, is full to capacity on all three floors....Tower and Liggett Halls, which heretofore have housed about ninety men...this year contain the quarters for about 130 men students," reported *Student Life*. Quickly, the University ended faculty rentals and doubled up on single rooms — but still had a waiting list of some 50 students. Even though Brookings authorized spending $50,000 to buy or lease a building near campus, an almost-frenzied search turned up nothing.

A new round of construction was clearly over-due if donors would only come forward. As an interim solution, the University threw up makeshift classroom space: North Hall, a squat, one-story building east of the Power Plant ("little more than an out size shanty," grumbled Langsdorf), which stood until 1928; a wooden biology building, later renamed Northeast Hall, on the site of present-day Compton Hall, which remained until 1932 and later served as architecture classroom space.

This increase in students meant a rapidly expand-ing faculty with 30 new appointments in 1920-21 alone. One was young Arthur Holly Compton, a promising Princeton Ph.D. who came to the Uni-versity as Wayman Crow Professor of Physics and head of the small department; years later, he returned as the University's chancellor. While Arts and Sciences was a particular beneficiary of this trend — with some 80 faculty in that school year and 29 departments — the growth was more gen-eral. By 1930, the University had almost three times as many faculty as it had in 1915.

Some faculty giants who had sustained the University during its darkest years were now dis-appearing. Calvin Woodward, the engineering dean and Manual Training School founder, died in 1914, and in 1923 the University honored him

Winter classes.
A mid-winter class meets in North Hall, a temporary build-ing constructed immediately after the end of World War I to house the rush of students. Constructed just before the 1919-20 school year, this build-ing — and several others — stayed in use until 1928 when the temporary buildings were razed to make room for more construction.
Photograph by Sanders and Melsheimer, 1923

Arthur Holly Compton (1892-1962).
Compton is fourth from the left in this 1923 photograph of the physics department faculty. Another noted mem-ber is Frank W. Bubb, third from the right.

Photos, WU Archives

135

with a bronze plaque mounted on University (now Brookings) Hall and a group of elm trees planted in the Quadrangle. Marshall Snow, the courtly Arts and Sciences dean and twice the acting chancellor, retired in 1911 and died in 1916. Two years later, former engineering dean Edmund Engler was dead; after leaving briefly to head Worcester Polytechnic Institute, he had returned in 1911 to become the loyal, efficient board secretary. Francis Nipher retired in 1914 after 39 years as a beloved physics faculty member, received an honorary LL.D. in 1915, and died in 1926.

Now came the dilemma: Who would replace them? Amid the post-war boom, some younger faculty were leaving to take better-paid, nonacademic jobs. At the medical school, a concerned Executive Faculty wrote the General Education Board (GEB), so often its funding source, that "it is becoming increasingly difficult…to retain or bring into the school the type of men necessary to maintain even an ordinary standard of medical education." Worried, Hall decided to mount a campaign for a $2 million salary endowment fund. With alumni help and $1.73 million from the GEB, the University raised $2.9 million. The average full professor's salary, previously $3,500 in the College, jumped to $5,000; Law went up to $4,500 and Medicine to $10,000. Hall was so struck by

Glasgow/Wilson family has multiple University connections

Sarah Louisa Glasgow Wilson, an 1876 Mary Institute graduate, came from a family with an extraordinary University pedigree. Her father, William Glasgow, Jr., was a charter board member; her twin brothers — Allen Cuthbert Glasgow, A.B. '75, and Frank Glasgow, A.B. '75, M.D. '78 — were early graduates. Her sister, Susan Glasgow, married Norman B. Carson, M.D. '68, medical school faculty member from 1898 to 1914. Other relatives — William Glasgow Bowling, A.B. '24, A.M. '25, and William Glasgow Bruce Carson, A.B. '13, A.M. '16 — were later faculty in the English department.

Sarah Louisa Glasgow Wilson (1858-1938).

After the 1914 death of her husband, Newton R. Wilson, E.M. '79, who had made a fortune in mining and lumbering, Sarah Wilson devoted herself to philanthropy. At the University, she funded part of the Women's Building, Wilson Pool, and Newton R. Wilson Memorial Hall for geology and geography. Later she provided a new home for Mary Institute.

At the Wilson Hall cornerstone-laying ceremony in May 1924, she explained her allegiance to Washington University: "During the seventy-one years' existence of this splendid university the attendance of members of our family as students has been continuous. Already twenty-one of our family have graduated from Washington and at present six of us are attending the university."

William Glasgow, Jr. (1813-1892).

William Glasgow Bowling (1902-1994).

Wilson Swimming Pool.

All photos, WU Archives

the alumni participation that in 1922 he organized an alumni office, which began publishing *Washingtonian* (later the *Alumni Bulletin* and now *Washington University in St. Louis Magazine*) in 1924.

MORE BUILDINGS RISE ON CAMPUS

Gradually, donors came forward with support for the much-needed buildings. In 1920, William Gephart persuaded the grieving Duncker family to memorialize their son Charles, A.B. '14, killed in the war, with a new building for the School of Commerce and Finance — particularly appropriate since their younger son, Henry, had been the school's first graduate in 1919. Brookings convinced Isabel Vallé January, later his wife, to fund a law school building, January Hall, in memory of her mother, Grace; its spectacular reading room was designed "in the style of the great halls of the Tudor period in England," said the *Hatchet*. Sarah Glasgow Wilson — daughter of William Glasgow, Jr., a charter board member — made the first of many gifts that earned her a nickname: "Lady Bountiful." This time, she gave $125,000 toward construction of the Wilson Swimming Pool, completed in 1922 and used by student swim teams that routinely won Missouri Valley Conference titles. Among the championship swimmers was I.E. Millstone, B.S. '27, later a trustee. The new indoor swimming pool, built in the 1980s, is named in his honor.

That was not all. Soon she announced her intention of donating $250,000 for a geology and geography building, Wilson Hall, as a memorial to her late husband, Newton R. Wilson, E.M. '79, a successful mining engineer. She aided another effort that was wending its way to completion.

The University women had undertaken their own fund drive for a Women's Building that would have space for social events, exercise, and dramatic performances. Eagerly determined, they held rummage sales, bridge parties, carnivals, and hot dog sales at athletic events. At one University football game, Sarah Wilson saw women selling snacks and asked the reason — then promptly contributed $25,000 toward the building campaign.

The new art building that Hall longed for was still a mirage, though University publications talked hopefully about plans for a three-building complex — to house Art, a museum, and Architecture — on the southeast corner of campus. Hall even asked Gabriel Ferrand, design professor and successor to Charles Abella, to create a plan for this new cluster. "This group of three buildings will make, perhaps, one of the most beautiful in St. Louis," said the *Hatchet*.

GOVERNOR HADLEY BECOMES CHANCELLOR

Hall was no longer in office when these projects came to fruition. Although the board had earlier fixed the faculty retirement age at 65, he was past his 68th birthday by 1923; presiding over Commencement as usual, he stepped down eight days later. His successor was Herbert Spencer Hadley, a Kansas native and Northwestern University Law School graduate. Unlike Hall, the lifelong academic, Hadley had lived in the public eye, winning state office in

Ridgley Library reading room, now Holmes Lounge.
WU Archives

January Hall reading room.
Originally the reading room for the School of Law, this space in January Hall now houses the East Asian Library.
WU Archives

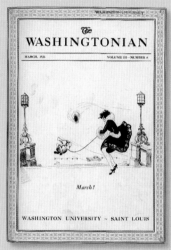

The Washingtonian,
March 1926.
WU Archives

Herbert Spencer Hadley (1872-1927).
When Hadley became the seventh chancellor, Robert Brookings called him a man of "courage, ability, and integrity."
Painting by Gustav F. Goetsch
WU Gallery of Art

137

Commencement 1927.

From left, Chancellor Herbert S. Hadley, Vice President of the United States Charles G. Dawes, and Robert S. Brookings: Dawes was the Commencement speaker.

Photograph by the *St. Louis Star*, 1927, WU Archives

Graduates serve in U.S. Senate

Three University graduates in a row were U.S. senators from Missouri. Selden P. Spencer, LL.B. '86, A.M. '16, was a lawyer who had earned an honorary M.D. from Missouri Medical College and taught medical jurisprudence there. A former state representative and circuit court judge, he was elected in 1918 to complete another senator's term, then reelected for his own six-year term in 1920.

Selden P. Spencer (1862-1925).
U.S. Senate Historical Office

After Spencer died, George H. Williams, LL.B. '97, also a Republican and a well-respected circuit court judge, was appointed to complete his term. But in 1926, Williams and Henry B. Hawes, LL.B. '96, squared off in an election for the next senatorial term. Hawes, a Democrat who had formerly been a state representative and Congressman, won the election and served until 1933, when he resigned to devote himself to the wildlife conservation movement and private legal work.

George H. Williams (1871-1963).
Used by permission, State Historical Society of Missouri

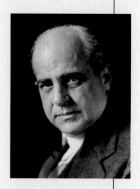

Henry B. Hawes (1869-1947).
Library of Congress

1900 as prosecuting attorney of Jackson County, and Missouri's attorney general three years later. A progressive Republican, he had earned a reputation as a crusader, targeting Standard Oil and other "malefactors of great wealth," as well as organized gambling. In 1908, he became governor at age 36 — the first Republican elected since 1870 — and narrowly missed being nominated for president. Then tuberculosis struck and he moved to Colorado in 1916 to find relief, soon recovering enough to serve as law professor at the University of Colorado.

Brookings learned of Hadley's availability and, behind the scenes, checked into his health; he also made certain that the Rockefeller family, funders of the GEB, bore no grudges over the Standard Oil prosecution. On November 10, 1923, Hadley was inaugurated during a sumptuous ceremony in Francis Gymnasium attended by representatives of 159 colleges and universities, 33 of them presidents or chancellors. "The fact that this was the first formal inauguration of a Chancellor of Washington University since 1892, added to the impressiveness of the ceremonies," said the *Hatchet*.

Ever gracious, Hall welcomed Hadley as his successor, and Brookings praised him as a man of "courage, ability, and integrity," careful to mention Hadley's recent book, *Rome and the World Today*, as a scholarly credential that might mollify faculty. In his own speech, Hadley showed little sympathy with scholarship for its own sake. While research adds to human knowledge, he said, it only touches a few students, so the key thing is teaching and preparing young people to become informed citizens. The University, he said, "should connect itself as far as practicable with the culture and civilization of which it is a part, and should impose no cloistered existence on either student or teacher."

BROOKINGS OPENS A NEW SCHOOL IN WASHINGTON, D.C.

As an example of this ethic, Hadley cited a new program of the University — the very program, in fact, that had probably convinced Brookings to recruit him. Just a few months earlier, Brookings had excitedly unveiled to the University board — which now included his own nephew, Harry Brookings Wallace — his plan for a Graduate School of Economics and Government to train young adults for public service. It would be integrated into two existing Washington, D.C.-based organizations, the Institute of Government Research and the Institute of Economics, both interests of Brookings. An enthusiastic board endorsed the new school the day after hearing his proposal.

In September 1923 it opened: a three-year program with up to 40 students — largely supported by fellowships that Brookings had established — who would spend the first year in St. Louis and then two years in Washington, D.C., living in a townhouse that Brookings had bought. Although some faculty opposed the idea, fearing the program would not be rigorous enough, others were intrigued. Leverett Lyon, an economist hired to succeed William Gephart as dean of the School of Commerce, resigned to join the faculty. Brookings appointed Warren Hamilton, formerly of Amherst, as professor of economics and liaison between the two campuses.

Harry Brookings Wallace (1877-1955).
Robert Brookings' nephew, Wallace carried on Brookings' work at the University, becoming a board member in 1923, its president from 1942-51, and acting chancellor in 1944-45. He received an honorary LL.D. degree in 1947.

Oil on masonite by Fred Conway
WU Gallery of Art

However, a power struggle developed between Hamilton and Hadley, prompting Brookings to assume leadership of the school and its board. That left the University, though nominally responsible, with no real authority over the school's affairs. When law professor Joseph Zumbalen raised concerns that the University's charter did not allow corporate activity outside of Missouri, a subdued board asked Brookings in November 1924 to incorporate his school separately. He did so; though in 1927, concerned about the inefficiency of sponsoring three Washington organizations, Brookings moved to consolidate them into one: The Brookings Institution.

University continues to honor legendary teacher Arnold Lien

A political science professor from 1924-52 who influenced generations of students, Arnold J. Lien was a gifted teacher, "singularly devoted to the truth — to the facts, regardless of any preconceived notions or popular ideas," said the *Alumni Bulletin* in 1958. Lien stayed up to the minute on world events. "It used to be said that if a revolution broke out in Afghanistan at 8:08 a.m., Prof. Lien would incorporate that fact and its implications in his lecture at 8:11." He taught far more than his subject. "A course from him was a course in life, a code of ethics," said the *Bulletin* adding: "Some have called him not a professor but an entire university."

Arnold J. Lien (1886-1963).
WU Archives

Today, Lien House on the South 40, part of the Robert S. Brookings Residential College, is named for him; the Arnold J. Lien Scholarships in the social and behavioral sciences, full-tuition academic scholarships with a stipend, are awarded annually to incoming College of Arts & Sciences students.

Lien House.
David Kilper, WU Photographic Services

THE UNIVERSITY ESTABLISHES A WEALTH OF EXPANDED PROGRAMS

This experience, though brief, left a lasting mark on the University. In 1923, amid the interest generated by Brookings' new school, three College departments — political science, economics, and sociology — were established as separate entities. Political science gained a new head in Arnold Lien, an inspirational teacher. Hadley, hoping to continue cooperating with Brookings' program, recruited a business school dean who was interested in public administration: Isidor Loeb, formerly head of the business school

Isidor Loeb (1868-1953).
After Leverett Lyon's resignation, Isidor Loeb became dean of the School of Business and Public Administration, serving until 1940.
WU Archives

at the University of Missouri–Columbia. In fact, Hadley endorsed a name change for the business school to reflect this new emphasis. In 1925, it became the "School of Business and Public Administration," offering bachelor's and master's degrees.

This revamped school also became the home of the University's latest social work effort. After the School of Social Economy ended in 1924, a group of donors offered to support a social work faculty member for a three-year period. Hadley agreed and hired former social service agency executive Frank Bruno, dynamic and determined, who moved to establish the program permanently. In 1927, he gained board approval for a bachelor's degree in social work, and soon persuaded Bettie Bofinger Brown, widow of George Warren Brown, founder of Brown Shoe Company, to endow the George Warren Brown Department of Social Work with a gift of $500,000.

Meanwhile, Hadley was forging ahead with curricular changes linked to his interest in public service. In 1924, he inaugurated a course in journalism, which he hoped would lead to a journalism school, and added required courses for freshmen and sophomores, especially political sci-

Frank Bruno (1874-1955).
A former Congregational minister, faculty member at the University of Minnesota, and executive officer of the Minneapolis Family Welfare Society, Bruno was appointed professor of applied sociology in 1925. He headed social work until 1944, placing it on a firm academic and financial footing.
WU Archives

ence. "We say to them, 'In your first year you must study your country's language, your country's history, and your country's government. You must also study a natural science, mathematics, and a foreign (or ancient) language,'" he said. He was concerned about the high dropout rate from the College, particularly among male students, so the University upgraded entrance requirements and in 1924 created the Freshman Advisory Council.

Another program, open to the public, pleased and astonished Hadley with its success. In 1924, the University formally offered its first summer school, though it had previously provided some summer sessions for handicapped veterans and engineering students needing remedial help. Many

---

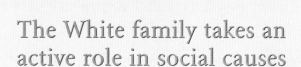

The White family takes an active role in social causes

As a student, Maria Bain, A.B. '16, was president of the Women's Union and member of Kappa Alpha Theta. Like her husband Park J. White, a pediatrician and medical school professor whom she married in 1918, she became a crusader for civil rights and social justice. The Park J. White Professorship in Pediatrics, held today by F. Sessions Cole, is named for him. Her sister, Katherine Bain (1897-1999), M.D. '25, was a pioneer in maternal and child health issues, and daughter, Katherine White Drescher, was a board member from 1985-89. At her 78th college reunion, Maria White — by then a widow — reconnected with a classmate, widower William Berry, B.S.Ch.E. '16, and that kindled a romance between the two, the last surviving members of their class.

Park J. White (1891-1987).
WU Becker Medical Library

Maria Bain White (1893-1997).
Maria (right) and friend in a cart when she was a student.
Courtesy of Katherine White Drescher

William Bixby provides a new home for the School of Fine Arts

William Keeney Bixby, prominent business-man and art patron, was generous to the University, which he served as board member from 1904 until his death, and president from 1928-30. Among his many gifts, he gave the new St. Louis Museum of Fine Arts in 1906 a fund for the purchase of American paintings; he also gave $250,000 toward the construction of an art school building, completed in 1926.

Another gift from Bixby, long active in the local Robert Burns Club, was the statue of the Scottish poet Robert Burns at the corner of Skinker and Forsyth. The eight-foot-tall bronze figure, which cost $10,000, was created by sculptor Robert Ingersoll Aitken.

Finally, Bixby donated much of his manuscript collection to the University, including letters and historical autographs

Bixby Hall.

of such prominent people as Samuel Clemens, Charles Dickens, Thomas A. Edison, Ulysses S. Grant, John Hancock, Oliver Wendell Holmes, Andrew Jackson, John Keats, Robert E. Lee, James Madison, Napoleon I and III, Henry David Thoreau, Leo Tolstoy, and Booker T. Washington.

William K. Bixby (1857-1931).

The cornerstone laying for Bixby Hall.
From left to right: Mrs. Edmund Wuerpel, Chancellor Herbert S. Hadley, School of Fine Arts Dean Edmund H. Wuerpel, donor William K. Bixby, and art professor Holmes Smith.

were skeptical: Who would come to steamy St. Louis in the summertime? Surprisingly, the first session attracted 534 students, and the program grew to nearly 1,000 students by 1930. Evening and weekend classes proved immense-ly popular, thanks to the tireless efforts of Frederick W. Shipley, director of the University's Extension Division, established in 1919. Shipley, a former classics professor, approached his recruiting with missionary zeal, and his classes, attended by the not-so-wealthy in the communi-ty, grew exponentially. Although the division

could not grant degrees, Shipley won permission in 1922 to award certifi-cates to students who had completed such sequences as accounting or home economics.

Law was still a problem. Hadley was often at odds with Dean Goode, who clung to the old curriculum and refused to consider the casebook method. His 1927 replacement, William G. Hale, a Harvard law graduate and former dean at Oregon State Law School, finally began to implement reform. New faculty helped the effort: Ernest B. Conant in 1917,

Frederick W. Shipley (1871-1945).
Shipley, a former classics profes-sor, was the energetic founding director of the University's Extension Division, established in 1919.

All photos, WU Archives

a Harvard LL.D., raised on the casebook; Ralph F. Fuchs, A.B., LL.B. '22, who also held a Ph.D. from the Robert Brookings Graduate School of Economics and Government; and Israel Treiman, A.B. '22, LL.B. '24, who received a Ph.D. from Oxford on a Rhodes scholarship — the first Jewish Rhodes scholar in the United States.

AT THE HEART OF THE NATION

All the while, buildings were rising on campus: January Hall completed in 1923, Duncker in 1924. "A graduate of the class of 1920 would not recognize the campus on his return," said the 1926 *Hatchet*. In 1926, Charles Rebstock, owner of a leading wholesale liquor company, gave $300,000 for a building to house zoology and botany, with a welcome $700,000 endowment to maintain it. A new Tudor Gothic smokestack and the first five of nine fraternity houses went up, all by 1925. At the May 1924 cornerstone-laying ceremony for Newton R. Wilson Memorial Hall, Hadley spoke elatedly about the prospects for Washington University to become "the typical American university" since it had "the culture and refinement of the East, the courage and vigor of the North, the frankness and freedom of the West, and the courtesy and

Charles Rebstock (1846-1928). Rebstock, board member from 1927-28, gave $1 million to the University in 1925: $300,000 for a new zoology and botany building and $700,000 for a maintenance fund. The Charles Rebstock Professorship in Biology, held today by Alan R. Templeton, was established the same year. In 1926, Rebstock said of his gift: "It is true that the active businessman enjoys making money. If broadminded enough to use a liberal part of it for educational, civic, and philanthropic purposes, he not only improves his citizenship, but he encourages others to follow his example."

Al Parker (1906-1985). A 1928 graduate of the School of Fine Arts, Parker was one of the most successful illustrators of the 1940s to '60s period, working for many popular magazines. For *Ladies' Home Journal*, he created a 13-year series of covers that depicted an idealized family life with mothers and daughters wearing matching outfits. He was named to the Illustrators Hall of Fame in 1965.

Charles Eames (1907-1978). Eames, an architecture student from 1925-27 and recipient of an honorary doctor of arts degree in 1970, was an architect and revolutionary designer who developed innovative furniture with his wife, Ray Kaiser. Best-known as the designer of the Eames chair, he also designed toys, buildings, and fabrics, and made educational films.

chivalry of the South. We have sunshine enough for sentiment and snow enough for courage, and we have the substantial foundations of industrial and agricultural wealth to justify our claim to leadership in material as well as in spiritual achievements."

To help realize this dream, board member William Bixby gave $250,000 toward a new School of Fine Arts building, though he insisted that some interiors from the British Pavilion be included in the design. Hadley was delighted; he and James Jamieson, still the University's architect, made hopeful plans for an arts and music campus along Forsyth. In designing Bixby Hall, Jamieson switched away from Collegiate Gothic to white stone and Tudor "to enhance the dominant character of the granite towers on the 'Hill,'" he said. When the building was finished in 1926, students and faculty were thrilled. "Professor Wuerpel is as pleased in his new surroundings as if he had suddenly discovered a Rembrandt," said *Washingtonian*.

Jamieson was indignant about another construction project. The eager Director of Athletics, William ("Big Bill") Edmunds, convinced Hadley that the University needed a new Field House for its basketball program, now relegated to the Coliseum downtown. In 1926, it was dedicated, with links to Wilson Pool and Francis Gymnasium; the three buildings, exclaimed the *Hatchet*, "formed the largest gymnasium unit in the world." But the Field House was too big for its space, Jamieson sniffed, and "its unfinished exterior makes it an eyesore."

In 1927, announcement came of yet another beneficence by Sarah Glasgow Wilson. She was

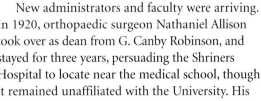

funding a new home for her alma mater, Mary Institute, on a 20-acre tract at the corner of Warson and Ladue roads, with a gift of $560,000. The school — which had a change of leadership in 1925 when Edmund Sears resigned after 34 years as principal — moved to its new site in 1930.

REMARKABLE PROGRESS AT THE MEDICAL SCHOOL

Through these years, the growth sweeping the Hilltop Campus was affecting the medical school as well. There was such demand for admission that the school increased its class size from 60 to 75, and finally to 82 by 1925. It raised admission standards, too, in 1929 becoming the first of the University's professional schools to require a bachelor's degree. Despite the early flurry of women applicants, there were still few women in the program, but the 1930 *Hatchet* bragged that the school was "without a doubt one of the best medical schools in the United States. Every medical student is a picked scholar….Only one applicant out of five is allowed to enter."

New administrators and faculty were arriving. In 1920, orthopaedic surgeon Nathaniel Allison took over as dean from G. Canby Robinson, and stayed for three years, persuading the Shriners Hospital to locate near the medical school, though it remained unaffiliated with the University. His successor was W. McKim Marriott, a Cornell medical school graduate and head of the Department of Pediatrics since 1917. For the next 13 years, Marriott did an effective, diplomatic job of moving the School forward and expanding facilities for clinical research, while keeping peace among the often-contentious faculty.

Within this faculty were some stellar recruits: David P. Barr, who replaced George Dock as Busch Professor of Medicine and department head; E.V. Cowdry, who came in 1928 as professor of cytology and shifted the major thrust of research in the anatomy department toward cell biology; Leo Loeb, who replaced Eugene Opie as Mallinckrodt Professor of Pathology in 1924 and made a national reputation in cancer research. Mildred Trotter, ultimately the first female full professor at the School of Medicine, came as a

Leo Loeb (1869-1959).
Loeb joined the medical school faculty in 1915, succeeding Eugene Opie in 1924 as professor of pathology. Loeb's research focused on tissue transplantation and tumor growth, and he discovered methods for establishing and sustaining *in vitro* tissue cultures. He was known as the founder of experimental cancer research.

David P. Barr (1889-1977).
A successor to George Dock as head of internal medicine, Barr enhanced the department's reputation in research, teaching, and patient care. He served as professor of medicine from 1924-41 and made major research contributions in the area of metabolic disease.

Jewish Hospital.
A 30-bed hospital opened in 1902 at 5815 Delmar Boulevard, then president Aaron Waldheim led the planning for a new building on Kingshighway, which was dedicated in 1927. The hospital became associated with the medical school in 1953; then in 1966 it became part of the BJC HealthCare system and was renamed Barnes–Jewish Hospital. Jewish Hospital has been known for its pioneering social services, including hospice care and its physical therapy program.

GRAHAM, ANDERSON PROBST & WHITE ARCHITECTS | NEW JEWISH HOSPITAL · ST·LOUIS · MISSOURI | S.S. GOLDWATER M CONSULTANT

researcher in 1920, earned her Ph.D. four years later, and began a nearly 50-year career in physical anthropology.

Others were engaged in groundbreaking research. In 1920, Joseph Erlanger and Herbert Gasser built their own cathode ray oscilloscope to record and analyze individual nerve impulses. George Bishop, who became a national leader in neuroscience, joined the medical faculty in 1921; Ethel Ronzoni, a specialist in carbohydrate metabolism and Bishop's wife, joined the department of biological chemistry in 1922, becoming one of the first female instructors in the school. The departments of bacteriology and pathology split in 1923, and Jacques Bronfenbrenner joined the faculty in

1928, doing important work on the prevention of syphilis. Harvey Howard, the flamboyant new head of ophthalmology, began investigations into trachoma, a common cause of blindness.

Thanks in large part to new grants from the GEB, which gave the School of Medicine some $6 million from 1919-31, buildings were going up. Eliza McMillan's bequest made possible construction of the McMillan Eye, Ear, Nose, and Throat Hospital, which began in May 1930. Family and associates of the late Oscar Johnson, a founder of International Shoe Company, donated $650,000 for construction of the Oscar Johnson Institute for Research in Ophthalmology and Otolaryngology. Frank Rand, the president, and Jackson Johnson, International Shoe board chairman — both of them University board members as well — gave $300,000, which helped fund a new Rand-Johnson surgical wing at Barnes Hospital.

Finally, after years of hoping, another GEB grant placed obstetrics and gynecology faculty on a full-time basis under Otto Schwarz, whose father, Henry, had led this department for years. Although it was not officially part of the University, the old St. Louis Maternity Hospital, where many faculty members had practiced, moved from its run-down Washington Avenue location to the Medical Campus. Eighteen years later, when the

hospital was foundering in debt, the University purchased it.

In 1923, Evarts A. Graham joined with Warren H. Cole, Glover H. Copher, M.D. '18, Sherwood Moore, M.D. '05, and scientists from the Mallinckrodt Company to develop a new technique, cholecystography, which allowed X-ray visualization of the gall bladder. With this success in mind, the GEB gave $750,000 to endow a new department of radiology — if the University could raise $250,000 for the building and equipment. In 1927, Edward Mallinckrodt, Sr. and Jr., jointly made this gift; an eight-story building went up north of Barnes Hospital, and the Edward Mallinckrodt Institute of Radiology was born under its first director, Sherwood Moore.

Dentistry was making progress, though slowly, under Dean Walter Bartlett, appointed in 1921. The school, still languishing in the dingy downtown building it had inherited from the School of Law in 1909, had lost students after extending its course from three to four years in 1917, and requiring one year of college starting in 1921. Amid these changes, the Dental Educational Council had lowered the school's "A" rating to "B," though it was restored in 1923. The University board, anxious to keep this from happening again, agreed in 1928 to give the school a new building on Scott Avenue — and enrollment began to rise.

THE END OF THE BROOKINGS ERA

By 1927 it was apparent that Hadley, having recovered from tuberculosis, was seriously ill with a heart condition. George Throop, a classics professor who had served as assistant to the chancellor since 1921, took over as acting chancellor while Hadley struggled to recover. In October 1927, when the Women's Building cornerstone finally was laid, Hadley was too sick to appear, and he died the following December. As Gov. Henry S. Caulfield, LL.B. '95, said in his eulogy: "There is not a resident of Missouri but who is better off that Herbert Hadley lived."

For the next year, Throop continued as chancellor while the board considered other candidates, including medical school dean W. McKim Marriott, law alumnus and former Secretary of War Dwight F. Davis, and botany professor George Moore. Yet this search was leaderless because the

ailing, 78-year-old Robert Brookings, who had hand-picked chancellors in the past, had gradually withdrawn from University affairs since his move to Washington, D.C.; in 1928, he finally resigned as board president and was named president emeritus. "As long as I live," he promised in his letter of resignation, "the University will always hold first place in my affections."

It was the end of an era. The board — led by his old friend William Bixby, who took over for

---

The Mallinckrodt family supports pediatrics, pharmacology, and radiology

Edward Mallinckrodt, Sr., founder of the Mallinckrodt Chemical Company, was a great friend of Robert Brookings and a board member from 1902-28. He was a generous donor to the medical school: serving on its reorganization committee, endowing the Edward Mallinckrodt Department of Pediatrics, and in 1919 helping to fund the Department of Pharmacology. He endowed the Edward Mallinckrodt Institute of Radiology, as well, but he did not live to see it built. His son Edward Mallinckrodt, Jr. (1878-1967), a board member from 1928-42, provided funds to complete the state-of-the-art building, the first of its kind in the world. Sherwood Moore (1880-1963), M.D. '05, was its first director, serving from 1930-49.

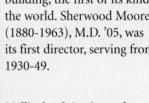

Edward Mallinckrodt, Sr. (1845-1928).
Painting by Irving R. Wiles
Mallinckrodt Institute of Radiology

Mallinckrodt Institute of Radiology in 1940.
WU Becker Medical Library

George Throop (1882-1949).
A professor of Greek and Latin, then assistant to the chancellor, Throop became acting chancellor during Herbert Hadley's final illness. He was named chancellor in 1928.
Oil on canvas by Charles F. Galt
WU Gallery of Art

Women's Building interior.
After years of fundraising by the women themselves, the Women's Building was finally completed in 1928. "The outer world is permitted to glimpse beauties, luxuries and attractions of which the half cannot be told," said *Washingtonian*.
WU Archives

Wulfing Coin Collection.
A St. Louis wholesale grocer, John Max Wulfing (1850-1929) was passionately interested in Greek and Roman coins. He built a collection, said *Washingtonian*, "second to only one other…in the United States." Shortly before his death, Wulfing — who had studied at Smith Academy — gave his collection to Washington University, along with an endowment to make additions possible. Originally, the collection consisted of 7,000 pieces, the oldest dating to 750 B.C., and it expanded greatly. Today, it includes more than 13,000 items, mostly ancient Greek, Roman, and Byzantine coins. For years, it was under the stewardship of classicist Kevin Herbert; today, it is under art history and archaeology faculty member Sarantis Symeonoglou.
WU Wulfing Collection

two years as president, though ill himself — joined in signing a letter of thanks for Brookings' extraordinary service. "It has been given to very few men," they wrote, "to accomplish in so brief a period of time for the cause of education, what you have succeeded in doing for our University." The next year, in an unprecedented gesture, Brookings was awarded the LL.D. and M.D. degrees, and University Hall was renamed in his honor. His old friend Henry Pritchett, who was in the audience, described the scene at Commencement as Brookings rose to speak, this time passionately appealing to young people to enter public life:

"His health was failing, but with the resolution of compelling devotion, he made his way to this platform….His plea was for the obligation of educated men and women to government….The ranks of his old associates were broken. Many of his colleagues were gone. Others had given to their limit. His own strength was spent; but his vision was clear. As he stood there, his classic profile turned to us, a splendid symbol of conviction and enthusiasm, his counsel never sounded more true or persuasive."

Within months of Brookings' resignation, faculty backing carried Throop to victory, and in

December 1928 he was named the University's eighth chancellor. A Tennessee native and Cornell Ph.D., he had come to the University in 1907, briefly resigned in 1918 to become assistant librarian in the St. Louis Public Library, and returned in 1921 to serve as assistant to Hall, then Hadley. In stark contrast to Hadley, Throop disliked dealing with the public (he held "the ideals of stern devotion to scholarship," said *Washingtonian*) and hated the details of his office (he felt "aversion to the trivial, the ephemeral, the showy or the merely expedient"). He named Walter McCourt as assistant chancellor to handle those responsibilities for him.

Throop's chancellorship got off to a difficult start. The new athletic director and football coach, Alfred Sharpe, was lobbying for a 30,000-seat stadium near Forest Park Parkway and Big Bend to replace overflowing Francis Field, but the project was abandoned when neighbors objected. Next came an extraordinary stroke of luck. In November 1930, Joseph Givens, an elderly St. Louisan who had never been asked for a donation, walked into the office of Charles Nagel, Bixby's successor as board president, with a surprising but welcome proposal. Givens, whose father, Joseph, had been architect and builder for the University's downtown campus, was ready to donate $800,000: half toward a new building for the School of

Dedicated staff members enhance the University

Grace Denison (1872-1955).

Adèle Starbird (1891-1987).

Charles Galloway (1871-1931).

Morris Boorstin (c. 1872-1935).

arly in the 20th century, several staff members — known to generations of students and faculty — performed invaluable service for the University.

In 1901, Grace Denison, A.B. '96, became secretary to Chancellor Chaplin, the first of five chancellors and four board presidents whom she assisted in her 40-year career. For many years the only secretary in the College and in Engineering, she helped faculty as well. "No one in the long history of the University ever worked harder or more loyally for its welfare than did Grace Denison," said Alexander Langsdorf.

Morris Boorstin (known tongue-in-cheek as "the Colonel") was a former army sergeant and chief custodian for the 1904 World's Fair, who performed the same role for the University, serving faithfully from 1905 until his death in 1935. In 1929, Gov. Henry S. Caulfield, LL.B. '95, gave Boorstin an honorary appointment as colonel on his personal staff to legitimize his title.

Adèle Chomeau Starbird was the widow of Robert Starbird, the University's first registrar in 1914; she was a well-loved dean of women, serving from 1931-59. A lecture in the Assembly Series, sponsored by the Washington University Woman's Club, is named for her. Starbird always balanced "good sense, compassion, and discipline," said William Danforth in 1988.

Charles Galloway, who attended Smith Academy, was the official 1904 World's Fair organist, then longtime University organist, giving recitals on Sunday afternoons. Altogether, 32 of his Graham Chapel concerts from 1914-18 attracted 18,000 people. A delighted Chancellor Hall praised his "superior rendition and his lucid interpretation." In 1941, his son Charles followed in his footsteps, becoming the new music director.

All photos, WU Archives

Architecture; and half in an appreciating trust fund for scholarship assistance. A stunned Nagel gratefully accepted.

New worries were on the way. however. October 29, 1929, had been "Black Tuesday" — the day of the catastrophic Wall Street crash. Early on, its impact on the University was not severe; in fact,

the newly elected president of the board, clinical surgery professor Malvern Clopton, declared boldly in February 1932 that the University had "been little hurt by the Depression." He spoke prematurely. Washington University, like all of the nation, faced hard times ahead. Ⓦ

William Glasgow Bruce Carson (1891-1976). Carson, A.B. '13, A.M. '16, a descendant of University charter board member William Glasgow, was first a student and then a beloved teacher who taught the legendary English XVI course for 28 years.

Walter Gustave ("Gus") Haenschen (c. 1890-1980). Gus Haenschen, ex-'12, became a composer, arranger, and orchestra leader for many well-known radio programs. As an engineering student at the University, he composed "The Moorish Tango" for *The Love Star* in 1914. One evening he played it at a party for two visiting New Yorkers. Weeks later, a music publisher invited him to New York and introduced him to producer Flo Ziegfeld, who liked the song, renamed it "Underneath the Japanese Moon," and added it to his 1914 Follies show.

Cast of *Captain Lettarblair*. Thyrsus performed Marguerite Merrington's play on March 29, 1910, at the Odeon Theatre in St. Louis. Gus Haenschen was the musical director for the group's sixth annual play.

Just before and after World War I, performing arts took center stage on campus as students clamored to take part in productions of all kinds: serious dramas and musicals; plays written in English or Greek; performances on an indoor stage or an outdoor lawn, or even at a downtown theater. Altogether, they added excitement to the growing social scene and made the University the liveliest place in the city for theatrical life.

Thyrsus was the premier drama group with a membership capped at 50 and a waiting list of hopefuls. Its first theater — Room 107 in Cupples II — had a 16-foot stage and space for a 70-member audience. While the tiny ladies' dressing room was carved out of one wing, men had to dress in a lavatory down the hall, dash outdoors, climb up a ladder through a window, then emerge breathless on stage to perform. This system led to mishaps, especially after a rain. "There was mud on every rung of the ladder," said faculty member William G.B. Carson, A.B. '13, A.M. '16, recalling his sophomore show. "As I descended to earth after my brief act, the tails of the dress-suit (my first) in which I was arrayed suffered damage from which they never recovered."

At its peak, Thyrsus put on two kinds of productions: monthly plays, often wild, spoofy "mellerdrammers"; and a spectacular annual play, often held downtown in the 1,200-seat Odeon Theatre. Student performers tasted the joys of stardom: They were excused from class on the day of the play, and the University hired a professional director to polish their acting skills. "When it was all over," said Carson, "the weary participants returned to a humdrum existence, cherishing handsome sweaters adorned with green and red masks, and were listed in the *Hatchet* as 'Wearers of the Mask.'"

In 1909, Fannie Hurst, A.B. '09, wrote the senior play, *The Official Chaperone*, then at the last minute made it a musical — the first at the University. Everything went smoothly, said *Student Life*, "until dress rehearsal when word came that the faculty refused to permit ballet costumes to be worn by the chorus." In the end, "the girls made their appearance in long tarleton skirts, none of which were more than four inches off the floor." Arthur Proetz, A.B. '10, M.D. '12, directed that musical, and the next year he and Hugh Ferriss, B.S. '11, wrote their own — the hugely successful *Quadrangle Town*. Three thousand flocked to see it in a tent next to Cupples II, and next season it returned to a sold-out Odeon, with songs played by a 25-piece orchestra conducted by Gus Haenschen, ex-'12. A key cast member was Erma B. Perham, who sang and danced the role of Fifi, "The Darling of McMillan"; another was Proetz, whom she later married.

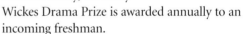

The Love Star and Quadrangle Town programs.
The success of musicals written by Arthur Proetz and Hugh Ferriss, including *Quadrangle Town*, led to establishment of the Quadrangle Club, which staged *The Love Star* in 1914.

On the heels of this success, a new drama group was born: the Quadrangle Club, which did *Pierrette* — another Proetz-Ferriss collaboration — in 1912; *The Sun of O-Gun* in 1913; and *The Love Star* in 1914, which fizzled when the lead comedian turned up drunk every night. Students tired of mounting a new musical each year and the Quadrangle Club faded, though it revived to do *Tame Oats* in 1926 (with young actor and later presidential adviser Clark Clifford, J.D. '28), *High Hat* in 1928, and *Down in Front* in 1940 (with a book by budding writer A.E. Hotchner, A.B. '40, J.D. '40). Quadrangle Club came back again after World War II, this time as a vehicle for Broadway productions.

In 1912, the Department of Greek managed a rare feat: performing Sophocles' *Antigone* entirely in Greek to an enthusiastic 900-member audience. Four years later, during Shakespeare's tercentenary, came an Elizabethan pageant that Chancellor Hall called "the most conspicuous single event of the year." Thyrsus ventured into the new medium of film in 1916 with its first silent movie, *The Maid of McMillan*, which opened at the Univee Surkuss. Students played the principal roles, including the female lead, Myrtle Maroon; Hall even made a cameo appearance.

During World War I, Thyrsus was relegated to the former YMCA hut, "one of the dreariest 'temples of the muses' this city has ever known," sighed Carson. A star from this period was Florence Walters, A.B. '23, who played Shakespeare's Juliet in 1923 opposite fine arts student Warren Hagee. After college, she acted for a time but quit to marry Hagee, deciding "that she would rather marry her Romeo," Carson said. Another

Actress Mary Wickes' career begins at Washington University

Mary Wickes as Amanda.
Wickes performed in the 1968 student production of Tennessee Williams' *The Glass Menagerie.*

M ary Isabella Wickenhauser ("Mary Wickes"), A.B. '30, got her start at the University. After graduation, she began her acting career as understudy to Margaret Hamilton in *The Farmer Takes a Wife*, giving up a graduate fellowship in political science. She went on to appear in 18 New York plays, more than 30 films, many television shows, and more than 300 stock company productions, including the Muny Opera in St. Louis.

In 1955, she received one of the University's first Distinguished Alumni Awards and in 1969 an honorary doctorate. She returned several times: in 1968 to play the role of Amanda in *The Glass Menagerie* and in 1972 as mistress of ceremonies at the dedication of Edison Theatre. Today, the Mary Wickes Drama Prize is awarded annually to an incoming freshman.

Mary Isabella Wickes (1910-1995).

When she died, she left a $2 million bequest to University Libraries, which created the Isabella and Frank Wickenhauser Memorial Fund for Television, Film, and Theatre, in memory of her parents. Her papers are in University Archives.

Florence Walters Hagee.
Florence Walters, A.B. '23, appeared as Juliet in the Thyrsus production of *Romeo and Juliet* in 1923; Warren Hagee played Romeo. She was an inspired actress, but she gave up a stage career to marry Hagee, a School of Fine Arts student.

All images, WU Archives

Oliver Nelson (1932-1975).
Nelson, who attended the University from 1954-57, was a well-known jazz musician and composer, who created the music for such television programs as *Ironside* and the *Six Million Dollar Man*. He was a visiting faculty member in 1969.
WU Archives

Morris Carnovsky (1897-1992).
Carnovsky, A.B. '20, a reknowned Shakespearean actor, volunteered to play the lead in *King Lear* on campus in 1976. The show had six sold-out performances and funded a drama scholarship.
WU Archives

Harold Ramis.
The producer, director, and screenwriter for Ocean Pictures, Ramis, A.B. '66, serves on the board of trustees.
WU Photographic Services

was Morris Carnovsky, A.B. '20, who became a leading Shakespearean actor and appeared in successful Hollywood films, including *Rhapsody in Blue* (1945), *Dead Reckoning* (1947), and *Cyrano de Bergerac* (1951).

Carson, known as "Pop" or "Boops," joined the faculty in 1919 and became "one of the truly beloved characters of the University," recalled writer Shepherd ("Ed") Mead, A.B. '36, best known for writing *How to Succeed in Business Without Really Trying*. In Carson's English XVI (now Drama 351) class, students wrote their own one-act plays, and at the end of the year, a jury chose three winners, which were produced by Thyrsus the following year. One well-known English XVI student was Mary Isabella Wickenhauser (later "Mary Wickes"), A.B. '30, who became a star on Broadway, on television, and in Hollywood, with films such as *White Christmas* (1954), *The Trouble with Angels* (1966), *Sister Act* (1992 and its 1993 sequel), and *Little Women* (1994).

Mead and A.E. Hotchner took English XVI in 1936, when an older student, Thomas Lanier ("Tennessee") Williams, joined the class. He wrote "the most wonderful, little fragile vignettes about a mother and daughter and a son in St. Louis," recalled Hotchner. "We took it for granted that he would turn in a play based on these people and that it would be hands-down the winner." Instead, he submitted *Me, Vashya* — "pretentious pap," said Hotchner. When Williams heard that his play was not a winner, "in a heat — I mean he really exploded — he picked up his books, stormed out of the class, out of St. Louis, and never came back to

Thomas Lanier ("Tennessee") Williams (1911-1983).
Williams, who attended the University for one year in 1936, contributed 20 poems to *The Eliot*, the University's literary magazine, but was crushed when his one-act play, *Me, Vashya*, written for English XVI, was unsuccessful. Yet, when he returned to the University in 1977 to give a talk, he still said that his "only happy times…[in St. Louis] were at Washington University." He is well known for his play *The Glass Menagerie* and for *A Streetcar Named Desire*, which won the Pulitzer Prize in 1948.
WU Archives

the class," added Hotchner. Williams eventually wove some of those vignettes into his play, *The Glass Menagerie*.

Meanwhile, music was attracting widespread interest on campus. By the mid-1920s, there was a chapel choir, Women's Glee and Mandolin Club, Uke Club, Banjo Club, the Amphion Musical Society. No music degree was offered yet, though courses were available

Student *a cappella* groups.
A wide variety of *a cappella* groups performed on campus during the sesquicentennial year. Here, the After Dark ensemble performs in Holmes Lounge.
WU Photographic Services

Tâm Minh Lê.
As a senior, Tâm Minh Lê, A.B. '96, now a choreographer and performer, was named Best College Dance Performer by *Dance Magazine*.
David Kilper, WU Photographic Services

through the Extension Division. Faculty dreamed of a new music building and concert hall, but the music department was not founded until 1947, and it only flourished after Leigh Gerdine became chair in 1950. Through these years, other arts groups were jostling for space. In 1937, Thyrsus moved to a new home — still too small — in Brown Hall (now Brown 100). In 1962, Annalise Mertz founded the Washington University Dance Theatre and five years later the first degree program in dance, holding rehearsals in the cramped Wilson Studio. Opera singers directed by Harold Blumenfeld practiced in several unsatisfactory rooms, like "a three-ring circus," he said.

During the post-war years, drama began a gradual decline, and by 1966, it was foundering. A council chaired by faculty member Egon Schwarz urged the creation of a Performing Arts area, established in 1968. Pressure was also mounting for a new theater, and that project joined forces with plans for a student union — all of which reignited interest in performing arts. Thyrsus won new recruits; South 40 residents put on *The Dutch Courtezan*; and students formed Kadadiz, which once again staged musicals, and revived the Bearskin Follies, a lively competition among fraternities and sororities to write and perform the best skits. In 1972, the 650-seat Edison Theatre was completed, giving the University its first dedicated performing arts space.

Performing Arts did not become a department until 1987, under the leadership of Henry I. Schvey. Meanwhile, many students studied with drama professor Herbert E. Metz, who directed Mary Wickes when she returned to campus in 1968 to star in *The Glass Menagerie*. He also taught Harold Ramis, A.B. '66, who launched

a career as writer, actor, and director by co-writing the comedy *National Lampoon's Animal House* in 1978, followed by such movies as *Ghostbusters* and *Groundhog Day*. Two classmates gravitated to Hollywood as well: Michael Shamberg, A.B. '66, who produced *The Big Chill, A Fish Called Wanda, Pulp Fiction, Reality Bites*, and *Erin Brockovich*; and Arthur ("Buzz") Hirsch, A.B. '66, producer of *Silkwood* and later a visiting professor.

Film was the medium of another graduate, Henry Hampton, A.B. '61. In 1968, he founded Blackside, Inc., then the largest African-American-owned film production company, which produced a series of well-respected documentaries. The best known is the award-winning *Eyes on the Prize* public television series, first aired in 1987. More than 35,000 items used to create the Blackside documentaries are now in the Henry Hampton Collection, a film and media archive at the West Campus Library.

Today, the University's music program includes more than half a dozen *a cappella* groups — including the "Pikers" for men, the "Greenleafs" for women, and the coed "Mosaic Whispers" and "Amateurs" — as well as the Pep Band, Jazz Band, Chamber Choir, Chamber Winds, Chamber Orchestra, Symphony Orchestra, and University Chorus. John H. and Jolly Stewart have developed a new tradition of opera on campus; Edison Theatre hosts theatre, dance, and music in its professional OVATIONS! Series, along with student productions. A young Film and Media Studies program exists in Arts & Sciences, and student drama groups on campus include the All-Student Theatre, along with a growing Performing Arts Department. Ⓦ

A.E. Hotchner.
Hotchner, A.B. '40, J.D. '40, a novelist and playwright, honed his writing as a student in English XVI. He wrote a student play, *Down in Front*, which made law professor Tyrrell Williams suggest that he consider a career outside of the law. Among his works are *Papa Hemingway*, a memoir of his friendship with Ernest Hemingway, and his autobiographical *King of the Hill*, made into a movie in 1993. Hotchner, who has funded the annual A.E. Hotchner Playwriting Competition, received an honorary doctorate in 1992. The A.E. Hotchner Studio Theatre, a 100-seat state-of-the-art black box theatre in Mallinckrodt Center, is named for him.
WU Archives

Henry Hampton (1940-1998).
Hampton, A.B. '61, told the story of the United States' great political and social movements through his documentaries, including *Eyes on the Prize* (1987) and *The Great Depression* (1993).
WU Libraries' Film & Media Archive

Robert Guillaume.
Star of television's *Benson*, Guillaume attended the University from 1956-57. He won Emmy awards in 1979 and 1985 and a Grammy for his reading of the *Lion King*.
WU Archives

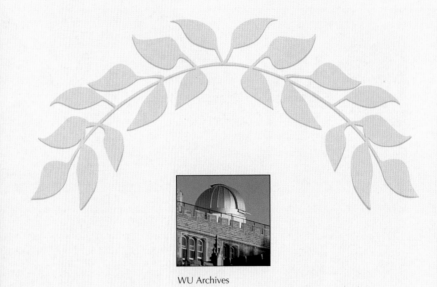

"THE EXIGENCY OF THE TIMES":
The Depression and World War II

1932-1945

A campus transformed by war. Within a year after the attack on Pearl Harbor, 600 ROTC trainees and 1,000 student reservists were on the Hilltop Campus.

WU Archives

"THE EXIGENCY OF THE TIMES"

In 1932, the coincidence of two key events — the 75th anniversary of Washington University's inauguration ceremonies and the bicentennial of George Washington's birth — seemed to cry out for a grand celebration. So in February, Missouri Gov. Henry S. Caulfield, LL.B. '95, addressed a convocation on campus, defying the Depression that was deepening all around him by focusing on happier things: the legacy of George Washington and the "inspiration of his splendid character." Congratulatory messages poured in from other universities and from politicians, including the country's beleaguered president, Herbert Hoover.

Previous pages:
Givens Hall.
Construction of Givens was made possible through a gift from Joseph Givens in 1930 to house the School of Architecture.

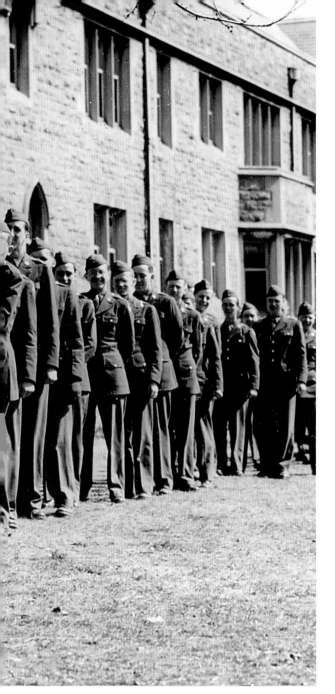

1932 ❧ 1945

1932   *The University celebrated the 75th anniversary of its inauguration ceremonies. William Greenleaf Eliot, Jr. — grandson of the co-founder — was the principal speaker.*

1933   *The University launched an aggressive student recruiting drive to keep enrollment from dropping further.*

1933   *Surgeon Evarts Graham performed the first-ever one-stage lung removal.*

1940   *The University broke ground for a cyclotron, which was completed in 1941.*

1942   *In the wake of Pearl Harbor, Base Hospital No. 21 was reactivated.*

1943   *By fall, half of the 8,905 students on the Hilltop were soldiers.*

1945   *Arthur Holly Compton was named the University's ninth Chancellor.*

Henry S. Caulfield (1873-1966). Caulfield, LL.B. '95, was governor of Missouri from 1929-33. He had previously served as a U.S. Congressman, judge of the Missouri Court of Appeals, and director of the St. Louis Public Library.

George O. James (1873-1931). Formerly Thayer Professor of Applied Mathematics, James was the beloved dean of the College of Liberal Arts for 17 years; he secured the University's first chapter of Phi Beta Kappa in 1914.

There was, after all, some cause for rejoicing. As Chancellor George R. Throop noted in a letter to alumni, the University had produced 15,000 graduates since it opened — a remarkable record of growth. "Yet its hold upon the past is so fresh that it still counts among the living a graduate of the first college class in 1862," he added, referring to 90-year-old Thomas Lamb Eliot, son of University co-founder William Greenleaf Eliot.

Over the previous year, some of the University's schools had taken significant steps forward. Board President Malvern Clopton had enriched the art collection with a dazzling assortment of woodcuts and etchings; Givens Hall was nearly complete. Although its outstanding dean, George O. James, had died suddenly, the College of Liberal Arts had exciting programs such as zoology, which was brimming with new research. The School of Law had named a strong new dean, faculty member Wiley B. Rutledge, Jr.; the School of Botany had lured lichen expert Carroll W. Dodge away from Harvard; and the Extension Division had acquired a new name — University College — as well as a promising affiliation with the Central Institute for the Deaf (CID). At the medical school, the Oscar Johnson Institute, McMillan Hospital Clinics, and Mallinckrodt

THE WHITE HOUSE
WASHINGTON

February 16, 1932.

My dear Dr. Throop:

I extend to you and your associates of the faculty and trustees of Washington University my cordial felicitations upon the celebration of the seventy-fifth anniversary of its inauguration, and my cordial good wishes for its continued growth in the high service of education.

Yours faithfully,

Herbert Hoover

Dr. George R. Throop,
Chancellor, Washington University,
St. Louis, Missouri.

Congratulatory letter from President Herbert Hoover.

All images, WU Archives

Harry Jones (1911-1993).
Jones, LL.B. '34, A.B. '37, graduated with high honors, after serving as editor-in-chief of the law review. He won a Rhodes Scholarship, joined the law faculty in 1935 as its youngest member, and later became a longtime law faculty member at Columbia University.
WU Archives

Institute of Radiology had officially opened.

Just as important, enrollment had not plummeted as it had at many universities. At the start of the 1931-32 school year, 3,438 students were registered, excluding University College, compared to 3,403 the year before. A few schools — Engineering, Graduate Studies, and Business and Public Administration — even showed a marked increase. "The temporary fluctuations in business are but ripples when they reach the educational mill pond," said *Student Life*, brashly confident.

Yet somehow the anniversary seemed muted, half-hearted. In the absence of an official event, students created their own "Eliot Day" on April 22, 1932, with a convocation featuring Harry Jones, LL.B. '34, A.B. '37 — a replacement for famous alumnus, Dwight F. Davis, LL.B. '03, who declined to appear — declaiming portions of the address

Wiley B. Rutledge, Jr. (1894-1949).
Rutledge joined the law faculty in 1926; in 1931, he became dean, then left five years later. From 1943-49, he served as an associate justice of the U.S. Supreme Court. Today, the Wiley Rutledge Moot Court Competition and the Wiley Rutledge Professorship in Law, held by John Owen Haley, are named for him.
WU Archives

Edward Everett gave at the University's gala inaugural ceremony in 1857. During Commencement weekend in June, students again provided the entertainment, performing a play with a Colonial-era theme. In a lone gesture of celebration, the administration had invited a speaker with impeccable credentials: Thomas Lamb Eliot's oldest son, William Greenleaf Eliot, Jr., A.B. '88. He concluded his speech by echoing a Civil War-era sermon of his grandfather's, who was in turn recalling some well-loved words of George Washington, written in 1777:

Malvern Clopton benefits the University – from medicine to art

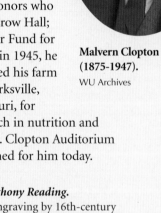

Malvern Clopton, board president from 1932-42, served as chief of the surgical service for Base Hospital No. 21 during World War I and afterward became professor of clinical surgery at the medical school. He was extraordinarily generous to the University. In 1930, he donated $300,000 toward the construction of the Rand-Johnson memorial surgical wing of Barnes Hospital; in 1931, he gave the University his valuable collection of etchings, woodcuts, and engravings;

in 1934, he was one of two donors who funded the construction of Crow Hall; in 1944, he created the Walker Fund for medical school support; and in 1945, he donated his farm in Clarksville, Missouri, for research in nutrition and health. Clopton Auditorium is named for him today.

Malvern Clopton (1875-1947).
WU Archives

St. Anthony Reading.
This engraving by 16th-century artist Albrecht Dürer was one of many works of art Malvern Clopton gave to the University.
WU Gallery of Art

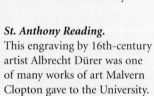

"I quote those simple and noble words again on this great day of the University's life, in this great year of the Nation's history: 'If new difficulties arise we must only put forth new exertions, and proportion our efforts to the exigency of the times.'"

THE UNIVERSITY ASKS FOR "HOARDED DOLLARS"

Behind the scenes, financial difficulties were emerging that *would* require extraordinary exertions. That spring, Throop and his board had quietly discussed making cuts they hoped would not be necessary, but in November 1932, writing in the *Alumni Bulletin*, Throop had bad news for his audience. The $250 annual tuition covered only half the cost of educating a student, he said; the other half came from endowment income — which had fallen by more than $200,000. Gifts were slumping, too, as everyone felt the economic pinch. One problem was the University's investment portfolio, heavily weighted toward real estate: commercial and residential buildings in St. Louis and Kansas City, rice lands in Arkansas, timber lands in Texas, and the Cupples Station warehouses in downtown St. Louis. Selling these properties was impossible in the midst of the Depression, and rental income had dropped as buildings lost tenants.

A month later, Throop announced retrenchments. Salaries for all faculty and staff, including the chancellor, would be cut by four percent, and a year later they dipped again by ten percent. On the Hilltop and at the medical school, faculty agreed to donate teaching services in 1934-35. At the June 1932 Commencement, Throop described a new Alumni Endowment Fund drive, developed by board member Daniel N. Kirby, A.B. '86, LL.B. '88 — but by the next spring, only 94 donors had given, for a modest $4,000. Since Kirby heard that many graduates wanted to donate and could not, he tried a new tactic: mailing chain letters to alumni groups, asking for $1 from as many people as possible. Now the fund grew a little faster, finally topping out at $11,091.50. "I am enclosing one of the hoarded dollars," said one alumnus. "Flatter than a pancake," admitted another, eking out a contribution anyway.

Daniel Noyes Kirby (1864-1945).
Kirby, A.B. '86, LL.B. '88, was an attorney, a part-time lecturer in the law school, and a member of the board. He left three-fifths of his estate to establish a chair honoring his former law partner, Charles Nagel; the chair is now held by Stephen H. Legomsky. The Daniel Noyes Kirby Professorship in Law was established in 1952 and is held by Rebecca Dresser.

STUDENTS "SKIMPING ON…FOOD"

In fall 1933 came a new worry: The daytime student enrollment had declined by 11 percent, reducing tuition income by nearly $100,000. Just as bad was the plight of current students, nearly half of whom would be forced to leave if they could not find part-time employment. "Many were making their way with the greatest difficulty," recalled engineering dean Alexander Langsdorf later, "even to the point of skimping on the food they ate." To attract new students and retain existing ones, the University embarked on a two-pronged effort. In a massive recruitment drive, it developed a pool of 28,000 high school seniors, mailed out catalogues, drafted alumni to talk to prospects, and brought students to campus for special events, such as an oratorical competition, afternoon teas, or "Engineer's Day." For the first time, the University opened the door to midyear admissions, allowing students to finish in three-and-one-half years.

For current students, administrators quietly reduced dormitory rates, provided cafeteria meals at cost, carved up scholarships into smaller pieces, and promoted the University's employment office, which kept a list of jobs: tutoring, office work, or childcare for women; hotel jobs, sales, or manual labor for men. One top woman student "holds in all five jobs — typing and clerical work afternoons, working with an author on his manuscript Sundays, and working for her room and board in between," said *Student Life*. In a given year, the employment office placed some 250 needy students and found full-time jobs for several dozen alumni. Government grants via the Federal Emergency Relief Administration provided part-time employment, paying an average $15 per month.

The University adopted a plan, proposed by its own chapter of the American Association of University Professors, in which 80 out-of-work adults would take under-enrolled, upper-level classes yet pay no tuition. More than two-thirds of the successful applicants, chosen from 400 hopefuls, had been forced to drop out of the University. Through this effort, the largest in the United States, the University was trying "to throw the whole weight of our equipment…into the struggle to preserve the morale and restore the sanity of society," said Throop.

Fundraising plea in the *Alumni Bulletin* in 1933.

GETTING "IN DUTCH"

These years were hard on Throop and his assistant chancellor, Walter McCourt, who loyally stepped in whenever key positions fell vacant. Years earlier, when Alexander Langsdorf resigned to take a job in industry, McCourt — already head of geology — had taken over for eight years until Langsdorf returned as engineering dean in 1928. Now in 1932, after George James' death, McCourt became dean of the College of Liberal Arts until the University filled the post with the popular Frederick Shipley, formerly dean of University College. Throop, too, faced these times with dogged determination, despite the increasing toll on his nerves. He once explained his stubborn devotion to duty by saying that "the first element of success is work, the second is work, and the third is work," recalled Langsdorf.

However, Throop and his dean of students, George S. Stephens, kept a tight rein on students — an unnecessarily restrictive attitude that repeatedly led to trouble. In spring 1932, *Student Life* protested that the administration was trying to curtail Sunday recreation, such as dancing, kite-flying, or tennis. Two years later, 400 students signed petitions hoping to rescind the rule forbidding ankle socks for women; when hot weather arrived, some boldly wore such socks on campus, but Stephens issued reprimands, and no one dared try it again. In 1936, a St. Louis newspaper reported with sly amusement that University women would now have to wear skirts: "Breeches, slacks or any kind of bifurcated outer garments are not for coeds," it giggled. Unlike male students, women were forbidden to smoke on many parts of the campus.

The administration also targeted student publications. Worried that *Student Life* was overly influenced by "Greek cliques," it handed control of the newspaper to a faculty-led committee. Later Throop and Stephens abolished *Dirge*, the campus humor magazine, out of concern for its risqué jokes. Said a student editorial, sadly: "The little humor magazine that got in Dutch had come to be looked upon as an institution at Washington, and its decease has caused not a few sorrowful gulps."

In an especially heavy-handed move, Throop cut off the scholarships of three students — undergraduates Donald Ellinger, A.B. '37, and Philip Monypenny, A.B. '36; and physics graduate student Harold Clark, A.B. '36, M.S. '37 — who had distributed letters to freshmen in 1936, advising them not to join ROTC. Worse still, *Student Life* was warned not to editorialize against this action, a move that caused the editor to resign and stirred up a firestorm of protest — along with a fundraising campaign that allowed the three students to complete their educations. Former board president Charles Nagel was exasperated at Throop's

Central Institute for the Deaf becomes a leader in educating deaf children

C entral Institute for the Deaf (CID), founded by Max Goldstein in 1914, was not originally connected with the University, though its building was adjacent to the Medical Campus. In 1931, that changed when CID and University College affiliated to offer a teacher-training course leading to a B.S. in Special Education. Students took their first two years at the University and their last two at CID.

Goldstein, an 1892 Missouri Medical College graduate and an internationally respected otologist and educator, invented one of the earliest hearing devices, "the simplex tube."

Max Goldstein (1870-1941).
WU Becker Medical Library

In 1939, at CID's 25th anniversary, visiting speaker Helen Keller praised the institute as "breaking trails for an understanding life for the deaf." Goldstein assembled a collection of 920 rare books on otology and deaf education, which CID donated to the University in 1977. In late 2003, the research and college-degree-granting programs of CID were slated to become part of the Department of Otolaryngology at Washington University School of Medicine.

The second CID building opened in 1929 at 818 S. Euclid Avenue.
Central Institute for the Deaf

handling of the matter. "It is one thing to admonish," he wrote to Wiley Rutledge, "it is quite another to impose a cash penalty which…gave an opportunity to the student body to express their views by reimbursing the student[s]."

DARK DAYS, BRIGHT MOMENTS

The University's aggressive recruitment campaign had stanched the loss of students — enrollment went up by 15 percent in 1934 and 11 percent in 1935 — but gifts were still way down, and so was endowment income. A new comptroller, Thomas Blackwell, helped by grabbing hold of the University's finances: centralizing purchasing, controlling expenses, taking charge of the budget. The problems continued, even after the 1933-35

trough of the Depression was past, and did not really end until World War II began. Starting in 1932, the University was embroiled in fighting two costly though ultimately successful battles, one in St. Louis and the other in Kansas City, to preserve the tax-exempt status of its commercial properties — fights that convinced the University to limit its city real estate acquisitions.

This ongoing crisis was bound to fray the University's academic fabric. Some faculty slots went unfilled; remaining faculty often waited years for promotion or turned to the lucrative pursuit of writing textbooks. A few sterling appointments took place, though, including sociologist Stuart A. Queen, who in 1935 headed a newly combined department of sociology and anthropology; Benno Lischer, who had earlier served as professor of orthodontics, as dean of the School of Dentistry in 1933; and George Mylonas, a well-known classical archaeologist, who chaired the Department of Art and Archaeology for the next 25 years.

Despite the efforts of its dean, W. McKim Marriott, the medical school was affected, too, with a 20 percent decline in spend-

ing from 1930-38 and a static, $4.5 million endowment. Rand-Johnson and McMillan Hospitals remained unfinished; "Depression Costs Washington U. Its Chief Eye Doctor" announced local headlines, in 1932, as ophthalmology head Harvey Howard resigned, saying his research had been curtailed. Although faculty could draw from a $240,000 research fund, established by the Rockefeller Foundation — the funding source that had replaced the General Education Board in 1929 — other support began to fall off. Important work by cytologist Edmund V. Cowdry into the roots of infantile paralysis was temporarily derailed when grant money from his New York funder disappeared.

One bright spot was the 1931 arrival of Carl F. Cori, with his equally distinguished wife, Gerty T. Cori, to head pharmacology in place of Herbert Gasser. Another was the quality of the student body, which continued strong and geographically diverse, drawing from 31 states and three countries in 1931. Soon the medical school began reaching out to alumni, offering postgraduate courses, and in 1938, a new program put down roots with establishment of the Elias Michael Professorship in Occupational Therapy. Three years later, the school decided to refine its entrance requirements, including personal qualities, such as "interest, initiative and industry, health and character."

Edmund V. Cowdry (1888-1975).
Cowdry, who became head of cytology in 1928, studied tropical diseases such as yellow fever and malaria and later specialized in cancer. He succeeded Robert Terry as professor of anatomy in 1941. In 1938, he became the first faculty member to receive funding from the National Institutes of Health (NIH).

Benno Lischer (1876-?).
Lischer, DMD '00, had been professor of orthodontics at the School of Dentistry from 1902-24, and returned in 1933 to receive a Distinguished Alumnus Award from the University.

A luminous moment came in 1933, when Evarts Graham, celebrated head of surgery, performed the first successful, one-stage pneumonectomy (lung removal) in medical history. The medical school and Barnes Hospital were national leaders in plastic surgery as well, primarily through the work of the "Three Bs": Vilray P. Blair, M.D. '93; James Barrett Brown, M.D. '23; and Louis Byars, M.D. '32. Ernest Sachs continued his pioneering work in neurosurgery and joined with others, such as neurologist Sidney I. Schwab, in establishing a neuropsychiatry department in 1938 using a $150,000 grant from the ever-helpful Rockefeller Foundation. On the medical side, researchers — such as pathologist Margaret Smith — played a crucial role in studying the 1933 St. Louis encephalitis epidemic. In 1936 Mallinckrodt Institute's Wendell G. Scott and director Sherwood Moore, M.D. '05, designed a kymograph, which can "record on X-ray film the beating of a heart," said the *Alumni Bulletin*.

Margaret Smith (1896-1970).
Smith was a pediatric pathologist who worked in the area of viral diseases. Her epidemiological studies helped trace the cause of the 1933 St. Louis encephalitis outbreak. The Margaret Smith Award is given to a sophomore woman medical student each year.

TRANSFORMATIONS ON THE HILLTOP CAMPUS

Givens Hall finally opened late in 1932, a long-held dream of its dean, Gabriel Ferrand, who had designed its sweeping staircase himself and saw the building as "acknowledgment of the noble desire to foster architectural progress." Arthur Hughes, who had succeeded Arthur Holly Compton in 1923 as Wayman Crow Professor of Physics, wanted the same acknowledgment for his own department, still languishing in cramped, outdated Eads Hall. His dream came true in 1933 when Edward Mallinckrodt, Jr., and Malvern Clopton donated $700,000 anonymously to construct a fine new physics building, named for University co-founder Crow. Eads Hall then became the home of psychology, education, and philosophy.

In 1935, work began on a social work building — funded by a bequest of Bettie Bofinger Brown in honor of her late husband, George Warren Brown — which included a 200-seat lecture hall and a 500-seat public auditorium. It had an unusual feature that she designed herself — a large, second-floor social room, still used today and known as Brown Lounge. The building, completed in 1937 and dedicated in a gala ceremony, was said to be the first in the United States built solely for the purpose of social work. At the beginning, it was big enough to accommodate other departments, too: history and political science on the first floor, and sociology and anthropology on the second.

Through these years, University College, with its popular evening and weekend courses, was the busiest school with 2,130 students in 1933. Under Shipley and then the new dean, classics professor Frank Debatin, A.B. '12, A.M. '13, it offered innovative courses, such as Chinese and Russian, and degree-granting programs: a B.S. in journalism,

Evarts Graham performs first successful lung removal

In 1933, a 49-year-old Pittsburgh physician, James Gilmore, was diagnosed with lung cancer and scheduled for surgery at Barnes Hospital. Evarts Graham, the Bixby Professor of Surgery, planned to remove a lobe of his left lung, but discovered during surgery that the cancer had spread further and that Gilmore's only hope was removal of his entire lung. The procedure — the first one-stage pneumonectomy in medical history — was a success: Gilmore lived another 30 years, cancer-free.

Later, Graham, in collaboration with Ernest Wynder, established tobacco's relation to lung cancer. Ironically, Graham himself — who had smoked for 50 years — died of lung cancer in 1957, six years before Gilmore. He had won a host of awards, including the prestigious Lister Medal in 1942; the Lister committee called him "the Dean of American Surgery." He also served as president of the American

Evarts Graham (1883-1957).
Herb Weitman, WU Photographic Services

College of Surgeons. After his death, the University's board paid tribute to Graham for "his brilliant and courageous achievements in surgery and medical research."

Graham's wife of 41 years, Helen Tredway Graham, was remarkable in her own right. She received a Ph.D. in chemistry and physics from the University of Chicago in 1915, then joined the Department of Pharmacology as an associate professor in 1925, becoming a full professor in 1955. One son, David T. Graham (1917-1999), was assistant professor of medicine from 1951-57.

Helen Tredway Graham (1891-1971).
WU Becker Medical Library

---

beginning in 1932; a cooperative arrangement with the School of Fine Arts, which did not offer its own degrees until 1941, to give bachelor's degrees to prospective art teachers; a master's degree in education, starting in 1936. In 1939, the creative Debatin — who was killed in an auto accident in 1940 — persuaded Throop to let him renovate the vacant Mary Institute building at Lake and Waterman for an Adult Education Center to house continuing education classes, a vocational guidance clinic, a photography program, and a performing arts venture — the St. Louis School of the Theater, in collaboration with the Little Theater. Under the deft management of business dean Isidor Loeb, the summer school was growing and had courses from every school; the English department offered 20 classes, the greatest number of all.

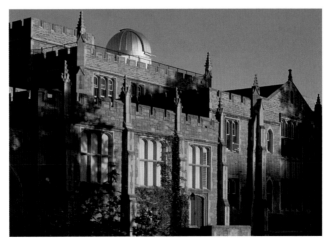

Wayman Crow Hall.
The new physics building opened in January 1934 with a ceremony attended by descendants of Wayman Crow. As Arthur Hughes planned it, the building's modular design can adapt to office, classroom, or laboratory space.
WU Photographic Services

Brown Hall.
Completed in 1937, Brown Hall became the new home for social work.
WU Archives

Other schools faced an array of problems, largely related to money. Despite talented faculty like Alexander Langsdorf, who developed an instrument to measure smoke, Engineering was falling behind. Chemical engineering had failed to win accreditation in 1937 because of aging laboratories and apparatus. While Architecture's move to Givens freed up space in Cupples I, the school lacked critical equipment, which Langsdorf listed in a troubling 1938 report to alumni. Three years later, an "angel" who had read Langsdorf's plea — Francis E. Schwentler, an engineer and 1888 Manual Training School graduate

"The three Bs" — national leaders in plastic surgery

From 1917 until his death, Vilray P. Blair, M.D. '93, was professor of clinical surgery at the medical school and chief of plastic surgery at Barnes Hospital, with a joint appointment in dentistry. He became the leading American surgeon in the young field of facial reconstruction. His operating room was unconventional, decorated with jungle scenes and cherubs. In 1938, the American Board of Plastic Surgery was founded in his St. Louis living room. His son, Vilray, Jr., an orthopaedic surgeon, was on the faculty from 1951-78.

In 1925, Blair hired plastic surgery fellow James Barrett Brown, M.D. '23, who succeeded him in

Vilray P. Blair (1871-1955).
WU Becker Medical Library

James Barrett Brown (1899-1971).
WU Archives

1940. Together, they revolutionized plastic surgery with a technique for split-thickness skin grafting. Brown became a world expert in head-and-neck abnormalities. During World War II, he was Chief of Plastic and Reconstructive Surgery for the U.S. Army, and afterwards was known as "miracle man" at Valley Forge Hospital, where his plastic surgery service performed some 15,000 operations on returning wounded. An award and a visiting professorship at the medical school are named for him today.

Louis T. ("Bill") Byars, M.D. '32, joined the plastic surgery division in 1934. A gifted surgeon, he was known for ear reconstruction; he served as a University board member from 1962-69. Others in the group were Frank McDowell, who joined in 1939, and Minot Fryer in 1946.

Louis T. ("Bill") Byars (1907-1969).
WU Becker Medical Library

stunned Langsdorf by donating the still-missing apparatus, at a cost of nearly $89,000.

Law felt the pinch, too. After Rutledge's departure, the obliging Tyrrell Williams became acting dean for a third time until Joseph A. McClain, a Yale J.S.D. and former dean at Mercer, took over in 1936. Believing that lawyers needed three things — "character, ability, and a sense of social responsibility" — McClain tried to create a legal aid office and summer law office apprenticeships for students but was frustrated by lack of money. Still, the school managed to establish a new *Washington University Law Quarterly* in 1936, the Order of the Coif in 1937, and a program change in 1939 that required law students to spend six years at the University, three of them at the law school. An ambitious 1938 fundraising campaign did not reach its million-dollar goal but raised half that — enough to provide a much-needed budget increase.

CAMPUS LIFE IN THE 1930S

The Depression was having an impact on athletics as well. In 1931, fencing was abolished; in 1933, the swim coach was released, but basketball quietly racked up a series of wins and football continued, though the team posted a weak 2-7 record in the 1931 season. Dismayed alumni were mollified when the popular James ("Jimmy") Conzelman, star quarterback of the 1919 Bears football team and former co-owner of a National Football League franchise team, was appointed head coach in 1932. He was, raved the *Post-Dispatch*, "one of the greatest football players and perhaps the most versatile athlete ever developed in the St. Louis

district." *Student Life* couldn't believe this stroke of luck. "The Administration Comes Through," read the jubilant headline.

Soon the University's football fortunes improved. In Conzelman's first season, the Bears beat the University of Missouri for only the third time in 25 years and then played teams from the Big Ten, such as the University of Illinois "Illini," and the Big Six, such as the Kansas "Jayhawks." In 1936, the Bears faced Notre Dame, but lost 14-6. From nearly 19,000 in 1932, attendance soared to 64,000 in 1933. That year's team included Captain Glynn Clark, A.B. '34, and Ray Hobbs, A.B. '36, who received honorable mention on the Associated Press All-American team. Clark and Dwight Hafeli, B.S. '37, later a coach himself, made the All-Missouri Valley teams.

On the buoyant pages of *Student Life*, which gleefully reported each athletic and social triumph, the Depression was little in evidence. Nearly every issue featured the crowning of a new Queen and her court: the Homecoming Queen, Hatchet Queen, Masque Queen, Beaux Arts Queen, May Queen, Engineer's Queen. In 1939, even the newspaper itself seemed a little fed up. With "this over-abundance of queens," it said, the University had become "the Hollywood of the mid-West," adding that there would soon be "20 or more ex- and contemporary queens stalking the campus byways." For men, there was a chance to become "Kampus King."

Students who could afford it joined sororities (11 on campus in 1933, pledging 135 new members) and fraternities (16, pledging 198), with a controversial "Hell Week" initiation for fraternity recruits. A 1934 editorial spoke of the great divide between the student "snobs" and the "underdogs":

> "The first…who, through fortunate circumstances, are provided with adequate resources, both financial and intellectual, to make the way easy…the second group is composed of people who, though very often equally as intelligent as the first, are handicapped by uncontrollable circumstances."

Despite larger ambitions, the University still drew 75 percent of its 1932 students from Missouri, 50 percent from St. Louis. Among the students were siblings, successive generations within families, and children of faculty. In 1932, Alice Trescott Chaplin, granddaughter of Chancellor Chaplin, was the May Queen, while John L. Horner, grandson of Chancellor Hall, was president of the Men's Glee Club, and his brother, Richard, became the newest Rhodes Scholar in 1935. Faculty children included Louise Berger, daughter of mechanical engineering professor Franz Berger, and Bessie Chambers, daughter of philosophy professor Lawson Chambers.

Joseph McClain (1903-1970). Named law dean in 1936, McClain urged the school to develop new courses in trial and appellate procedures.
WU Archives

Washington University vs. Notre Dame. The official program for the October 10, 1936, Bears football game at Notre Dame Stadium.
WU Archives

Five University wartime heroes

Capt. Richard A. Sutter (c. 1909-1999).
WU Archives

With three volunteers from Battery "B," Capt. Arthur E. Huff, B.S.C.E. '32, restored the American flag to a 100-foot flagpole on the highest point of Corregidor while under heavy fire in April 1942. He won the Silver Star for this action. Captain Huff died a prisoner of the Japanese, when the ship in which he was imprisoned was sunk en route to Japan in December 1944.

Maj. Gerald H. Hoffman, B.S.C.E. '30, took part in the Bataan Death March and was incarcerated in a Japanese prison camp, where dysentery eventually caused his death. Major Hoffman was one of several University men lost on Bataan. A bench in the Quadrangle honors him today.

Lt. Cdr. McClelland Barclay, an art student on the University's downtown campus, became one of the nation's best-known commercial artists for magazines like *The Ladies' Home Journal* and *Saturday Evening Post*. A 51-year-

Capt. Arthur E. Huff (1908-1944).
WU Archives

Maj. Gerald H. Hoffman (c. 1910-c. 1944).
WU Archives

old naval reservist when war broke out, he volunteered for active duty, served as a combat artist in the Pacific Theatre, and died when his landing craft was torpedoed by a Japanese submarine.

In 1942, Capt. Richard A. Sutter, A.B. '31, M.D. '35, of the U.S. Army Medical Reserve Corps, landed at Normandy two months after D-Day and supported combat troops during the Battle of Northern France, the Battle of the Bulge, and later action. Promoted to lieutenant colonel, he received the Bronze Star. In 1985, Sutter and his wife established the Richard A. and Betty H. Sutter Visiting Professorship in Occupational and Industrial Medicine at the medical school.

Lt. Cdr. C. Barber Mueller, M.D. '42, took part in the Marshall Islands campaign and the invasions of Saipan and Tinian, but said in a 1945 *Globe-Democrat* article that six hours on Iwo Jima were worse than all the rest: More than one-third of his corpsmen were among the casualties, and he was struck by mortar shell fragments. Mueller is the author of a biography: *Evarts A. Graham: The Life, Lives, and Times of the Surgical Spirit of St. Louis* (BC Decker: 2002).

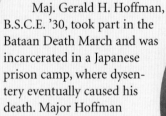

Lt. Cdr. McClelland Barclay (1891-1943).
Bettman/CORBIS

Lt. Cdr. C. Barber Mueller.
WU Becker Medical Library

By then, women were peppering the faculty: Jessica Young Stephens, A.B. '14, who taught a popular astronomy course; others in chemistry, applied sociology, zoology, French, nursing, weaving, pathology, commerce, and finance. Winifred C. Magdsick, A.B. '31, A.M. '32, Ph.D. '34, a psychology faculty member, became assistant dean in 1939 — the first woman administrator. More women than ever were studying in the professional schools. In 1935 Law had 12, and in 1939 Medicine had 23

— five Phi Beta Kappas among them — "and we are not a down-trodden group," declared one.

"THE WAR GOD AWAKENS" AGAIN

Editorials in *Student Life* had begun to detail, with growing dread, new troubles brewing in Europe and Manchuria. Memories of World War I, only two decades past, were still fresh enough that the University solemnly marked Armistice Day each

November. Was it possible that the country would soon be drawn into a new conflict? History faculty member Roland Usher, who had predicted war in 1914, now returned to KSD radio and the lecture circuit, though in 1932 he still hoped that war could be averted. Some students signed up with ROTC or the Pershing Rifles, while others joined the active peace movement, calling ROTC "an instrument of the War Department" which "inculcates a spirit of militarism among students."

By 1934, the editorials were taking a more anxious tone. "The War God Awakens," announced one, fretting about student involvement. Students staged strikes against potential conflict and held well-attended peace rallies. In 1935 Roland Usher changed his mind, saying that war was now possible, and the 1936 peace rally was the biggest yet, with a parade of 70 cars from campus groups, decorated in red, white, and blue. ROTC, on the other hand, soon had remodeled facilities in Cupples II and an arsenal of equipment; in 1938 alone, its enrollment grew by 70 percent. "No one wants war," said Major Harrison Cochran, new ROTC head, "but if it comes the trained man will stand a better chance for survival."

Gradually, as the European conflict widened, student and faculty attitudes shifted. Late in 1938, Usher was arguing for U.S. involvement: "We can stay out of world events," he said grimly, "but we can stay out only at a price." Early in 1939, a student editorial noted "a marked abatement" in campus pacifism and later that year another condemned other schools for their "naïve peace demonstrations." Law dean Joseph McClain and faculty member E.E. Hilpert resigned from the local America First Committee in 1941, after Charles Lindbergh made anti-Semitic remarks. "To characterize one's political opponents by calling names or according to racial origin or religious affiliation is wholly inexcusable," Hilpert said.

June 1941.
Wartime propaganda posters were on display in the Ridgley Library reading room.
Photo by Frank Darr

That spring, University juniors became the first U.S. students to donate the proceeds from their prom to British war relief, and letters flooded in from politicians endorsing their effort: British prime minister Winston Churchill, British ambassador Lord Halifax, President Franklin D. Roosevelt. Architecture student Adrienne Palan was crowned Hatchet Queen at the ball, which attracted 2,000 people — including the entire faculty — to hear "King of Swing" Benny Goodman play in Convention Hall. As one student wrote: "The dance was on the colossal side" and "a magnificent success."

Student interest in national politics also heated up. In a 1932 campus straw poll, Republican incumbent Herbert Hoover beat Roosevelt in the race for president; so did Alf Landon in 1936. On October 18, 1940, students turned out to gawk as Republican Wendell Willkie made a brief speech from the Brookings Hall steps during a trip to St. Louis sponsored by Edgar Queeny, Monsanto Company president and a University board member. Soon after, another poll showed 56 percent of students favoring Willkie, with 36 percent for Roosevelt, five percent undecided, and three percent for socialist Norman Thomas, who had been a frequent lecturer on campus.

Just days before Willkie's visit, male students and faculty from 21 to 36 lined up in the old Brookings chapel to register for the first peacetime draft. Already, students were leaving to enlist; 39 enrolled in a Civilian Pilot Training Program sponsored by the Civil Aeronautics Authority. Carolyn Lorenz, A.B. '42, a business student, was the only woman to sign up — and early in 1940 she beat all the men in the flight program by becoming the first trainee to "solo." Peace week in 1940 had a somber, demoralized tone. "As the long-mobilized armies of Europe finally come to grips in the first really decisive action of the present war," said *Student Life*, "there is a new note of grim reality added to the more academic discussions of the past several years. War is here — now."

Peace Day 1936.
The third annual Peace Day featured a 70-vehicle motorcade through the western part of the St. Louis region, including parts of the Hilltop Campus. The peace movement eroded rapidly as the war engulfed Europe, but still managed to maintain a presence until Pearl Harbor.

Benny Goodman swings.
The 1941 Junior Prom, featuring Benny Goodman and his band, was a stupendous success — "the junior prom we've always dreamed about," said one student. Its proceeds went to British war relief; the British Ambassador, Lord Halifax, sent a note thanking the students for "sympathiz[ing] so ardently with the causes for which the entire British Commonwealth of Nations is at war."

All photos, WU Archives

165

A Cyclotron for Peace — and War

In 1938, physicist Arthur Hughes strongly recommended to Chancellor Throop that the University build an 80-ton cyclotron to produce radioisotopes that could be used in medical and biological research. To help plan the project, he visited the handful of other U.S. centers that already had cyclotrons, among them the University of California, and there he met with cyclotron inventor Ernest Lawrence, who received the 1939 Nobel Prize for his work. Lawrence strongly backed Hughes, writing in 1939 that Washington University "offers an ideal set-up for a medical cyclotron project." Convinced of its potential, Mallinckrodt Institute director Sherwood Moore applied for funding to the Rockefeller Foundation, which granted $60,000 in 1939 — provided that the University bear operating costs for seven years.

Langsdorf and Hughes — University fathers and sons

Alexander Langsdorf, Sr., was engineering dean during the war years; his son, Alexander Langsdorf, Jr., A.B. '32, physics instructor on the Hilltop Campus and applied physicist at Mallinckrodt Institute of Radiology, came to the University in 1941 from the University of California to help design and build its new cyclotron, then he moved on to the Metallurgical Laboratory in Chicago, directed by Arthur H. Compton.

The cyclotron was a special project of Arthur Hughes, Wayman Crow Professor of Physics and department chair from 1923-55, who urged the University to build it in 1939. In 1943, he left for 15 months on a top-secret assignment: serving as assistant director of the Los Alamos atomic energy project. After the war, he returned to the University, along with an outstanding group of Los Alamos chemists.

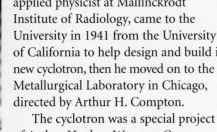

Alexander Langsdorf, Jr. (1913-1996).
WU Archives

One son was J. Peter Hughes, B.S.B.A. '43. The other, David F. Hughes, A.B. '42, a physics major, wrote about his father's cyclotron for *Eliot* magazine. It took 16 and one-half months to produce its "first baby proton beam. If you've ever seen a young boy with his first electric train, you will have a little idea of the radiant joy in their faces." The cyclotron itself "is pretty awe inspiring....It is ninety five tons of copper, lead, brass, and iron....Most of this weight is in a gigantic magnet fifteen feet high."

During the war, David Hughes became a naval aviator, losing his life on a mission off the coast of Hainan Island in January 1945; he earned the Distinguished Flying Cross and two Navy Crosses for heroism. During flight training, he kept a journal that eloquently chronicles his feelings about the war, life and death, and his own future. In April 1943, after a near-miss, he wrote: "I am living on borrowed time....Every second person you meet has cheated death in some manner or other. Every tenth person is dead....I don't think any of us is afraid of death itself, we just hate to leave this transitory life with so much left undone."

David Hughes (1920-1945).
Courtesy of J. Peter Hughes

University cyclotron.
Through the work of Arthur Hughes and others, ground was broken for a cyclotron on the Hilltop Campus in 1940. It became operational late in 1941.
WU Archives

Nervously, the University broke ground early in 1940 for an underground chamber just west of the Power Plant on the Hilltop Campus. Lawrence sent two young physicists, Robert L. Thornton and Alexander Langsdorf, Jr., A.B. '32, to oversee the cyclotron's design, construction, and operation. Its 78-ton steel magnet, bragged *Student Life*, "is the second largest in the country." Late in 1941, it was finished and "within a month after the first test run was made, the cyclotron had developed the highest intensity of bombarding particles ever attained with an instrument of its size," wrote the senior Langsdorf proudly.

Meanwhile, Arthur Holly Compton, now on the University of Chicago faculty, was working on a top-secret project that would soon depend on Washington University's cyclotron. In fall 1941, he wrote that a bomb "of superlatively destructive power" could be built if only enough uranium were available.

December 7, 1941

Then came the surprise attack on Pearl Harbor — and lingering isolationism soon evaporated. "Lick Hell Out of 'Em," thundered *Student Life*, in a strident new voice. "There is no recourse, no answer, but war." With this new reality came the sense that the innocent old world had changed forever. As Tom Ottenad, A.B. '43, later recalled: "Pearl Harbor forced upon us…the realization that what affected one part of the world affected another and that we, university and students alike, were parts of the world. It forced upon us the realization that we were lagging far behind."

It was time to catch up, and quickly. Throop, speaking to a crowd that filled every seat in Graham Chapel and spilled into the aisles, announced a month later that Washington University was on a wartime basis. To help male students finish undergraduate degrees before they were 21 and eligible for the draft, the University offered an accelerated, two-and-two-thirds-year schedule featuring three semesters and year-round classes; the medical and dental school calendar speeded up as well, with three years to a degree. A newly formed Civilian Defense Council (later the War Emergency Council) signed up volunteers immediately. The curriculum, especially in University College, now included war-related courses: world weather; nautical astronomy; the history of Germany, France, and Italy; and unfamiliar languages such as Japanese, Russian, and Chinese.

Physical education for men became mandatory as old activities were suspended. The University's vibrant social life dwindled; baseball, swimming, golf, and tennis ended for the duration — so did the football program, which had lost Jimmy Conzelman in 1940 in a controversial, forced resignation that left students angry. Frank ("Butch") Loebs, an All-American end who had coached for three years under Conzelman, briefly became head coach, promising a squad that was "tough and colorful." During these years, Wilson ("Bud") Schwenk, B.S.B.A. '42, was the team's star, setting three national records, and in December 1941 the Student Senate voted to permanently retire his number, 42.

Despite appeals by administrators not to rush off and enlist, students left in droves, stripping fraternities to the bone. Within a year of Pearl Harbor, 1,400 students and graduates were in active service with the armed forces, ROTC had 600 trainees, and 1,000 student reservists were on campus. While faculty who had fled Nazi oppression were arriving, others were departing to fight, teach in Army ground schools, or take a war-related assignment. English professor John F. McDermott, for example, left to do military intelligence work. Meanwhile, University botanists scoured South American jungles for sources of rubber and quinine. In 1943, Alice Schriver, director of physical education, was commissioned a lieutenant in the WAVES, the first woman faculty member in the armed forces.

Notices soon appeared of University men serving in celebrated actions, such as the Battle of Midway or the bombing of Holland. Some were killed: Lieut. Donald V. Urquhart, A.B. '41, in a bomber crash; Lieut. Richard L. Root, ex-'41, in the Philippines; Ensign Philip Joyce, ex-'42, who had a destroyer escort vessel named for him. Others, like Lieut. Milton Modalsky, LL.B. '38, on board the sunken destroyer *Blue*, were missing in action. Closer to home, St. Louis Mayor William Dee Becker, LL.B. '01, and Thomas Dysart, LL.B. '03, president of the St. Louis Chamber of Commerce, were killed in the crash of an Army glider at Lambert–St. Louis Field.

At the medical school, the much-honored Base Hospital No. 21 was reactivated within weeks of Pearl Harbor, and 60 officers, soon joined by 55 St. Louis nurses, were sent to Fort

Wilson ("Bud") Schwenk. Schwenk, B.S.B.A. '42, was a baseball player and football star who dominated for the Bears, offensively and defensively, from 1939-42, setting three national records. In his honor, the Student Senate voted to retire his number, 42.
WU Archives

Alice Schriver. In 1943, Schriver became the first woman faculty member in the armed forces.
WU Archives

Croix de guerre. French Gen. Georges Marie Revers presents the Croix de guerre to 21st General Hospital commander Col. Lee D. Cady, M.D. '22, in July 1945.
WU Becker Medical Library

W. Randolph Lovelace II (1907-1965).
Lovelace, A.B. '30, a Mayo Clinic surgeon, developed a strong interest in aviation medicine, winning the Robert J. Collier Trophy of the National Aeronautic Association in 1940. He was a co-developer of the oxygen mask that crews used on high-altitude missions during World War II. In 1964, he became Director of Space Medicine in NASA's Office of Manned Space Flight.
Courtesy of New Mexico Museum of Space History

Benning, Georgia. While one part of this group became the 21st Station Hospital and served in Eritrea, Persia, and Palestine, most of it formed the 21st General Hospital under Lt.Col. Lee D. Cady, M.D. '22, and, as the front advanced, served three different overseas locations: Bou Hanifia, in North Africa; Naples, Italy; and Mirecourt, France. Altogether, the medical team — which included neurosurgeon Capt. Henry G. Schwartz, ophthalmologist Capt. E.B. Alvis, and cardiologist Maj. Joseph Edwards — treated 65,503 patients, both Allied war wounded and POWs, winning the *Croix de guerre avec palme* in 1945 and a host of other citations: 70 Bronze stars, 21 Legion of Merit medals, and nine Purple Hearts.

ON THE HOMEFRONT

Amid these tidings of war came a heartening piece of home news: Wallace and Lucille Renard were donating $250,000 for a neuropsychiatry department endowment fund and named professorship. On the Hilltop, social work — up to then a department within the business school — was working toward a final separation in 1945, creating the George Warren Brown School of Social Work. This move fulfilled the long-held wish

War Service Honor Roll.
Student Life editor Shirley Parks wrote that the newly mounted honor roll in Ridgley Arcade was dedicated "to the men upon whom we have placed the burden, the suffering, the sacrifice, the Hell of war…who will bring the dawn of hope, the light of Victory, and the sunshine of peace."
WU Archives

of social work's guiding spirit, Frank Bruno, who retired a few months later; Benjamin E. Youngdahl, a faculty member since 1939, became dean of the new school.

In 1942, just months after the cyclotron was completed, the government's Office of Scientific Research and Development contracted with the University to use it for another purpose: producing plutonium for Compton's Metallurgical Laboratory team in Chicago from uranium refined at

Students train on an obstacle course (above and right) in April 1943.
WU Archives

Mallinckrodt Chemical Works in St. Louis. The amount supplied by the University was miniscule but significant, providing more than half of all that was needed by the end of that crucial first year of 1942. Compton later said that "the availability of a sufficient quantity of plutonium for microanalysis in 1942 shortened the time required for the development of the entire project by many months."

Until 1943, when he was called to a secret, top-priority assignment in Los Alamos, New Mexico, Arthur Hughes took charge of the St. Louis cyclotron group, and then Frank W. Bubb, B.S.M.E. '16, A.M. '17, head of applied mathematics, took his place. Other ties developed to the Los Alamos project, where the first atomic bombs were built: Radiation biologist Louis H. Hempelmann, Jr., A.B. '34, M.D. '38, instructor in radiology, became director of the Health Division at Los Alamos, and other faculty members monitored fallout from the experimental blast at Alamogordo. H.W. Fulbright, A.B. '40, M.S. '42, Ph.D. '44, and Arthur Knudsen both served as physicists for the University's cyclotron, then moved over to Los Alamos. Martin Kamen, later associate professor of biological chemistry, was the chemist in charge of uranium recovery and processing at the University of California's Radiation Laboratory.

On campus, students and faculty rolled bandages, gave blood to an active blood bank and held USO dances. To rally support for war bonds, movie stars Gene Tierney, Errol Flynn, and Anthony Quinn appeared at the Field House. The Chancellor's residence, now Alumni House at 6510 Wallace Circle, became the headquarters of a Red Cross unit, while scrap metal drives confiscated familiar objects, such as the old radio tower atop Eads Hall and the locomotive rim on Francis Field, used to chime the Bears' touchdowns.

Meantime, some schools — especially Engineering — were booming, with a record number of students in fall 1942. On the other hand, Law was down to 28 in 1943 from a pre-war average of 150; Saint Louis University closed its law school completely and sent the remaining students to Washington University. The 1942 summer school was "more important than at any time in its history," said the *Hatchet*, with 2,600 students registered from 34 states. With nearly 200 faculty away, all these courses strained the remaining faculty to the limit. "Physicists are now worth their weight in gold," grumbled Throop, "and mathematicians are not far behind."

Soon the campus filled up with special programs, such as the Engineering, Science, Management War Training Program (ESMWT), administered by the U.S. Office of Education, which brought evening students to campus for defense training courses. In 1943, hundreds of Army Air Force cadets and meteorological students, Army basic and advanced engineering students, Army premedical students, and others began arriving, taking over men's dormitories and fraternity houses. With Architecture below 40 students, Givens became a barracks; McMillan also fell to the men — its women residents moved off campus to temporary quarters at 22 Kingsbury Place or the Usona Hotel at Kingshighway and Waterman. In August 1943, there were 8,905 students, and half the student body was made up of soldiers.

With internment of people of Japanese descent under way on the West coast, the first group of Japanese-American students, assigned to the University by the National Japanese-American Student Relocation Council, came to campus in fall 1942. There were 28, scattered through eight different programs; 23 eventually graduated. "The attitude of the University is that these students, if American citizens, have exactly the same rights as other students who desire to register in the University," said Throop. The Japanese-American students faced no restrictions on campus, living in the dorms and enrolling in extracurricular activities as they wished.

In October 1942, the University paused to dedicate a War Service Honor Roll, hung in the Ridgley Arcade. By 1943, it listed 2,530 students and alumni, with 29 among the dead and 13 prisoners of war or missing in action. Six former University students were captured on Bataan alone. Like others, *Student Life* editor Shirley Parks was moved: "These men have gone before us, they have stood where we are standing, they have walked where we are walking, they have laughed as we now laugh, they have cried in sorrow as we are crying." Eventually, 5,723 Washingtonians served and 150 were lost in the war effort.

David P. Wohl, Sr. (1886-1960) and David P. Wohl, Jr. (left). David P. Wohl, Jr., a World War II bombardier, was lost in action over Berlin in 1944. His father, founder of the Wohl Shoe Company, honored his son's memory through generous gifts that made possible construction of the David P. Wohl, Jr. Memorial Hospital and the David P. Wohl, Jr.–Washington University Clinics Building. He was a board member from 1950 until his death.

Painting of David Wohl Sr. by C.J. Fox. Painting of David Wohl Jr. by Charles F. Galt.

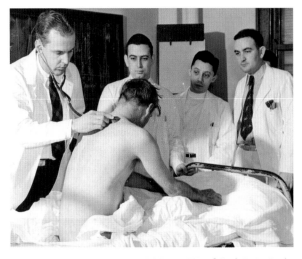

W. Barry Wood, Jr. (1910-1971). At age 32, William Barry Wood, Jr. (far left), became head of internal medicine, one of the youngest men in the nation to hold such a position. He spent 13 years at the University, attracting a superb group of house officers, among them Robert J. Glaser, Edward Reinhard, and Llewellyn J. Sale, Jr.; he also did research on the host response to pneumococcus. He left in 1955, after turning down the chancellorship.

All images, WU Becker Medical Library

The End of the Throop Era

All the while, Throop's unrelenting efforts to improve the University's finances continued. In 1939, the board hired a professional fundraising firm, Tambyln and Tambyln of New York, to survey the University's needs. The results were disquieting. Compared to similar institutions, the University was close to the bottom in everything — endowment, income, and salaries — and a $10 million endowment drive was needed. At Harry Brookings Wallace's prodding, the board instead created the Sustaining Associates Fund in which local businesses made ongoing pledges of support.

This idea clicked, and from 1941-45 unrestricted gifts to the Fund averaged $100,000 each year.

Even that did not resolve the University's fiscal difficulties, however, and the problems were further complicated by a growing dispute between Throop and Philip Shaffer, who had again become dean of the medical school after W. McKim Marriott's 1936 departure. Shaffer, determined to move his school forward, had secured from the Rockefeller Foundation a $450,000 "transfusion fund," designed to bolster the University's core clinical departments with ten years of supplemental support. After that, warned the Foundation, the University would have to make up the difference — but Shaffer was undeterred. Throop, increasingly frustrated in his own attempts to place the entire University on a firmer footing, was furious at Shaffer's efforts, which he felt were at cross-purposes with his own. In a red-hot 1943 letter, he snapped at Shaffer: "I have your letter…and as usual do not agree with you. I suggest that, if you are so desirous to spend money, you go out and collect it yourself."

A year later, Throop retired. His loyal lieutenant, Walter McCourt, had died in 1943; his dean of students, George Stephens, who had added the role of dean of the College of Liberal Arts, had died in 1940; Malvern Clopton, who had served as board president for most of Throop's tenure as chancellor, had resigned in 1942; and other long-time deans had stepped down, notably business dean Isidor Loeb in 1940. While new leaders had come along to take their places — business dean William H. Stead, College of Liberal Arts dean William Glasgow Bowling, graduate dean Richard F. Jones, and the new board president Harry Brookings Wallace — Throop's long era had passed.

Wallace was quickly named acting chancellor, then he and board members Daniel Kirby and Daniel Catlin worked with Shaffer and Evarts Graham to improve the medical school's financial condition. A $1.5 million infusion from old friends Edward Mallinckrodt, Jr., and Malvern Clopton helped; so did a guaranteed appropriation from the University's endowment income, and a brand-new reserve fund. On the Hilltop, a committee headed by John M. Olin launched an effort to stabilize Engineering, and by 1944 it had raised enough funds to increase the school's budget.

That year, good news arrived from Stockholm for Joseph Erlanger, professor of physiology and medicine. He and former faculty member Herbert Gasser, who had become director of the Rockefeller Foundation, won the Nobel Prize for their research into the functions of single

---

Architecture alumni found internationally prominent firm

Gyo Obata, B.Arch. '45, came to the University from California in 1942, just as his family, like many other Japanese-Americans, was about to be confined in an internment camp. He has said that he is grateful to the University, which was one of the few in the Midwest to accept Japanese-American students.

In fact, all three founding partners of the architectural firm Hellmuth, Obata + Kassabaum, Inc. (HOK), established in 1955, were University graduates. George Hellmuth, B.Arch. '28, M.Arch. '31, won the Steedman Traveling Fellowship; George Kassabaum, B.Arch. '47, joined the faculty for four years after his graduation and served on the University's board from 1976 until his death.

Another HOK tie to the University is Jerome J. Sincoff, B.Arch. '56, retired chairman, HOK Group, Inc., who received the 1999 Dean's Medal for service to the School of Architecture. He was a board member from 1997 to 2001.

George Hellmuth (1907-1999).

Gyo Obata.

George Kassabaum (1920-1982).

All photos, WU Archives

nerve threads. In 1943, a Nobel Prize had gone to another scientist with past University connections: biochemist Edward A. Doisy, faculty member from 1919-23, for discovering the chemical nature of vitamin K.

A New Day Follows the End of War

The war had actually helped the University's financial situation, providing more than $1.5 million in Army contracts — nearly one-third of its income. Further, it had radically changed the role of women, who were going to the law school and medical school in greater numbers and entering the engineering school for the first time. Atomic scientists had demonstrated that technology and applied science would dominate the future. In many ways, a new era was dawning, but who would lead the University into it?

Wallace plotted a shrewd campaign to recruit Arthur Holly Compton, a national figure with impeccable scientific and community credentials, including a leadership role in the National Council of Christians and Jews. In summer 1944, Wallace sent Evarts Graham and Frank Bubb to Chicago to woo Compton. Back again, Graham reported that Compton was intrigued by the challenge of rebuilding the School of Engineering; he had also remarked that the College of Liberal Arts was the University's backbone and hinted that it might need strengthening, especially in chemistry, biology, and physics. Graham was impressed. Compton, he said, "would be an excellent man as chancellor. The prestige associated with his name would also be a splendid thing for the University."

So Wallace persisted, and his work culminated in an exciting announcement on April 20, 1945: Arthur Holly Compton would be the University's new chancellor, pending completion of his war work. Days later came an even more momentous event: V.E. Day, the end of the European phase of the war. "Dashing out of classes and laughing excitedly, a large number of students raced to the Quad May 7 and held an impromptu snake dance in celebration," said one article. A service of thanksgiving took place at Graham Chapel and classes were canceled. V.J. Day was still ahead, but the end of the long war was at last in sight.

For years, University publications had been filled with war news, and now it was nearly time to turn a fresh page. Those who fought were not forgotten, however. As the 1943 *Hatchet* said in its dedication:

"To those heroic alumni of Washington who have died by the sword in World War II, that we who follow might not live under one." Ⓦ

NOBEL LAUREATES WITH WASHINGTON UNIVERSITY AFFILIATIONS

Arthur H. Compton (1892–1962)
Physics, 1927
"For his discovery of the effect named after him"
Faculty of Arts and Sciences, 1920-23 and 1945-62; Chancellor 1945-53

Edward A. Doisy (1893–1986)
Physiology or Medicine, 1943
"For his discovery of the chemical nature of vitamin K"
Faculty of Medicine, 1919-23

Joseph Erlanger (1874–1965)
Physiology or Medicine, 1944
"For...discoveries relating to the highly differentiated functions of single nerve fibres"
Chair, Department of Physiology, 1910-46

Herbert S. Gasser (1888–1963)
Physiology or Medicine, 1944
"For...discoveries relating to the highly differentiated functions of single nerve fibres"
Faculty of Medicine, 1916-31

Carl F. Cori (1896–1984)
Physiology or Medicine, 1947
"For...discovery of the course of the catalytic conversion of glycogen"
Faculty of Medicine, 1931-84

Gerty T. Cori (1896–1957)
Physiology or Medicine, 1947
"For...discovery of the course of the catalytic conversion of glycogen"
Faculty of Medicine, 1931-57

T.S. Eliot (1888–1965)
Literature, 1948
"For his outstanding, pioneer contribution to present-day poetry"
Smith Academy graduate, 1905; grandson of co-founder William Greenleaf Eliot, Jr.

Arthur Kornberg
Physiology or Medicine, 1959
"For...discovery of the mechanisms in the biological synthesis of ribonucleic acid and deoxyribonucleic acid"
Chair, Department of Microbiology, 1952-59

Severo Ochoa (1905–1993)
Physiology or Medicine, 1959
"For...discovery of the mechanisms in the biological synthesis of ribonucleic acid and deoxyribonucleic acid"
Faculty of Medicine, 1940-42

Alfred D. Hershey (1908–1997)
Physiology or Medicine, 1969
"For...discoveries concerning the replication mechanism and the genetic structure of viruses"
Faculty of Medicine, 1934-50

Luis F. Leloir (1906–1987)
Chemistry, 1970
"For his discovery of sugar nucleotides and their role in the biosynthesis of carbohydrates"
Faculty of Medicine, 1944

For more historical information about faculty and alumni honors, refer to http://library.wustl.edu/units/spec/archives/facts/.

Earl W. Sutherland, Jr. (1915–1974)
Physiology or Medicine, 1971
"For his discoveries concerning the mechanisms of the action of hormones"
M.D. '42; Resident in Internal Medicine, 1943-45; Faculty of Medicine 1945-53

Christian de Duve
Physiology or Medicine, 1974
"For...discoveries concerning the structural and functional organization of the cell"
Faculty of Medicine, 1946-47

Daniel Nathans (1928–1999)
Physiology or Medicine, 1978
"For the discovery of restriction enzymes and their application to problems of molecular genetics"
M.D. '54

Hamilton O. Smith
Physiology or Medicine, 1978
"For the discovery of restriction enzymes and their application to problems of molecular genetics"
Washington University Medical Service, 1956-57

Paul Berg
Chemistry, 1980
"For his fundamental studies of the biochemistry of nucleic acids, with particular regard to recombinant-DNA"
Faculty of Medicine, 1954-59

George D. Snell (1903–1996)
Physiology or Medicine, 1980
"For...discoveries concerning genetically determined structures on the cell surface that regulate immunological reactions"
Faculty of Arts and Sciences, 1933-34

Stanley Cohen
Physiology or Medicine, 1986
"For...discoveries of growth factors"
Faculty of Arts and Sciences, 1953-59

Rita Levi-Montalcini
Physiology or Medicine, 1986
"For...discoveries of growth factors"
Faculty of Arts and Sciences, 1948–present

Edwin G. Krebs
Physiology or Medicine, 1992
"For...discoveries concerning reversible protein phosphorylation as a biological regulatory mechanism"
M.D. '43; Resident in Internal Medicine, Research Fellow in Biological Chemistry, 1945-48

Douglass C. North
The Bank of Sweden Prize in Economic Sciences in Memory of Alfred Nobel, 1993
"For having renewed research in economic history by applying economic theory and quantitative methods in order to explain economic and institutional change"
Faculty of Arts and Sciences, 1983–present

Robert F. Furchgott
Physiology or Medicine, 1998
"For...discoveries concerning nitric oxide as a signalling molecule in the cardiovascular system"
Faculty of Medicine, 1949–56

"Refugees from Everywhere": New Faculty Members in the Pre- and Post-World War II Period

Gerty (1896-1957) and Carl Cori (1896-1984).

The Coris did their work in a second-floor laboratory in the medical school's South Building. A later member of the research team, William H. Danforth, described it in a 1984 eulogy of Carl Cori: "The Cori department was no research factory with people following detailed protocol laid out by others; it was a collection of extremely talented individuals doing their own work with their own hands."

Herb Weitman, WU Photographic Services

From the end of World War I until shortly after World War II, thousands of intellectuals migrated from Europe to America. They were graduate students and faculty members; artists, musicians, physicians, scholars, and writers. Some were fleeing political oppression; many were Jews escaping religious persecution. A few arrived in the 1920s; still more after the Nazis rose to power in 1933, and they kept coming through the post-war reconstruction of Europe — a vast, talented stream of émigrés that transformed academic and cultural life in the United States. At least 15 came to Washington University, where they had a major impact as teachers and researchers.

Carl and Gerty Cori, who came to the United States in 1922 and to the University in 1931, were the first of these immigrants on campus. Even then, they were scientists of some distinction. In Carl Cori, said the *Alumni Bulletin*, the medical school "obtains one of the leading authorities on carbohydrate metabolism and on the action of insulin and of epinephrine on the body"; his wife and collaborator, Gerty Theresa Radnitz Cori, "is also a scientist of eminence." Carl was hired as head of pharmacology, later biological chemistry, presiding with steely determination, while Gerty was given the title "research associate," only changed to associate professor in 1944.

Viktor Hamburger (1900-2001).

A founding father in the field of developmental neurobiology, Hamburger was a faculty member from 1935-2001. He won many honors, including election to the National Academy of Sciences and the American Academy of Arts and Sciences, and being awarded the National Medal of Science.

Herb Weitman, WU Photographic Services

Gábor Szegö (1895-1985).

Szegö, a brilliant mathematician, left Nazi Germany in 1934 and taught at the University until 1938.

Bust by Gyofri Lajos
David Kilper, WU Photographic Services

The Coris had met at the University of Prague: her family was Jewish, while his was not. They married in 1920 shortly after receiving their medical degrees and accepted positions in Vienna, but to be hired, Carl had to prove he was of Aryan descent. At the same time, the dissolution of the Austro-Hungarian empire had led to food shortages, and Gerty was sent back to Prague, suffering from a vitamin-A deficiency. When a chance came to move to the United States, they took it willingly.

At Washington University, they researched the mechanism of blood glucose regulation, the so-called "Cori Cycle." A breakthrough came in 1936 when they discovered a new compound — the "Cori ester" — formed by an unknown enzyme, and went on to crystallize this enzyme, phosphorylase, in 1941. Six years later they won the Nobel Prize in Physiology or Medicine, sharing it with Bernardo A. Houssay of Buenos Aires. Meanwhile, the Coris nurtured brilliant young scientists, including some who themselves had

fled repressive regimes. In fact, recalled Arthur Kornberg, a visiting investigator in 1947: "They welcomed refugees from everywhere to join them. Unlike the prevailing culture in American academia, they showed no discrimination toward men or women, husbands with scientist wives, Jews or gentiles."

Among these protégés was Luis Leloir, a research assistant in 1943, who had worked in Houssay's Buenos Aires research institute until Juan Perón forced it to close. Eventually, Leloir returned to Argentina to head a biochemical laboratory, and in 1970 became the first Argentinian to win a Nobel Prize in Chemistry. Another was Severo Ochoa, who had left Madrid in 1936 at the outbreak of the Spanish Civil War, and, under the Rockefeller Foundation Refugees Program, spent 1941-42 in the Coris' laboratory. Subsequently he chaired the New York University biochemistry department and, with Kornberg, won the 1959 Nobel Prize in Physiology or Medicine. A third, Christian de Duve, spent six months with the Coris in 1947 as a Rockefeller fellow, collaborating with Earl Sutherland, M.D. '42, winner of a 1971 Nobel Prize. Eventually de Duve returned to Belgium, his childhood home, to start a research laboratory, sharing his time with Rockefeller University in New York. He won the Nobel Prize in Physiology or Medicine in 1974.

After the Coris, the next refugee was Gábor Szegö —"one of Europe's most distinguished mathematicians," said the *Alumni Bulletin* — who joined the faculty in 1934. A Hungarian by birth and a Jew, he had previously taught at the University of Königsberg and was officially on leave; however, he did not go back. Instead, he spent four years at Washington University with the support of outside funding, and directed the first four doctoral graduates in mathematics. But the financially strapped University could not offer him a permanent appointment and in 1938 he left for Stanford, where he spent his career. A bust of

Later World War II émigrés enhance University faculty

Years after World War II, faculty members arrived who had been shaped by the war as children. One was Egon Schwarz, professor emeritus of German and Rosa May Distinguished Professor Emeritus in the Humanities, who taught at the University for 32 years. He and his family, natives of Vienna forced to flee Europe in the 1940s, emigrated to South America and then to the U.S. He joined the faculty in 1961.

Egon Schwarz.
WU Photographic Services

Gustav Schonfeld, the Samuel E. Schechter Professor of Medicine, and a well-known lipid expert, was born in Czechoslovakia. During the war, all the Jews in his town were sent to concentration camps;

Schonfeld's family was among them, and his infant brother died in Auschwitz. But he and his parents survived and in 1946 emigrated to St. Louis, where he earned his bachelor's degree from the University in 1956 and his M.D. in 1960. He joined the University faculty in 1972, later chairing the Department of Internal Medicine.

Gustav Schonfeld.
WU Photographic Services

Szegö (above left) stands on the Hilltop Campus near Crow Hall.

Viktor Hamburger came next, a native of Germany with a 1925 zoology doctorate from the University of Freiburg. He had received a Rockefeller fellowship to study at the University of Chicago in 1932, but was warned not to return — Hitler was targeting German universities and Hamburger, who had Jewish ancestry, was not welcome. He joined Washington University's zoology department in 1935, chaired it from 1941-66, and was granted emeritus status in 1968, having earned an international reputation for his work in experimental neuroembryology. He continued to work in his campus lab until the 1990s. In October 2000, researchers from around the country gathered in St. Louis for a symposium

The Cori lab team.
Members of the Cori lab, which included three other Nobel Prize-winners, reunited at a 1976 symposium held in honor of Nobel Laureate Carl Cori. From left: Arthur Kornberg, Severo Ochoa, Cori, and Luis F. Leloir.
WU Becker Medical Library

Dietrich Gerhard (1896-1985). Gerhard, a history professor, wrote in 1966: "I am convinced that living and studying in a foreign country is essential to the training of educators and scholars." WU Archives

Herbert (1906-1986) and Liselotte (1903-1994) Dieckmann. Herbert Dieckmann left the University in 1950 for Harvard, but Liselotte stayed on to become professor in the German department in 1947 and head from 1963-67, retiring in 1971. In 1996, her colleague, William Matheson, created the Dieckmann-Matheson Fund for the Support of Comparative Literature to assist graduate students; the Liselotte Dieckmann Scholarship Program in Arts & Sciences is named for her today. Photos, WU Archives

honoring Hamburger on his 100th birthday. As biologist David Kirk noted: "In the late '30s, there were six people in the world doing neuroembryology, and Viktor was friends with all of them. Today, about 20,000 neurobiologists attend their annual flagship meeting, and about one quarter…consider themselves developmental neurobiologists. Every one of them owes a lot to Viktor."

In 1936, another immigrant appeared: Dietrich Gerhard, a lecturer at the University of Berlin in the early 1930s when intellectual freedom began to be repressed. At Washington University, he taught European and Russian history for 30 years, serving as history department chairman in the mid-1950s. From 1955-61, Gerhard became an academic ambassador to his native country by accepting a concurrent position: director of the Institute for American Civilization at the University of Cologne. Active in the Fulbright program, he ardently believed in cross-cultural experiences for faculty and students.

Husband-and-wife Herbert and Liselotte Dieckmann arrived in 1938; they had left Germany in 1933 and spent time in Istanbul before emigrating to the United States. Herbert rose to professor and chair of the Romance languages department, leaving in 1950 for Harvard; Liselotte, who had earned her Ph.D. from the University of Heidelburg in 1927, joined the German department in 1944. After Herbert's departure, she stayed on for the rest of her career, becoming chair of the department in the mid-1960s when few women held such positions, as well as first chair of the Committee on Comparative Literature.

In 1941, Horst W. Janson — a Russian native who left Germany in 1935 in repudiation of Nazi

---

Horst W. Janson's art legacy

In spring 2002, an exhibit, *H.W. Janson and the Legacy of Modern Art at Washington University in St. Louis*, opened in New York with 21 masterworks acquired by Horst W. Janson, art history faculty member at the University from 1941-48 and curator of the art collection from 1944-48.

Glass and Bottle of Suze by Pablo Picasso (Spain, 1881-1973). WU Gallery of Art

Horst W. Janson (1913-1982). WU Archives

religious persecution and cultural policies — joined the University's art faculty after receiving his Ph.D. from Harvard. Soon he discovered its large art collection, mostly stored at the City Art Museum (now the Saint Louis Art Museum) since there was no museum on campus. As its new curator, he established temporary exhibit space in Givens Hall and de-accessioned 120 paintings, including Frederic Remington's *Dash for Timber* and 500 other artifacts — almost a sixth of the collection. With $40,000 from this sale, he bought 40 modernist paintings, sculptures, and prints by Georges Braque, Alexander Calder, Willem de Kooning, Jean Dubuffet, Max Ernst, Juan Gris, Henri Matisse, Pablo Picasso, and others — "the finest collection of contemporary art assembled on any American campus," he said. Janson left the University in 1948, and today is remembered for his seminal textbook, *History of Art.*

Rita Levi-Montalcini.
Levi-Montalcini came to the University in 1947. She and Stanley Cohen later isolated nerve growth factor (NGF), a discovery that won them the 1986 Nobel Prize in Physiology or Medicine.
WU Photographic Services

The next émigrée, Rita Levi-Montalcini, came from Italy where she had received her M.D. in 1936 from the University of Turin and remained on staff. After Mussolini issued his racial and anti-semitic laws in 1938, she was discharged and moved to Belgium; then when German invasion threatened, she returned to Italy and set up a laboratory in her home. In 1947, Viktor Hamburger, who had seen two of her articles, invited her to the University for a semester, and she stayed to become in 1958 the first woman in Arts and Sciences promoted to full professor. Working in Hamburger's laboratory, she and biochemist Stanley Cohen, faculty member from 1953-59, began research that led to the discovery of nerve growth factor, important for its potential to revive damaged neurons; the two won the 1986 Nobel Prize in Physiology or Medicine for this work. In 1961, Levi-Montalcini began dividing her time between St. Louis and Rome, receiving emerita status in 1977. In her memoir, she called her University period "the happiest and most productive" of her life.

In 1946, the University acquired a 1943 Max Beckmann painting, *Les Artistes mit Gemüse (Artists with Vegetable)*, or *Four Men Around a Table*; in 1947 the artist himself — already well known, said a local newspaper, as the "leader of the German Expressionist artists" — joined the art faculty as a visiting professor to teach advanced students. Beckmann, a native of Germany, had been fired in 1933 from the Frankfurt academy where he taught, and soon his art was labeled as degenerate by the Nazis; fleeing to Berlin, the Netherlands, and briefly Paris, he finally came to St. Louis, where he taught for two years and then left for the Brooklyn Museum Art School. In 1948, the City Art Museum held the first U.S. retrospective of his work.

In 1949, classicist Ernst Abrahamson made his way to St. Louis. Born in Berlin, he had to earn his Ph.D. in Prague in 1934 because he was forbidden to study in his native country. Driven from teaching jobs in Italy and France, he came to the United States in 1939, eventually becoming professor of classics and comparative literature at the University.

The last of these immigrants was Gustav Kurt Mesmer, a German native who had received a Ph.D. from the University of Göttingen; while teaching in Darmstadt, he refused to join the Nazi party and after the war cooperated with the Americans in reinstating civilian authority. In 1950, he came to Washington University as a visiting professor of applied mathematics, two years later was named chairman of the department, and in 1957 began directing Engineering's graduate division; he remained in both positions until 1964, when he was named Distinguished Professor of Engineering, retiring ten years afterward.

Today, some engineering freshmen receive Gustav Kurt Mesmer scholarships, and many alumni gratefully remember him: a kind, fair-minded man, whose motto was "praise loudly and criticize softly." One student, Robert Yeager, B.S. '64, recalled that after a particularly difficult exam, Mesmer offered students the chance to come to his office and answer three questions, and if they did so correctly, earn an "A" after all. Yeager, a scholarship student dependent on doing well, nervously decided to try. "Handing me a piece of chalk, [Professor Mesmer] asked me to go to the chalkboard. I don't remember the problems, but I got them right," recalled Yeager years later. "Herr Yeager," Mesmer said, "you get your 'A.'" Ⓦ

***Les Artistes mit Gemüse (Artists with Vegetable)* or *Four Men Around a Table*, 1943.**
German Expressionist artist Max Beckmann spent two years at the University teaching advanced art students. He received an honorary degree in 1950.
WU Gallery of Art

Ernst Abrahamson (1905-1958).
Abrahamson, professor of classics and comparative literature, joined the faculty in 1949. When he died, Thomas Hall said, "To say of a lost friend 'He was a great teacher' is to say that. . .he achieved the greatest possible happiness, the surest immortality."
WU Archives

Gustav Kurt Mesmer (1905-1981).
Mesmer was head of the Department of Applied Mechanics from 1952-64, director of the Sever Institute of Technology from 1957-64, and Distinguished Professor of Engineering from 1964-74. Students recall that, in his classes, they enjoyed being "Mesmerized."
WU Archives

175

David Kilper, WU Photographic Services

CHAPTER NINE

"A GREATER DESTINY":
The Compton and Shepley Era

1946-1962

1946 ✣ 1962

1946 *Arthur Holly Compton was inaugurated as the ninth chancellor on February 22. He established athletics on a "strictly amateur" basis with no athletic scholarships.*

1947 *A record number of students, 13,204, enrolled in the fall as returning World War II veterans entered colleges nationwide.*

1952 *The College of Liberal Arts became the last academic unit to desegregate, permitting the admission of African Americans.*

1953 *Compton resigned as chancellor just before the board approved a capital campaign.*

1954 *Board President Ethan A.H. Shepley was appointed the University's tenth chancellor.*

1959 *Chancellor Shepley received the Alexander Meiklejohn Award for Academic Freedom from the American Association of University Professors (AAUP).*

Chancellor's medallion.
During Compton's 1946 inauguration, Board President Harry B. Wallace placed a gold-and-silver medallion around the chancellor's neck. Wallace had commissioned the piece, embossed with the University seal, which was wholly created at the University: designed by Mrs. W.F. Richter, faculty member in the School of Fine Arts; executed by her colleagues Naomi M. Walsh and Mary L. Lischer, A.B. '36, A.M. '37; and cast at the School of Dental Medicine.

"A Greater Destiny"

On the sunny morning of February 22, 1946 — the 93rd anniversary of the University's founding — a 600-person procession marched out of Francis Gymnasium to the joyous beat of music played by the Saint Louis Symphony Orchestra. Leading the way were 260 robed academics, 40 college presidents among them — a group, said one newspaper, rivaling "ancient Athens in the number of distinguished scholars." Next came faculty, students, alumni, and finally the star of the day: new chancellor Arthur Holly Compton, accompanied by the slight, beaming man who had hired him, Board President Harry Brookings Wallace.
As the parade entered the Field House, the crowd of 4,500 people rose to its feet and cheered. Officially, it was an inauguration, said Engineering Dean Alexander Langsdorf, but it had all the earmarks of a "coronation."

Carl F. Cori (1896-1984), Joseph Erlanger (1874-1965), Gerty T. Cori (1896-1957), and Arthur H. Compton (1892-1962) (from left to right).
Current faculty members when Compton was inaugurated as chancellor, all four scientists were awarded the Nobel Prize (in 1947, 1944, 1947, and 1927, respectively).

Previous pages:
Blewett Hall. Blewett is part of the complex of buildings that houses the Department of Music in Arts & Sciences and was built as Chancellor Houston's residence.
Facing page: One of the grotesques inside Graham Chapel, beneath the organ; the organ and Blewett Hall were gifts of Avis Blewett.

Photos, WU Archives

Joyce C. Stearns (1893-1948).
Named dean of faculties in 1945, Stearns had "a personality of exceptional charm and absolute integrity," said Alexander Langsdorf. Ethan Shepley called him "an ideal dean," adding that "he was very fair but very firm."

WU Archives

Chemists from Manhattan District staff.
Four of the chemists Chancellor Compton recruited to the faculty in 1946, shown in 1982, are (left to right) Lindsay Helmholtz, Arthur Wahl, Sam Weissman, and David Lipkin.

Herb Weitman, WU Photographic Services

An evening of music.
Chancellor Compton entertains students with his bandolin at an outdoor gathering in 1949.

WU Archives

By this time, Compton was no longer new at his job. He had begun work in July 1945, but for months he and physicist Joyce C. Stearns, once his right-hand man at the Metallurgical Laboratory in Chicago and now his dean of faculties, had been splitting their time between St. Louis and the remaining work on the Manhattan Project. At first, that meant keeping the deeply held secret that atomic bombs would be dropped on Japan in hopes of ending the war. After the blasts at Hiroshima and Nagasaki, then the Japanese surrender on August 15, Compton's role in the war effort had emerged into the public spotlight — and his already-bright reputation acquired even more luster. The University benefited greatly from his prestige, since it "must have real class to be able to attract a man of his position and ability," said board member Ethan A.H. Shepley.

In October 1945 Compton had assured the board that his war-related work was finally at an end; however, he actually continued to juggle consulting commitments for much of the next year.

He also tried, unsuccessfully, to parlay his government and corporate contacts into programs for the University: a biomedical research venture at Los Alamos; an atomic energy institute on campus; the short-lived Washington University Research Foundation (WURF), which he hoped would channel major research funds to technology experts on the faculty.

The months before his inauguration, though, had seen remarkable progress in faculty recruitment. He and Stearns, formerly the Met Lab's

shrewd personnel director, had already snared six chemists, veterans of the Manhattan staff, to replenish the University's depleted department. Joseph Kennedy, department chair, was first, and by December 1945 offers had gone out to five others: Lindsay Helmholz, David Lipkin, Herbert A. Potratz, Arthur C. Wahl, and Samuel I. Weissman. They would soon be joined by a talented crew of physicists — George Pake, Henry Primakoff, Robert D. Sard, and Eugene Feenberg — along with Walter Leighton, head of the newly merged mathematics and applied mathematics department.

So on that February morning, Compton had good reason to be in a celebratory mood. Sharing his joy were wartime colleagues Enrico Fermi and Vannevar Bush, both receiving honorary degrees, and James Conant, president of Harvard, who were there to hear Compton's inaugural address. Later that day, J. Robert Oppenheimer, Major General Leslie R. Groves, and other top Manhattan Project personnel — the largest group of them ever assembled — gathered for a gala dinner. Compton himself, one of those who had advised President Harry S Truman to drop the bomb on Japan, proposed a toast: that "the atomic bomb never again be used in war."

Now, at the climax of the morning inauguration, Compton leaned forward as Harry Brookings Wallace, predicting that the University was "on the threshold of a new period of development," slipped a chain around his neck. Suspended from it was the new chancellor's medallion, which Wallace had commissioned at his own expense. The board had "unlimited confidence" in Compton, Wallace declared, adding that "we will do everything in our power to strengthen your hands."

Barry Commoner takes part in survey to measure nuclear fallout

Barry Commoner joined the University in 1947 as professor of plant physiology and spent 34 years on the faculty. He became a pioneer in the environmental movement, called by *Time* magazine in 1970 the "Paul Revere of Ecology." In 1966, he founded the Center for the Biology of Natural Systems, the first of its kind in the nation, bringing together physical and social scientists.

Survey request card illustration. The card gave basic information about Strontium 90 and the study. It made an offer, "Send a tooth – Get a button!"

Barry Commoner.

Concerned about the effect of nuclear fallout, he helped found the St. Louis Committee for Nuclear Information in the early 1950s. In 1958, he and dental professor Harold Rosenthal did the St. Louis Baby Tooth Survey, collecting nearly 300,000 teeth in order to measure the radioactive material, especially strontium 90, absorbed by humans. They found that the amount was directly related to the level of nuclear testing in the year of a child's birth. When the project ended in 1970, the remaining 85,000 teeth were stored at Tyson Research Center, where they were rediscovered in 2001. The teeth are now housed at the Radiation and Public Health Project in New York.

Forgotten for the moment were the gathering storm clouds: student and alumni dissatisfaction over the controversial new football policy, and increasingly vocal demands from the community for the University to desegregate. Soon after the ceremony, a leading black newspaper commented bitterly that no one listening to the inaugural rhetoric would "have suspected that the University had abandoned the liberal policy with which it was founded and had disavowed the principles upon which [it] was built — education for all people."

In his inaugural address, Compton spoke of other goals for the University: the need for more and better students; the importance of productive scholarship; the increasing role of graduate study; the urgent need for new buildings, especially a student union; the desperate lack of faculty housing. As the ninth chancellor, he had a lofty vision: to educate young men and women who would, amid the coming atomic age and its dangers, build a better community and world. "The goal before us," he said with hopeful enthusiasm, "is education for a greater destiny."

Housing for faculty.
In 1945 and 1946, 50 prefab housing units were built to house new faculty members. Each had a living room, kitchen (including a china closet with a door that doubled as a table), two bedrooms, and a "bathroom with plumbing." *Student Life* joked that these units bore "a resemblance to chicken coops."

All images, WU Archives

Avis Blewett (1860-1946).
Ben Blewett (1856-1917), A.B. '76, A.M. '80, St. Louis public schools superintendent, told his sister, Avis, that he wanted his estate to go to the University. She donated the Graham Chapel organ in 1946 and close to $1 million in gifts, which made possible the founding of the music department and its home in Blewett Hall. The Avis Blewett Professorship of Music is held today by Hugh J. Macdonald.
WU Archives

One of his goals — a larger student body — was already being realized. A tidal wave of returning veterans, eager for education and bankrolled by the government's 1944 "G.I. Bill of Rights," was hitting schools around the country. In spring 1946, enrollment was up 39 percent as 9,159 students registered for courses; by fall 1946, it had risen to 12,300, with men outnumbering women 3 to 1; and the peak finally came in fall 1947 as 13,204 students enrolled. English professor William Glasgow Bowling was quickly named the first dean of admissions.

To cope with this onslaught, Compton reorganized the administration, appointing Charles Belknap, retired president of Monsanto Chemical Company, to the new office of vice chancellor. Meanwhile, Stearns focused on the faculty, pushing for new tenure rules and broader membership in the Faculty Senate. He began recruiting at all levels, hiring biologist Thomas S. Hall, molecular biologist Barry Commoner, economist Werner Hochwald, and political scientist Merle Kling, A.B. '41, A.M. '41, Ph.D. '49. Hall soon led a new "Basic College" program in the College of Liberal Arts that allowed some students to spend their first two years in interdisciplinary courses.

To attract faculty, the University dangled a tantalizing inducement: the offer of housing, then in desperately short supply in St. Louis and around the country. In December 1945, workers quickly assembled 20 temporary housing units on the northwest end of campus or "North Forty"; another 30 went up the following spring. That May, groundbreaking took place on more faculty quarters: a 69-unit set of buildings, later known as the Millbrook Apartments, which occupants wryly dubbed the "Comptontration Campus." A nursery school opened in the McMillan basement in January 1947, then moved to space in the Millbrook development.

Student housing was a thornier issue, since twice as many students applied for rooms as there were places available. Men doubled up in dormitories, and fraternities offered space to non-members; the University housed women at 5058 Washington, 5531 Maple, 5521 Waterman, and 4607 McPherson, while juniors and seniors were allowed to find off-campus housing themselves. With the spike in enrollment, the lack of an adequate student union became a sore point again. The administration, pleading lack of money, refurbished the basement of Liggett Hall early in 1948 and added a sunken patio.

With the help of outside gifts, other Hilltop buildings sprang up. In 1946, construction began on a radiochemistry laboratory, funded by Monsanto and located near the now-famous cyclotron, newly dedicated to peacetime uses. There was hope of an engineering building, one of Compton's cherished desires, after an Illinois Supreme Court ruling in 1946 gave the University $1.25 million from the estate of textbook publisher Henry Edwin Sever. Thanks to a gift from Avis Blewett in 1945, increased the next year by a bequest from her estate, music moved into 6500 Forsyth. The University built the house for Chancellor David Houston, later sold it, and reacquired it as "Blewett Hall."

Bernard Becker arrives as head of ophthalmology

Bernard Becker.
WU Becker Medical Library

I n 1953, the medical school appointed Bernard Becker to succeed Lawrence Post as the head of ophthalmology. He chaired the department until 1988: expanding its training program, building its faculty, earning acclaim for his own glaucoma research. During the 1950s, he fought to integrate hospital wards and private rooms; McMillan became the first of the affiliated hospitals to integrate its private service. Becker also chaired the committee that oversaw construction of the eight-story medical school library — later renamed in his honor — completed in 1989; two endowed professorships are also named for him. He donated his own collection of rare books on ophthalmology to the School of Medicine library.

Becker Medical Library.
Robert Boston, WU Medical Public Affairs

Hallowell Davis (1896-1992).
Davis came to the medical school in 1946 as professor of physiology and research professor of otolaryngology, then directed research at Central Institute for the Deaf until 1965. The world's leading authority on the ear and hearing, he was awarded the National Medal of Science in 1975.
WU Becker Medical Library

PROGRESS ON THE MEDICAL CAMPUS

Just as Chancellor Compton was arriving, Philip A. Shaffer was ending his second term as medical school dean, giving way to pathologist Robert A. Moore. Shaffer left behind a long, distinguished record of service to the University. M. Kenton King, later dean himself, wrote: "No one stands above Philip Shaffer as the architect and builder of this School in its first quarter century." Before retiring, Shaffer summed up his dreams for the medical school: stronger clinical and laboratory staffs; a firmer plan for the school's financial support; and an active building program. In short order, all these goals were on their way to being fulfilled.

New faculty members soon joined the school, among them otolaryngologist and Central Institute for the Deaf (CID) research director Hallowell Davis; Ira J. Hirsh, psychoacoustics specialist and later CID director; David Goldring, who founded the Division of Pediatric Cardiology; Arthur Kornberg, head of microbiology, who shared the 1959 Nobel Prize; and Bernard Becker, head of ophthalmology. A school of physical therapy, previously sponsored by Barnes Hospital, was transferred to the medical school. Among several shifts in leadership, Oliver Lowry took over in pharmacology; Harvey L. White in physiology; Hugh Wilson, M.D. '26, at Mallinckrodt Institute of Radiology; Edward Dempsey in anatomy; and Carl Moyer in surgery.

They came to a medical school flush with applicants. Before the war, an average 800 students applied each year for admission, but in 1948-49, that total shot up to 3,200 — 78 percent of them veterans. Most departments now had active internship and residency programs, and the demand was growing for postgraduate training. In the past, the School of Medicine had offered short, refresher classes, while candidates for other graduate work applied through the School of Graduate Studies. In spring 1946, the medical school established its own Division of Postgraduate Studies, with classes from one week to nine months in length.

Barnard Hospital affiliates with Washington University

Barnard Hospital.
WU Becker Medical Library

In 1908, George D. Barnard, impressed by the work of the St. Louis Skin and Cancer Hospital, founded three years earlier, donated $130,000 for a new 44-bed building, which was renamed in his honor. When he and his wife died, they left much of their estate to the hospital, which offered free cancer care to indigent patients. For years, Barnard shared faculty with the School of Medicine, including E.V. Cowdry, director of research. In the 1940s, Cowdry and others nudged the hospital, which was struggling financially, toward affiliation with the University; despite controversy, even litigation, the affiliation took place in 1952. Barnard's new, five-story building was dedicated in 1954 on the medical center campus with 40 inpatient beds and free outpatient care for up to 12,000 people a year.

George D. Barnard (1846-1915).
David Kilper, WU Photographic Services

Shaffer's second goal, financial restructuring, was more problematic, but he had a bold idea that Moore pushed forward. Along with tuition, endowment, and gifts, Shaffer envisioned a fourth source of income: faculty-staffed clinics, not only for the indigent, but also for paying patients. Despite some alumni protests, the board voted its guarded approval of the idea, and by the early 1950s the annual income from this practice had soared to $1.4 million.

The strong clinical research program Shaffer hoped for was under way, in part with funds from private foundations. Increasingly, help was coming from a new source, the federal government — much of it through the National Institutes of Health (NIH), which had joined forces with the National Cancer Institute in 1944 and soon

Hugh Wilson (1902-1978).
WU Becker Medical Library

The first three women complete engineering degrees

Doris Millner.

S oon after the war, three women were the first to graduate from the engineering school: Irma Amoratis, a civil engineer, in 1947; Elizabeth Samann, a chemical engineer, in 1948; and Doris Millner, a mechanical engineer and also the "Engineers' Queen," in 1949. Of the 32 students in her class, Samann was the first to get a job; Millner was the only woman student in all her engineering classes.

B. Blair Gullion (c. 1901-1959). Washington U.'s new athletic director in 1946, Gullion was president of the National Association of Basketball Coaches. He implemented Chancellor Compton's decision to abolish athletic scholarships.

embraced a host of specialized institutes. By the 1950s and '60s, this support expanded enormously, ushering in, says historian Kenneth Ludmerer, "a golden era of American medical research."

In 1948, one government agency — the United States Public Health Service — gave the medical school $450,000 toward a cancer research building. Two further additions to the cancer program were in the offing. The Barnard Free Skin and Cancer Hospital, which provided free cancer care for the indigent, affiliated with the University in 1948 and moved from Washington Avenue to the Kingshighway campus in 1954. Since Barnard was small, the University needed another cancer hospital; a federal grant, matched by funds from the Wohl Foundation, provided it in the David P. Wohl, Jr., Memorial Hospital. This facility nearly doubled in size with completion of the David P. Wohl, Jr. Memorial–Washington University Clinics building in spring 1961.

"Can't Cheer a Cyclotron to Victory"

For Compton, fresh from epochal decisions about the atomic bomb and filled with plans for world peace, it must have been deflating to find students, alumni, even board members preoccupied with the future of football. The University had not fielded a team since 1942, and many were hungry for gridiron glory. Shortly after their arrival, Compton and Stearns — aided by a committee that included Ethan Shepley — began to study the matter. They had four choices, Shepley recalled: continue to pretend they had an unsubsidized team; move into the expensive world of "big-time" football; abandon intercollegiate football; or switch to amateur football, with "a strictly unsubsidized group of athletes, playing for the fun of it."

Two threads in Compton's own background surely tugged him in opposite directions. At the College of Wooster, he had played left tackle on the football team, but later had taught at the University of Chicago, which had pulled out of the Big Ten and abolished football. Late in 1945, a deciding nudge came from the "Ivy League agreement," in which eight eastern universities promised to keep intercollegiate football "in fitting proportion" to academic life — with no post-season play and disapproval of athletic scholarships. During a January 1946 meeting of the National Collegiate Athletic Association (NCAA) in St. Louis, Compton praised this middle ground. "They have wisely chosen not to throw the baby out with the dirty bath water," he said.

However, alumni were grumbling, students were staging football rallies, and *Student Life* was demanding an answer to the "Pigskin Puzzle" — what *was* the University's football policy? Compton invited the heads of seven Midwestern schools to St. Louis to consider forming a mid-American federation, linked to the Ivy League, to sponsor amateur athletics. This proposal proved unsuccessful, but Compton forged on alone. In February 1946, just before his inauguration, *Student Life* announced "W.U. Endorses Football on an Amateur Basis," though the sport did not resume right away because the University was hunting for two key figures — an athletic director and football coach — to develop a "strictly amateur" team.

At first, *Student Life* responded respectfully to this decision: "Despite severe criticism and

pressure from outside [Dr. Compton] has declared his policy on athletics. It seems safe to assume that he will meet future problems in the same fearless way." Yet by October, with no coach and Homecoming canceled, students were resentful. "Will Washington U. put a football team on Francis Field next year, or will the dandelions grow more frequent and the grass grow taller?" the newspaper asked. Another editorial traced the flagging school spirit to the lack of a team, noting impatiently: "We can't cheer a cyclotron to victory."

Behind the scenes some board members, too, were feeling exasperated as coaching prospects faded away, but in December 1946 Compton had his new athletic director: B. Blair Gullion, an all-American basketball star at Purdue and now president of the National Association of Basketball Coaches. In turn, Gullion recruited football coach Wilbur C. ("Weeb") Ewbank, who stayed for two successful years before joining the National Football League in 1949. A year after the change, although Compton insisted he was pleased, complaints from alumni continued; even Shepley later called the amateur policy "a good deal of a flop" because "students haven't rallied around it."

"PINK GRANITE"

While dealing with this highly public issue, Compton was quietly taking a stand on the status of nuclear scientist Martin Kamen. In 1940, Kamen and a fellow scientist had isolated the radioactive isotope carbon-14, used for radiocarbon dating. As a wartime researcher at Oak Ridge National Laboratory and the University of California–Berkeley, Kamen and his group did groundbreaking research that made possible the mass production of Uranium 235. In 1996, he won the Enrico Fermi Award for lifetime achievement in energy research.

At Berkeley, he met two Russian officials at a party given by his friend, violinist Isaac Stern, and helped one find radiation treatment for a

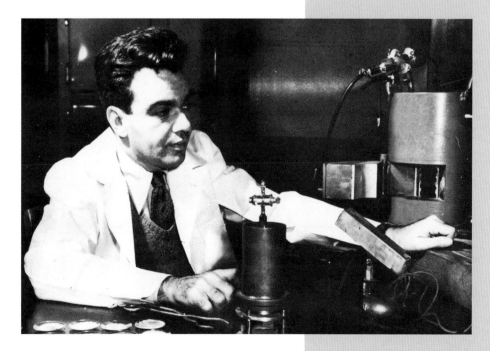

friend with leukemia; the grateful official invited him to dinner at a restaurant, where the FBI observed them talking. Amid swirling innuendo, he was fired in July 1944 — and could not find another academic position until Compton hired him in 1945 to run the University's cyclotron program. Kamen stayed until 1957, with Compton's steadfast support, despite a well-publicized 1948 appearance before the House Un-American Activities Committee.

In another politically charged move, Compton appointed the liberal Stuart Queen as dean of the College of Liberal Arts — and late in 1946,

conservative board member Edgar M. Queeny had had enough. He fired off an angry resignation letter denouncing the elevation of "Russophiles" to positions at the University. "I am certain that it never crossed Robert Brookings' mind, when he chose pink granite for Washington University's towers, that its color would become symbolic," he said. Compton went to see him, hoping to convince him that a University should encourage "impartial, vigorous, high-quality study of social and economic problems from varied angles," but Queeny was unappeased. He resigned from the board of directors — and Compton's appointments remained in place.

Lion fountain, gift of the class of '09, in the Brookings Hall archway.
David Kilper, WU Photographic Services

Historian of freedom believes Washington University is "a noble treasure"

J. H. ("Jack") Hexter taught at the University from 1957-64, including three years as history department chair, before moving to Yale. He returned in 1978, eight years later founded the Center for the History of Freedom, then retired in 1990.

In his 1972 book, *The Vision of Politics on the Eve of the Reformation*, he wrote:

"It is not, I believe, customary to dedicate a book to an institution. The place of Washington University in my heart and life has been such, however, that nice customs can curtsey to it….Washington University was neither a very rich school nor a very big one. It was just a great one. Its excellences shone out in that fine and magnanimous man, Ethan Shepley…and in a multitude of my colleagues whom I remember still with the warmest affection. The people of St. Louis have a noble treasure in their midst."

J. H. ("Jack") Hexter (1910-1996).
WU Archives

SEGREGATION AT THE UNIVERSITY

Compton's fearlessness deserted him, however, in dealing with the University's segregation. The last African-American student had matriculated in 1895; none had been admitted since, though some had inquired about coming. In 1928, Frank Bruno tried unsuccessfully to move the University toward admitting black social work students; beginning in the 1930s, medical school professor Park J. White became a perennial gadfly, urging integration. He convinced the Campus Y to sponsor forums featuring such speakers as attorney Sidney Redmond.

During World War II, some black students came to campus through Engineering, Science, Management War Training Program (ESMWT) evening classes, and others wished to follow. In an action sponsored by the National Association for the Advancement of Colored People (NAACP), four black students tried to enroll in the 1945 summer school but were refused admission; the NAACP, represented by attorneys David Grant and George L. Vaughn, joined the city of St. Louis in a suit, ultimately unsuccessful, that contested the University's tax exemption. Acting Chancellor Harry B. Wallace responded tersely, saying that since the University had received its charter from the state, it had "followed the policy of the State educational institutions as to segregation."

By 1946, students were beginning to speak out. After the Ink Spots, a black musical group, performed at a rally for world relief, one *Student Life* letter writer noted the irony: "Why should they have come here in order to help us in this campaign, while if they asked for admittance as students, their requests would have been rebuffed?" University war veterans weighed in, opposing "the type of discrimination which we fought against," as letters poured in from citizens, some of them alumni, in favor of speedy integration. In a memo to the board, Compton expressed his own philosophical support for integration. "From the purely educational point of view," he wrote, "there is no doubt that academically qualified negro students should be admitted to the University." Yet he failed to take the next bold step, saying instead that he would leave any decision to the board, that he had not "lived in the St. Louis community long enough to sense adequately the local social attitudes."

Students kept up the pressure, their polls repeatedly showing majority support for integration. In October 1946, social work dean Benjamin Youngdahl made one of several requests to admit blacks to his school, saying his faculty had "unanimously and vigorously" recommended it. That same month, Compton outlined his vision for the University, at one point declaring that "our geographical location and the composition of our population make us a natural center for advance toward a solution of inter-racial and inter-religious relationships." He failed to address desegregation, though, and a few weeks later told the faculty that, in light of other goals, "perhaps the lesser objective, such as this one of admitting negroes, might have to be sacrificed."

On behalf of the administration, Charles Belknap surveyed the deans in spring 1947. Youngdahl, Willis Reals of University College, and Kenneth Hudson of the School of Fine Arts argued for immediate desegregation; Wayne Townsend in Law and Louise Knapp in Nursing were opposed; several preferred a gradual approach. Medical Dean Robert Moore, who favored the admission of qualified students, wanted to begin by establishing a postgraduate program for black physicians at Homer G. Phillips Hospital — but events moved up his timetable. That June, ophthalmology professor Lawrence Post found he had inadvertently accepted a black physician, James Nofles, to a three-week postgraduate course. The board, which had already discussed the acute shortage of black physicians, now decided to make the best of things and announced that the medical school was desegregated. Arguing a similar shortage of social workers, Youngdahl finally prevailed and

in December 1947 his school desegregated; the Graduate School of Arts and Sciences followed in May 1948.

Still, the controversy was not over. Other schools, including the College of Liberal Arts, did not yet admit black students — and the University had faced some embarrassment on account of its policies. In fall 1947, Florence S. Frank left $15,000 to the law school on condition that there be no discrimination in admission. At first, the University accepted the money, then returned it amid jibes from local newspapers. This case, said the *Post-Dispatch*, "will cause many people to inquire by what logic the directors feel that the university can render unusual service to the education of Negroes in the medical school; but do not feel the same way about the law school."

"CHANGE EVERYWHERE" ON THE HILLTOP CAMPUS

In a 1950 reminiscence, Fannie Hurst, A.B. '09, described the transformation of the campus where she had once been a student. "Change everywhere," she wrote. "New buildings, formalized landscaping. Trees that you knew as saplings have become adult. A city has sprung up where the one-time Missouri terrain rolled out to horizon." *Student Life* believed the change included a new academic direction. In a choice of what disciplines to favor and fund, the article contended, "WU chose science."

Benjamin Youngdahl (1897-1970).
The well-respected dean of social work from 1945-62, Youngdahl was president of the American Association of Social Workers and the National Conference of Social Work, and a long-standing national committee member of the American Civil Liberties Union. The Benjamin E. Youngdahl Professorship in Social Development, held by Michael Sherraden, honors him today.
WU Archives

Sever Hall.
The cornerstone for the Sever Institute of Technology building was laid in 1948, and occupancy began in 1950. The building was made possible by a bequest from Henry Edwin Sever (1866-1941).
David Kilper, WU Photographic Services

Louderman Hall.
William M. Louderman (1868-1952) participated in the ceremony for the laying of the cornerstone in 1951. In addition to his gift for the construction of the building, he left a bequest as an endowment for its operation and maintenance.

David Kilper, WU Photographic Services

Michael Friedlander.
He joined the faculty in 1956 and began the University's first balloon flights for cosmic ray detection. Since then, his research interests have included infrared astronomy and archaeoastronomy. A local and national AAUP leader, he formerly chaired the Department of Physics in Arts & Sciences.

WU Archives

There was some evidence to back this up. Except for two ROTC Quonset huts and a small student activities center west of McMillan, most new buildings on campus were science-related. Engineering had Sever Hall, completed in 1950, and Sever funds had made possible a program begun two years earlier: the Henry Edwin Sever Institute of Technology — Engineering's new graduate school — with master's and doctoral-level courses. It was directed by Lawrence Stout, formerly head of chemical engineering, who had replaced Alexander Langsdorf as dean in 1948.

The chemistry department had Louderman Hall, dedicated in 1952, with an underground laboratory, a three-story tower, and the first elevator on campus. Compton had persuaded William Louderman, an 1886 Manual Training School graduate and investment house president, to fund its construction. This project displaced the old observatory, which moved to the roof of Crow Hall, while chemistry's former home, the aging Busch Hall, was renovated for economics and history.

The medical school had a cancer complex in the offing, a fresh contract with

Barnes Hospital in 1949, and several new programs: a pioneering exchange with Thai hospitals; a gerontology division, begun in 1947; and a division of psychosomatic medicine under psychiatrist George Saslow. On February 21, 1950, the medical school marked the 50th anniversary of the merger of its two 19th-century predecessors in a gala celebration. Abraham Flexner received an honorary LL.D., presented by Philip Shaffer, one of the first faculty hired after the 1910 reorganization.

Quietly, though, one old scientific program disappeared: the Henry Shaw School of Botany. In March 1950, its dwindling undergraduate degrees were discontinued, and a revised botany curriculum was incorporated within the College of Liberal Arts.

New Faculty in the Non-science Areas

Yet progress took place in areas other than the sciences, too. In 1947, the College of Liberal Arts hired philosophy professor Huston Smith, whose introductory religions course first turned into a popular program on St. Louis public television station, KETC-TV, and eventually into a widely read book. Two years later came what *Student Life* called "the largest administrative turnover" in the University's history, when biologist Thomas Hall succeeded Stuart Queen as college dean, and new department heads were named, among them Guy Cardwell in English, Marion E. Bunch in psychology, and Philip de Lacy in the newly reorganized classics department.

In coming years, Hall hired key faculty: Leigh Gerdine in 1950 to head the music department, which began offering the bachelor of music degree in 1953; Isidore Silver in Romance languages in 1950; Thomas H. Eliot in 1952 as chairman of political science; physicist Michael Friedlander in 1956; and J. H. Hexter in history in 1957. Hall fought successfully to retain archaeologist George Mylonas, whose discoveries at Mycenae, Eleusis, and Attica drew the attention of other universities. In 1950, he recruited Jarvis Thurston and his wife Mona Van Duyn — the first in a spectacular group of writers attracted to the University. In 1950, A. Gwendolyn Drew, hired as associate professor of physical education in 1946, became the first woman named a full professor on the Hilltop Campus.

A. Gwendolyn Drew (1907-2001).
Drew was named professor of physical education in July 1950. In 1985, an award was created in her honor to recognize students with strong academic standing who have contributed to varsity athletics.

WU Archives

Writers bring distinction and honors to Washington University

In 1950, Mona Van Duyn and Jarvis Thurston were the first of the prominent writers to arrive at the University, bringing their literary magazine *Perspective: A Quarterly of Literature.* In 1960, Donald Finkel joined them and so did novelist Stanley Elkin; in 1969, poet Howard Nemerov and writer William Gass became faculty members. This group received many honors. Nemerov was poet laureate of the United States in 1963-64 and 1988-90, received the Pulitzer Prize and the National Book Award in 1978, the National Medal of Arts in 1987, and the National Book Critics Circle Award in 1995, as did Gass in 1985, 1997, and 2003; Elkin in 1982 and 1996. Gass was awarded the PEN Award in the Art of the Essay category in 2003. Van Duyn, who was poet laureate in 1992-93, won the Bollingen Prize, the National Book

Gerald Early.
Joe Angeles, WU Photographic Services

Howard Nemerov (1920-1991).
David Kilper, WU Photographic Services

Award in 1971, the Pulitzer Prize in 1991, and received an honorary degree from the University.

Other writers have since achieved national prominence. Gerald Early became a faculty member in 1982 and won the National Book Critics Circle Award in 1995. John Morris (1931-1997) was a poet and English department member from 1967-95. Carl Phillips, professor of English and of African and Afro-American Studies in Arts & Sciences, won the 2002 Kingsley Tufts Poetry Award. Early now heads the Center for the Humanities in Arts & Sciences, founded by Gass in 1990 as the International Writers Center.

Stanley Elkin (1930-1995).
Herb Weitman, WU Photographic Services

With Alexander Langsdorf's 1948 departure as head of engineering and architecture, the School of Architecture acquired its own dean: Joseph Murphy, B.Arch. '29, M.Arch. '34, professor of design since 1935. Four years later he gave way to Kenneth Hudson, dean of the School of Fine Arts, who took over both schools. Fine Arts, meanwhile, hired its first female full professor in Virginia Fel'Dotto, instructor in fashion design; in 1945, Philip Guston became the first faculty member to have a work — a painting

entitled *If This Be Not I* — added to the University's collection.

Law added faculty, too, including Arno Becht in 1940, William C. Jones and Frank W. Miller in 1948, and Gray L. Dorsey in 1951. In 1952, Wayne Townsend stepped down as dean, replaced by John Ritchie from the University of Virginia. In Business, Leslie J. Buchan became dean, adding a master's in business administration program in

Huston Smith.
A native of China, where his parents were missionaries, Smith joined the University faculty in 1947. His popular religion class became a KETC television course, "Religions of Man," and a book in 1958.
Herb Weitman, WU Photographic Services

Mona Van Duyn.
Van Duyn's first book of poetry,
Valentines to the Wide World,
appeared in 1959. Author of
eight more books of poems,
Van Duyn is a highly respected
editor and an experienced
teacher of younger writers.
The Mona Van Duyn Papers
are housed at Washington
University Libraries.
WU Photographic Services

1950; economics shifted over to the College of Liberal Arts. University College was booming with new programs in physical education, librarianship and, in cooperation with KMOX, radio education.

LEAN TIMES AGAIN

In contrast to the excitement at the start of Compton's chancellorship, the early 1950s were a time of stagnation. Joyce Stearns had died in 1948 and Shepley recalled, "Arthur never found anybody capable of…doing the job the same way." Enrollment was dropping, as the number of veterans diminished and the pool of potential freshmen — those born during the Depression — shrank. Some students left for a new conflict in Korea, and in December 1950, *Student Life* spoke of a "Not-So-Merry Christmas," saying: "On a distant peninsula men are slaughtering each other in what appears to be only the prelude for a wider, bloodier war."

Compton, who had persuaded the board to adopt a deficit budget in 1948 in order to build new programs, was facing a financial crunch, though he increased tuition repeatedly. That March, Leslie Buchan, by now vice chancellor and dean of faculties, took a controversial cost-cutting step: In a memo to faculty, he announced that they were appointed for 12 months, could be called on for summer duties, and could not do outside work without the dean's approval. The faculty was outraged, the American Association of University Professors (AAUP) — whose Washington University chapter, founded in 1916, was rapidly growing — protested, and within a year, Buchan had resigned.

Meanwhile, some areas expanded while others contracted. In 1951 came a welcome donation: Irene Walter Johnson, widow of shoe manufacturer Oscar Johnson, gave $240,000 to help fund a new building for the programs in occupational therapy and physical therapy. In 1949, after a 90-year affiliation, the University officially separated

Rabbi Robert P. Jacobs (1908-2002).
Al Gerber, S. Charles Baer, Jacobs, and Sander Zwick (left to right) attend the groundbreaking for Hillel House, January 1966. Rabbi Jacobs, M.S.W. '56, the founding director of the Hillel Student Center in 1946 and later executive vice president of the St. Louis Rabbinical Association, won many honors for his work in interfaith relations.
WU Archives

from Mary Institute, its only remaining secondary division. The University briefly considered closing the School of Dentistry in 1953, but instead upgraded the school's laboratory space, adding a research wing.

All the while, student activities continued: Compton played his banjo-mandolin at the annual freshman picnic; *Quirk*, a humor magazine, came and went; the Quad Shop, renamed the Q-X, was a popular meeting place; and students rejoiced in 1952 when Saturday classes were eliminated. With the support of Compton and Huston Smith, campus religious organizations — Christian Science, Newman (for Catholic students), Baptist, Methodist, Presbyterian — were all growing. In 1946, Hillel opened its first chapter under the leadership of Rabbi Robert P. Jacobs, M.S.W. '56. Subsequently, it added Hillel House at 6142 Pershing, breaking ground on a new Forsyth location in 1966.

The board saw the departure of longtime members. In November 1951, Ethan A. H. Shepley, Sr., succeeded Wallace as president. William H. Danforth, member since 1925, became emeritus

Senator Robert A. Taft (1889-1953) enjoys a football game with E. Shepley and A. H. Compton.
Taft (center, in hat), Republican Senator from Ohio and son of President William H. Taft, visited campus during the 100th anniversary year of the University's founding.
WU Archives

in 1950, as did Admiral Ben Moreell, B.S.C.E. '13, LL.D. '42, while new members included Meredith C. Jones, LL.B. '17, in 1950. During his tenure, Shepley reorganized the board, adding more alumni and changing its size.

INTEGRATION AT LAST

In December 1947, newspaper headlines announced that President Truman's Commission on Higher Education had issued a report calling for the repeal of state laws requiring segregation in education — but a minority group made up of three southerners, plus Arthur Holly Compton, strongly dissented. They proposed that inequalities be removed gradually, "within the established patterns of social relationships." Some letter writers were incredulous. "If Washington University wants to line up with some university in Arkansas or Mississippi or Georgia, that's its business," wrote one, "but…the great liberal universities such as Harvard, Yale, Columbia, and Chicago are much better company."

As 1949 began, much of the University was still segregated, though the first full-time black social work students — Lily Holland, Leona Evans, and Fredda Witherspoon — had enrolled to earn a master's degree. Walter White, executive director of

the NAACP, spoke on campus in January, urging students to take a stand — and in spring 1949 some students formed the Student Committee for the Admission of Negroes (SCAN), under the leadership of Jack P. Davidson, Jr. In March, the board announced the opening of all graduate programs except dentistry, and that opened, along with the summer school, the following year.

In May 1949, SCAN sponsored a three-day poll on undergraduate desegregation in which 31 percent of the student body participated. The results, sent to Compton via telegram, showed more than 3-to-1 in favor of admission. That year, pediatrician Helen Nash became the first African-American woman to join the attending staff at St. Louis Children's Hospital, and Ernest S. Simms was appointed to the medical school's research staff — the first African American to hold a full-time academic appointment at the University. By 1950, more blacks were enrolling in Hilltop graduate programs, among them Raymond R. Palmer, the first to earn a master's degree in English, who reported in the *Post-Dispatch* that "everyone was friendly, not in an apologetic, sympathetic, or tolerant manner, but in true democratic spirit."

Now *Student Life*, under a new series of editors, cried out for change. Dean Thomas Hall, too, asked Compton to admit minority students to the College "without discussion or debate." In 1951, Edgar Thomas, who had attended New York University, became the first black to enroll in the medical school, though the first to graduate was James L. Sweatt III, M.D. '62. That same year, four philosophy department members polled College of Liberal Arts faculty — and 130 responded with support for immediate desegregation. By now, all the deans favored admission. "ADMIT NEGROES,"

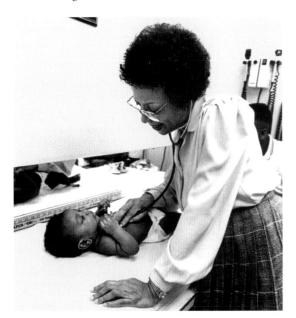

Helen Nash.
A 1945 Meharry Medical College graduate and resident at Homer G. Phillips Hospital, Nash was the first African-American woman pediatrician to join the attending staff at St. Louis Children's Hospital. She became president of its staff in 1977 and served as acting dean of minority affairs.
WU Becker Medical Library

Students march in 1949 to support undergraduate desegregation.
WU Archives

James L. Sweatt III.
Sweatt, M.D. '62, the first African American to graduate from the School of Medicine, went on to become a thoracic surgeon in Dallas.
WU Becker Medical Library

Ernest St. John Simms (1917-1983).
In 1949, Simms was appointed to the medical school's research staff working first in surgery, then microbiology, in the laboratories of Arthur Kornberg and Herman Eisen. He was named research assistant professor in 1968 and finally, after a letter-writing campaign by leading scientists, associate professor in 1971.
WU Becker Medical Library

Thomas S. Hall (1909-1990).
Hall, a University student from 1926-28, professor of biology from 1946-78, and dean of the College of Liberal Arts from 1949-61, was awarded the William Greenleaf Eliot Society "Search" award in 1970 for his distinguished service. The Thomas S. Hall Book Collection and Display in the Biology Library honors him today, as does the Hall lecture that is part of the Assembly Series.
WU Archives

African-American student Jesse Swanigan admitted to the College

Jesse C. Swanigan was among the first group of African-American students admitted to the College of Liberal Arts after its desegregation in 1952. He had to interrupt his education to take a job, but completed his B.S. in 1966 through University College; later he worked at McDonnell Douglas and as an adjunct finance professor at the University of Missouri–St. Louis.

Jesse Swanigan (seated toward center).
Courtesy of Jesse Swanigan

Today, he recalls that first semester in 1952. "You had to try to live up to the standards of the University and also to being a representative of the African-American race, so you were carrying two burdens," he says. But he does not remember any problems with students or faculty; in that regard, it was "smooth sailing," he says, "and as I think back on it now, that is surprising, considering the times."

individual person [it] was and is a product of its age and environment."

By the next fall, 24 black students had been offered admission as undergraduates. The first to graduate, in August 1953, was Edgar Thomas, who had transferred from the medical school. Other early graduates included Charles Lewis, Jr., A.B. '56; Mary Alice Franklin, A.B. '56; Kenneth A. Davis, B.S.M.E. '57; and Vivian Wilkerson, B.M. '56, M.M. '61. Another critical step remained, though: much to the embarrassment of the University's housing staff, the dormitories were still segregated.

A New Century Begins

In 1952, the University began planning for a major event: the 100th anniversary of its founding, to be commemorated with a year of activities. Another event was in the offing: a centennial fund drive to shore up the University's finances. Compton, weary from his various struggles, increasingly came to believe that he was not the person to lead this new effort. He had succeeded in some of his goals, failed in others; most of all, recalled Ethan Shepley, he had seen a university with "no evidence of real life in it, [and] converted it into an institution that…was definitely going places."

On April 10, 1953, at a specially called board meeting, Compton tendered his letter of resignation just days before the board approved the capital campaign. He wished to step down by the end of the year, he said, to take a round-the-world tour, but he offered to return in a scholarly capacity to study the relation of science to human affairs. The board obliged, naming him Distinguished Service Professor of Natural Philosophy, and asked Shepley to appoint a committee to seek a new chancellor. Chairing it was William Akin, president of Laclede Steel Company and board member since 1949; a faculty committee, headed by Evarts Graham, provided advice.

Abram L. Sachar (1899-1993). Sachar, A.B., A.M. '20, speaker for the Second Century Convocation; his wife Thelma Horwitz Sachar (1906-1997), A.B. '25; and David P. (1886-1960) and Carlyn H. Wohl (1894-1987) (seated left to right) were guests February 20, 1955, at the residence of Chancellor Shepley (standing). A writer on Jewish history and onetime national director of B'nai B'rith Hillel Foundations, Sachar became founding president of Brandeis University in 1948, serving as president until 1968 and chancellor until 1982.
WU Photographic Services

demanded *Student Life* in February 1952 for the third semester in a row.

Finally, on May 10, 1952 — a few months after Shepley became board president — the College did, with no warning and little fanfare. Congratulatory letters flooded in from graduates, such as Joy Guze; faculty, such as Park White; and members of the black community, such as Henry W. Wheeler, who called the step "long overdue." The Urban League's executive director M. Leo Bohanon, who had been prodding Compton to act, took a conciliatory tone: "Perhaps some will say that Washington University is not entitled to any special thanks for doing what should have been done at the very beginning of its existence. I choose to differ…not unlike the

Second Century Convocation.
Prominent alumni, chosen after a nationwide polling of University alumni, were honored with citations at the Second Century Convocation in February 1955.

W. Barry Wood, Jr., Busch Professor and head of internal medicine, was the frontrunner for the job. That spring, Shepley found him "very much interested" — but he asked to consider the matter over the summer, and by fall had decided to stay in medicine. With time growing short before Compton's departure, the committee asked Shepley to fill in as acting chancellor while it kept looking. Many prominent names were on the list, mostly from Harvard — Erwin N. Griswold, dean of the School of Law; McGeorge Bundy, associate professor of government; Archibald Cox, professor of law — but the top prospect seemed to be Arthur Flemming, president of Ohio Wesleyan University, who later became U.S. Secretary of Health, Education, and Welfare.

Behind the scenes, a groundswell of support was rising for another candidate: Shepley himself. As Graham put it, "the enthusiasm for his candidacy has grown like a rolling snowball." When Shepley heard that the faculty and board had endorsed him, he was dumbfounded. As he remembered it later: "Evarts said to me, 'Ethan, I don't know whether you have sold these fellows a gold brick or not, but they all want you to stay on this job.'...I said, 'It's been a very interesting assignment. I've loved every bit of it. I've found it fascinating. But I've never contemplated leaving the law.'" In the end, he accepted "with happiness and humility" and took office in March 1954, receiving the gold medallion during the June Commencement.

Although Shepley was a lawyer, not an educator, he was a man of good will and unshakable integrity — known as "Mr. Republican," recalled Thomas Eliot, and "as respected as any man in St. Louis." He had deep University roots on both sides of his family. His paternal grandfather, John R. Shepley, was a board member from 1866 until his 1884 death; his father, John F. Shepley, received a law degree in 1882.

Ray Charles performs at a senior dance in the 1950s.
In 1954 Charles had his first big hit, "I Got a Woman," which marked the beginning of a new genre, "soul," by combining the blues with gospel.
Photo by T. Mike Fletcher

Eleanor Roosevelt (1884-1962).
Chancellor Shepley hosts humanitarian Roosevelt on campus to give an Assembly Series address. A popular speaker and prolific writer, Roosevelt was the niece of President Theodore Roosevelt and the wife of President Franklin D. Roosevelt.

All photos, WU Archives

John M. Olin Library.
Olin Library, completed in 1962, was said by *Student Life* to have "integrated the campus. It provides a focal point, a meeting place." In 2004, the refurbished Olin Library will be rededicated with a revised exterior and rebuilt interior.
WU Archives

His maternal grandfather, Ethan Allen Hitchcock, was a board member from 1907-09 and brother to Henry Hitchcock, the law school's founder and first dean. His mother, Sarah Collier Hitchcock, came from the family that had endowed the Collier Professorship in 1868, while an uncle, Charles Nagel, served on the board from 1892 to 1940. Ethan Shepley himself had studied at Smith Academy, then Yale, and had returned to the University for his law degree in 1922.

THE JOHN M. OLIN LIBRARY RISES

Shepley hit the ground running with several major actions. As an early order of business, he desegregated the dormitories, thus completing at last the University's integration. Within days of his election, he asked psychology chairman Marion Bunch to head a committee to study the University's goals and capital needs; the committee's report, issued after 16 months, became what Shepley called "our institutional bible." He named geologist Carl Tolman, dean of the Graduate School of Arts and Sciences since 1946, as vice chancellor and dean of faculties. However, the looming issue ahead was the new fund drive — and Shepley made the troubling discovery that several uncoordinated offices were handling preparations. He promptly consolidated them into one, University Development, and appointed

Alpha Chi Omega dance, 1949.
WU Archives

E. H. Hopkins to head the effort. Privately in 1954 — then publicly with a four-day convocation in February 1955 — the University launched the three-year, $20 million Second Century Campaign, the second-largest capital fund drive conducted by any U.S. university at the time.

Evidence was mounting that some campaign funds should be used for a new library. The Bunch committee made it a top priority, along with higher faculty salaries, and the College of Liberal Arts faculty endorsed a library building as "the greatest physical need of the University." At a board meeting, Shepley heard Thomas Hall describe the inadequacies of Ridgley — it was "built to accommodate 70,000 volumes for a student body of 300, and we now had a student body of 5,000 and a collection of volumes of…over a half a million" — and he was sold. "I wanted that library building in the worst way," he recalled.

Staffed by dozens of volunteers, the campaign moved forward with clockwork precision. Within months, Shepley could announce that the University would build its new library; by spring 1956, he could promise the faculty a three-year plan to raise their pay by up to 40 percent. Within a year, the campaign had reached its $20 million goal. Altogether, it garnered $22 million, with the welcome help of nearly $5.5 million from the Ford Foundation.

John M. Olin, a board member since 1942, had listened attentively to Hall's description of the old library's shortcomings. Hall noticed Olin, too — "a rather serious-looking man sitting over at the corner of the table," who asked how much the library would cost. Hall said it would take $5 million — $3 million to build and $2 million more to endow — but Olin's only reply was "Grumph." When Shepley went to see Olin subsequently, Olin said he would donate stock worth $1.25 million and hinted at more — a hope that went unful-

The Olins and Shepley.
Left to right, Spencer T. (1900-1995) and John M. (1892-1982) Olin converse with Chancellor Shepley at the Second Century Convocation in 1955.
WU Archives

filled when Olin's alma mater, Cornell University, asked him to fund its library, too. Finally, a $1 million gift from Karl Umrath supplemented the Olin money, and groundbreaking took place in 1960 for the John M. Olin Library, designed by Murphy and Mackey and completed in 1962.

New Buildings and New Leadership on Both Campuses

A spate of other building got under way with the Hugo F. Urbauer Hall for engineering; the Adolphus Busch III Laboratory of Biology for molecular and cellular biology; and the Syma Busiel Astronomical Observatory on the Crow Hall roof. The art collection, long on loan to the Saint Louis Art Museum, finally acquired exhibit space in the new Steinberg Hall, designed in 1956 by young architect Fumihiko Maki, who was chosen four decades later to design the Sam Fox Arts Center. Other additions included the Gaylord Music Library, a new home for the chancellor at 6420 Forsyth, and the Julius and Freda Baer Memorial to house KETC-TV, which showcased faculty in its programming. Soon the Ford Foundation funded University College's Civic Education Center, which aired public affairs programs on KETC.

In 1950, Hall began meeting with Liberal Arts colleagues in a process, funded by the Carnegie Corporation, to seek consensus on undergraduate education. Their report, drafted by Huston Smith, led to the adoption of a curriculum in 1955 that balanced required courses with some choice, particularly in the last two years of study. It reached a national audience when it was published in 1955 as a book: *The Purposes of Higher Education*. Hall promoted two collaborative efforts: a Social Science Institute in 1957, organized by newly hired sociologist Nicholas J. Demerath; and the Graduate Institute of Education in 1956, under Robert J. Schaefer.

Other schools had new leadership. Weary of their feuding, Shepley asked Lawrence Stout, engineering dean, and Willis Reals, University College dean, to step down. Ross Trump, business dean since 1954, eliminated a nine-year-old retailing program, established the Graduate School of Business Administration, dropped "public administration" from the graduate division's title, and launched cooperative programs with universities in Korea and Tunisia. Joseph R. Passonneau, architecture dean since 1957, reduced the undergraduate curriculum from five years to four; added graduate studies, including a program in urban planning and design; and hired George Anselevicius and Constantine Michaelides, both of whom succeeded him as dean. In the law school, Milton Green became dean in 1953, hiring Hiram Lesar, who became his successor, and librarian Jean Ashman, the first woman in the school to hold faculty rank.

Despite a quick succession of deans — Carl V. Moore replacing Robert Moore in 1954 for one year, Oliver Lowry in 1955, Edward W. Dempsey in 1958 — the medical school was expanding. Thanks to Spencer T. Olin, brother of John, and to fund drive chairman Samuel B. Grant, A.B. '18, M.D. '20, a dormitory rose on Scott Avenue late in 1958, and the school continued to receive funding from David Wohl. The major addition to the medical center was Jewish Hospital, a neighbor since 1927. In 1953, the directors of Jewish Hospital agreed to an "association" with Barnes, and eventually to membership in the Washington University Medical School and Affiliated Hospitals (WUMSAH), a formal umbrella organization for medical center institutions, established in 1962.

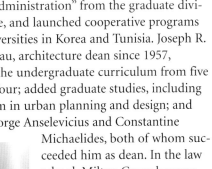

Carl Tolman (1897-1995).
Tolman joined the faculty as a geology professor, served as dean of the Graduate School of Arts and Sciences, as vice chancellor and dean of faculties, then as the University's 11th chancellor during 1961-62.
Herb Weitman, WU Photographic Services

Steinberg Hall.
Japanese architect Fumihiko Maki designed Steinberg Hall, which was funded by Mrs. Etta Steinberg in memory of Mark C. Steinberg and dedicated in May 1960.
David Kilper, WU Photographic Services

Joseph Passonneau.
Passonneau was appointed to the architecture faculty in 1956, became acting dean in 1956, and served as dean from 1957-66. He revamped the undergraduate curriculum in architecture and began an advanced graduate program in urban planning and design.
WU Archives

Chief Justice Earl Warren.
In 1955, Warren spoke at the Second Century Convocation.
WU Archives

195

Daniel Nathans (1928-1999) and Mildred Trotter (1899-1991). Nathans, M.D. '54, shared the 1978 Nobel Prize for "the discovery of restriction enzymes and their application to problems of molecular genetics." He once credited a summer's work with Oliver Lowry as teaching him the joy of research. Trotter, who specialized in physical anthropology, was a longtime faculty member at the School of Medicine.
WU Archives

"Pink Parasites." An anti-Communist picket protests against faculty members who supported scientist Linus Pauling by signing a petition that called for a ban on atmospheric nuclear testing.
St. Louis Post-Dispatch photo Courtesy of Missouri Historical Society, St. Louis

Chancellor Shepley (left) with Edward U. Condon (1902-1974). Shepley appointed Condon to chair the physics department in 1956. Shepley's steadfast support for Condon despite attacks from anti-Communist groups was, in part, what led to his being given the Alexander Meiklejohn Award for Academic Freedom in 1959.
WU Archives

KEEPING FREEDOMS FROM ERODING

The opening speaker of the 1955 Second Century Convocation was Earl Warren, chief justice of the U.S. Supreme Court. His topic, the "Blessings of Liberty," had been much on the minds of Americans throughout the Communist witch hunts of the McCarthy era, and it was the theme of this celebration. "Powerful forces are at work in the world both to preserve liberty and to extinguish it," said Warren, adding: "We do have a battle today to keep our freedoms from eroding."

Already, the University itself had been accused of subversive activity in a 1950 *Saturday Evening Post* article that called it a link in a nationwide system of colleges used by the Communist Party. In 1953, Compton revealed that he had felt "the stinging blows…of America's neo-fascists" as part of a smear campaign that tried to tie him to Communist-sponsored groups. A month later, he refused to let a Party member participate in a forum discussion. While *Student Life* agreed, saying the appearance would do "little good," others argued that this decision hampered freedom of speech. "Since when is the way of truth and wisdom 'to refuse to listen'?" asked Charles Klotzer, A.B. '54. In spring 1953, the University Senate appointed a committee to help protect faculty members against "attacks upon their legitimate freedom."

As chancellor, Shepley was a steadfast defender of these principles. He staunchly supported Merle Kling, whose wife came under investigation, and in 1960, when the *St. Louis Globe-Democrat* attacked 140 faculty members for signing a petition in support of scientist Linus Pauling that called for a ban on nuclear testing, Shepley replied with an eloquent defense: "We are proud of our faculty and proud of their willingness to speak out on controversial issues — even when others, including members of our Board of Directors, may be in complete disagreement." In protest, the St. Louis chapter of the Committee for Outlawing the Communist Party posted pickets around the Hilltop Campus with signs that read: "Down with Pauling's Pink Parasites."

Already Shepley had shown his resolve in 1956 when he hired atomic scientist Edward U. Condon as physics department chairman despite charges — repeatedly refuted — that Condon was, according to the House Un-American Activities Committee chairman, "one of the weakest links in our atomic security." The conservative *Globe-Democrat* and its publisher, Richard Amberg, berated the University editorially, and "I finally had to have a showdown with Mr. Amberg," recalled Shepley, "in which I told him that I had read the entire transcript of the loyalty hearing and…there wasn't a scrap of evidence to question Condon's loyalty."

Condon stayed — and the University's AAUP chapter, headed by Barry Commoner, nominated Shepley for the coveted Alexander Meiklejohn Award for Academic Freedom, which he received in 1959 at the AAUP national meeting. As Commoner explained then, the award demonstrated that Shepley's actions had "consistently revealed an unqualified faith in the value of academic freedom as a way of life for the University."

A NATIONAL STUDENT BODY

The committee suggesting Second Century goals had listed "dormitories" as crucial to the University's future. Since David Houston first envisioned his "University for the Southwest," every chancellor had tried to broaden the geographical reach of the student body, still largely composed of "streetcar" students. This process, which accelerated under Compton, took a giant leap forward under Shepley, who saw the financial value of attracting out-of-state applicants and knew that an infusion of able students would have a stabilizing effect on the faculty, giving them added reason to stay in St. Louis.

Accommodating these students, however, meant residence hall construction south of Forsyth. The planning process, begun in 1957, unfolded quickly. First, the University applied to the Housing and Home Finance Agency (HHFA) for a building loan, next Hellmuth, Obata + Kassabaum (HOK) was chosen as the architect, then the first group of dormitories — Liggett, Koenig, Umrath, Rubelmann, plus half of Wohl Center — went up from 1958-60. Three more stages of construction followed: Lee, Beaumont, Hitzeman, Myers, and building H from 1960-62;

Shepley House.
Completed in 1998 as part of
the William Greenleaf Eliot
Residential College, this resi-
dence house on the South 40
honors the memory of
Chancellor Shepley.
David Kilper, WU Photographic
Services

"ONE HELL OF A MAN"

By 1960, with new financial problems looming and some faculty
complaining that they needed
stronger academic leadership,
Shepley was approaching his June
1961 retirement date — completely exhausted. After "a very, very
happy six years," he recalled, "the
last year and a half were unfortunate; I shouldn't have stayed that
long, because it was a tough
grind." The University, he said,
was ready for new leadership.
"Someone who could analyze the
goals and objectives and spot the
weaknesses. Also one who would
be able to attract scholars that I
couldn't attract at all….What they
needed was someone who could
lift that faculty up and give their morale a boost."

The University began the search process again
— and it was a long, messy struggle. The first
committee consisted of too many potential
candidates and resigned en masse; one outside
prospect, Roger Revelle, director of the Scripps
Institute of Oceanography, turned the job down;
and faculty began choosing sides as
the hunt narrowed to four likely candidates. Finally, Carl Tolman, vice
chancellor and dean of faculties, was
appointed chancellor for 1961-62 —
and despite Shepley's initial insistence
that an outsider would be best, the
choice ultimately fell to an insider:
Thomas H. Eliot, who had succeeded
Thomas Hall as dean of the College
of Liberal Arts in 1960 and then
served as Tolman's vice chancellor
and dean of faculties.

Shepley subsequently returned as
board chairman, but a *Washington
University Magazine* commentary
gave him much higher marks as
chancellor than he had given himself. Calling him "one of the great
figures" in University history, the
article praised his support of academic freedom,
efforts to raise academic standards, success in
garnering financial support, and sterling character. "Shepley's influence will continue to be felt,
thank heaven, and the University will continue
to benefit from his kindness, his wisdom, his
humanity, and the noble tradition he represents,"
the article said, concluding:

"He is one hell of a man."

Shanedling, Dauten, Rutledge, and the Shepley
high rise from 1963-64; and the Eliot high rise
by the mid-1960s.

Women began vacating McMillan Hall,
which became the home of economics, anthropology, sociology, and education, and men left
Umrath (Lee), which now housed the student
health service. To help fill the South 40 resi-
dences, Oliver W. Wagner, formerly University
registrar, took over undergraduate recruitment
efforts, which included a promotional blitz and
hundreds of secondary school visits, some far
from St. Louis. Further, he tackled the problem
of increasing student aid, partly alleviated by
new federal loans and work-study programs.
Little by little, the number of out-of-town
undergraduates rose; within five years, the average Scholastic Aptitude Test (SAT) score went up
by 150 points.

The new dormitories opened to a host of
problems: unfinished rooms, muddy yards,
noisy conditions, a lack of support services. In
1960, a panty raid grew into a melée that had to
be quelled by the Clayton police. Quickly, Leigh
Gerdine convened a faculty committee that recommended the addition of a head faculty resident, faculty fellows in the halls, and interior
modifications, such as sound-deadening materials. When this plan was adopted, political scientist William Chambers became the first Master
of Forsyth Houses, with 17 fellows and as many
graduate students to assist him. The Congress of
the South 40, organized in 1959, improved the
residence hall culture, too, sponsoring dances,
films, and intramural sports.

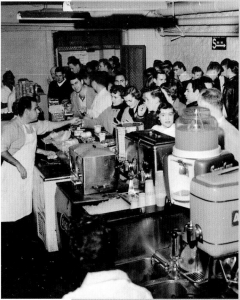

The Quad Shop.
Located in the basement of
South Brookings, the Quad
Shop was a popular gathering-
place for students following
World War II.
Herb Weitman, WU Photographic
Services

"THE NOBLE QUALITIES OF THE BEAR": ATHLETICS AT WASHINGTON UNIVERSITY

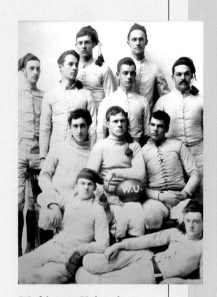

Washington University football team.
The 1890-91 University football team, wearing liberty caps. Intercollegiate football was introduced in 1890.

In 1946, Chancellor Arthur Holly Compton embraced amateur athletics — crushing the hopes of alumni fans, nostalgic for the pre-war days of big-time football. Local newspapers applauded the change: The *St. Louis Star-Times* titled its editorial, "Staying Out of the Mastodon Market." And on September 27, 1947, with B. Blair Gullion as athletic director and Wilbur C. ("Weeb") Ewbank as the new football coach, the "rusty gates of Francis Field swung open and a throng of 9,000 swarmed in to witness the...49th year of football," said *Student Life*.

Some rocky days lay ahead before the athletic program settled comfortably into its current National Collegiate Athletic Association (NCAA) Division III niche, acquired adequate funding and facilities, and joined with eight like-minded schools in establishing the University Athletic Association (UAA), but the University was firmly committed to amateur athletics. "We

Frank H. ("Doc") Ewerhardt (1877-1948).
Ewerhardt, M.D. '10, was athletic director from 1904-13.

believe that the philosophy of playing without athletic scholarships has high merit academically and ethically," said then-Chancellor William H. Danforth in 1986, at the time of the UAA founding.

By 2003, the University's program had grown to include 18 varsity teams — nine each for men and women — with a solid record of achievement: 11 NCAA team national championships, 285 All-America awards, and four NCAA individual national titles. In recent years, several programs have emerged as stand-outs. Volleyball has won seven Division III national championships and 15 of the past 16 UAA titles. In 2003, both basketball programs were again UAA champions, and the women narrowly missed winning their fifth NCAA title. Since 1988, men's track and field teams have accrued a combined total of 14 UAA indoor and outdoor titles, while the women swept their indoor-outdoor championships from 2000-03. Overall, from 1978 to the end of the 2002-03 winter season, varsity teams racked up 3,446 wins, 1,612 losses, and 71 ties — a .673 winning percentage.

19TH-CENTURY ATHLETICS

Athletics began on the University's downtown campus, which had no playing field and only a small gymnasium. Baseball started in 1867, but in 1870 the *Irving Union* reported that "foot-ball mania has seized the students, and every day they may be seen on 17th Street, rushing after a ball." In 1884, the Washington University Athletic

Smith Academy baseball team.
The Smith Academy boys organized a baseball club called the "Olympics," and their success sparked interest among the Collegiate students, who formed a club in 1867 with nine players.

1903 track team.

According to the 1905 *Hatchet*, members of the track team were William L. Hall, '04, *Captain*; W.W. Brey, '03; E.F. Sessinghaus, '03; Sears Lehmann, L., '03; S.E. Eliot, '05; J. Laichinger, '05; T.P. Moore, '05; A.R. Skinker, '05; S.P. Smith, '05; Walter Heimbuecher, '06; Walter Krause, '06; and Harvey Lamb, '06.

Association was born, and it sponsored intramural contests until 1890, when the first intercollegiate football match took place between the University and the Missouri Tigers.

No player, including star halfback Charles Reber, A.B. '91, ever forgot that thrilling game in which the University men, wearing tasseled red hats, prevailed 28-0 against the Tigers, in black and gold. "We didn't have padded uniforms like they have now," recalled Reber years afterwards. "Just wore canvas trousers and sweaters….When we had any money we bought shoes with cleats, but that wasn't very often."

Soon entrepreneurial students decided to cash in on the football craze. From gate receipts, they bought uniforms, hired coaches, and paid the players a little something, often enhancing the team with a few "ringers" from the outside. By 1899, the faculty was up in arms, "opposed to the semi-professional manner in which the football games were conducted," said *Student Life*. The University cracked down with new rules and a committee to promote amateur athletics.

1900-1920

The early years saw attempts at other sports — crew, track, hockey — but the next surge in athletics came after the move to the new campus. Football started up with a lopsided 1905 victory in which the University team, now called the "Pikers," defeated Westminster College 59-0. By then they had an athletic director, Frank H. ("Doc") Ewerhardt, M.D. '10, but were so poor, he said, that one season they had only a single football; baseball disappeared completely from 1910-14. In 1908, the University hired its first full-time football coach, Francis Cayou, who stayed until 1913.

Soon Monroe Cuming ("Poge") Lewis, LL.B. '16 — an outstanding pitcher as well as captain of the football team — emerged as one of the University's greatest athletes; his kicking helped defeat Missouri and Saint Louis University in 1915. To sponsor more football stars, the enterprising new athletic director, physician and former University of Michigan (Wolverine) tackle William ("Big Bill") Edmunds, began soliciting private donations. By the time Edmunds left in 1917, however, he had managed only one winning season in four.

Tennis was flourishing, crew had some good years, and men's basketball began in 1903, improving in 1919 under director Richard Rutherford and talented guard Oliver Kraehe, LL.B. '22, who shot one memorable goal just as a light fuse blew in Francis gymnasium. The University women formed an athletic association in 1911, and their sports roster grew to include baseball, track, field hockey, basketball, and swimming.

Francis Cayou (1875-1948).
Cayou, who was born at the Omaha Indian Reservation near Decatur, Nebraska, came from Wabash College in 1908 to coach football and stayed until 1913. From 1920-23, he was athletic director at Great Lakes Naval Training Station.

Washington University at 150
as of February 22, 2003

VARSITY SPORTS

Men
Baseball
Basketball
Cross Country
Football
Indoor Track and Field
Outdoor Track and Field
Soccer
Swimming and Diving
Tennis

Women
Basketball
Cross Country
Indoor Track and Field
Outdoor Track and Field
Soccer
Softball
Swimming and Diving
Tennis
Volleyball

INTRAMURAL AND CLUB SPORTS

Arm Wrestling
Badminton
Basketball
Billiards
Bowling
Crew
Cross Country
Flag Football
Golf
Inner Tube Water Polo
Racquetball
Soccer
Softball
Swimming
Table Tennis
Tennis
Track and Field
Ultimate Frisbee
Volleyball
Wallyball

The legendary 1923 football victory over Mizzou.

1916 Women's field hockey team.

All photos, WU Archives

199

James ("Jimmy") Conzelman (1898-1970). During his time at the University, Conzelman played football two years and moved on to professional football until 1929, when a knee injury ended his career. In 1932 he came back to the University as coach, compiling a six-year record of 32-16-2 and winning two straight Missouri Valley Conference titles. In 1940, he became coach of the Chicago Cardinals, and he was elected to the Pro Football Hall of Fame in 1964.

THE 1920s AND EARLY 1930s

By 1923, Rutherford had left and a new coach had failed to ignite the football team, now playing high-powered opponents in the Missouri Valley Conference. Under pressure from alumni, Chancellor Hadley rehired Big Bill Edmunds. At first his approach seemed to fizzle; in a game against the Kansas Jayhawks, the University received "the most terrific walloping" — 83-0 — "in the history of Conference football," said *Student Life*. A week later, however, the team rallied, "administering a convincing 13-7 licking to the Tigers. Just how the miracle was accomplished no one knows."

Edmunds did not stop at football: He talked Hadley into building an 8,000-seat field house, largely for basketball and track. At the gala ded-

ication in January 1926, undergraduate juniors in the law class presented the school with a live bear mascot for its newly retitled teams. Hadley explained the name change in his speech. With the whole animal world to choose from, he said, Missouri's founders had placed two bears on the state seal. Now the University would pay "a belated but deserved tribute to their wisdom and to the noble qualities of the bear. May he always lead us to deserved victory."

Two years later, new Chancellor George Throop dismissed Edmunds and his football coach for hiring paid athletes. The new director, Alfred Sharpe, had big dreams: a stadium seating 30,000, even 50,000 people, near the corner of Big Bend and Forest Park Parkway. But neighbors objected, the Depression intervened, and the expansive plan was abandoned. In 1929, the University installed floodlights on Francis Field, and the football team played its first night game.

While football garnered most attention, other teams were quietly doing well. Basketball teams won three conference titles and even played Notre Dame in 1936. Swimming improved, too, thanks to the new Wilson Pool; between 1926 and 1947, teams won the Missouri Valley Conference every time but once. Tennis continued strong, track and cross country had successful years — only baseball was sputtering. In 1924-25, said the *Washingtonian*, 78 percent of University men were taking part in some form of campus athletics.

"Whitey" becomes the team mascot

The dedication of the Field House in January 1926 marked another first — the initiation of "Whitey," the University's official bear mascot; he was given by the Whiteacres, a junior law organization, in honor of the athletic teams' name change from "Pikers" to "Bears." The cub (right) lived in the Washington University stables, in care of a keeper, and paraded around at sports events; but as he got larger, his care became more difficult and, eventually, he was given to the St. Louis Zoo Bear Pits. "The sultan of our athletic events…is now enjoying a well-earned rest with his brethren," said *Washingtonian*.

"Whitey" drawings from the 1927 *Hatchet*

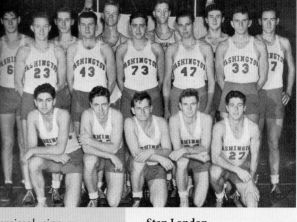

THE GLORY DAYS OF FOOTBALL

One star of Rutherford's football teams — 6-0 in 1918 and 5-1-1- in 1919 — was the charming quarterback, James Gleason Ryan Dunn ("Jimmy") Conzelman. When the University invited him back as coach in 1932, during the depths of the Depression, he was just the spark that the team and city needed. For seven exciting years, he recruited top players; scheduled tough conference, Big Ten, Big Six, and other opponents, such as Duquesne, Southern Methodist, Notre Dame, even Army; and managed to compile a respectable 40-35-2 record. In 1933, 63,422 people watched the University's home games — an increase of some 44,000 over the year before.

Sometimes he bent rules to get players he wanted, but among his "Iron Men" were football legends: tackle Glynn Clark, A.B. '34; running back "Bucking" Joe Bukant, A.B. '36, A.M. '48, who later played five years in the National Football League (NFL); end Dwight Hafeli, B.S. '37; powerful center Alviero Iezzi, B.S.B.A. '37; "Bounding" Bob Hudgens, D.D.S. '38, an All-American running back; quarterback Dick Yore, A.B. '39, M.D. '43; and Wilson ("Bud") Schwenk, B.S.B.A. '42, a basketball and baseball stand-out, who led the nation in 1941 in total offense and passing. Conzelman's recruiting sins were mitigated by the results, said longtime *St. Louis Post-Dispatch* sports editor, Bob Broeg, in 1990: "Many a hard-nosed kid with soft pockets got his education from a university of lofty ideals and used it to become doctors, dentists, lawyers, educators, civic leaders, etc. Many wouldn't have had a chance without Conzelman."

Eventually, the downtown alumni sports crowd turned against Conzelman, and in 1940 he was fired. Players were outraged by Conzelman's dismissal, signing a petition printed in the *Post-Dispatch*, while students staged a "We Want Jimmy" parade — all to no avail. To his horror, Throop discovered that some of the alumni subsidies Conzelman had solicited to cover expenses had not been paid, and the hard-pressed University had to pick up the tab. "Washington University has its choice," said the *Globe-Democrat* grimly, "continuation of [subsidized] football or elimination."

POST-WAR SPORTS

As chancellor, Compton picked a third course: shifting to amateur athletics. Under Ewbank, the football program racked up a 9-1 record in 1949; one key player was Charles Winner, M.S.H. Phys. Ed. '50, a running back who married Ewbank's daughter and, in time, succeeded his father-in-law as coach of the New York Jets. Athletic director Blair Gullion coached basketball and that team improved, with help from engineering student Jim Barton. Briefly, a medical student coached baseball: Stan London, M.D. '49, who subsequently became team surgeon for the baseball Cardinals. After Ewbank's departure, Gullion recruited Irv Uteritz ("Utz"), then former North Carolina coach Carl Snavely. His key players included Jim Burst, B.S.I.E. '55, who scored 30 career touchdowns; Don Polkinghorne, A.B. '59, who carried the ball a record-breaking 21 times for 367 yards in his final game; and Mel Siegel, A.B. '56, who signed with the Philadelphia Eagles after graduating.

On the women's side, some 70 percent of students took part in sports by 1950; one star was Jacqueline Bickel Schapp, B.S. '47, M.S. '54, captain of the field hockey and basketball teams. However, women's sports halted in 1955 and did not resume for 13 years. With the budget squeeze of the 1960s and early '70s, the men's program entered a

Stan London.
London, M.D. '49 (front row, far left), a star in basketball and baseball, later became a national standout in handball. He was longtime team surgeon for the St. Louis Cardinals baseball team.

Charles Dallan ("Dal") Maxvill.
Maxvill, B.S.E.E. '62, playing shortstop and hitting over .300, helped the University's baseball team to four winning seasons. He played professional baseball for 14 seasons, 11 of them with the St. Louis Cardinals. In 1978 he joined the coaching staff of the New York Mets, returned as a Cardinals coach in 1979-80, then became third base coach for the Atlanta Braves from 1982-85. He was general manager of the Cardinals from 1985-94.

Bleacher Collapse.
In November 1947, the Bears scored an early touchdown in a football game against Grinnell College and the 2,200-member crowd jumped to its feet, causing two sections of makeshift wooden bleachers to collapse and injuring 22 people, one seriously. Sturdier bleachers quickly replaced them. "It May Take an Atomic Bomb to Make New Bleachers Collapse," quipped *Student Life*.

All photos, WU Archives

201

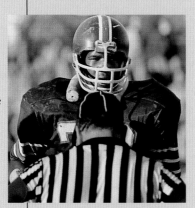

Shelby Jordan.
Jordan, A.B. '74, is the only football player in University history to have played in a Super Bowl and one of only a few to be drafted into the NFL. He played professionally for 13 seasons and appeared in the 1983 Super Bowl with the Los Angeles Raiders.
WU Archives

Women's soccer.
Christyn Chambers (center), A.B. '01, earned first team University Athletic Association honors in 1998, 1999, and 2000, as well as first team All-America honors in 1998.
WU Photographic Services

Kevin Suiter.
Suiter, B.S.B.A. '88, two-time Division III All-America basketball guard, liked the scholar-athlete concept. "Basketball is for four years," he once said. "An education is forever."
WU Photographic Services

bleak period, too, in which Chancellor Thomas Eliot considered dropping varsity football and *did* drop basketball in 1971, over student protests. Still, "Battling Bear" football squads under popular Dave Puddington, coach from 1962-67, provided exciting moments, as did All-American soccer star Majid Kria, B.S.B.A. '63; and winning baseball teams that featured shortstop Dal Maxvill, B.S.E.E. '62.

Into the 1970s, the athletics program still languished — even its new title, the Department of Sports and Recreation, seemed lackluster. Amid a series of coaches, football was able to attract some key players, notably defensive linebacker Shelby Jordan, A.B. '74, who later played 13 seasons in the NFL, including a 1983 appearance in Super Bowl XVIII with the Los Angeles Raiders; Marion Stallings, A.B. '75, defensive back; and David Bolton, B.S. '84, M.E.M. '89, a wide receiver in football, as well as national champion in the decathlon. One milestone came in 1973 with the formal beginning of Division III athletics.

1980s: A New Beginning

The long-neglected athletic facilities were by now in poor repair and badly out of date. One hour after John Schael, former University of Chicago associate athletic director, took over the program in 1978, a county health inspector closed Wilson Pool. With added stimulus from Title IX of the Higher Education Act of 1972, Schael reinitiated women's sports and hired full-time coaches, among them Mark Edwards, A.B. '69, who restarted men's basketball in 1981. Schael helped plan the first major expansion of the University's athletic facilities in more than 50 years — and the handsome $13 million Athletic Complex opened in 1985. In that year, Hartwig ("Harry") Kisker, dean of students, with the support of Schael and Chancellor William Danforth, initiated talks that led to the 1986 formation of the University Athletic Association, a group that believes "student-athletes are just that — students first and athletes second."

Amy Sullivan Nordmann.
A two-time, first-team All-America selection, Nordmann, A.B. '94, M.D. '99, helped the Bears capture three NCAA Division III national volleyball championships. She was a member of the undefeated 1992 squad.
Joe Angeles, WU Photographic Services

At the same time, Schael's new coaches were busy building their programs. Edwards soon chalked up 18 winning seasons, setting a team record for wins (25-2) in 2001-02 and advancing to the "Sweet 16" of the NCAA Tournament. Teri Clemens arrived in 1984 and retired 14 years later, after her volleyball teams had won seven of the previous 10 national titles and she was five-time Division III coach of the year. Nancy Fahey came in 1985 to coach basketball, was named coach of the year in 1998-99

and again in 1999-2000, and by 2001-02 had a 377-64 record, having taken her team to four straight national titles. Its 81-game winning streak is the longest in NCAA women's basketball. In 2002, Larry Kindbom, head football coach since 1989, led the Bears to their second UAA championship and tenth winning season in a row.

These years were marked by memorable players. In basketball, Kevin Suiter, B.S.B.A. '88, was a two-time All-American guard; Debbie Michelson, B.S.B.A. '92, was an outstanding tennis player. Women's basketball had the 1998 and 1999 NCAA champions Emily Harold, Emily Nolan, Sue Tucker, Tasha Rodgers (Division III Player of the Year in 2000-01), and Alia Fischer (who was Player of the Year for the three years preceding Rodgers). In 1998 and 1999, Emily Richard captured national track-and-field titles. Volleyball had All-American players Lori Nishikawa Price, A.B. '90; Amy Sullivan Nordmann, A.B. '94, M.D. '99; Amy Albers Laczkowski, B.S.B.A. '95; and senior setter Rebecca Rotello, named Division III National Player of the Year in 2003. Linebacker and biomedical engineering major Brandon Roberts won the 2002 HealthSouth Draddy Award — the "Academic Heisman" — as the nation's top scholar-athlete, the first non-Division I player to receive the award.

The athletic program attracted supporters, as well, including two couples — Stanley, A.B. '35, and Lucy Lopata; Art, B.S.B.A. '49, and Marge McWilliams — who have established annual basketball

tournaments. I.E. Millstone, B.S. '27, a former championship swimmer himself, donated funds for the Millstone Pool, while William K. Y. Tao, M.S.M.E. '50, supported the refurbishing of the tennis courts, now called the Tao Tennis Center. In 1991, a nine-foot bronze statue of two bears was installed in front of the Athletic Complex — a tribute to sports enthusiast and former University trustee, George H. Capps, A.B. '39, J.D. '39.

Two other key boosters have been William Danforth and his wife, Ibby, who won the athletic department's Distinguished Service Award in 1995 for helping to revitalize the sports program. Now Chancellor Mark Wrighton is an avid fan: attending games when he is in town and, when he is not, calling the 24-hour sports hotline or visiting the athletics Web page for the latest scores, from as far away as China.

For more on the history of athletics at Washington University, refer to bearsports.wustl.edu.

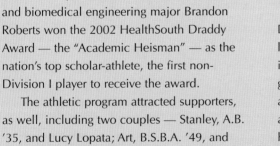

A "TAKE-OFF" UNIVERSITY

1962–1978

Seventy by 'Seventy. Chancellor Eliot announces the start of the Seventy by 'Seventy campaign at a special convocation in Graham Chapel in 1965.
WU Archives

A "TAKE-OFF" UNIVERSITY

In July 1962, the 12th chancellor of Washington University took office: former vice chancellor and dean of faculties, Thomas Hopkinson Eliot. Like tenth chancellor Ethan A.H. Shepley, he was a lawyer — a 1932 Harvard law school graduate — who had left a prominent law firm to come to the University. They were alike in another respect: Each aspired to political office. Three times Eliot had run for Congress from Massachusetts, winning his 1940 race. In 1964, recovered from his labors as chancellor, Shepley tried unsuccessfully to become Missouri's governor.

Previous pages:
A detail on Francis Gymnasium.

1962   *Thomas H. Eliot became the University's 12th chancellor.*

1964   *The position of vice chancellor for medical affairs was created with Carl V. Moore the first to hold it. He was succeeded in 1965 by William H. Danforth.*

1964   *About 67 percent of entering freshmen came from outside the St. Louis area.*

1965   *In February, Chancellor Eliot launched the "Seventy by 'Seventy" campaign.*

1966   *The College of Liberal Arts was renamed the College of Arts and Sciences.*

1968   *In December, black students staged a sit-in in Brookings.*

1970   *In the wake of the May 4 students' deaths at Kent State, WU's Air Force ROTC building was set on fire.*

1971   *On July 1, William H. Danforth became the University's 13th chancellor.*

1978   *The University marked its 125th anniversary.*

1962 entering class.
Chancellor Eliot and his wife, Lois (right), greet students at the freshman picnic.
Herb Weitman, WU Photographic Services

The resemblance ended there: the two differed sharply in background and politics. While Shepley was a lifelong St. Louisan, connected by blood and friendship to the city's elite, Eliot was bound to his native Boston, where his grandfather had been longtime Harvard president Charles W. Eliot, a distant cousin of William Greenleaf Eliot and friend of Robert Brookings. Eliot, unlike Shepley, was a New Deal Democrat, who had spent heady days in Washington drafting the Social Security Act of 1935 and then, as counsel to the Social Security Board, defending it before the U.S. Supreme Court. "For such a man," wrote President John F. Kennedy in his congratulatory letter, "the past is prologue and, still youthful in years and outlook, I know he will lead Washington University to days of even greater distinction."

In fact, Shepley initially opposed Eliot's appointment as chancellor because he was concerned that Eliot's liberal politics would lead to conflicts with conservatives on the board. As Eliot later noted, Shepley worried that "I would not be able to talk the same language as John Olin." However, board members were "terrifically impressed," recalled Shepley, with the "businesslike way" in which he had handled things as vice

Thomas Hopkinson Eliot (1907-1991).
Eliot was the 12th chancellor of Washington University, serving from 1962-71. A graduate of Harvard in 1928 and its law school in 1932, he came to the University in 1952 as chairman of political science, becoming dean of the College of Liberal Arts, vice chancellor, and dean of faculties in 1961 and chancellor in 1962.

Oil on canvas by Fred Conway
WU Gallery of Art

Ethan Shepley, Thomas Eliot, and James S. McDonnell.
In May 1965, Shepley, chairman of the Seventy by 'Seventy campaign, meets with Chancellor Eliot and McDonnell, chairman of the board of trustees.
WU Archives

chancellor, and James S. McDonnell, chairman of McDonnell Aircraft Co. and board member since 1960, became a leading advocate for Eliot's candidacy. When Eliot declared he would only take the job if the board raised funds for him to hire top-notch faculty and staff, McDonnell and Morton D. May, president of the May Department Stores Company, buttonholed fellow members to find the needed support.

At the height of the late-1960s campus unrest, Eliot sometimes clashed with local businessmen on the board, who could not understand why he did not deal more harshly with student protesters and why he often sought compromise instead of

confrontation. Such disputes may have been exacerbated by Eliot's own tendency, borne of years in politics, to savor a good fight. Though a "man of real ability," Shepley said, Eliot was "one of the tough ones…who never hesitated to tell you what he thought."

Eliot first did so in his eloquent, unusually specific, inaugural address. Unlike Shepley, who never dreamed of setting an academic course for the University, Eliot had one clearly in mind: He wanted to give all undergraduates a solid liberal education, erase "obsolete curricular boundaries" between disciplines, and turn the professional schools into graduate programs only. The University should not grow much larger, he said; rather, it should "stress quality rather than quantity," offering moderate-sized classes and personal attention. "This will not be a simple task," he warned. "It will demand of us ingenuity, imagination, and innovation."

INGENUITY IN RECRUITMENT

Eliot's first task was to build a strong administrative team. Since he loved the "representational" or external side of the chancellor's role, he created the job of provost to share the inside work. This person would function, he said, as his "alter ego," making "decisions which I would not second guess and who wouldn't second guess mine." For this position, Eliot tapped George E. Pake, physics chairman from 1952-56, who had moved to Stanford but now came back — with even better results than Eliot had hoped, taking a special interest in the sciences, engineering, and government relations.

Carl Dauten (1914-1976).
A faculty member in the business school for 30 years, Dauten, A.B. '36, A.M. '39, Ph.D. '44, was a key administrator for 14, and executive vice chancellor for the last seven. At his death, Chancellor Danforth called him a man of "total integrity."
WU Archives

For an associate provost, Eliot turned to the business school and Carl Dauten, respected professor of finance and banking; for his own assistant, to political scientist Lattie F. Coor, Jr., A.M. '60, Ph.D. '64, later vice chancellor. Within months, Eliot had created another post, dean of the Faculty of Arts and Sciences, and here he managed a coup that impressed even *Time* magazine, which called him in May 1963 "a ferocious faculty raider." Historian Jack Hexter had proposed "a crazy notion" — hiring eminent

The last streetcar.
In February 1963, the last streetcar to campus stopped running. It was the end of an era for many nostalgic alumni, said Frank O'Brien (1920-77), A.B. '42, editor of the *Washington University Magazine*:

"An old, old friend has finally passed away….If it weren't for the trolley, it is doubtful if some of us would even be alumni today. In times past there were a variety of lines to campus…. Today a growing number of students come to the campus by jet and ocean liner from all over the world. The days of the 'streetcar college' are gone."

In 2006, new MetroLink light rail service will run along this same right of way.
Herb Weitman, WU Photographic Services

George Pake.
A Harvard Ph.D. at age 24, Pake came to the University in 1948 as assistant professor of physics, becoming department chair four years afterwards. He left for Stanford in 1956 but returned as provost in 1962, later adding the title of executive vice chancellor. He stepped down to become Mallinckrodt Distinguished University Professor in 1969; in 1970, he left academia for Xerox Corporation. He served on the University's board from 1970-87, when he was named an emeritus trustee.
WU Archives

historian Robert R. Palmer from Princeton — and Eliot pounced. When Palmer accepted, said Eliot, "it did the job that was so desperately needed, which was to reestablish the great confidence of the faculty in themselves and in the institution."

With his team in place, he attacked weaknesses on the faculty — and no one, at any institutional or seniority level, was off limits. When he was chairman of political science, Eliot had already hired Robert Salisbury, and now he moved to shore up philosophy and economics, where early appointments included Harold J. Barnett and Murray Weidenbaum, who became department chairman and founder of the Center for the Study of American Business. As director of the Graduate Institute of Education, Eliot named Judson Shaplin from the Harvard School of Education. Soon classics, art and archaeology, Romance languages, and botany were on his list for change.

In fall 1962, Eliot took a hard look at Engineering and found it "in a sorry mess," with a divided faculty, outdated curriculum, and dwindling enrollment. Immediately, Pake brought in a team of outside advisers whose recommendations led to a leadership change. The

new dean, James McKelvey, M.S.Ch.E. '47, Ph.D. '50, formerly chairman of chemical engineering, took office amid some opposition, but before long managed to build the school — now renamed Engineering and Applied Science — by actively recruiting students, appointing more than 30 faculty members in three years, and focusing on up-and-coming fields, such as computer science. Research funding exploded, and so did new ties with industry, including a 1965 research collaboration with Monsanto. By 1968, the *Washington University Magazine* could title an article: "Engineering Renaissance."

As part of his personnel changes, Eliot took aim at the board of directors — called "trustees" after 1965 — broadening its membership base. Moving outside the reliable pool of local business leaders, he chose trustees with national scope, such as Clark M. Clifford, LL.B. '28, former special counsel to the president, and Paul A. Freund, A.B. '28, Harvard law professor. Within a few years, these men — firm Eliot supporters — would be of key importance, backing him at moments of crisis. In October 1963, he persuaded James S. McDonnell to succeed Shepley as board president.

MEDICAL CRISIS BREWING

Eliot's focus then shifted from the Hilltop to the medical center, where a colossal conflict was about to unfold. At the heart of the dispute were two formidable personalities: Edgar

M. Queeny, who had retired from Monsanto and had become board chairman of Barnes Hospital in 1961; and Edward W. Dempsey, dean of the medical school since 1958. At first the two men got along well; together they helped to shape Washington University Medical School and Affiliated Hospitals (WUMSAH) and bring Jewish Hospital into the group. Queeny even tried to persuade Dempsey to resign as dean and become WUMSAH director, but Dempsey cordially declined.

Setting up his office in the hospital, Queeny devoted himself full time to his new job, along

Murray Weidenbaum.
Weidenbaum (right), converses with Paul McCracken, Chairman of the Council of Economic Advisers under Nixon. The Edward Mallinckrodt Distinguished University Professor, Weidenbaum served for two years as Assistant Secretary of the Treasury for Economic Policy in the Nixon administration and was chairman of President Ronald Reagan's Council of Economic Advisers from 1981-83, becoming one of the principal architects of "Reaganomics." In 1975, he founded the Center for the Study of American Business, renamed the "Murray Weidenbaum Center on the Economy, Government, and Public Policy" in 2000.
WU Archives

James M. McKelvey.
McKelvey, M.S.ChE. '47, Ph.D. '50, formerly chairman of chemical engineering, became dean of Engineering and transformed the school. Today he is a senior professor.
David Kilper, WU Photographic Services

with his close friend Robert
Otto, former president of
Laclede Gas Co., who moved in
next door. "I don't suppose there
was anything about this huge
complex of buildings that Edgar
Queeny didn't become familiar
with," recalled Ethan Shepley. He
overhauled hospital maintenance
procedures, instituted pay raises,
and forced telephone operators
to improve their manners, literally overnight. As a personal gift,
he donated a four-story addition
to the Rand-Johnson wing of the hospital and
funded construction of Queeny Tower, begun in
1963. "Queeny was doing a magnificent job in
getting the hospital facilities operating on a
better basis," said Shepley.

Then a rift developed between Queeny and
Dempsey. Queeny, "a very brilliant, ruthless, and
ferocious antagonist," said Eliot, "decided that
come hell or high water, he was going to make
Barnes pay for itself." He began demanding more
income from the medical school, trying to cut the
house staff, and threatening to close unprofitable
clinics that treated the indigent. As pathology professor Margaret Smith said in an irate letter to the
Post-Dispatch, the hospital facilities would soon
"resemble those of a financially oriented hotel
catering to those with well-lined pocketbooks."

Queeny then decided to offer space in
Queeny Tower to private physicians
who were part-time faculty members
— but *he,* not the full-time faculty,
would choose who got it. The very
idea of competition so close at
hand angered the faculty, especially
the surgeons, struggling to maintain their own clinical practices.

"Two men who had been great
admirers of each other now became
so bitter in their personal relations
that, literally, they found it difficult to sit
in the same room," said Shepley. Others were
drawn into the Dempsey–Queeny fray: Eliot,
denounced by both sides when he tried to inter-
cede; and the medical school's Executive Faculty,
especially its "kitchen cabinet" made up of its
most influential members, all heads of major
departments — Carl Cori in biochemistry, Carl V.
Moore in internal medicine, Carl Moyer in surgery, and Oliver Lowry in pharmacology. Dempsey
reported to them on his disagreements with Queeny,
and at first they supported him; in fact, Carl
Moyer resigned from the University in 1964,
furious with Queeny and the Barnes board.

In January 1964, Eliot had had
enough. He named a "Committee of
Four," headed by Robert Brookings
Smith, great-nephew of Robert
Brookings, to resolve the differences.
Working quickly, the committee
recommended the appointment of
two referees — Joseph C. Hinsey,
Ph.D. '27, director of Cornell
Medical Center, and John H.
Knowles, M.D. '51, chief executive
officer of Massachusetts General
Hospital — to make a site visit and
suggest constructive change. By
April 1964, Hinsey and Knowles produced their
report, which made a central recommendation:
create a new position, vice chancellor for

medical affairs,
and fill it with
someone who
could work with
the dean and the
Barnes director
"in attaining a
coordinated pro-
gram." Without
consulting any-
one, Queeny and
J.S. McDonnell
chartered a plane,
flew to Boston,
and offered the
job to Knowles,
who turned
it down.

Under pres-
sure, Carl Moore
— respected on
all sides, but
unwilling to leave
his own beloved
department — agreed in June 1964 to take the
job for one year and "live for the day," he wrote,
"when I can give the job up." As vice chancellor,
he represented the medical school in all external
matters, especially in dealing with the hospitals.
That meant a shrinking of the dean's responsibility — another blow for Dempsey, who left abruptly in August to become special assistant to the
secretary of the Department of Health,
Education, and Welfare. Associate Dean M.
Kenton King became acting dean; then early in
1965, Cori came into King's office. "He kept pac-
ing back and forth in front of the desk. He said,
'We have decided we want you to be the dean.
Will you accept?'" recalled King, who was
stunned, but said yes.

Meanwhile, the regular medical faculty, expressing a lack of confidence in the medical school's leadership, had formed a Faculty Council, a move that angered the Executive Faculty, though King was able to defuse that crisis. In December 1964 came the welcome announcement that Barnes and the medical school, on the brink of divorce only months earlier, had signed a 30-year agreement. Now it was necessary to hunt for a successor to Carl Moore as vice chancellor. In spring 1965 Carl Cori made a recommendation: a young associate professor who had worked in the Cori lab — William H. Danforth.

NEW PROGRAMS AND BUILDINGS ON THE HILLTOP

While the medical school's problems distracted Eliot, they did not halt change on the Hilltop Campus, and before long Eliot had made some progress toward the goals he had laid out. Among the interdepartmental offerings, which already included molecular biology and comparative literature, were new programs such as Asian studies. Though Fine Arts and Engineering refused to abandon undergraduate education, as Eliot had hoped, Law agreed to admit only college graduates after 1968.

Graduate programs saw particularly dramatic growth — and that meant more faculty. In the decade after Eliot took office, faculty in the College of Liberal Arts — renamed the College of Arts and Sciences in 1966 — grew from 240 to 355. Some were hired for new departments, such as Russian, established in 1965, or anthropology, split off from sociology in 1967. The new dormitories on the South 40 were filling up with undergraduates and, beginning in 1962, faculty member Burton M. Wheeler took over for three years as Master of Forsyth Houses, directing a stimulating program of student activities.

Sterling Schoen helps establish Consortium for Graduate Study in Management

Sterling H. Schoen (1918-1999).

In 1964-65, research by Sterling H. Schoen, professor of management at the business school from 1950-88, showed a dearth of African Americans in the top ranks of Fortune 500 companies. He decided the remedy was to provide full scholarships for them in M.B.A. programs, then jobs on corporate management tracks. Provost George Pake gathered a meeting of educators and business leaders, enthusiastic about Schoen's plan.

Indiana University and the University of Wisconsin signed on to the effort, and Schoen — aided by faculty colleague William Emory and Wallace L. Jones, a Ph.D. candidate in education — established the Consortium for Graduate Study in Management, funded by a $400,000 Ford Foundation grant matched by corporate contributors. In 1967, the first class was admitted: 21 African-American men, seven at each school.

The Consortium, which Schoen directed until 1980, grew to include nine other universities. It admitted its first women in 1971, and eventually added Hispanics and Native Americans to the program. By the time of Schoen's death, it had brought more than 3,000 minority men and women into management positions. Wallace Jones (1934-1997), Ph.D. '90, served as its associate director, executive director, then chief executive officer in 1990, succeeded by Phyllis S. Buford in 1996.

Burton M. Wheeler.
Professor of English and religious studies, Wheeler served in other key roles, including Master of Forsyth Houses, dean of the College of Arts and Sciences from 1966-78, and University grand marshal. A student, Elizabeth Knoll, A.B. '78, called him "the ideal of an academic administrator, with a sense of duty and honor and service to the community, whose integrity — and good judgment — everyone recognized and respected." A residence house on the South 40 and two academic awards are named for Wheeler, now professor emeritus.

Photos, WU Archives

The recruitment of minority students was initiated, thanks to the efforts of admissions staff member Margaret Dagen, who came in 1963 and began seeking out African-American students in inner-city schools. Two years later, the Work-Study Career Scholarship Program started: a collaboration with local businesses,

Gloria W. White (1934-2003).
White, A.M. '63, M.J.S. '80, vice chancellor for human resources and affirmative action officer, retired in 1997 after three decades of service to the University in many different roles. William H. Danforth praised her, saying: "her wisdom, courage, and common sense have guided us all."
WU Archives

funded by a $150,000 grant from the Rockefeller Foundation, which offered outstanding high school graduates a daytime job and scholarship help to attend University College in the evening. Originally, it was directed by Charles Thomas, then by a talented new staff member, Gloria W. White, A.M. '63, M.J.S. '80, who took over in 1968.

In 1967, the business school pioneered an effort, spearheaded by faculty member Sterling Schoen, to recruit minorities into the Master of Business Administration program; soon it grew into the Consortium for Graduate Study in Business. Upward Bound, a program to prepare promising high school students for college, came to campus that same year. Meanwhile, the University adopted a new policy in 1963, denying recognition to any social organizations that followed discriminatory practices.

McMillen Hall.
WU Archives

New buildings were going up and old space was being renovated. The old Ridgley Hall reading room took on new life as the Mary Brooks Holmes Lounge. In 1965, George Pake won a $3.9 million grant from the National Science Foundation, half of it to help construct buildings in engineering and chemistry: Bryan Hall, funded partly by noted dietician Mary DeGarmo Bryan, A.B. '12, in honor of her late husband, Charles W. Bryan, Jr., B.S.C.E. '12; and McMillen Hall, named for St. Louis executive George F. McMillen, who gave $1 million toward its construction. The Arthur Holly Compton Laboratory of Physics, Beaumont Pavilion, and Monsanto Laboratory for the Life Sciences went up in these years. In 1963, the University acquired from the government a 2,000-acre section of the Tyson Valley Powder Farm, which was renamed the Washington University Tyson Research Center. Finally, plans got under way for the long-awaited student union and performing arts building, opened in 1973 as Mallinckrodt Center.

The University was becoming more widely known, even garnering a few national accolades. One Princeton publication labeled it the "Most Alive University in the Middle West," and former chancellor candidate McGeorge Bundy became a cheerleader, praising it in two national magazines. In *Harper's*, he wrote that the University, like Brown and Vanderbilt, had joined Yale and Princeton on "the mountain tops"

Washington University Tyson Research Center.
Located above the Meramec River, 25 miles southwest of St. Louis, the 2,060-acre Tyson Research Center was developed by the Army during World War II as an ammunition storage site. The University acquired Tyson in 1963 and used it for library storage, a sculpture program, ecology research, and as a wildlife sanctuary. Adjunct professor Richard Coles directed it for 25 years, in 1995 biology professor Owen Sexton became director, then evolutionary biologist Jonathan Losos took over in 2000, followed by Peter Morin in 2003. The Field Science Program at Tyson involves thousands of St. Louis K-12 students in nature and science experiences each year.
David Kilper, WU Photographic Services

Monsanto Laboratory for the Life Sciences.
David Kilper, WU Photographic Services

of higher education. *Time* magazine described the school in 1963 as one of four "Take-Off Universities."

Shepley's nationalization push was definitely showing results. In 1956, fewer than 20 percent of freshmen came from outside the St. Louis area, but by 1964 that total had risen to 67 percent. As the proportion of students from Missouri and Illinois dropped — from 78 percent in 1959 to 38 percent in 1969 — more came from the east coast, especially New York and New Jersey: up from less than 3 percent in 1959 to 19 percent by 1969. In 1966, Eliot declared victory, a little prematurely: "Financial problems are far from solved, but the change to a national university of established high repute, begun twenty years ago, is completed."

Beaumont Pavilion.
David Kilper, WU Photographic Services

SEVENTY BY 'SEVENTY

Financial problems were indeed very far from solved. Faculty and staff members, graduate assistants, and South 40 residence halls all came at a price — and Eliot was willing to take a few risks to pay for them. "As an administrator," recalled Thomas Hall, "either you are a deficit spender or you're a sound dollar man who wants to keep the bills paid....Chancellor Eliot was a leader who believed in a safe and creative amount of deficit budgeting." In projecting the 1964-65 budget, Eliot presented the board with the probable need for $1.74 million in special gifts, just to balance the books. Though pleased with Eliot overall, the board decided it needed a greater role in the planning process, and in 1965 formed a budget committee, headed by I.E. Millstone, B.S. '27. However, two lean years of unrestricted giving had left an accumulated $3.4 million deficit by 1966 — and Robert Palmer, frustrated by the need for retrenchment, left for Yale and was replaced as dean by political scientist Merle Kling.

Privately, Eliot had been planning a major fund drive: consulting professional fundraisers, forming a trustees' committee on planning and development, and convening faculty planning councils to formulate strategies for change. Late in 1964, the University filed a major proposal with the Ford Foundation,

Herbert F. Hitzeman, Jr.
Herb Weitman,
WU Photographic Services

which was offering challenge grants to universities; behind the scenes, Eliot pulled every string he could to ensure its success. The happy news came in June 1965 that the University had received $15 million — its largest gift ever, and the fifth-largest granted by Ford in that competition. There was just one catch: the award had to be matched by three times as much support from private sources.

On a wintry morning in February 1965, Eliot held a convocation in Graham Chapel to kick off an important initiative: a major campaign known as "Seventy by 'Seventy," which aimed at raising $70 million by 1970, with $56 million of it earmarked for the Hilltop Campus. But who would lead it? Already, Eliot had locked horns with board chairman McDonnell, who, Shepley said, had tried to be "the chief executive of the University," not fully understanding the chancellor's function; in 1966, McDonnell stepped down from the board, though he remained generous to the University. After board members David Calhoun and Charles Thomas turned him down, Eliot asked Ethan Shepley to head the drive, and Shepley loyally, though wearily, agreed. "I'd run out of steam," he remembered. He already had "hounded all these prospects" before, and "my shoe leather was worn awfully thin."

The campaign was fraught with problems. Eliot hesitated to ask strangers for money even though, as Shepley told him, exasperated, anyone in St. Louis would be flattered to receive a call from the University's chancellor. The professional fundraisers were unsatisfactory, and the development office was in tatters until Herbert F. Hitzeman, Jr., B.F.A. '53, took over in 1968 and reorganized it from the ground up. Thanks largely to his efforts, backed by the fundraising skills of trustee Edward A. O'Neal, Monsanto board chairman from 1965-68, the University reached its goal in May 1969, a year before the scheduled completion. Leading the way were McDonnell gifts of $6 million and Danforth gifts of more than $4 million.

Still, Seventy by 'Seventy left issues behind. Unrestricted gifts fell critically short of hoped-for goals, and after 1970 the University faced

I.E. Millstone.
Millstone received a B.S. in engineering and architecture in 1927 and an honorary degree in 1994; his late wife, Goldie Gollin Millstone, was a 1928 graduate. Appointed to the board in 1964, he became a life member in 1980. His construction company built some of the South 40 residence halls. In 1970, the Millstone Lounge and Plaza were named in his honor, as was the Millstone Pool in the new Athletic Complex, completed in 1986.
David Kilper, WU Photographic Services

Merle Kling.
Kling, A.B. '41, A.M. '41, Ph.D. '49, joined the political science faculty in 1946. Twice dean of the Faculty of Arts and Sciences, he became the University's provost in 1976, retiring in 1983. The Merle Kling Professorship of Modern Letters in the Department of English in Arts & Sciences is held today by Gerald Early.
WU Archives

Researchers develop a biological approach to mental illness

Eli Robins (1921-1994).

From the late 1940s on, the University's psychiatry department stood for something revolutionary: a strong investigative interest in the genetics of mental disorders and a belief that they should be diagnosed and treated like physical illness. This biological approach to mental illness, known as the "Washington University School of Psychiatry," changed the entire field.

Key figures in devising this approach were: Edwin Gildea (1898-1977), psychiatry department head from 1942-63, who promoted biochemical studies of the brain despite the prevailing emphasis on Freudian theory; Eli Robins, Wallace Renard Professor of Psychiatry and head of psychiatry from 1963-75, when illness forced him to step down; Samuel B. Guze, M.D. '45, Spencer T. Olin Professor of Psychiatry, vice chancellor for medical affairs from 1975-89, and department head from 1975-89 and 1993-97; and George Winokur (1925-1996), professor of psychiatry and director of residency education from 1966-71.

They developed standard diagnostic criteria for psychiatric illnesses, reflected in the American Psychiatric Association's groundbreaking third edition of the *Diagnostic and Statistical Manual of Mental Disorders* (DSM–III), published in 1983. In 1972, Guze, Donald Goodwin (1932-1999), and Robert Woodruff (1935-1976), both faculty members until 1976, co-authored a well-known textbook *Psychiatric Diagnosis*. Today, the Samuel B. Guze Professorship, donated by Guze and his wife Joy, is held by Charles F. Zorumski, chairman of the department.

Samuel Guze (1923-2000).

At the 1977 unveiling of a portrait of Eli Robins, Samuel Guze said: "We have stood consistently for the medical model in psychiatry, for the importance of systematic data, for a broad spectrum of research....We speak for and defend psychiatric patients and their families. We do not blame them for their disorders. We do not ignore or demean their suffering by denying the reality of psychiatric illness."

Photos, WU Becker Medical Library

---

the devastating loss of the Ford subsidy, which had accounted for $3 million a year in income. Now dramatic new cuts were on the table: the basketball program ended after the 1967-68 season, the nursing school closed in 1969, and the dental school narrowly escaped closing in 1967, saved by a rush of faculty and alumni support. To attain more solvency, Eliot proposed continuing the campaign through 1970, as planned, to try to add to the $70 million.

SOCIOLOGY AND LAW

Two University programs were having both academic and financial trouble. One was the sociology department, chaired from 1959-64 by Alvin Gouldner, a brilliant though abrasive scholar who recruited new faculty comprising, said one article, a kind of "Who's Who in Sociology." In 1963, Gouldner also founded a new journal, *Trans-action*, to translate social science research into lay terms; it was increasingly successful but required major University subsidies. The first crisis occurred in 1966 after Gouldner returned from a leave and tried to reassert control over the journal and its able managing editor, Leonard Zweig, thus polarizing his department. Eliot stepped in, appointing Gouldner, who withdrew from the department, to a research professorship.

A new student center.
Students gather in Bowles Plaza, adjacent to Mallinckrodt Center, completed in 1973.
WU Photographic Services

In May 1968, mysterious notes attacking Gouldner appeared on departmental bulletin boards, and he attributed them to a doctoral candidate, R. Laud Humphreys, whom he confronted in a violent episode. During an inquiry by the administration, Humphreys' own dissertation, on homosexual encounters in public places, came under scrutiny, with the University expressing concern over legal issues related to data collection. Fearing similar problems, Eliot and Pake asked the National Institute of Mental Health (NIMH) to hold up a $1.2 million grant to Lee Rainwater, Humphreys' adviser — though, after an NIMH investigation, it was reinstated. A deeply divided sociology faculty, feeling "under attack," began to disperse: Rainwater to Harvard, taking his research grant with him. The University sold *Trans-action*, whose annual deficit had reached $204,000.

University scientists conduct space-related research

In the late 1960s and 1970s, an interdisciplinary group of faculty was engaged in space-related research. Among them were Robert M. Walker, who came in 1966 as McDonnell Professor of Physics; Martin H. Israel, who joined the physics department in 1968; and Raymond E. Arvidson, who came to geology, which was renamed earth and planetary sciences in 1974. In that same year, the McDonnell Center for the Space Sciences — the vision of William Danforth, James S. McDonnell, and Walker — was established with a major gift from the McDonnell Aerospace Foundation.

Walker, Center director from 1974 to 2000, was a member of a NASA committee that advised on the distribution of lunar samples. After the first moon rocks came back in 1969, his laboratory played an important, ongoing role in studying them to measure the history of solar radiation and cosmic rays.

In another NASA-sponsored project, Israel, now professor of physics, headed a group of six scientists from the University and elsewhere who built an instrument that was launched in 1979 and operated successfully in orbit for nearly two years. Its purpose was to study the chemical composition of heavy, high-energy cosmic rays.

Arvidson, now the James S. McDonnell Distinguished University Professor and chair of earth and planetary sciences in Arts & Sciences, was one of 20 members of the Viking Lander Imaging Team, charged with photographing the terrain of the planet Mars and analyzing the photos as they were beamed to earth from the lander cameras. He serves on the Athena science team for the 2005 Mars rover mission.

A fourth faculty member pursuing space-related research was Larry A. Haskin, the first Ralph E. Morrow Distinguished University Professor in Arts & Sciences, who used electrolysis to simulate "moon-mining": separating raw materials from lunar samples. After chairing the Planetary and Earth Science Division at Johnson Space Center in Houston, he joined the Department of Earth and Planetary Sciences in 1976, serving as its chair until 1990.

A piece of the moon.
University scientists in the McDonnell Center researched material that astronauts gathered on the moon, including this "moon doughnut."
WU Archives

Raymond E. Arvidson working in the lab with students.
WU Photographic Services

For some time, the School of Law had been stagnating. As chancellor, Shepley said, "I was deeply troubled over the law school, and didn't know quite what to do about it." Too many of the tenured faculty were "not doing any creative work at all — no publications of any significance." During the deanship of Milton Green, friction over salary issues developed, precipitating his departure. Then in 1965, with Hiram Lesar as dean, the school faced another crisis: two successive graduating classes had a large number of graduates who failed the Missouri Bar examination — 10 of 50 in 1964 and 21 of 49 in 1965. "The faculty is just as baffled as I am," said Lesar.

While he was political science chairman, Eliot had served for several years in the law school as Charles Nagel Professor of Constitutional Law — a controversial appointment with some faculty, who opposed his selection as chancellor. Eliot continued to take a strong interest in the law school; in a 1964 report, he described his goals for its improvement, including more faculty and better students, a new LL.M. degree, and a building to replace the hot, crowded January Hall. Already, the school had made some headway in faculty recruiting with the appointments of Daniel Mandelker and Jules Gerard in 1962; David Becker in 1963; and Dale Swihart in 1965.

Mudd Hall.
The School of Law was housed in Mudd Hall from 1972-97, when Anheuser-Busch Hall was completed. The building has since been replaced by the Charles F. Knight Executive Education Center for the Olin School of Business.

David Kilper, WU Photographic Services

By 1967, Lesar was able to report that 51 of 56 graduates had passed the Bar exam.

Amid Seventy by 'Seventy, the board announced in July 1965 an upcoming architectural competition for adjoining law and social science buildings, to cost $3.5 million. Soon 115 teams had submitted entries, to be judged by a team consisting of Eliot; G. Holmes Perkins, architecture dean at the University of Pennsylvania; and Chicago architect Harry Weese. The winner was a contemporary structure designed by Dolf Schnebli, Swiss architect and visiting professor in the architecture school, in collaboration with two faculty members: George Anselevicius, who served as dean of the school from 1968-73, and Roger Montgomery.

Eliot wanted to break ground immediately, but only after the Seeley J. Mudd Foundation gave the University $1.75 million in 1970 was financing in place. Even so, the project was hobbled by economies that did away with key design elements — such as the red-chip granite exterior — that would have improved its function or appearance. As it was, the poor acoustics, leaky roof, and stark appearance made it roundly hated from the start. One faculty member, recalling its cave-like spaces, said he was always afraid to look at the ceiling for fear "stalactites had begun to form"; others called it, tongue-in-cheek, "Eliot's Revenge." More law students did arrive, however — 538 in 1972, up from 251 in 1969.

MEDICAL HEALING

Over these years, the tempestuous medical situation had calmed down, thanks to the peace-making efforts of William H. Danforth, new vice chancellor for medical affairs. When James S. McDonnell asked him to take the position, Danforth, a young cardiologist, was not at all sure he wanted it. Some people on the Medical Campus did not know him, recalled M. Kenton King. Once he accepted the

P. Roy Vagelos.
Vagelos came to the University from the National Heart Institute, serving as professor and head of biological chemistry from 1966-75. Later, he served as chairman and chief executive officer of Merck & Co, Inc. The Roy and Donna Vagelos Professorship in Biochemistry and Molecular Biophysics, held by Gabriel Waksman, honors him today.

Joe Angeles, WU Photographic Services

Jessie L. Ternberg.
Ternberg, M.D. '53, who joined the medical faculty in 1959 and became chief of pediatric surgery at St. Louis Children's Hospital in 1972, was the first female surgical resident at Barnes Hospital, the first female surgeon on the medical faculty, and the first woman elected head of the Faculty Council. In 2002, she served as honorary grand marshal at Commencement.

Joe Angeles, WU Photographic Services

appointment, with concurrent election as president of WUMSAH, several "were at first surprised, but a little bit later wondered: 'Why didn't I think of that?'" Edgar Queeny liked him, so did James McDonnell; Danforth and King decided that "the vice chancellor was supposed to function as Mr. Outside, and the dean, Mr. Inside….He and I were almost an ideal twosome," King said.

Danforth quickly set to work. To qualify for federal funds aimed at combatting heart disease, cancer, and stroke, he forged a relationship with Saint Louis University's medical school and successfully applied for a regional planning grant. His strong relationship with McDonnell helped secure the $4.7 million gift that made possible the spectacular, nine-story McDonnell Medical Sciences Building, which received additional funding from a $4.3 million grant from the National Institutes of Health. Construction got under way in 1967 with a festive "launching" ceremony. When the building was completed in 1970, it provided much-needed space for preclinical departments and brought a 25 percent increase in the medical school's entering class.

Danforth and King participated in searches that led to the appointment of department chairs: P. Roy Vagelos for

Robert Lee.
M. Kenton King and William Danforth recruited Lee to boost African-American student enrollment at the School of Medicine.

Tom Heine, WU Medical Public Affairs

Joseph Ogura (1915-1983).
Ogura arrived in 1945 as a resident and stayed to become a faculty member, then head of otolaryngology from 1966-82. Widely known for his pioneering surgical technique and research, he won the American Laryngological Association's coveted "triple crown": the James Newcomb Award in 1967, the Casselberry Award in 1968, and the DeRoaldes Gold Medal in 1979. The Department of Otolaryngology library and an annual lectureship are named for him.

WU Becker Medical Library

biological chemistry in 1966; Philip R. Dodge for pediatrics, Walter F. Ballinger II for surgery, and Carlton C. Hunt for physiology and biophysics, all in 1967; W. Maxwell Cowan for anatomy in 1968; and James C. Warren for obstetrics and gynecology in 1971. In two internal changes, Joseph Ogura rose to head of otolaryngology in 1966, and in 1970, neurology head James O'Leary stepped down, replaced by William M. Landau, M.D. '47. They administered a school that was increasingly complex, with income rising from $4.8 million in 1955-56 to $15.5 million in 1964-65. Government grants to the University were up from $1.53 million in 1956 to $14.6 million the following decade, with the lion's share going to the medical school.

Through these years, the school was engaged in new initiatives. In 1967, the Executive Faculty approved a major revision of the curriculum, including an elective fourth year. A Division of Health Care Research was founded in 1969, due largely to Danforth's efforts. Women were making strides; in 1972, Jessie L. Ternberg was named chief of pediatric surgery at St. Louis Children's Hospital and three years after that, professor of surgery in pediatrics. Two African-American medical staff — Henry Nichols, a resident in pathology, and John Arradondo, a house officer — led the call for greater participation of black students. Together, King and Danforth recruited Robert Lee as assistant dean for minority affairs, and worked to boost enrollment. Julian C. Mosley, Jr., M.D. '72, the second African-American graduate of the school, helped to establish a tutorial program to help bridge the gap for bright, motivated students who lacked the necessary training.

W. Maxwell Cowan (1931-2002).
Cowan, a neuroanatomist who helped to shape modern neuroscience as a field, became professor and head of the Department of Anatomy in 1968. He eventually renamed it the Department of Anatomy and Neurobiology. After leaving the University for the Salk Institute in 1980, he came back for a year as provost, before becoming vice president and chief scientific officer at the Howard Hughes Medical Institute.
WU Archives

"Mr. Mac"

J ames S. McDonnell or "Mr. Mac," founder and board chairman of McDonnell Douglas Corporation, was an extraordinary benefactor to the University, providing funds for the McDonnell Center for Space Sciences, the McDonnell Medical Sciences Building, the McDonnell Department of Genetics, the McDonnell Laboratory of Biochemical

James S. McDonnell (1899-1980).
Herb Weitman, WU Photographic Services

Genetics, the McDonnell Center for Studies of Higher Brain Function, and the McDonnell Laboratory for Psychic Research. At the time of his death, gifts from McDonnell, his family, the McDonnell Foundation, and the corporate foundation, totaled more than $28 million.

McDonnell served as trustee from 1960-66, and chairman during the last three years of that time, as well as board member of WUMSAH from 1963-66 and its chairman from 1964-66. He received an honorary doctorate in engineering in 1958, and in medicine in 1977. In 1969, the medical school Executive Faculty named him an honorary member.

At his death, Chancellor William H. Danforth said: "Washington University has lost its most important benefactor. The world has lost one of the truly great leaders of this or of any age."

A lab in the new McDonnell Medical Sciences Building, 1970.
David Kilper, WU Photographic Services

More construction began to take place. In 1969, Mallinckrodt Institute of Radiology — now directed by neuroradiologist Juan M. Taveras — added four more floors, as well as a five-story extension designed to house a linear accelerator. A 12-story East Pavilion, jointly financed by Barnes and the medical school, got under way, and the medical school acquired the five-acre St. John's Hospital property on Audubon Avenue for future expansion.

Start of the "Troubles"

Amid a turbulent era on campuses across the nation, Eliot faced the greatest and perhaps most successful test of his leadership during the late-1960s period of student unrest. Eliot often referred to this era as the "time of troubles" or "the troubles." He walked a fine line, buffeted by largely irreconcilable forces. To one side was a sharply divided student body: a few committed to violent protest; others to peaceful demonstration; still others, rejecting all of it, to getting an education. On another side was the board of trustees, still composed mainly of local business leaders, furious with the activist students. There were the Clayton police, ready to invade campus, though their presence was inflammatory and often unwanted. Finally, there was the faculty, some, but not all, sympathetic to student demands. Eliot himself lacked key help in dealing with crises since George Pake, his provost, was put off by student activism; instead, William Danforth — though officially tied to the medical school — stepped in to fill that gap.

The chancellor and his successor.
Chancellor Eliot (right) was succeeded by William Danforth (left) on July 1, 1971.
Herb Weitman,
WU Photographic Services

The lightning rod for student unhappiness over growing U.S. involvement in Vietnam and Cambodia was the University's ROTC program, founded in 1922 and headquartered in two Quonset huts — one Army, one Air Force — at the north end of campus. The existence of these huts, so close at hand, provided a constant irritant and reminder of the war strategy, as did the University's involvement, through its trustees and investments, in companies that were alleged to be part of the "military–industrial complex." The growing struggle nationally for civil rights paralleled, and sometimes intermingled with, the anti-war activism.

Eliot, who was personally opposed to the war, shifted tactics to meet the changing needs of this difficult period. At times he was the diplomat, listening carefully to students and staunchly defending their First Amendment rights; at others, he was the lawyer, initiating legal action against those who committed violent offenses. Once he became openly angry — when he ordered the Clayton police chief off campus, as television cameras recorded the incident — but he could quietly overlook gross offenses. At one board meeting, said King, "the students were banging on the door, trying to interrupt the meeting. Eliot went over himself and opened the door. I saw a student hit him on the arm with his fist. Eliot never mentioned it. He knew what would happen if he reported that a student had struck him. The board would overreact."

At some level, he even enjoyed the whole fray. As he remembered: "In some ways it was a good time…much of the time I felt rarin' to go." During the tense spring of 1970, he commiserated with another college president by phone about broken windows on both campuses. Still, said Eliot, "It's a beautiful day, and…I feel like the horse in the Bible, who, when he hears the sound of the trumpet, he gets up on his hind legs and says, 'Ha, ha.'"

The Early Troubles: 1965-68

With 1964 came passage of the Gulf of Tonkin resolution and the first flickerings of activism on campus with the Student Peace Union (SPU), led by Ted G. Goertzel, A.M. '66, Ph.D. '70. In fall 1965, after the bombing of North Vietnam, students founded the University's chapter of Students for a Democratic Society (SDS), which joined the SPU in picketing a speech by Vice President Hubert H. Humphrey; two key SDS members were Richard ("Terry") Koch, A.B. '73; and Devereaux Kennedy, A.B. '69. With five other students, they caused a brief stir by applying unsuccessfully for recognition as the University branch of the radical W.E.B. DuBois Club, but Eliot defused the crisis by ending official recognition of student groups.

That year, two "teach-ins" took place on campus: marathon discussions of American policy on Vietnam, tied to a national teach-in in Washington, D.C. An anti-war faculty group, the Foreign Policy Round Table — led by Robert Buckhout, Dan Bolef, William Caspary, and Barry Commoner — organized the first one. Their failed invitation to presidential adviser McGeorge Bundy attracted national attention when he replied that if the letter had come "to me for grading as a professor of government, I would not be able to give it high marks," a response that a *Time* magazine writer called "churlish."

Over the next two years, events escalated, nationally and locally. Irate alumni complained to Eliot about a California newspaper article in which Kennedy, elected student body president in 1967, called for "the overthrow of the U.S. Government." That fall, some students held a "love-in" on campus; others traveled to Washington to march on the Pentagon. Fearing violence, Eliot canceled a Dow Chemical Co. recruiting visit in November, though members of the graduate business faculty signed a petition wanting Dow to come. In February 1968, Dow did appear, and 60 students — with Commoner as their spokesman — forced the recruiter off campus, an action that earned four, including Terry Koch and George Lipsitz, A.B. '68, letters of reprimand.

Month by month the situation grew more tense, yet Eliot could say in June 1968 that "thus far…we have been lucky." He had formulated a policy of "fairness, firmness, and willingness to discuss all relevant issues," though he was prepared to call police if injury to persons or property were imminent. He warned students that "disrupting regularly scheduled University activities is a serious offense" — and such offenses would result in a penalty, "normally, suspension or expulsion."

THE HEIGHT OF THE CRISIS: 1968-70

In November, Richard Nixon was elected president and, said *Student Life*, "frustration, disgust and despair were the pervading sentiments of WU students." Attempts were made to ignite the Army ROTC building. In early December senior Michael Siskind, A.B. '73, an SDS member, was arrested and charged with possession of three firebombs. The following February, he pleaded guilty to "intent to destroy federal property," and was sentenced to five years in prison.

Early on December 5, 1968, a member of the Association of Black Collegians (ABC) — Elbert A. Walton, Jr., M.B.A. '70 — was arrested for

Vice President Hubert H. Humphrey (1911-1978).
In 1965, Humphrey delivered the Benjamin Youngdahl lecture, while some students picketed his talk.

October 15, 1969, Vietnam Moratorium.
Students skipped classes to attend day-long workshops and rallies in which they planned anti-war activities. George Wald, a Harvard professor, spoke at an evening meeting in the Field House.

parking violations and said he was beaten by campus police. That afternoon, 40 ABC members occupied the campus security office in Busch Hall, demanding disciplinary action against the officers. Next door in North Brookings, 300 white students who had failed to take over the ROTC rifle range as they had planned — an effort in which Ken Holder, A.B. '71, was arrested — stormed the second floor, occupying Eliot's outer office; their position, presented by Ben Zaricor, A.B. '72, later president of the new Student Union, was support for the black students and abolition of ROTC. The next day, the black students moved to North Brookings basement and outlined their grievances through ABC president Robert Johnson, who asked the white students to leave. Many moved over to Holmes Lounge, where they discussed war-related issues with Arts and Sciences faculty, who voted on December 7 to end academic credit for ROTC.

Literature table.
Members of Students for a Democratic Society presented information about the war in Vietnam during the October 1969 Vietnam Moratorium.

The black student sit-in continued for nine days — a period marked by the release of Johnson's lengthy "Black Manifesto" and a productive meeting between Johnson and Eliot, who said that plans for a black studies program would begin right away. As he wrote, Eliot respected the black students and their protest, which taught the University a great deal. "The great tact and sagacity" of trustee and Harvard law professor Paul Freund, A.B. '28, who came quickly to town to act as mediator in the dispute, said Eliot, "led to a harmonious and constructive outcome."

All photos, WU Archives

219

However, other events began to escalate. Early in 1969, a staff member was assaulted during a protest outside a trustees' meeting. In May, students and faculty cast their votes in a referendum on keeping ROTC on campus, with 69 percent, mostly from business, engineering, dentistry, law, and medicine, in favor of retaining it in some form. That October, a letter from Eliot appeared in the *New York Times* expressing publicly for the first time his own opposition to the war. Ending it, he said, would permit students to get back to learning "with a renewed conviction that their work will be worthwhile."

unsympathetic: "Little boys who play with matches sometimes get their fingers burnt, and college radicals who play at revolution sometimes collide with disagreeable reality."

National news, particularly the tragic death of four students on May 4 at Kent State University, sparked new violence. That evening, nearly 2,000 protesters marched to the Air Force ROTC hut, broke into the building, and set fire to it. When firefighters arrived, rock-throwing demonstrators chased them away, but more came, reinforced by police, and a cherry bomb exploded at their feet. Two students were charged with violating the anti-riot clause of the 1968 Civil Obedience Act: Lawrence Kogan, A.M. '71, M.S.W. '74, Ph.D. '91, who was sentenced to a five-year prison term, reduced to 90 days, and Howard Mechanic, A.B. '70, who fled after his appeals were exhausted to avoid serving his five-year sentence. Five other students faced charges in the incident.

After the fire, Eliot and President Paul C. Reinert, S.J., of Saint Louis University decided to move their ROTC programs off campus to a shared location, although many on the University's board were opposed to giving in to the protesters. At a tense meeting on July 14, Clark M. Clifford, LL.B. '28, former Secretary of Defense, gave a stirring speech in favor of moving ROTC — and the motion squeaked past by only two votes. "What the administration would have done if the vote had gone the other way I don't know," Eliot said. "We all felt sure that keeping ROTC on campus would lead to renewed violence." Even so, there *was* more violence: On March 8, 1971, two bombs exploded in the new ROTC complex. But that was the last of the major incidents.

The William H. Danforth Era Begins

At the end of the Seventy by 'Seventy drive, Eliot declared his intention to retire, though he kept close tabs on the hunt for his replacement. Eliot had his own favorite: William H. Danforth, who had restored order to the medical school and helped him steer a course through the "troubles." Tipping his hand, Eliot had appointed Danforth

On February 23, 1970, the Army ROTC building sustained heavy damage in a fire, to the cheers of some 200 students. A month later, 150 students broke into South Brookings, ransacking files; five were arrested and one, Robert Zeffert, was injured. Amid other episodes, Eliot canceled classes on March 27, then four students, represented by law professor Gray Dorsey, filed a $7.7 million lawsuit against him for failing "to prevent the repeated disruption" of University activities. That April, senior Ken Holder was sentenced to six months in jail for spilling red paint in Olin Library under the portrait of munitions maker John M. Olin to symbolize, he said, that the library "was built on blood." In a controversial move, Eliot suspended 15 students for disrupting ROTC classes, though two were ultimately acquitted and ten placed on probation. Angry students threatened a strike, but the *Post-Dispatch* was

Student protest.
When recruiters from Dow Chemical Co. came to campus in February 1968, students protesting the company's manufacture of napalm forced them off campus.

Black student sit-in.
William B. Pollard III, A.B. '70, a leader of the Association of Black Collegians that staged the nine-day December 1968 sit-in in North Brookings, meets with Chancellor Eliot. At Commencement 1970, Pollard gave the student address.

Photos, WU Archives

What happened to those charged in the burning of the Air Force ROTC building?

Howard Mechanic, A.B. '70, a senior, already under court order to stay away from the ROTC building, was there on the night of May 4. He was charged with throwing a cherry bomb at police and firefighters. The first person in the U.S. convicted under the 1968 Civil Obedience Act, he was sentenced to the maximum penalty of five years in prison and a $10,000 fine. Faculty members — primarily English professor Carter Revard, who took out a second mortgage on his house — posted Mechanic's $10,000 bond, but Mechanic disappeared. University faculty and administrators, along with Mechanic's father, contributed to a fund to save Revard's home. For 28 years, Mechanic lived under a pseudonym, Gary Tredway, in Scottsdale, Arizona, then turned himself in to authorities after his identity came to light during a run for political office. President Bill Clinton pardoned Mechanic just before leaving office in January 2001.

Others charged were:

Joel Achtenberg, A.B. '68: Tried for sabotage and destruction of government property, he was initially sentenced to 15 years, but an appeals court granted him a new trial, and he was acquitted in 1973.

Napoleon Bland: The only African-American student charged, Bland (now Abdur Rahim) pleaded guilty to one charge of attempted sabotage and was sentenced to ten years, serving four years and seven months before he was paroled in 1976.

William Bothwell, A.B. '72: He was charged with violating the anti-riot section of the 1968 Civil Obedience Act, but the charges were dropped in March 1971.

Joseph Eisenberg: Convicted of sabotage by Judge William H. Webster, he was sentenced to a year in prison, six months of it suspended.

Lawrence Kogan (c. 1944-2003), A.M. '71, M.S.W. '74, Ph.D. '91: He was found guilty of violating the anti-riot section of the 1968 Civil Obedience Act, served 90 days in prison, then was placed on probation. Kogan was pardoned by President Ronald Reagan December 17, 1981.

Michael Rudofker: He pleaded guilty to destruction of federal property, was sentenced to ten years and a $10,000 fine, but was released from the federal penitentiary on probation after serving 60 days.

Howard Mechanic.
WU Archives

Air Force ROTC building burns.
Firemen are silhouetted against the burning building on May 5, 1970.

L. T. Spence, *St. Louis Post Dispatch*

---

to key positions, including the head of a committee on University goals and objectives in 1968. The medical school was pleased by the idea of Danforth's succession. "By this time," recalled M. Kenton King, "he was a seasoned administrator."

In addition, Danforth's family had recently performed a vital service for the University. With

the Ford Foundation grant on the verge of expiring and draconian cuts under way, in June 1970 the Danforth Foundation, which he chaired, had made a gift of $15 million, two-thirds for the Hilltop and one-third for the medical school. It would not solve any long-term needs — reserve funds were exhausted and Eliot was concerned

Happy Burt Wheeler Day.
On May 11, 1971, hundreds of members of the University community gathered in the Quad to honor Wheeler, then dean of the College of Arts and Sciences. Planned by College students and faculty, Burt Wheeler Day included speeches, volleyball and softball games, tug-of-war contests, a picnic (right), and a dinner in the dean's honor.

Blimp on the Quad, March 1970.
To enhance people's awareness of their environment and to inspire spontaneity, architecture students Jay Steinhour and Brooks Bond constructed a pneumatic, air-supported "ground blimp" out of polyethelene squares. One such spontaneous event, a "nude-in," appeared in a front-page photo in the *St. Louis Globe-Democrat.*

All photos, WU Archives

that further budgetary cuts would leave his successor "a mortally injured University" — but it was a crucial stopgap. As trustee chairman Charles A. Thomas said, "the very existence of the University was at stake."

Late in 1970, *Newsweek* reported that Danforth was on a list of finalists to succeed Nathan Pusey as president of Harvard. There seemed to be no time to lose. At a specially called board meeting in December, Eliot moved to "unanimously and enthusiastically appoint William Henry Danforth Chancellor of Washington University, effective July 1, 1971" — and the trustees gladly concurred. As Charles Thomas said: "His experience, ability, personality, and character make him perfectly suited for this post." While some people might view this result as inevitable, said history professor and search committee member Peter Riesenberg, "if there was anything inevitable about the whole thing, it was in the quality of the man."

NOT COUNTERREVOLUTIONARY TO SAY HELLO

Maybe it was disillusionment, maybe exhaustion, but the campus shifted gears in 1971 to a quieter, though less conservative, life. A *Post-Dispatch*

reporter noted a "sharp fall-off in political activity, revived interest in sports, a growing taste for booze." Dress codes and curfews for women had disappeared, residence halls were coeducational, fraternities lost members. After the ROTC fire, students had even held a nude-in on the Brookings Quadrangle, and in May 1971, they turned out again for a "Happy Burt Wheeler Day," honoring the beloved dean of Arts and Sciences.

Old-fashioned schoolwork was on the increase, and the usage of Olin Library went up 20 percent during 1971-72. The innovative General Studies Program, started in Arts and Sciences in 1968, was attracting students to courses on local history, coins, or Karl Marx. In his Founders Day speech on February 22, his first major address since becoming chancellor, Danforth noted this change: "The tenseness and anger of the late 1960s is gone. As a recent graduate wrote, 'It is no longer counterrevolutionary to say hello to an administrator.' Students have rediscovered the joy of learning and going to college."

Some political disputes remained, however, among them a 1972 controversy over a gift of 38,000 shares of McDonnell Douglas stock to the University. Danforth defended the $1.4 million gift, intended to create a new genetics department. "A university cannot do all things to better man's condition," he said. "It must do well what it alone as an institution can do: advance learning and treasure thought in a troubled world." For that, private generosity was essential, he said, since the University "faces financial challenges as critical as any in the history of American higher education."

THE TASKS AHEAD

Better than anyone else, he knew what those challenges were. Quite simply, said Danforth in the 1972 annual report, the University's problems were caused "by a declining rate of growth in income coupled with an increasing rate of growth in costs." Inflation was gripping the economy, private gifts were down, government support had dropped 25 percent in the past year alone. To cope, he said, they had cut faculty positions, deferred crucial maintenance, and increased tuition — yet a deficit remained. "We are going to have to look for help from other sources," he warned.

That meant a new fund drive, which began in 1973 with the exciting news of a $60 million endowment grant from the Danforth Foundation — to be matched by private funds, dollar for dollar, before 1978. By 1974, the fund drive had raised $35 million; by 1975, $45 million. The largest single gift, $4.4 million, came from a trust established by Malvern Clopton, board president from 1932-42. In July 1976, the University announced that the $60 million matching goal had been surpassed two years ahead of schedule. Danforth's tone was relieved, but cautious. This money would not increase the operating budget, he said, but without it, the University faced "a major dismantling" of programs. "With it we can plan for the decades ahead with reasonable certainty."

BUILDING A TEAM AND A PROGRAM

Like Eliot, Danforth faced the task of assembling an administrative team. The old group was fast disappearing — George Pake had left, Lattie Coor became president of the University of Vermont in 1976, and Carl Dauten died that year — but Merle Kling, previously dean of the Faculty of Arts and Sciences, came back in 1973, and in 1976 became

provost. Robert L. Virgil, Jr., M.B.A. '60, Ph.D. '67, formerly a faculty member in the business school, became vice chancellor for campus affairs; Ralph E. Morrow, who was dean of the Graduate School of Arts and Sciences, became dean of the faculty in 1979 and provost in 1984. In 1977, John Biggs was named vice chancellor for administration and finance, and began instituting major reforms.

Several new deans emerged during the early 1970s: Constantine E. Michaelides in Architecture, Roger DesRosiers in Fine Arts, and Shanti K. Khinduka in Social Work. Law, now in its new building, had faced a problem in 1971 when six African-American students said they had failed because they were "placed in a kind of environment where [they] couldn't excel." Three were readmitted and the dean, Hiram Lesar, announced a new scholarship policy for needy black students. Lesar left in 1972. An interim dean, Lewis ("Red") Mills, resigned in 1973, replaced by Edward T. ("Tad") Foote, formerly University vice chancellor and general counsel, who set the school on a new course: raising student morale, involving alumni in the school, and recruiting a host of faculty, including Merton C. Bernstein, A. Peter Mutharika, D. Bruce La Pierre, Charles R. McManis, John Drobak, Ronald Levin, Susan Frelich Appleton, and F. Hodge O'Neal, the George A. Madill Professor of Law and an authority on close corporations.

Two milestones occurred in 1974: the Spencer T. Olin Fellowship Program for Women in graduate and professional studies was created, as was the McDonnell Center for the Space Sciences. Funded by nearly $5 million in gifts from the McDonnell Aerospace Foundation and directed by Robert Walker, the McDonnell Professor of Physics, it placed the University among a handful of major centers for study of the universe.

Impromptu concert.
Student musicians perform on the lawn by Blewett Hall in 1971.
WU Archives

Building rapport.
Early in his term as chancellor, William Danforth pauses for a conversation with a student. By 1971, the time of student unrest was largely over.
WU Archives

Commencement 1976.
New graduates gather with their family and friends.
WU Photographic Services

Edward T. ("Tad") Foote.
Dean of the School of Law from 1973-80, Foote left to become president of the University of Miami. William Danforth called him "an extraordinary leader" who had "enthusiasm, good judgment, and [a] sense of direction" for the school.
WU Photographic Services

"First Lady of Song" receives honorary degree.
Ella Fitzgerald, a popular jazz singer for more than half a century, was given an honorary doctor of fine arts degree at Commencement 1974. At left is Grand Marshal Robert W. Reinhardt.
Herb Weitman,
WU Photographic Services

Paul Lacy.
Lacy (second from right), professor emeritus of pathology and immunology, was chair of the Department of Pathology from 1961-85. His research centered on islets, the cells of the pancreas that produce insulin, and led to a successful transplantation of islet cells into a diabetic patient in 1990.
WU Archives

PET scanner.
PET was developed by Michel Ter-Pogossian and a collaborative team, including Jerome Cox, Carol Higgins, Ed Hoffman, John Hood, Sr., Nizar Mullani, Michael Phelps, Marcus Raichle, Donald Snyder, and Michael Welch.
WU Becker Medical Library

MEDICAL FACULTY CHANGES

At the medical school, one urgent task was replacing Danforth as vice chancellor and head of WUMSAH (renamed Washington University Medical Center in 1972), and Samuel Guze got the job. Unlike Danforth, he had a second role, serving in 1975 as Spencer T. Olin Professor of Psychiatry and head of the department. With the departure of Juan Taveras, Mallinckrodt Institute of Radiology (MIR) needed a new head, and in 1971 the choice fell to the promising but little-known Ronald G. Evens, A.B. '60, M.D. '64, who had graduated first in his medical school class and who is now president of Barnes–Jewish Hospital. In 1974, neurology and neurosurgery formed a joint department under William Landau and Sidney Goldring, brother of pediatric cardiologist David Goldring. After Carl Moore's death in 1972,

David Kipnis.
Currently Distinguished University Professor of Medicine, Kipnis served as chair of the Department of Medicine from 1972-92. He is internationally known for his pioneering research into the molecular mechanisms underlying diabetes.
WU Photographic Services

David Kipnis became the new chair of medicine, building the department dramatically. When Oliver Lowry, the last of the old kitchen cabinet, stepped down in 1976, pharmacology got a new head in Philip Needleman.

These new department heads began recruiting their staffs — an easier task with the inducement of prime laboratory space in the new McDonnell building. Anesthesiology, a newly independent department, had to develop from scratch, under the leadership of C.R. Stephen. Surgery, however, had difficulty recruiting full-time faculty because the part-time staff was so large, and there were not enough patients to go around. Over time, Walter Ballinger let the part-time staff diminish, setting the stage for a major rebuilding of the full-time faculty in the 1980s.

In 1973, P. Roy Vagelos and Danforth developed an idea that caught hold: build a joint Division of Biology and Biomedical Sciences from six preclinical areas of the medical school plus the biology and anthropology departments in Arts and Sciences on the Hilltop Campus. After Vagelos left the University in 1975, replaced in biochemistry by Luis Glaser,

Maxwell Cowan took over the program; in 1977, Robert Thach, who had headed the division's molecular biology graduate program, became chair of biology. Vagelos also founded the Medical Scientist Training Program (MSTP), subsequently strengthened by a $30 million grant from the Spencer T. and Ann W. Olin Foundation.

OTHER CHANGES AT THE MEDICAL CENTER

New research was bringing recognition to the medical center. At Mallinckrodt, Michel Ter-Pogossian, M.S. '48, Ph.D. '50, and a collaborative team, pioneered the development of positron emission tomography (PET); MIR installed a second cyclotron in the subbasement of Barnard for its use — the only center in the world with two. Psychiatry was doing pioneering work into the biological roots of mental disorders, while Louis V. Avioli and others were studying bone disease. Paul E. Lacy, chair of pathology, was studying insulin-dependent diabetes; in 1967, he had discovered a method to isolate islet cells, a landmark accomplishment that he would build on to develop the process of islet cells transplantation.

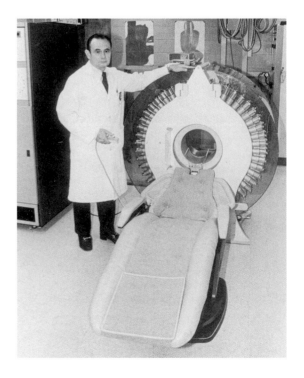

However, the medical center took a hard look at its nearby community and found troubling urban decay just to the north. Danforth enlisted the help of real estate developer Raymond H. Wittcoff, today an emeritus trustee, and Richard A. Roloff, B.S.I.E. '51, today an executive vice chancellor. In 1972 they were asked to plan and implement the redevelopment of the neighborhood, working with Team Four, Inc. Soon the Washington University Medical Center Redevelopment Corporation was approved by the city and embarked on a bold renewal effort in a 36-block, 280-acre area surrounding the medical center. With leadership from director Jerry King, the corporation acquired buildings and attracted developers and private owners to this area, winning both national accolades and imitators.

In a $50 million initiative, Barnes Hospital broke ground for its 17-story West Pavilion, with four floors being added to the East Pavilion. Indigent care was increasing, at a cost of $7.6 million in 1977, up from $5.4 million in 1973. Under the leadership of Carlos A. Perez, director of the Radiation Oncology Center, the Cancer Information Center opened in 1977 — the first of its kind in the nation — serving 877 patients in its first year alone. At the medical school, an all-time high of 547 students enrolled in 1976-77 — a 70 percent increase over the 1962 total — including 125 women and 49 black students. The school had become increasingly selective, choosing the 120 first-year students that year from among 6,078 applicants.

Happy anniversary!
For the University's 125th Anniversary, a highlight of the celebration was a 125-square-foot cake.
WU Photographic Services

OLD DREAMS AND NEW

In 1978, the University marked its 125th anniversary with a month of festivities, including a 125-square-foot birthday cake. At the law school, a "Quest for Equality" series brought in speakers with earlier University associations, including Paul Freund, A.B. '28, now Carl M. Loeb University Professor of Law Emeritus at Harvard; and two former chancellor candidates, both former U.S. Solicitor Generals: Archibald Cox and Erwin Griswold. The medical school, too, hosted a speaker with past ties, Juan Taveras, now radiologist-in-chief at Massachusetts General Hospital. In October, FBI director William Webster, J.D. '49, gave the Founders Day address.

Cutting the anniversary cake.
Chancellor and Mrs. Danforth (left) join with Edward Lindley Bowles (1897-1990) B.S.E.E. '20, for whom Bowles Plaza is named, to begin the festivities.
Peter Zimmerman, WU Photographic Services

Danforth saw this anniversary as a new beginning, a moment in which to ponder the past and prepare for two daunting challenges ahead. A major financial campaign must begin soon, preceded by a giant planning effort to "better understand ourselves and better set overall goals for Washington University," he said. His words were both a rallying cry and a warning of the vast undertaking to come — a critical step in turning the still-struggling school into a top-flight University. (WU)

125th Anniversary crowd in Bowles Plaza.
WU Photographic Services

William H. Webster.
Webster, J.D. '49, was the Founders Day speaker in 1978.
WU Archives

DREAMING TALL: WILLIAM HENRY DANFORTH

William Henry Danforth, the elder (1870-1955).
The grandfather of Chancellor Emeritus William Danforth, one of his slogans was: "Aspire nobly, adventure daringly, and serve humbly."
WU Archives

Elizabeth Danforth's birthday, 1994.
Herb Weitman, WU Photographic Services

Each Thanksgiving that he spent as chancellor, William H. Danforth wrote a letter to alumni — and not the typical, year-end fundraising appeal. These were personal reflections on the past year, with quotes from his favorite writers (Toynbee, de Tocqueville, Marcus Aurelius), gentle stories about his grandchildren, and frequent references to the University's founding values, such as faith, modesty, hard work, self-sacrifice, hope, perseverance. Between the lines, they revealed something about their author: his extraordinary devotion to Washington University. Its progress measured his progress; its values were a road map for his life, too. Readers who supported the University he loved became, in effect, members of his extended family. In a 1977 letter, he recalled two of his greatest heroes, William Greenleaf Eliot and Robert S. Brookings, explaining their dedication — and, in the process, his own:

> "From time to time, I try to figure out how our predecessors did it....They shared a grand dream that knowledge was better than ignorance, that humankind could be bettered by education. They did not feel that they were building for themselves but for their fellow humans and those who would come after. They believed that they could influence the future. And they did."

In the Navy.
Danforth spent two years as a Navy doctor during the early 1950s.
Danforth family photo

An earlier dreamer was his grandfather, the original William Henry Danforth, who hailed from Charleston, Missouri, where his father Albert, a former Confederate soldier, was bank president and owner of a prosperous general store. Sickly as a child, William was spurred to action by a teacher who dared him to become "the healthiest boy in the class." He did so through exercise and sheer determination,

"Danforth men marry well."
In 1950, William Danforth married Elizabeth ("Ibby") Gray, who has been his "true partner," he has said.
Danforth family photo

developing an iron constitution and a missionary zeal for self-improvement. Traveling to
St. Louis at age 14, he graduated from the
University's Manual Training School in 1887
and its mechanical engineering program in
1892. Then he set out to make his fortune,
founding a feed business in 1894 that grew into
the world-famous Ralston Purina Company (now
Nestlé Purina PetCare Company).

There were obstacles along the way. When
the 1896 tornado leveled his new business, he
stoically borrowed $10,000 and built it again.
At the same time, he developed words to live
by: "Stand tall. Think tall. Smile tall. Live tall."
In his inspirational 1931 book, *I Dare You*, he
outlined his four-part philosophy. "You have a
four-fold life to live: a body, a brain, a heart and
a soul…." he wrote. "To use and develop them
is not a task….It is a golden opportunity."
Through the American Youth Foundation, which
he helped found in 1924, he dared children to
live full, balanced lives; for almost 40 years, he
wrote a Monday Morning Message, exhorting
Ralston employees to do the same.

He passed on this philosophy to his grandson
and namesake, born in 1926. When Danforth
was 12, his grandfather asked him to fetch the
dictionary, then instructed him to cut out the
word "impossible" — thus banning it from their
lives forever. Other lessons stuck, too. "To his
younger sister and brothers, Bill seemed to take
our grandfather's dare literally, especially the
part about standing tall," said his brother, former U.S. Senator John C. Danforth, in 1995.
"It was more than his physical height. To us he
was a big person: high-minded, soft-spoken, brilliant, and persuasive."

Their father, Donald, who took charge of
Ralston Purina in 1932 and greatly expanded its operations, helped to shape his son's life.
Quiet, thoughtful, less flamboyant than his
father, he never said a negative word about anyone. "When I was about 14," Danforth once
recalled, "I learned from my mother there was

Honors for Ibby Danforth

To honor their longtime
member, the Woman's Club
of Washington University
created the Elizabeth Gray Danforth
Butterfly Garden on Forsyth
Boulevard, dedicated in 1996.

Another group, the Women's
Society of Washington University
(WSWU), has named a scholarship
in her honor; it is given to outstand-
ing St. Louis Community College
District transfer students. In 2003,
the Jane and Whitney Harris St.
Louis Community Service Award,
which supports local charitable
organizations, was presented to the
Danforths, who asked that the
$25,000 award be added to the
WSWU Elizabeth Gray Danforth
Scholarship Fund.

**Elizabeth Gray Danforth
(standing, center).**
A 1946 graduate of John
Burroughs School, she has
served as a member of its board
of trustees and its alumni board.
In 1989, she and her sister, Mary
Jane Gray, M.D. '49, won the
John Burroughs Outstanding
Alumni Award. A 1950 graduate
of Wellesley College, she has
also served as president of the
Wellesley Club of St. Louis and
received the St. Louis Wellesley
Award in 1983.

Ibby's Garden.
The Elizabeth Gray Danforth Butterfly Garden
was a gift of the Woman's Club of Washington
University in 1995 when William Danforth
retired as chancellor. Mrs. Danforth at the dedication (above); a butterfly takes advantage of
the garden (left).

Photos, WU Photographic Services

someone my father didn't like. I could hardly
believe it. I thought he liked everyone." Donald
Danforth and his wife, Dorothy, raised their four
children — William; Dorothy; Donald, B.S.B.A.
'55; and John — in a large home in Clayton's
Brentmoor Park.

Graduating from St. Louis Country Day
School in 1944, Danforth spent a year at
Westminster College then transferred to
Princeton, finishing early in 1947. During these
years, friends introduced him to Elizabeth
("Ibby") Gray, three years his junior, a John
Burroughs alumna and Wellesley student, who

**The future chancel-
lor as a toddler.**
Danforth family photo

Physician Danforth.
Danforth, a cardiologist, rose to the rank of associate professor in the School of Medicine before being named vice chancellor for medical affairs.
WU Archives

1977 Man of the Year.
The *St. Louis Globe-Democrat* named Danforth its Man of the Year for 1977. In a January 1978 address, Danforth said, "This award being given to a chancellor of Washington University....signifies a healing of the strained relations between the university and community that occurred in the 1960's....For that I am thankful."

St. Louis Globe-Democrat photo, from the Collections of the St. Louis Mercantile Library at the University of Missouri-St. Louis

also loved hiking, skiing, and canoeing. In 1950, during his last year at Harvard Medical School, they were married. While he was reticent, she was outgoing, sociable; she became a "true partner," he has said, and living proof of his aphorism that "Danforth men marry well." In coming years, he and Ibby raised four children — Cynthia, David, Maebelle, and Beth — making their home in a sunny, contemporary house in Ladue, close to his old high school.

Following an internship at Barnes Hospital and two years of service as a Navy doctor during the Korean War, he returned to the University for his residency and never left. Although tempted by a year in pediatrics, he switched to internal medicine, followed by a cardiology fellowship in 1957-58 and basic research in the Cori laboratory. From instructor in medicine, he rose to assistant professor in 1960, associate in 1965 — the well-worn path of academic advancement.

All that changed when James S. McDonnell, another of his heroes, convinced him that administrative work could be just as creative, and he agreed in 1965 to become vice chancellor for medical affairs. To seal the bargain, the previous vice chancellor, Carl V. Moore, took Danforth to meet the indomitable Barnes Hospital board chairman, Edgar M. Queeny. They sat silently for a time; a man of few words, Queeny had nothing to ask and only one thing to say: "Call me Edgar." But that low-key meeting signaled the start of a new era in School of Medicine–Barnes Hospital relations, strained to the breaking point

On-campus gatherings.
Chancellor Danforth met regularly with students and faculty, often welcoming new students and their parents.
WU Photographic Services

a year earlier. Though he could have ducked the task, Danforth chose to stand beside Chancellor Thomas Eliot during the student unrest on the Hilltop Campus. When it was time to seek the University's 13th chancellor, he was the universal choice.

Some wondered why he wanted the job at all. Community relations were badly strained in 1971; the University was in a financial crisis. When Danforth's own father asked why he would quit medicine for the headaches of university administration, he quickly replied: "Didn't you raise us all to take on challenges?" But, unlike Eliot, Danforth had long-standing ties to local business leaders; soon he strengthened community connections, launched successful new fund drives, and oversaw the allocation of major grants to the University from the Danforth Foundation, which he chaired from 1966-97.

By the time of his retirement from the chancellorship in 1995, his list of accomplishments was legion: 70 new faculty chairs, for a total of 110; a $1.72 billion endowment, seventh largest in the nation; dozens of new buildings added; and triple the previous number of gift-supported scholarships. At Founders Day in 1972, he had declared that the University must secure a place among the country's "30 to 35 first-rate universities" — and by every national measure it had far surpassed that modest goal. He had managed to endure the job's relentless demands — one semester he confessed to having spent only two full evenings at home — to become one of the longest-serving chancellors or university presidents in the United States.

Asked by a recent alumnus to name his greatest achievement, he pointed a finger at the speaker and said simply: "You." Nearly 60,000 students had graduated during his chancellorship, and "Uncle Bill" knew many personally, thanks to campus events that he and Ibby attended faithfully. As she once said, "He never says no to a student. All they have to do is walk into his office." During the 1970s, he began an annual tradition of telling bedtime stories on the South 40. One favorite came from his own family: a man dies and sees a table laden with food, but the would-be diners can only look on longingly, since their arms are stiff, unbending rods. Nearby is another table with more rod-armed people, but they are happy and well-fed. The secret? Each person has learned to feed his or her neighbor.

Among his many awards, he was named "Man of the Year" in 1977 by the *St. Louis Globe-Democrat*. Like another of his heroes, Chancellor Ethan Shepley, he won a signal honor: the Alexander Meiklejohn Award, given by the American Association of University Professors in 2000 for his unwavering support of academic freedom. Danforth — who kept on his wall a framed copy of the *Post-Dispatch* cartoon drawn at the time of Shepley's award, showing a flag labeled "The Blessings of Liberty" flying from Brookings Hall — had earned this distinction many times over. When he was still new on the job, for example, the trustees wanted to deny tenure to a "leftist" professor, an outspoken Hilltop scientist whose views Danforth himself did not share. Yet he stood his ground, the board relented, and the faculty member got tenure.

In his work for charitable boards and cultural organizations, local and national, he followed his grandfather's prescription for community service: "Catch a passion for helping others, and a richer life will come back to you." Though not musical himself, he has actively supported the St. Louis Christmas Carols Association, another favorite family cause. He has been a widely respected leader in race relations. In 1996, he was named mediator in the St. Louis public school desegregation lawsuit, helping to broker a 1999 settlement and obtain continued state funding.

In 1994, at age 68, he announced his intention to retire, and, the following spring, the leave-taking began. Students, who had celebrated Danforth's birthday every April since 1991, held the "biggest party for the best chancellor." At his final Commencement in June 1995, graduates gave him a giant diploma and a giant Washington University bear; Ibby received an honorary doctorate. Trustees launched a student scholarship fund — the William H. and Elizabeth Gray Danforth Scholars Program — which has since garnered $5.785 million in gifts or pledges; two donors made gifts of $2 million in his honor; and the William Greenleaf Eliot Society established a successful $25,000-per-year Danforth Circle of giving. Staying on as board chairman, Danforth finished his term in 1999, and more honors followed: the trustees named him "chancellor emeritus" and he received his own honorary degree. He continues to serve as the board's vice chairman.

Many times through those 24 years, he could have gone elsewhere, even to the top position at the National Institutes of Health (NIH). Instead, like William Greenleaf Eliot and Robert S. Brookings, his legacy is Washington University. As he said in his final Thanksgiving letter in 1994: "As I see it, we have been giving back to a world that has treated us well....We have strengthened a university that will keep alive our ideals, hopes, and dreams for generations to come." Ⓦ

CHAPTER ELEVEN

DOING SOMETHING IMPORTANT:

Building a
Major University

1978-1995

Chancellor William Danforth with students at Homecoming 1994.
Danforth had a special rapport with students, who called him "Uncle Bill" and "Chan Dan." They honored him prior to his retirement as chancellor with a "Birthday Bash" they called the "biggest party for the best chancellor."
Doug Miner, WU Photographic Services

Previous pages:
Francis Gymnasium.

DOING SOMETHING IMPORTANT

On November 10, 1977, 66 people — all with ties to Washington University — converged on the elegant Greenbrier resort hotel, tucked away in the remote Allegheny Mountain town of White Sulfur Springs, West Virginia. Some had feared that this trustee retreat, held so far away, would be a dismal failure, but the response was enthusiastic. Chancellor William H. Danforth, several staff members, school deans, and 30 of the 41 University trustees had made their way to this spot, most with their spouses. For two intense days, they immersed themselves in the University: discussing its strengths and weaknesses, then plotting the next crucial steps for a school that was little known nationally and seriously under-endowed.

1978 1995

1981 *The ten task forces of the Commission on the Future of Washington University reported their findings to the Board of Trustees.*

1983 *On May 2, the $300 million ALLIANCE FOR WASHINGTON UNIVERSITY campaign went public.*

1987 *The ALLIANCE campaign concluded on December 31, having raised a record-setting $630.5 million.*

1992 *The University hosted the first-ever presidential debate with three candidates: President George H.W. Bush, Arkansas Gov. Bill Clinton, and independent candidate H. Ross Perot.*

W.L. Hadley Griffin (1918-1997). Griffin, LL.B. '47, LL.D. (honorary) '90, president and chief executive officer of Brown Shoe Company, chaired the Commission on the Future of Washington University and served as a trustee for more than 30 years. The W.L. Hadley Griffin Student Commons in Anheuser-Busch Hall is named for him today.
Joe Angeles, WU Photographic Services

The recently concluded $120 million fund drive had helped relieve the University's immediate financial crisis, but its endowment — worth $147.4 million at the start of Danforth's term of office — had risen to a mere $176.7 million by the end of fiscal 1976. Faculty salaries lagged behind those at competing institutions, new buildings were sorely needed, and tuition was rising each year without a corresponding investment in student activities. In sports, for example, there was still no men's basketball team, and the athletic complex was shabby. The impact of this lean student life was painfully evident: just two-thirds of undergraduates stayed to graduate, and freshman enrollments were sagging. From 1971-77, the 3,000 Arts and Sciences undergraduates

dropped to around 2,400 — a trend that led to a stinging loss of tuition income.

It was clear to Danforth and his advisers, particularly Herbert F. Hitzeman, Jr., the visionary vice chancellor for university relations, that a major infusion of capital was needed from a fund drive that would dwarf all others in University history. Already, they were setting the stage for such an effort, working to increase the number of donors and raise more money, particularly in the all-important area of unrestricted giving. The key,

Reaching an ALLIANCE campaign milestone.
Holding high the latest total are (left to right) George H. Capps, A.B. '39, J.D. '39, campaign general chairman; W.L. Hadley Griffin, LL.B. '47, chairman of the board of trustees; and Herbert F. Hitzeman, Jr., B.F.A. '53, director of the campaign.
Herb Weitman, WU Photographic Services

233

Outdoor classroom.
In 1978, students take advantage of architect Walter Cope's vision for the campus' planned quadrangles: "Each will develop a character of its own. These are the outdoor rooms, with the sky for the ceiling."
WU Archives

Campus gathering places.
Students take a break between classes outside Olin Library in 1979.
WU Archives

Hitzeman believed, was alumni support. He reshaped the alumni program: dissolving the old Alumni Federation and forming a larger, more active Alumni Board of Governors; revitalizing Founders Day and the reunion program; and enlisting alumni to help with student recruitment. When it was time to ask for money, he did it in new ways, using phonathons and letting alumni give directly to the schools from which they had graduated. While some 5,000 alumni had given $689,000 to the University in 1970, that number had risen to 12,800 and $1.4 million in just seven years.

Still, 44,000 alumni were not giving anything to the University, and many other prospects — individuals, corporations, and foundations — were yet to be tapped. Soon the University would have to look to these sources and more for the financial push ahead. At Greenbrier, Hitzeman told the crowd that this time was fast approaching: "As surely as we are meeting here today, there is another major fund drive in our future. When we get to it, we must be ready….The time to begin getting ready is right now."

First, as Chancellor Danforth advised the assembled crowd, they needed to prepare the ground, building "a larger constituency than we have, one that is interested and informed, a constituency on whom we can count both for honest evaluation and criticism and for moral and especially financial support," he said. How to do it? The answer was a daring new approach: a Commission on the Future of Washington University. Like the campaign ahead, this task would not be easy, Danforth warned these trustees — the very group he counted on to spearhead the effort. "We are about [to embark on] a large undertaking….We in our University and in our community need to be examples of what confidence, dedication, and hard work can produce."

THE COMMISSION LOOKS AT THE FUTURE

This new commission was formally constituted early in 1979 — ten task forces, each assigned to a school or major service area of the University. They were chaired by trustees with impeccable credentials, including FBI director William H. Webster, J.D. '49, on the law task force; Hellmuth, Obata + Kassabaum, Inc. president George E.

Kassabaum, B.Arch. '47, in architecture and fine arts; former provost George E. Pake, who had become a Xerox vice president, in Arts and Sciences. The committees they headed had 18-24 members — alumni and other experts from around the country — 270 people in all. Overseeing this sprawling effort was W.L. Hadley Griffin, LL.B. '47, president and chief executive officer of Brown Shoe Company and a trustee since 1967.

For 28 months, the task forces studied the University, talking to faculty, students, deans, and alumni, and in 1981, compiled a report with nearly 200 recommendations aimed at strengthening the University. Certain themes were consistent: higher faculty salaries, interdisciplinary approaches to learning, better student recruitment, new sources of financial support. The Arts and Sciences task force targeted a need for new facilities, especially in physics, chemistry, earth and planetary sciences, and psychology; law noted tactfully that "the Mudd Law Building has a potential yet to be realized." Medicine found a school "with a well-deserved and recognized national reputation," but in need of careful planning for "a decade of dwindling government resources."

Two reports were the hardest hitting of all. The Student Life Task Force, chaired by John R. Barsanti, Jr., B.S.I.E. '49, J.D. '52, declared that extracurricular life on campus had suffered from "benign neglect," and pointed to a critical need for new housing, more student activities, and renewed athletics ("the facilities would suffer in comparison with most high schools," the report said). Business, chaired by Charles F. Knight, chairman and chief executive officer of Emerson Electric Co., stated flatly that the University's program "does not rank among the leading business schools in the United States." Strengthening it would take a new building, better faculty, a leap into executive education — and money, lots of it. "The historic approach… of operating from tuition income and trying to improve incrementally ('bootstrapping') will not accomplish the task," the report said bluntly.

At a closing dinner in December 1981, board chairman George H. Capps, A.B. '39, J.D. '39, thanked task force members for such valuable input. In fact five years later, the University instituted a "National Council" for each school, the libraries, and student activities, to continue the same kind of dialogue. On this night, Capps announced the formation of a follow-up committee to set financial goals based on the Commission's findings. As Danforth had previously told the trustees, their work was far from over; to create the kind of University they had envisioned, they needed to remain involved. Together, he said, "let us do something really important."

Studying aging and Alzheimer's disease

I n 1979, neurologist Leonard Berg, A.B. '45, M.D. '49, in collaboration with Martha Storandt, A.B. '60, Ph.D. '66, and Jack Botwinick of the Department of Psychology in Arts & Sciences, received a five-year grant from the National Institute of Mental Health to study the natural history of Alzheimer's disease — and the Memory and Aging Project was born. In 1985, the medical school was selected as one of five new Alzheimer's Disease Research Centers (ADRC), with Berg as principal investigator, and given a series of major research grants from the National Institute on Aging. Berg, who developed a Clinical Dementia Rating System to distinguish between stages of Alzheimer's disease and normal aging, stepped down as ADRC director in 1997; he transferred leadership to Eugene M. Johnson, Jr., the Norman J. Stupp Professor of Neurology, and John Morris, the Harvey A. and Dorismae Hacker Friedman Distinguished Professor of Neurology. Today, Morris is also director of the Memory and Aging Project and the Center for Aging, established at the University in 2002.

Leonard Berg.
Berg, now professor emeritus of neurology, explains a "draw-clock" test to a research participant at the Alzheimer's Disease Research Center.
Joe Angeles, WU Photographic Services

John Morris.
Morris was named director of the University-wide Center for Aging, made possible in 2002 with a gift from Harvey A. and Dorismae Hacker Friedman.
Robert Boston, WU Medical Public Affairs

THE ALLIANCE CAMPAIGN SETS A NEW RECORD

Out of the public eye, work on the giant fund drive — the ALLIANCE FOR WASHINGTON UNIVERSITY — had already begun. During fiscal year 1980, eight donors had come forward with gifts totaling more than $80.6 million, a promising start. Danforth, Hitzeman, and the special committee considered a $250 million campaign, but knew that even this ambitious goal fell short of the needs they had identified. Then in January 1982, the Danforth Foundation announced a powerful new incentive: a $45 million challenge grant to be matched three-to-one from private sources by the end of 1987. That March, the trustees' own development committee made a bold proposal for a $300 million campaign — a goal, wrote Hitzeman, that the board "viewed with considerable astonishment." However, the arguments for it were compelling, and the trustees approved it unanimously.

The sparkplug of the ALLIANCE was George Capps, president of Capitol Coal and Coke Co.,

Thach brothers.
All members of the faculty, the Thaches are (left to right) Bradley T., Robert E., and W. Thomas, Jr.
Robert Boston, WU Medical Public Affairs

Three Thaches join the faculty

Three Thach brothers, Oklahoma natives, are University faculty members, two at the medical school and one on the Hilltop Campus. W. Thomas Thach, Jr., the oldest, is professor in the departments of anatomy and neurobiology, neurology, and biomedical engineering, as well as physical therapy. Next is Robert E. Thach, dean of the Graduate School of Arts & Sciences and professor of biology. Youngest is Bradley T. Thach, M.D. '68, professor of pediatrics and a Sudden Infant Death Syndrome researcher, who completed his internship and residency at Barnes and Children's hospitals.

Robert Thach was first to join the faculty, recruited in 1970 by P. Roy Vagelos, then head of the biological chemistry department. Thomas came in 1975 at the urging of W. Maxwell Cowan, head of anatomy and neurobiology. The next year, Bradley came back in pediatrics after a year at Harvard's medical school — thus reuniting the siblings.

who stepped down as board chairman — replaced by W.L. Hadley Griffin — to head the effort. Capps "lived the program," said Hitzeman. At the end of the campaign, Danforth described Capps as the board's "greatest fund-raiser." Other trustees filled key slots on his leadership team. The two executive committees — Capital Resources and Annual Programs — were chaired respectively by Richard F. Ford, managing general partner, Gateway Associates, L.P., and Zane E. Barnes, chairman and chief executive officer of Southwestern Bell Telephone Co.

On May 2, 1983, at a gala dinner, the board went public with plans for the fund drive, the largest ever between the coasts: $200 million for endowment and facilities, and $100 million for annual operations and special programs. At the time, commitments exceeded $142 million — and in another year, thanks to the work of some 3,200 volunteers, the news looked even better: $201.7 million in gifts and pledges from nearly 42,000 donors. In December 1985, Capps could tell the board that the Danforth Foundation's challenge had been met more than two years early. Then in June 1986, he made a stunning announcement: the campaign had reached its overall goal 18 months ahead of schedule, with $301.2 million pledged by 50,627 donors. The University was one of only four nationwide to have completed drives of this size.

Some trustees must have breathed sighs of relief, but six days after Capps' announcement, the Danforth Foundation provided a new grant of $100 million, earmarked for the endowment — and it reinvigorated the campaign. In October 1986, buoyed by $55 million more in Danforth Foundation funds, the drive became the first in the nation to exceed $500 million; in December 1987, the first to exceed $600 million. In the end, the ALLIANCE raised $630.5 million: $387.1 million for endowment, $55.5 million for facilities, and $187.9 for operating purposes. There were 233,115 gifts from 60,752 donors — 71 of whom had given more than $1 million. The endowment had jumped from $245.5 million in 1980 to $1.2 billion in 1987, seventh largest in the United States.

In a jubilant 1987-88 letter, Danforth noted another welcome statistic: undergraduate applications had gone up 60 percent over the previous two years. Partly this growth was due to an aggressive, decade-long marketing effort, launched by Hitzeman, who had folded the University's public relations effort into the development office. In 1980, he had hired M. Fredric Volkmann as director of public relations, charging him with increasing the University's name recognition. The next year, they organized the Public Relations

Understanding air pollution

eginning in the 1970s, the Center for Air Pollution Impact and Trend Analysis (CAPITA) — a multidisciplinary team of researchers from bioengineering, mechanical engineering, chemistry, and mathematics — worked toward a better understanding of air pollution. Rudolf B. Husar was the director; others were faculty members Edward S. Macias, Noor Gillani, and Warren White, plus research associates Janja Husar and Geoffrey Cobourn. With funding from the Environmental Protection Agency, they established a clearinghouse for air pollution literature, a databank of pollution-related statistics, and interdisciplinary research projects. They were among the first, for example, to document multi-state haziness as an indicator of pollution.

Studying air pollution.
The CAPITA group in 1980 included (left to right) Geoffrey Cobourn, research associate; Rudolf Husar, director and professor of mechanical engineering; Janja Husar, senior research associate; Warren White, professor of mechanical engineering; Noor Gillani, associate professor of mechanical engineering; and Edward Macias, associate director and associate professor of chemistry.
WU Archives

Council, chaired by Charles Lipton, then chairman of the board of Ruder-Finn, Inc., a public relations firm in New York City, which advised Volkmann to embark on some first-ever market research, as well as visits with more than 200 journalists nationwide to learn what would help raise the University's public profile. The result was the development of a program promoting news coverage of faculty research and scholarly activities.

WILLIAM DANFORTH: NO LONGER A NEWCOMER

While the Commission and then the ALLIANCE progressed, Danforth was gaining confidence as a leader. His speech-making had markedly improved; so had his selection of staff members. In his 1981 Thanksgiving letter to alumni, he wrote: "Ten years is a long time to be a university chancellor or president. I have evolved from

Centenarian celebration.
Chancellor William Danforth congratulates 101-year-old Maria Bain White, A.B. '16, (right) and 100-year-old William C. Berry, B.S.Ch.E. '16, when the two met again at their 78th class reunion in 1994. Between them is 100-year-old Elmyra Sewing Johaning, A.B. '15.
WU Photographic Services

Washington University becomes a leader in computing

In 1964, the NIH-funded Biomedical Computer Laboratory (BCL) was founded by electrical engineering faculty member Jerome R. Cox, Jr., in the old Shriners Hospital. Soon a second group, the Computer Systems Laboratory (CSL), was established nearby by William N. Papian and Wesley A. Clark, also new engineering faculty, formerly at MIT. Clark and Charles E. Molnar (1935-1996), who came to the University from MIT in 1966, were co-developers there of the first personal computer — LINC (Laboratory Instrument Computer) — tested and refined at Washington University.

BCL and CSL began a collaboration that put the University at the forefront of biomedical computing efforts nationally. In 1972, Molnar took over from Clark at CSL, and in 1975 medical faculty member Lewis J. Thomas, Jr., succeeded Cox at BCL. A spinoff company, Tripos, Inc., was launched in 1979 by CSL's Garland R. Marshall, a medical school faculty member, to develop computer-aided drug design software for the pharmaceutical industry. In 1984, Molnar combined the CSL and the BCL into the Institute of Biomedical Computing (IBC), a joint venture of the engineering and medical schools, which pioneered advanced computing and engineering techniques in biomedical sciences.

A researcher works in the Biomedical Computer Laboratory.
WU Archives

The IBC ceased operation, but a successor program is the Center for Computational Biology (CCB) — affiliated with biomedical engineering, biochemistry and molecular biology, and genetics — focusing on bioinformatics and computational biophysics.

Wesley A. Clark.
WU Archives

The LINC computer.
Tested and refined at Washington University, it was state-of-the-art in the late 1960s.
WU Archives

Cox, the Harold B. and Adelaide G. Welge Professor of Computer Science from 1989-98, and now a senior professor, has since collaborated with Jonathan S. Turner, B.S. '77, the Henry Edwin Sever Professor of Engineering, and Guru Parulkar, professor of computer science. Work they did in the engineering school's Applied Research Laboratory on Internet routers and switching systems became the basis for a company — Growth Networks, Inc. — sold to Cisco Systems, Inc. in 2000.

Engineering faculty members Jerome Cox, Guru Parulkar, and Jonathan Turner (left to right) in the Applied Research Lab.
Joe Angeles, WU Photographic Services

being a newcomer to being a senior chief officer of a major university."

He had balanced the competing demands of town and gown, defending the academic freedom of faculty while smoothing ruffled community feathers. When one donor threatened to withhold a gift unless outspoken faculty member Barry Commoner was fired, Danforth replied firmly that a university must tolerate divergent opinions. Both he and his wife Elizabeth ("Ibby") had endeared themselves to students by their warm interest: attending campus events, greeting them by name, listening attentively to their concerns. Relations with the board of trustees, enlarged and diversified under his leadership, had grown collegial, mutually respectful.

Just before the ALLIANCE began, weighed down by financial worries, he had fretted that "too much concern with nuts and bolts can inhibit vision." In a letter to faculty, he quoted from John Steinbeck's account of King Arthur and his knight-turned-administrator, Sir Kay, who mourned the effect that his career shift was having on his character: "A heart that will not break under the great blows of fate can be eroded by the nibbling of numbers, the creeping of days, the numbing treachery of little-ness….To you war is fighting; to me it is so many ashen poles for spears or so many strips of steel."

In 1984, two-thirds of the way into the drive, Danforth's tone was more optimistic as he moved from a preoccupation with numbers to the business of education. "My spirit is buoyed in the faith that we shall reach our goal," he wrote that Thanks-giving, expressing gratitude for three new buildings, 11 professorships, and 50 endowed scholarships.

In late 1987, just shy of ending the ALLIANCE, he could see the lasting benefit of counting those ashen poles: "An institution, like a human being, usually defines its character…from the cumula-tive effect of thousands of decisions," he wrote. "If these decisions are shaped by a coherent set of principles, a character of significance and influ-ence will likely emerge." What emerged in this case was a vision, he said, "of having here in St. Louis one of the world's greatest universities."

ADVANCES AT THE MEDICAL SCHOOL

The first of the three buildings mentioned in Danforth's Thanksgiving letter to get under way was the $55 million Clinical Sciences Research Building (CSRB), the largest project in the medical school's history. Ten stories high and nearly 400,000 square feet in size, it linked hospitals with pedestri-an bridges and provided research facilities for seven clinical departments. Other projects followed quickly. In 1985, the East Building, formerly an A&P bakery, underwent major renovation for the use of several departments, especially Mallinckrodt Institute of Radiology (MIR). By 1987, more than 30 medical school buildings were scattered across 50 acres. Adjacent to the medical school, a new $84 million St. Louis Children's Hospital, more than twice the space of the previous facility, was dedicated in 1984; Ronald G. Evens, already MIR director, assumed its presidency in 1985.

New department heads, too, were transforming the medical center. In 1981, Gerald D. Fischbach came from Harvard to head anatomy, while Samuel A. Wells, Jr., arrived from Duke and built

John W. Olney.
Olney, who became the first John Feighner Professor of Neuropsychopharmacology in 1999, established that glutamate can kill nerve cells in the brain by overstimulating them — a process he calls "excitotoxicity."
WU Archives

Ronald G. Evens.
President of Barnes-Jewish Hospital since 1999, professor of radiology, and adjunct professor of medical economics, Evens, A.B. '61, M.D. '64, has been president and chief executive officer at St. Louis Children's Hospital, 1985-88; vice chancel-lor for financial affairs, 1988-90; and Elizabeth Mallinckrodt Professor, head of radiology, and director of Mallinckrodt Institute of Radiology, 1971-99.
Oil on canvas by Gilbert Gordon Early
Mallinckrodt Institute of Radiology

$55 million Clinical Sciences Research Building.
Chancellor Danforth, George Capps, general chairman of the ALLIANCE campaign, and Herbert F. Hitzeman, Jr., senior vice chancellor for university relations, examine a model of the structure to be built on the Medical Campus.
Herb Weitman, WU Photographic Services

William A. Peck.
A well-known expert on osteoporosis and on issues related to academic medicine, Peck (right) served as vice chancellor (executive vice chancellor from 1993) and dean of the School of Medicine from 1989 to 2003, and in a continuing role as the Alan A. and Edith L. Wolff Distinguished Professor in Medicine. Together with Timothy Eberlein, Peck signs the beam topping off a new medical center building.
Robert Boston, WU Medical Public Affairs

Emil Unanue.
Succeeding Paul Lacy as head of the Department of Pathology in 1985 was Unanue, the Edward Mallinckrodt Professor and a leader in the field of immunology. In 1995, he won the Albert Lasker Basic Medical Research Award.
WU Medical Public Affairs

up surgery, depleted of its part-timers, with a large full-time staff. The next year, John M. Fredrickson took over otolaryngology. Others took the place of longtime faculty members, now retiring, among them Philip D. Stahl in cell biology and physiology; Emil R. Unanue in pathology; Harvey R. Colten in pediatrics; C. Robert Cloninger in psychiatry; and Ralph G. Dacey in neurosurgery. In 1989, William A. Peck, an osteoporosis expert, became vice chancellor for medical affairs and then dean, replacing both Guze and M. Kenton King, whose roles were now combined.

Faculty engaged in seminal research, often supported by grants from the National Institutes of Health (NIH). Cardiology chief Burton Sobel and collaborators, including Philip A. Ludbrook, developed a new clot-dissolving agent, tissue plasminogen activator (t-PA). Unanue, an immunopathologist, studied the cellular basis of

the immune response; endocrinologist William H. Daughaday researched metabolism and growth disorders; and John W. Olney, a pioneering neuroscientist, established glutamate as a major excitatory transmitter in the brain. While biochemist Philip W. Majerus was studying the cellular response to hormonal signals, his colleague, Carl Frieden, was looking at the relationship between protein structure and function. With help from McDonnell Douglas engineers, pediatric plastic surgeon Jeffrey Marsh and radiologist Michael W. Vannier produced three-dimensional images from computed tomography (CT) scans to plan corrective surgery for patients with craniofacial deformities.

This research got a further boost from new ties with industry, which drew some criticism nationally. University officials staunchly defended the partnerships, denying any hint of undue corporate influence. In 1981, the medical school joined forces with Mallinckrodt, Inc., which provided $3.9 million for research into the production of genetically engineered antibodies. A historic $23.5 million agreement with Monsanto, formalized the next year, led eventually to more than $100 million in biomedical research projects — the largest research venture linking an American company and a university. University scientists collaborated with Hoffman-LaRoche, Inc. to investigate nerve cell injury and conducted research into treatments for cardiovascular and inflammatory diseases with Sphinx Pharmaceuticals Corp.

On the faculty side, new chairs were being endowed, such as the Fred C. Reynolds Professorship of Orthopaedic Surgery, held by Paul R. Manske, and named for Reynolds, orthopaedic division chief for 17 years. On the student side, more than ever were applying: In 1985-86, the medical school enrolled 119 out of more than 5,000 applicants. In the Spencer T. and Ann W. Olin Medical Scientist Training Program (MSTP), one of the largest such programs in the world, there were 91 M.D./Ph.D. students. With a $30 million ALLIANCE-related

William H. Daughaday.
Daughaday (left), the Irene and Michael Karl Professor of Endocrinology and Metabolism, was a faculty member from 1947-94 (now professor emeritus) and a pioneer in the study of human growth hormone's role in health and disease. He received an honorary degree from the University in 1997.
WU Archives

Clinical Sciences Research Building, dedicated October 17, 1984.
Robert Boston, WU Medical Public Affairs

gift in 1987 from the Spencer T. and Ann W. Olin Foundation, the MSTP was able to fund as many as ten new students each year.

Not long before the 1980 death of James S. McDonnell, the McDonnell Foundation made another spectacular gift to the School of Medicine: $5.5 million to establish the McDonnell Center for Studies of Higher Brain Function. The Foundation continued to be generous, donating $5 million to the Center in 1984 through a gift to the ALLIANCE, and in 1988 giving $1.8 million to establish the Center for Genetics in Medicine, which soon got involved in mapping the human genome.

A LIVELIER STUDENT LIFE

After the Clinical Sciences Research Building, a second major facility — the most popular among students — emerged from the ALLIANCE. As T-shirts with red-and-green lettering proclaimed at the April 1983 ground-breaking: "I'm Getting an Athletic Complex at Washington University." The new $13 million complex — including a multipurpose gym, swimming pool (replacing Wilson Pool, which was torn down), and racquetball and squash courts — was designed to wrap around the existing structures, which were completely refurbished. The seating capacity of the field house was 4,200.

Homecoming 1982.
Revived in 1978, Homecoming was once again a popular student activity.
WU Archives

Danforth believed that student life needed a lift, and the rehabilitation of the sports program was just one item on his list. New student housing went up on the South 40, the expanded Millbrook Apartments opened to students instead of faculty, and fraternity houses got make-overs, as Greek

241

Carnival!
Every April, Washington University students host Thurtene Carnival — the oldest student-run carnival in the nation — and raise funds for charity.
WU Archives

life made a strong comeback. Although student Lori Tenser, A.B. '84, wrote in a 1984 *Washington University Magazine* article, that "sometimes I think [the University] is a haven for the criminally studious," student activities were gaining momentum, thanks in part to the efforts of Hartwig E. ("Harry") Kisker, dean of student affairs since 1978.

Homecoming, which had faded from the student scene, came back to life in 1978, and campus events — such as the Walk-In Lay-Down (WILD), annual TANG party, Washington University Olympics, Thurtene Carnival, and South 40 Formal — attracted large crowds. By the mid-1980s, the University had some 200 student organizations: literary (*Student Life, Hatchet, Cadenza*), musical (*a cappella* groups that included the Greenleafs

and the Pikers), social action (the Environmental Action Group, Students Together Against Racism), pre-professional (Pre-Law, Society for Women Engineers), and purely fun (Ballroom Dance Club, Society for Creative Anachronism). Under the leadership of John Schael, athletics got a fresh start, including men's basketball and women's sports. Many students took part in two governing bodies — Student Union and the Congress of the South 40 — or reached out to the community through programs such as those sponsored by the Campus Y.

Some won nationwide academic competitions. University teams, tutored by physicist Carl Bender and mathematician Edward Wilson, excelled in the prestigious William Lowell Putnam Mathematical Competition, taking first or second place seven times from 1976-86. In 1983, four business seniors were first in the University of Virginia's McIntire Commerce Invitational, a University team ranked second place nationally in the College Bowl in 1984, and School of Law teams won National Mock Trial competitions. Individual students

Simon Hall.
Completed in 1985 to house the business school and named for donor John E. Simon, Simon Hall became the largest building on the Hilltop Campus at that time, with 130,000 square feet of floor space.
David Kilper, WU Photographic Services

received Rhodes, Marshall, and Beinecke scholarships, Andrew W. Mellon Graduate Fellowships, National Science Foundation Fellowships, Barry M. Goldwater Scholarships, and Fulbright awards.

Through these years, several frightening crimes took place on and near campus that led to the installation of blue light security phones in 1979. Two years later, unexplained fires damaged some University buildings and destroyed the Sigma Alpha Epsilon fraternity. Yet the emphasis on student activities was working, and late in 1983 Danforth was able to report that "student morale on campus is high this year."

THE BUSINESS SCHOOL MOVES FORWARD

Groundbreaking for the third ALLIANCE-funded building, a $13-million home for the business school, took place in October 1984. Since 1961, students and faculty had been wedged into Prince Hall, a renovated dormitory, and they had longed for this day. The building — named John E. Simon Hall for the business leader and Smith Academy graduate whose campaign contribution helped make it possible — was more than three times the size of Prince and, at the time, the largest academic building on the Hilltop Campus. Simon Hall represented an aesthetic shift from Mudd Hall, Eliot Hall, and Mallinckrodt Center: a return to red granite and limestone building materials and a nod to the Collegiate Gothic tradition. Buford Pickens, professor emeritus and former dean of architecture, was ecstatic: "With Simon Hall, we're back on track," he said in 1986.

This building, completed in 1985, was just one evidence of progress. Under the leadership of former faculty member Robert L. Virgil, Jr., M.B.A. '60, Ph.D. '67, who had become acting dean in 1977 and then dean in 1979, the school was forging ahead with new programs. In 1980, it inaugurated the Institute of Banking and Financial Markets, directed by Jess B. Yawitz, who became the first John E. Simon Professor of Finance; a microcomputing development program, led by faculty member Lyn D. Pankoff, in 1982; an executive MBA program in 1983; a new Center for Business, Law, and Economics, with a grant from Mark E. Mason, A.B. '51, and his wife, Myrna, in 1990; and a Management Center, led by Russell Roberts, in 1991. Student enrollment grew and so did the faculty, with new members such as Nicholas Dopuch, later the Hubert C. and Dorothy R. Moog

The Master of Liberal Arts program begins

Students in a Master of Liberal Arts seminar.
WU Photographic Services

T his popular part-time graduate program — the only one of its kind in the St. Louis area — began in 1980, developed under the leadership of Robert C. Williams, dean of University College and professor of history. Program students take part in interdisciplinary seminars, organized into four categories: Ideas and Inquiry, The Creative Imagination, Science and Human Values, and Historical Understanding. Two graduates of the program, who have both served as trustees, are: Lee M. Liberman, A.M. '94, chairman emeritus of Laclede Gas Co.; and William E. Cornelius, A.M. '83, retired chairman and chief executive officer of Union Electric Co.

Robert L. Virgil, Jr.
Virgil, M.B.A. '60, Ph.D. '67, with his wife, Gerry, received the "Search" award from the William Greenleaf Eliot Society in 2001. He joined the business school as a faculty member in 1964, later serving as acting dean from 1977-79, dean from 1979-92, and executive vice chancellor for university relations from 1992-93, when he was named a principal in Edward D. Jones & Co. (now Edward Jones). A trustee, Virgil has served as chair of the Sesquicentennial Commission.
Joe Angeles, WU Photographic Services

Professor of Accounting, and Philip H. Dybvig, later the Boatmen's Bancshares Professor of Banking and Finance.

With the help of strong alumni giving, the school took off financially. From 1980-93, revenues rose from $3.7 million to $21.96 million, and its share of the endowment from $1.1 million in 1980 to $77.4 million in 1994. In 1987, the John M. Olin Foundation pledged $15 million if a similar amount could be raised from private

Douglass C. North.
North, the Spencer T. Olin Professor in Arts & Sciences, received the 1993 Nobel Prize in Economic Sciences, with Robert W. Fogel, "for having renewed research in economic history by applying economic theory and quantitative methods in order to explain economic and institutional change."
Joe Angeles, WU Photographic Services

James E. McLeod.
McLeod, who came to the University in 1974 as an assistant professor of German, was named assistant dean of the Graduate School of Arts and Sciences from 1974-77, then assistant to Chancellor Danforth from 1977-87. From 1987-92, he was director of the African and Afro-American Studies Program, then became dean of the College of Arts and Sciences. Chancellor Wrighton named him vice chancellor for students in 1995.
Joe Angeles, WU Photographic Services

sources — a challenge that the school met, renaming itself for Olin. There was an upsurge in endowed professorships: from one in 1981 to 12 by 1994.

CHANGES IN ARTS AND SCIENCES

Through the 1980s and early 1990s, other schools had changes in leadership, programs, and facilities — and sometimes all three, especially Arts and Sciences. Here the picture was complicated by a new factor: In 1983, Arts and Sciences, Fine Arts, and Architecture were all placed on the "reserve" system, which meant they were largely fiscally independent units, responsible for attracting income and living within their means. These three were the last of the University's schools to shift to this system. Medicine had been the first in the 1940s, Social Work and Law in the 1950s, Dentistry in the 1960s, Engineering in 1973, and Business six years later. In 1983, the changeover was controversial, with some arguing that these alumni might be less able than physicians or business executives to provide the needed support.

Yet the change was less bumpy than many had feared, as funds from the ALLIANCE helped smooth the transition. Arts and Sciences received a financial lift in 1981 from the addition of a new program. Some years earlier, University College had spawned the broader School for Continuing Education, but this operation got into financial trouble, with some noncredit programs draining away income.

Through a reorganization in which Robert Williams became dean, the unprofitable programs were discarded, while engineering, business, and architecture classes shifted over to their respective schools to administer. University College, the profitable core that remained, was the piece that joined Arts and Sciences, along with an exciting new interdisciplinary graduate program, the Master of Liberal Arts (MLA), begun by Williams in 1980.

Slowly, Arts and Sciences began to rally, with full-time student enrollment — down to around 2,400 in 1985 — beginning to rise, along with faculty hiring and salaries. Among the recruits of this period were Douglass C. North in 1983 as Henry R. Luce Professor of Law and Liberty; Roy Curtiss III, as chair of biology; Peter Heath in 1986 as the first tenure-track professor in Arabic; and Thomas Eagleton, former U.S. senator, to become University Professor of Public Affairs in 1987. Roger N. Beachy, who joined the biology faculty in 1978, eight years later became director of the Center for Plant Science and Biotechnology, a collaborative effort with the Missouri Botanical Garden and the University of Missouri-Columbia.

Ralph E. Morrow (1920-2001).
David Kilper, WU Photographic Services

New administrators came onto the scene. Merle Kling, retiring longtime executive vice chancellor and provost, was replaced in 1984 by Ralph Morrow, former dean of the Faculty of Arts and Sciences, who was succeeded two years

T.S. Eliot centenary conference.
The English department hosted a scholarly conference in 1988 to re-examine the work of T.S. Eliot, a Smith Academy graduate and grandson of University co-founder William Greenleaf Eliot.
WU Photographic Services

later by former anatomy head Maxwell Cowan, returning from the Salk Institute. Cowan left again to become vice president and chief scientific officer of the Howard Hughes Medical Institute, and Morrow came out of retirement to fill in before chemistry chair Edward S. Macias took over in 1988. Another key appointment was James E. McLeod, who became dean of the College of Arts and Sciences in 1992, replacing Linda Salamon. One unsuccessful choice was Richard N. Rosett, who replaced Morrow as dean of the Faculty of Arts and Sciences in 1984 but ran into problems, including his controversial refusal to grant tenure to a popular young history professor and an acrimonious dispute over changes he made at Olin Library. He left abruptly in 1987.

A number of areas were clearly showing signs of progress. Music reinstated its long-inactive bachelor of music degree, while Romance languages, under chair James F. Jones, Jr., introduced the "Dartmouth" method, which reversed the downward spiral of enrollments in some language courses. During his tenure, Jones recruited visiting professors such as Peruvian novelist Mario Vargas Llosa and Mexican novelist Carlos Fuentes. For biology and earth and planetary sciences, there was a new building named for James S. McDonnell. The Graduate Institute of Education became the Department of Education. In 1988, English sponsored a spectacular T.S. Eliot centenary conference; two years later Arts and Sciences established a Teaching Center under mathematics professor Robert N. McDowell.

Changes in Architecture, Engineering, Fine Arts, and Law

Architecture, led by Constantine E. Michaelides, dean from 1973-93, began the 1980s by celebrating the 50th birthday of Givens Hall with a ceremony honoring former deans and longtime design professor Leslie Laskey. The school established an "Architecture Discovery" summer program under Iain Fraser for high school juniors and by 1985 a 3+4 program with several other colleges. In 1986 it received its first endowed chair, the Ruth and Norman Moore Professorship in Architecture, held by art historian Udo Kultermann until his 1994 retirement. Faculty member Donald Royse took a leave from 1990-93 to serve as the first director of urban design for the City of St. Louis, overseeing the design and construction of such projects as MetroLink.

In 1981, Engineering granted a record number of undergraduate degrees, most of them in electrical engineering, to students from 37 states

and 14 countries. That same year Lopata Hall was dedicated, thanks to a gift from Stanley L. Lopata, A.B. '35, and his wife Lucy; later, an addition, given by Edward L. Bowles, B.S.E.E. '20, served as a laboratory for the Institute of Biomedical Computing. A gift from the estate of Harold D. Jolley, B.S.C.E. '11, led to the construction of Jolley Hall, dedicated in 1990. The school incurred deficits when sponsored research fell off and the School of Technology and Information Management (STIM), the new continuing education program, lost money. On the other hand, when Christopher I. Byrnes, former chair of systems science and mathematics, took over as

Constantine E. Michaelides as a new dean, 1974.
When he stepped down in 1993, Michaelides, who had been dean since 1973 and a member of the architecture faculty since 1960, was the longest-serving dean at the University. In collaboration with private firms, he was also the architect for four University buildings: McMillen, Bryan, Lopata, and Harold D. Jolley halls. Today he is dean emeritus.
Herb Weitman, WU Photographic Services

Leslie J. Laskey.
Laskey, senior professor of basic design (now professor emeritus of architecture), was an influential teacher in the School of Architecture.
Herb Weitman, WU Photographic Services

tled years later, with exhibits by faculty members William Fett and H. Richard Duhme. Another well-known art faculty member, Arthur Osver, retired in 1981. The overcrowded school, which had previously sent some of its graduate programs to Tyson Research Center, then to a University-owned warehouse downtown, desperately needed a second home. In 1984 it found an answer: Lewis Center, built in 1909 by University City founder E.G. Lewis, was now fully renovated for its use. Falling enrollment plagued the school in the mid-1980s, and longtime dean Roger DesRosiers left. In 1989, new dean Joe Deal took his place; that same year enrollment — down to 232 in 1986-87 — climbed to over 300. Noted fashion designer Carolyne Roehm, B.F.A. '73, gave a $100,000 gift in 1989 to make possible the new Carolyne Roehm Electronic Media Center at the art school. In 1987, the nearby Gallery of Art mounted the successful "Paris in Japan" exhibition of late 19th- and early 20th-century oil paintings by Japanese painters who studied in France.

Law dean Edward T. ("Tad") Foote had moved the school forward by appointing 14 of its 27 faculty members, building a new wing on Mudd Hall, and instituting an improved system of student recruitment. In 1978, amid a growing number of female law students, faculty member Kathleen Brickey became the first woman to receive tenure and, subsequently, the first to hold a named chair. When Foote left in 1980, another of his hires, F. Hodge O'Neal, took over as dean for five years, bringing in more faculty, such as Stephen H. Legomsky and Stanley L. Paulson; in 1984, D. Bruce La Pierre helped mediate the St. Louis landmark desegregation case as a court-appointed special master. Next Philip D. Shelton stepped in briefly as acting dean, followed in 1987 by Dorsey D. Ellis, Jr. Ellis, too, hired new faculty — including Daniel L. Keating, Clark Cunningham,

Dorsey D. Ellis, Jr.
Ellis, now the William R. Orthwein Distinguished Professor of Law, served for 11 years as law school dean, stepping down in 1998.
WU Photographic Services

engineering dean from the retiring James McKelvey in 1991, he inherited a school with a stable undergraduate enrollment and more student aid than ever, thanks to a plan suggested in 1974 by William K. Y. Tao, M.S.M.E. '50, for funding "term-endowed" scholarships through individual annual gifts of $2,500 or more.

In 1978, the School of Fine Arts — renamed the School of Art in 1994 — celebrated the renovation of beautiful Bixby Gallery, which would be disman-

"Paris in Japan."
The Gallery of Art exhibit received national coverage and went on to the Japan House Gallery in New York in December 1987 and to the Wight Art Gallery at the University of California, Los Angeles in 1988.

Woman Reading, 1908. Oil on canvas by Yamashita Shintaro Bridgestone Museum of Art, Ishibashi Foundation, Tokyo

Shanti K. Khinduka.
Dean since 1974 of the George Warren Brown School of Social Work, Khinduka — also the George Warren Brown Distinguished University Professor — has led the school to national prominence. The school draws a substantial number of international students to St. Louis.
WU Archives

Kathleen F. Brickey.
The James Carr Professor of Criminal Jurisprudence, Brickey, who first came to the School of Law in 1976, is a noted expert on corporate criminal liability and corporate and white-collar crime.
Joe Angeles, WU Photographic Services

Richard Lazarus, Kimberly J. Norwood, Stuart Banner, and Kathleen Clark — but Ellis's defining activity was a $40 million campaign, chaired by William Webster, J.D. '49, to replace the increasingly inadequate, always unpopular, Mudd Hall — this time with a building in the Collegiate Gothic style, named Anheuser-Busch Hall in recognition of the company's support.

Under the deft management of Shanti K. Khinduka, its dean since 1974, Social Work remained strong despite declining student enrollment and federal grants. One major effort of the 1980s was the search for more scholarships; another was an emphasis on faculty research. Already the school had faculty with strong reputations such as Martha Ozawa, who became the Bettie Bofinger Brown Professor of Social Policy and an expert on the U.S. public assistance network. During this decade, the school updated the curriculum, added a computing facility, and inaugurated a new Center for American Indian Studies, donated by Kathryn M. Buder. More international students were attending the school, due in part to faculty member Richard J. Parvis, who retired in 1987. By 1994, the school ranked as one of the top two social work schools in the nation.

MINORITY RECRUITMENT GAINS STRENGTH

Recruitment of minority students, which had begun under Chancellor Thomas Eliot, now moved forward in every school. The law school created the Walter Moran Farmer Scholarship for African-American students; the business school continued its leadership of the Consortium for Graduate Study in Management and, under the sponsorship of the Urban League, hosted a Minority Youth Entrepreneurship Program. Engineering held an "Access to Engineering Institute" through its Joint Undergraduate Engineering Program with the University of Missouri–St. Louis. On the Hilltop, the Chancellor's Graduate Fellowship Program aided African Americans seeking doctoral degrees, as did new scholarships at the medical school, created through a $600,000 grant in 1990 from the Monsanto Fund for minority students enrolled in the Medical Scientist Training Program. The first Monsanto Scholar was Roderick L. McCoy, M.D., Ph.D. '98.

Around campus were other efforts toward greater inclusiveness. The Black Studies Department (renamed African and Afro-American Studies), began in 1970 under the leadership of psychology

Buder Center for American Indian Studies scholar Wendy Nunez.
Nunez, of the Nez Perce Tribe, won second place in the Jingle Dress competition at the 2002 Pow Wow sponsored by the George Warren Brown School of Social Work.
Mary Butkus, WU Photographic Services

The John B. Ervin Scholars Program begins

**John B. Ervin
(1916-1992).**
WU Archives

I n fall 1987, the first group of John B. Ervin Scholars arrived on campus, chosen from 305 applicants. They were initiating a program, directed by James McLeod and Dorothy Elliott, that awarded up to ten scholarships, covering tuition plus a $2,500 stipend, to exceptional African-American students each year. Students were selected on the basis of academic achievement, leadership skills, and community service.

Among that group was Christopher Warlick, A.B. '91. While working in the laboratory of genetics professor Helen Donis-Keller, he discovered two genetic markers — named CW1 and CW2 in his honor — that might figure in a genetic heart ailment. He was the only undergraduate to present a paper at the American Society of Human Geneticists' meeting in 1990. A star on the football team, he had to skip a key game to present the paper. After graduation, he continued on to an M.D./Ph.D. program at the University of Minnesota.

Since that initial group of scholars, the program has produced doctors, lawyers, architects, engineers, psychologists, historians. Trina Williams, B.S.B.A. '92, was one of 20 students named to *USA Today's* All-USA Academic First Team in 1992. She served in the Peace Corps in Ecuador, won a Rhodes Scholarship in 1994, and eventually returned to the University to receive a doctorate from the George Warren Brown School of Social Work in 2003.

The program honors John B. Ervin, a beloved educator, associate dean of

University College from 1965-68, then dean of the reorganized School of Continuing Education from 1968-78. The John B. Ervin memorial bench on the Brookings Quadrangle, purchased with gifts from the Ervin Scholars, is named for him; the Ervin Scholars hold a memorial event at the bench each year.

In 2001, a $25 million gift from Enterprise Rent-A-Car Co. established the Enterprise Rent-A-Car Endowed Scholarship Fund, designed to support 30-40 African-American and financially disadvantaged students. Half of them are selected on the basis of John B. Ervin Scholars program criteria and the others on the basis of financial need. Approximately ten percent of Enterprise Scholars are graduates of St. Louis area high schools or community colleges.

Christopher Warlick in the lab, 1990.
While he was an undergraduate, Warlick, A.B. '91, uncovered two genetic markers that are named for him.
Joe Angeles, WU Photographic Services

Trina Williams.
Named a Rhodes Scholar in 1994, Williams later returned to Washington University to earn a Ph.D. in social work.
Joe Angeles, WU Photographic Services

professor Robert Williams; in 1992, Gerald Early, who had joined the English department faculty a decade earlier, became its director. The medical school opened an Office of Minority Affairs, headed by Robert Lee. Danforth stood firmly behind these efforts, aided by campus leaders James E. McLeod, director of African and Afro-American Studies from 1987-92, then dean of the College of Arts and Sciences; and Gloria W. White, named human resources' associate vice chancellor in 1981 and vice chancellor in 1988.

Yet minority undergraduate enrollment was down in the mid-1980s, with only 36 black students entering as freshmen in 1986. A signal effort in reversing this trend was the John B. Ervin Scholars Program for Black Americans, initiated that year with strong support from Chancellor Danforth and funding from the Danforth Foundation. Its name honored John B. Ervin, associate dean and then dean of the School of Continuing Education from 1965-77, and afterwards vice president of the Danforth Foundation. Spearheading this recruitment program, among the first of its kind in the United States, were McLeod, who became its director, and Dorothy Elliott, its assistant director. Adrienne Glore, associate dean of students, soon joined the Ervin committee to help plan program activities for these scholars, selected for academic achievement, leadership, and community service.

PROGRESS CONTINUES AT THE SCHOOL OF MEDICINE

In 1991, the School of Medicine marked its 100th anniversary with a three-day commemoration; an entire issue of the *Journal of the American Medical Association* was devoted to it. The school had much to celebrate. After years of waiting, the medical school had its new library building, later named for longtime ophthalmology head Bernard Becker. In March 1992, the medical school and Barnes Hospital negotiated another operating agreement, and that November Barnes and Jewish hospitals affiliated, creating Barnes-Jewish Inc. The next year Barnes and Jewish combined with Christian Health Services to form BJC Health System, a regional network of hospitals and other medical facilities. In 1994, St. Louis Children's Hospital also joined BJC.

New research grants supported projects at the medical school, which received $26 million from the NIH in fiscal 1989 — one of the top five medical schools in NIH awards. With a $2.3 million NIH grant in 1990, the school became one of the first four to take part in the federally funded Human Genome Project; that same year, geneticist Robert H. Waterston received $3.8 million from the NIH to develop large-scale DNA sequencing methods. Psychiatrist Theodore Reich was exploring genetic factors involved in alcoholism, depression,

John P. Atkinson.
A noted rheumatologist and researcher, Atkinson, now the Samuel B. Grant Professor of Medicine, served as director of the rheumatology division and Howard Hughes investigator from 1976-92, and head of internal medicine from 1992-96. He received the nation's top award for arthritis research, the 1991 Lee C. Howley, Sr. Prize from the Arthritis Foundation.
Robert Boston, WU Medical Public Affairs

Marcus Raichle.
Raichle, professor of neurology, of radiology, of anatomy and neurobiology, of psychology, and co-director of the radiological sciences division at Mallinckrodt Institute of Radiology, has been a pioneer in using PET to determine which areas of the brain are active during specific tasks.
Robert Boston, WU Medical Public Affairs

Susan Mackinnon.
In 1996, Mackinnon, the Sydney M. Shoenberg, Jr. and Robert H. Shoenberg Professor of Plastic and Reconstructive Surgery, successfully treated patient Rebecca Case, who had been injured in a riding lawn-mower accident, by transplanting nerve tissue from a cadaver donor and from Rebecca's legs into the child's left arm.
Joe Angeles, WU Photographic Services

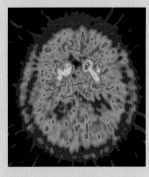

PET scan showing activity in the brain.
Courtesy of Joel Perlmutter

and bipolar disorder; biochemist Stuart Kornfeld was studying basic cell biology; nephrologist Saulo Klahr was investigating the causes of kidney disease. In 1994, biochemist Gary K. Ackers received a $7.5 million grant from the National Heart, Lung, and Blood Institute to fund the development of hemoglobin for artificial blood. Medical imaging pioneer Marcus E. Raichle was using PET to study the neural processes underlying language development.

Around the medical center were researchers named as investigators by the prestigious Howard Hughes Medical Institute. One was Stanley Korsmeyer, chief of the division of molecular oncology, who was doing landmark research on the identification of genes that control apoptosis or programmed cell death — work that might shed new light on the causes of cancer. Another was John P. Atkinson, director of the rheumatology division and Howard Hughes investigator

from 1976-92; he was studying the complement system, proteins critical for the host's response to many infectious organisms, including the development of immunity.

Breakthroughs were occurring on the clinical side as well. Joel D. Cooper, pulmonary transplant surgeon, performed the first successful double-lung transplant in 1988 and developed lung-volume-reduction surgery in 1993 for emphysema patients. Susan Mackinnon, head of plastic and reconstructive surgery, was the first in the world to perform a nerve transplant from a cadaver donor. Using minimally invasive techniques, surgeon Ralph V. Clayman, with Louis Kavoussi and Nathaniel Soper, performed the world's first laparoscopic nephrectomy for low-grade renal cancer. In 1989, William Catalona initiated a study that established prostate-specific antigen (PSA) as a screening test for prostate cancer, and in 1993 the medical school, with Gerald Andriole as principal investigator, was chosen as one of nine sites nationally to participate in the largest randomized, prospective cancer screening study ever undertaken for prostate, lung, colorectal, and ovarian (PLCO) cancers.

Along with the successes, there were problems to address. Having helped stabilize the area north of the Medical Campus, the Washington University Medical Center Redevelopment Corporation, under executive director Eugene Kilgen and then Brian Phillips, began work on a $186 million plan to revitalize Forest Park Southeast, an economically depressed and increasingly crime-ridden neighborhood south of the medical center. By 1992, the federal government was providing some $144 million in research grants to the University, but that year allegations surfaced that the Department of Psychiatry had misallocated some NIH funds. After an investigation by an outside accounting firm, the University sent a check back to NIH for more than $400,000.

McDonnell Medical Sciences Building.
Robert Boston, WU Medical Public Affairs

St. Louis Children's Hospital.
The hospital became part of BJC Health System (now BJC HealthCare) in 1994.
Robert Boston, WU Medical Public Affairs

Joel Cooper.
Cooper (second from right), the Evarts A. Graham
Professor of Surgery, who pioneered a lung-volume-
reduction procedure for patients with emphysema,
makes hospital rounds with student interns.
Joe Angeles, WU Photographic Services

Managing health-care costs became a major
challenge of this era. With a grant from the Metropolitan Life Insurance Company, the medical
school launched an experimental prepaid group
practice in 1969, organized by Gerald I. Perkoff,
director of the new division of heath care research
— despite the opposition of some medical faculty,
who feared that its cost might compromise traditional academic areas. In fact, the program was
profitable, and in 1973 this Medical Care Group
(MCG), with pediatrician Lawrence Kahn as its
medical director, broadened its patient base from
the original experimental group, moving to its
own office on Audubon. In 1979, the growing
practice became independent, though part- and
full-time medical center physicians continued to
provide clinical services. It has since undergone
more changes and today continues as Esse Health
Care Group, though it is no longer affiliated with
Washington University.

THE LOSS OF THREE PROGRAMS

In 1989, the difficult choice was made to close
two academic programs. One was the 124-year-
old School of Dental Medicine, which had a
shrinking applicant pool, declining research
funds, and rising costs — all of which led to high
tuition. Some faculty, including dean Richard J.
Smith, who shifted to the anthropology department, remained on campus; others retired or left.
Two years later, students in the school's final class
received their degrees, and the first dental school
west of the Mississippi closed its doors.

The Faculty of Arts and Sciences voted 116 to
114 to eliminate the Department of Sociology, a
long-beleaguered program with a dwindling faculty. By the time of the closing, the 18 full-time

members of the mid-1960s had shrunk to seven,
only three of them tenured, with no tenured
appointments made after 1975. Yet the decision
to close was controversial; students protested,
and the national press trumpeted the story.
Martin H. Israel, dean of the Faculty of Arts and
Sciences since 1987, said: "We must allocate our
resources selectively to areas…likely to move us
to new levels of excellence." To replace sociology,
Arts and Sciences inaugurated an interdisciplinary Committee on Social Thought and Analysis
with anthropologist John Bowen as chair.

Another controversial program quietly met its
end in the mid-1980s: The McDonnell Laboratory
for Psychic Research (MacLab) was established off
campus in summer 1979 with a five-year, $500,000
grant from James S. McDonnell and directed by
physics professor Peter R. Phillips. In 1983, the
program attracted national publicity when James
Randi, professional magician and outspoken para-
psychology critic, revealed an elaborate hoax: He
had sent two teenage magicians to fool MacLab
staff by claiming to have psychic powers. Phillips
replied that while they were initially deceived,
they had moved to correct their errors. *Discover*
magazine called the incident an example of "the
carelessness and wishful thinking that pervade
psychic research."

THE END OF AN ERA

Overall, the University's campuses
were expanding — and in creative
new ways. In 1990, the University
acquired a complex in nearby
Clayton that included the old
Famous-Barr building; this "West
Campus" facility soon housed various University offices, including the
International Writers Center,
founded in 1991 by William Gass;
the Lifelong Learning Institute,
begun in 1995 by a group led by
former trustee Henrietta Freedman,
A.B. '75; the Nancy Spirtas
Kranzberg Studio for the Illustrated
Book; and the library annex. Two
years later, the University sold the
old Cupples warehouses downtown
and acquired the former Blue
Cross/Blue Shield building at 4444
Forest Park Parkway. More build-
ings were coming in the future as part of a giant
construction effort headed by Richard Roloff,
B.S.I.E. '51, who joined the University administration in 1991 as executive vice chancellor. A
building for psychology and the long-awaited law
building were two of those in the offing.

William Gass.
Gass, the David May
Distinguished University
Professor Emeritus in the
Humanities, has received many
awards, most recently the 2003
PEN/Spielvogel Diamonstein
Award in the Art of the Essay
category and the 2003 National
Book Critics Circle Award for
his book, *Tests of Time*. Gass
was the founding director of
the International Writers Center
in Arts & Sciences.
Joe Angeles, WU Photographic
Services

Commencement 1995.
Presiding over his last
Commencement ceremony as
chancellor, William Danforth
was given a larger-than-life
stuffed bear by the Class of 1995.
Herb Weitman, WU Photographic
Services

251

Sandra Day O'Connor.
The first woman to become a justice on the U.S. Supreme Court, O'Connor has given keynote addresses at the Olin Fellows Conference and at the dedication of Anheuser-Busch Hall.
WU Archives

In 1992, Washington University received international attention when it played host to a presidential debate, the first to feature three candidates: President George H.W. Bush, Arkansas Gov. Bill Clinton, and H. Ross Perot. Other people in the public eye were making their way to the University: Rosalynn Carter in 1985 and former president Jimmy Carter in 1991; Supreme Court justice Sandra Day O'Connor in 1990 for the annual Olin Fellows Conference, sponsored by the Mr. and Mrs. Spencer T. Olin Fellowship Program for Women; presidential candidate Walter Mondale in 1984; U.S. Sen. Paul Simon (1928-2003) to receive an honorary degree at the 1986 Commencement; President George H.W. Bush in 1989 with his "thousand points of light" message about volunteerism — his first visit to a college campus after his inauguration; U.S. Sen. Bill Bradley in 1994; First Lady Hillary Rodham Clinton in March 1994 to discuss health-care reform; the chancellor's own brother, U.S. Sen. John Danforth, at Commencement 1995. In 1994, U.S. Olympic Festival events took place on campus and around the St. Louis region with current and future Olympic stars.

In spring 1994, William H. Danforth announced his intention to retire after the 1994-95 school year.

October 11, 1992. The presidential debate held in Washington University's Field House featured (left to right) independent candidate H. Ross Perot, Arkansas Gov. Bill Clinton, and President George H.W. Bush.
Herb Weitman, WU Photographic Services

The University hosts the first debate of the 1992 presidential campaign

In October 1992, Washington University played host to the first nationally televised three-person presidential debate in U.S. history. Candidates President George H.W. Bush, Arkansas Gov. Bill Clinton, and H. Ross Perot squared off in the Field House, which was transformed in only one week into a high-tech television studio. A live audience of 600 — including 250 University students — a 1,000-member media pool in the recreational gym, and a televised audience of more than 100 million people watched the debate, which addressed topics such as military spending and the candidates' patriotism. The debate was sponsored by the Commission on Presidential Debates.

First Lady Hillary Rodham Clinton. On March 15, 1994, Clinton spoke in the Field House about health-care reform.

Joe Angeles, WU Photographic Services

"I succeeded Tom Eliot in 1971, thinking I should stay for a decent period, perhaps three to five years," he wrote to alumni and friends. "Now, about one-third of my lifetime later, it is time. When I became chancellor, the students seemed so young; today, the parents also seem young; no one should stay until the grandparents look young." The University formed a search committee to hunt for a successor.

In 24 years, Danforth had fixed many of the problems he had targeted, such as undergraduate student retention. By 1992, he could report that 93.4 percent of freshmen who enrolled in 1991 came back the following year, and more than 84 percent of those who entered the University in 1987 had graduated in 1992. The number of undergraduate applications by 1993 had increased more than 50 percent over the previous decade, and 84 percent of freshmen ranked in the top 20 percent of their high school class.

The University had grown and flourished under his leadership. In a 1994 letter to alumni, he said of his accomplishments: "I believe that great universities are to the modern world what gothic cathedrals were to the late Middle Ages, symbols of our ideals and of our deepest aspirations. I like to think that all of us, like the mostly anonymous stone masons and architects of those days, add our bit to an enduring structure, a structure that will keep alive for generations after we are gone our hopes and our sense of what is right and beautiful." Now, to provide a blueprint for the next chancellor, he launched a major planning effort reminiscent of the Commission study more than a decade earlier: Project 21.

At the gala dinner that marked his departure, William M. Van Cleve, J.D. '53 — his close friend and board chairman — served as master of ceremonies, introducing speakers who praised Danforth and his wife for their extraordinary service. As James McLeod said, "Bill is like the compass of Washington University — in times of turmoil, you know where he is….He takes care to preserve our fundamental values and

Students volunteer to help victims of the flood of 1993

In summer 1993, the Mississippi and Missouri rivers poured over their banks, spreading across thousands of acres and wreaking havoc with low-lying communities. University students formed a response committee that funneled volunteers to a range of projects: building sandbag levees, collecting school supplies for displaced children, serving meals at shelters, shoveling mud from flooded homes. At Homecoming '93, students sold tickets to a paper airplane toss across the South 40 "swamp," and proceeds benefited relief efforts. Fraternities and sororities organized fundraisers, while the Performing Arts Department in Arts & Sciences donated the proceeds from a play, Sam Shepard's *Buried Child*, to the Salvation Army for flood relief.

Providing service, August 1993. Then-freshman Kati Gardos, A.B. '97, was among the volunteers who helped carry mud from flooded homes in West Alton, Missouri. The grateful daughter of one flood victim wrote to Chancellor Danforth: "They had the worst job anyone can imagine…[but] stuck with it until the end…. Sorry they didn't leave as clean as they came to us."

David Kilper, WU Photographic Services

objectives: He does not forget them; he does not compromise them." Hearing these tributes, the ever-modest Danforth quoted writer Howard Nemerov who quipped, after winning the Pulitzer Prize, "Overestimated at last." Then Danforth spoke movingly of the value of education — the noble enterprise to which he had dedicated so much of his life. "I've loved being a part of that effort," he said. "No one has been more fortunate than I." Ⓦ

LIVING LONGER, LIVING BETTER: LIFE SCIENCES AT WASHINGTON UNIVERSITY

Genome Sequencing Center.
Washington University's center played an important part in sequencing the human genome.

Robert Boston, WU Medical Public Affairs

Frank C-P Yin.
Yin, chair of biomedical engineering, was also named the Stephen F. and Camilla T. Brauer Professor of Biomedical Engineering in 1998. He has made pioneering contributions to the fields of biomechanics and cardiovascular research.

Joe Angeles, WU Photographic Services

S everal previous University chancellors — astronomer William Chauvenet, Nobel Prize-winning physicist Arthur Holly Compton, engineer Winfield S. Chaplin, geologist Carl Tolman, and physician/researcher William H. Danforth — have been scientists themselves. From the earliest days to the present, faculty have achieved national prominence for groundbreaking scientific and medical research. In 1995, chemist Mark S. Wrighton

became chancellor and began to build on an increasingly important aspect of that research through new programs and community collaborations. "We at the University," he said in 2003, "together with people in the corporate world, civic leaders, and government leaders in the region, have all been focused on strengthening our life sciences."

What are "life sciences"? This category includes research aimed at improving human health through advances in several areas: biotechnology and bioinformatics, especially tracing the genetic causes of disease; biomedical engineering, applying engineering principles to problems in biology or medicine; the environment, discovering ways to create a sustainable world; and plant biotechnology, developing plants that are genetically altered to resist pests and producing foods or plant-based pharmaceuticals that offer health benefits. More broadly, life sciences include the study of interrelationships among all the biological components of life, including human behavior.

Among the University's life sciences programs, the most prominent is the Genome Sequencing Center (GSC), established in 1993, one of the two top centers of its kind in the United States and among the top three in the world. It was a leader in the Human Genome Project: the global effort, completed in spring 2002, to spell out the three billion chemical letters in the human "genome" or genetic blueprint. With this sequence in hand, the GSC will next move on to more large-scale mapping — in chickens and chimpanzees, for example — and to applied genomic research that promises to shed new light on human diseases and their treatment.

In 1990, the University helped convince the international community to launch the ambitious genome-sequencing effort. Together with the Sanger Centre in England, University scientists first tackled the *C. elegans* roundworm genome, completing it in 1998 with the GSC providing half the sequence. By June 2000 the

Robert H. Waterston. Former head of genetics and director of the Genome Sequencing Center, Waterston oversaw the completion of a draft sequence of the human genome.

Mary Butkus, WU Photographic Services

consortium of collaborators — with the University among its leaders — had finished a working draft of the human genome. In the end, the GSC supplied more than 20 percent of the sequence data to the Human Genome Project, including several key elements: the early map used and the entire sequencing of chromosomes 2, 4, 7, and Y. It also played a major role in the sequencing and mapping of the mouse genome.

Amid the federal grants that supported this project, the University received the largest in its history. In 1999, Robert H. Waterston, the James S. McDonnell Professor, head of the genetics program, and director of the GSC, was awarded a five-year, $218.4 million grant from the National Human Genome Research Institute of the NIH, part of a $581.7 million grant to three institutions sequencing major parts of the genome. To perform this sophisticated work, the GSC has used robots, state-of-the-art sequencing machines, and advanced computer technology to turn out 40 million base letters daily. More than 300 scientists, engineers, and technicians have staffed this 24-hour-a-day effort, now directed by geneticist Richard K. Wilson.

On the Hilltop Campus, a 40-year-old collaboration between engineering and medicine merged in 1996 into an interdepartmental program in biomedical engineering, headed by mechanical engineer Salvatore Sutera. A year later, it took more formal shape when the Department of Biomedical Engineering was born with Frank C-P Yin, a physician and engineer recruited from Johns Hopkins, as its chair. Yin also took charge of the Institute of Biological and Medical Engineering, developed under the leadership of computer scientist Jerome R. Cox, Jr., which

would work with the department to administer biomedical engineering graduate programs. Late in 2002, the department got another boost with the completion of Uncas A. Whitaker Hall for Biomedical Engineering, supported by a $10 million grant from the Whitaker Foundation. In less than a decade, biomedical engineering had become one of the University's most sought-after programs, with one-third of freshman engineering students expressing interest in this area of study in 2003.

For the past decade, another popular undergraduate major or minor has been environmental studies, an interdisciplinary program in Arts & Sciences combining elements of anthropology, biology, economics, earth and planetary sciences, law, political science, environmental regulation, and engineering. Students, who choose a natural science or social science track, have studied the impact of lead smelter pollution in southeastern Missouri or wolves and bison in Yellowstone National Park, among others.

The sequenced genome. Genome Sequencing Center director Richard K. Wilson and co-director Elaine Mardis are leading the center into a new era of genomic medicine, applying all that has been learned about human genetic makeup to the understanding of specific diseases.

Robert Boston, WU Medical Public Affairs

Pathfinder Program. Students in the four-year Pathfinder Program in Environmental Sustainability in the College of Arts & Sciences conduct electrical resistivity measurements at Lake Waiau, Hawaii.

Photo courtesy of Professor Raymond E. Arvidson

Ralph S. Quatrano.
Quatrano (right), a well-known plant biologist, became chair of the University's biology department and Spencer T. Olin Professor in Arts & Sciences in 1998. He is in the Goldfarb Plant Growth Facility with Glenn Stone, associate professor of anthropology, and Elizabeth Stoll, A.B. '03.
Joe Angeles, WU Photographic Services

Interdisciplinary Environmental Clinic.
In front of the Supreme Court building in Jefferson City, Missouri, law student Colleen Williams (second from left), J.D. '02, and environmental studies student Rachel Permut (second from right), A.B. '02, pose with Sierra Club clients they represented through the Interdisciplinary Environmental Clinic, Terry Spence (left) and Scott Dye (right).
WU School of Law

Donald Danforth Plant Science Center.
Gathering at the 1999 groundbreaking for the center are (left to right) Roger N. Beachy, president of the center; Chancellor Emeritus William H. Danforth; former U.S. Sen. John Danforth; and Peter Raven, Engelmann Professor of Botany and director of the Missouri Botanical Garden.
Joe Angeles, WU Photographic Services

Another environmental option for undergraduates is the Pathfinder Program in Environmental Sustainability, directed by earth and planetary sciences faculty member Raymond Arvidson. Here students select a science or engineering major and combine that with a four-year experience in environmental studies, including fieldwork in the Mojave Desert and in Hawaii. Additional environment-related programs thrive around the University, including the law school's Interdisciplinary Environmental Clinic, founded by Maxine Lipeles; and engineering's environmental engineering program, directed by Pratim Biswas.

The University, which in 2001 decided to invest up to $40 million of its endowment in local venture-capital funds, has reached out to the community to form partnerships that further life sciences. In 1999, groundbreaking took place on the $146 million Donald Danforth Plant Science Center in Creve Coeur: a nonprofit research institution and partnership that includes Washington University, the Missouri Botanical Garden, the University of Missouri–Columbia, the University of Illinois at Urbana–Champaign, Purdue University, and Monsanto Company. Its mission is to focus on basic plant research and use discoveries to develop new products and technologies and its president is biology faculty member Roger N. Beachy, former head of the University's Center for Plant Science and Biotechnology. The Center and the University's biology department, chaired since 1998 by Ralph S. Quatrano, have already embarked on collaborative efforts in plant science research.

In January 2003, the Danforth Foundation, which had given $60 million to fund the Plant Science Center, announced it would spend $117 million to develop life sciences in St. Louis. Since 2000, William H. Danforth had chaired the Coalition for Plant and Life Sciences, a group of university and corporate supporters of biotechnology — including Washington University — hoping to attract investment capital for start-up plant and life science ventures throughout the area. The goal is to create a "biobelt" in and around St. Louis, a region that has five universities engaged in life sciences research. At the School of Medicine, for example, researcher Ming You is collaborating with the Missouri Botanical Garden and the Danforth Plant Science Center on cancer-prevention strategies involving plant products. In fiscal year 2002, the medical school received $328 million in life sciences research grants from the National Institutes of Health, in addition to other grants and contracts from private sources.

A robust biobelt is also the goal of two young business incubators: the Nidus Center for Scientific Enterprise in Creve Coeur; and the Center for Emerging Technologies, established in 1995 near the medical school. At the Center for

Emerging Technologies, Christopher I. Byrnes, engineering dean, has served as board chairman; a number of its start-up firms have been created by University faculty or collaborate with University physicians. One company, Stereotaxis, works with University physicians on developing magnetically guided surgical tools; Orion Genomics, co-founded by Richard K. Wilson, hopes to identify the functions of genes that will improve the world's food supply; and Symbiontics Inc., co-founded by molecular biologist Stephen Beverley, looks toward targeted delivery of therapeutic enzymes. In 2003, the School of Medicine and Barnes–Jewish Hospital received $2.8 million from the National Cancer Institute to continue work on a new imaging technique; related discoveries will go to Kereos, Inc., a biotech company in the Center founded by physicians Gregory Lanza and Samuel Wickline, for development into commercially viable treatment methods.

Technology transfer is a growing need for University researchers who want to see their discoveries reach the public. To help faculty license their findings, the University provides assistance through the Office of Technology Management, founded in 1997 and now directed by Michael Douglas, which helps transfer technology to private companies while generating income for the University to support research and education.

To create a new generation of entrepreneurs ready to assist in developing new businesses, the John M. Olin School of Business established the Skandalaris Program in Entrepreneurial Studies — a program that built on the success of the school's Hatchery entrepreneurship class — with the help of a $3 million pledge from Robert and Julie Skandalaris in 2001. A year earlier, the couple had donated $1 million for a new seed capital fund that would supply start-up funds for entrepreneurial business students.

In programs such as the Center for Aging, under John C. Morris, life sciences-related researchers are studying the process of aging, both its problems and healthy, productive aging. The George Warren Brown School of Social Work is looking at the social phenomenon of aging and offering students the chance to become geriatric social workers; since 1994, it has also been the home of the Center for Mental Health Services Research, funded by the National Institute of Mental Health and founded by faculty member Enola Proctor.

Social work practicum. At the Crown Center for Senior Living, participants knit blankets for the Linus Foundation, which distributes them to needy children. Social work student Rebecca Fierberg (standing) started the group during her practicum.
Joe Angeles, WU Photographic Services

The psychology department in Arts & Sciences is continuing to examine the cognitive aspects of aging. With funding from the National Institute on Aging, the medical school is looking at aging in patients with Alzheimer's disease and in healthy adults. Architect Carl Safe and his students are designing environments for senior citizens, while the Lifelong Learning program in University College, led and attended by older adults, offers students intellectual stimulation and growth. Ⓦ

Christopher I. Byrnes. Byrnes (right), dean of the School of Engineering and Applied Science and the Edward H. and Florence G. Skinner Professor of Systems Science and Mathematics, tackles a project with then-graduate student Wei Lin, D.Sc. '93 in systems science and mathematics.
WU Photographic Services

CHAPTER TWELVE

A GOLDEN AGE
OF GROWTH

1995-2003

Mark S. Wrighton.
He took office in 1995 as the University's 14th chancellor with an inaugural address entitled: "Learning and Discovery: Gateways to the 21st Century."
Dan Donovan, WU Photographic Services

A GOLDEN AGE OF GROWTH

*W*ho could ever replace William H. Danforth as chancellor? A 24-member search committee, headed by board chairman William Van Cleve and faculty member James W. Davis, began its difficult task in May 1994. They knew the competition was stiff for the best candidates; among the nation's 3,800 colleges and universities, Van Cleve recalled, as many as 1,000 were engaged in a similar search. The committee — made up of faculty, graduate and undergraduate students, alumni, trustees, and administrators — wanted to find someone who appealed to the University's diverse constituencies. Only an academic would do, they decided — ideally a scientist or doctor, most acceptable to the strong-willed medical faculty.

Previous pages:
Anheuser-Busch Hall.
Completed in 1997 for the School of Law, the 175,000-square-foot facility is named in recognition of a gift from the Anheuser-Busch Foundation in honor of longtime executive Fred Kuhlmann, J.D. '38.

1995 ~~~ 2003

1995   *Mark S. Wrighton became the University's 14th chancellor on July 1st; his inauguration took place on October 6.*

1996   *The newly formed International Advisory Council for Asia held its first meeting in Taipei, Taiwan, with founding chairman Shi Hui Huang presiding.*

1998   *The public announcement of the Campaign for Washington University, with a goal of $1 billion, came at a gala dinner in September.*

2000   *The Trustees raised the goal of the Campaign to $1.3 billion.*

2000   *On October 17, the University hosted the internationally televised final debate of the season between presidential candidates Al Gore and George W. Bush.*

2003   *The University turned 150 on February 22 — George Washington's birthday and the date that the charter incorporating Eliot Seminary was signed into law.*

William M. Van Cleve (1929-2003).
Van Cleve, J.D. '53, was elected trustee in 1983, board chair from 1993-95, and was named a life trustee in 1995. He was founding chair of the law school's National Council. His wife, Georgia Dunbar Van Cleve, A.B. '51, attended the law school for one year while an undergraduate senior. The Dunbar–Van Cleve Professorship in Arts & Sciences, held by John R. Bowen, is named for them today.
WU Photographic Services

James W. Davis.
Davis, a retired professor of political science, has served as director of the Teaching Center, associate provost, associate dean for Arts & Sciences, vice chancellor, and acting dean of the School of Art.
WU Photographic Services

The committee attacked its job aggressively, writing 8,000 letters to solicit nominations; they ran advertisements in national newspapers, called friends, and consulted with John Chandler, former Williams College president and chair of Duke University's successful presidential search. In the end, they compiled a list of 350 candidates, then took a closer look at a small group of semifinalists. A staff member of the Consortium on Financing Higher Education, headquartered at Massachusetts Institute of Technology (MIT), was impressed by the MIT provost, Mark S. Wrighton, and gave his name to an acquaintance on the Washington University committee. Soon a subcommittee

was flying to Boston to meet Wrighton in a harborfront hotel.

By that point, they were all familiar with his academic background. With a bachelor's degree in chemistry from Florida State University in 1969, he had earned a doctorate at age 22 from California Institute of Technology (Caltech), before joining the MIT faculty, becoming a full professor at 28. At the time 45 and MIT's CIBA-Geigy Professor of Chemistry, he had already amassed 14 patents, some 300 publications, and numerous awards, including a MacArthur Prize Fellowship (the so-called "genius grant") in 1983. Trustees on the committee were pleased by his experience in

261

Sampling Mocha Mark.
During the festivities surrounding his inauguration, Chancellor Wrighton joined students to taste the special flavor of frozen custard, "Mocha Mark," created in his honor by Ted Drewes, A.B. '50.
Doug Miner, WU Photographic Services

Inauguration Day, October 6, 1995.
A caricature of Chancellor Wrighton and the Corvette he owned then, drawn by Gary Karpinski, B.F.A. '74, encourages students to attend the inaugural events.
David Kilper, WU Photographic Services

Washington University at 150
as of February 22, 2003

The *Campaign for Washington University* had raised:
$1.317 billion in gifts and pledges;
115 new endowed professorships;
400 new endowed scholarships;
$93.2 million toward the Annual Fund goal of $100 million

working with such companies as GTE and General Electric, as well as his extensive government work.

Yet the committee did not know what Wrighton would be like in person. Articulate? Poised? In charge, able to handle a roomful of contentious academics? In ways hard to quantify, were he and Washington University a good fit? The group filed into the hotel meeting room, where Wrighton was waiting. Within 30 seconds, by one recollection, he was leading the session, with a presence, poise, and responsiveness that impressed the contingent. The group left feeling, somehow, that he was "one of us."

From then on, he was a top choice, as the committee whittled down the list. Two candidates — former law dean Edward ("Tad") Foote and former University financial officer John Biggs — took themselves out of consideration. In the end, the top three, as reported by the *St. Louis Business-Journal*, were Wrighton, one internal, and one external candidate. When the final vote came, nearly a year after the search committee began its work, the committee and the board selected Wrighton unanimously.

INAUGURAL FESTIVITIES FOCUS ON LEARNING AND DISCOVERY

Wrighton accepted with pleasure; he had aimed at finding a presidency or chancellorship in a top-20 research university and was drawn to Washington University in part by its trajectory of growth. At his inauguration as the University's 14th chancellor in October 1995, Wrighton received the golden Chancellor's medallion and — in an echo of a presentation made at William G. Eliot's 1872 inauguration — an elegant new copy of the University's Charter, crafted by School of Art faculty members Douglas Dowd and Sarah Spurr.

In his address, Wrighton outlined the themes that were to guide him as chancellor: building on the partnership with St. Louis; forging stronger international ties; recruiting new faculty, especially women and minorities; improving facilities; strengthening interdisciplinary programs; addressing complex problems, local and national, with energy and creativity. "The Brookings Hall arch as the entrance to the Quadrangle is a tangible gateway to an institution with an important mission. We have the responsibility to encourage learning and discovery — the figurative gateways to a 21st century better than the 20th," he said. Wrighton praised Danforth's leadership, and Danforth returned the compliment, noting his successor's "wide-ranging intellect, his quick, retentive mind, his imagination," as well as "his reputation for integrity and the admiration of those who worked most closely with him." He predicted that, during Wrighton's era, the University would experience its "golden age."

Amid the inaugural festivities were lighthearted moments. St. Louis frozen custard maker Ted Drewes, A.B. '50, concocted a new flavor for the events, "Mocha Mark," and in a campus raffle two students, Hubert Chuang, M.D. '02, Ph.D. '02, and Allyson F. Jacobson, A.B. '96, won rides to Drewes' shop in the chancellor's prized 1984 bronze Corvette. At the student-sponsored Inaugural Gala, held in the Athletic Complex, Wrighton danced cheerfully with students, one of whom proclaimed him "awesome, very personable."

PLANNING EFFORTS FOR THE NEXT CENTURY

Mark Wrighton's era of leadership continues today, so it is impossible to fully assess his accomplishments or his legacy. Yet even now, at the time of the University's 150th anniversary, it is possible to see that he has followed the blueprint he laid out at his inauguration. He has had something else to guide him: the results of an extended, two-part planning effort that began in 1989 with a "Committee to Prepare for the 21st Century," convened by Danforth and chaired by then-provost Edward S. Macias.

This group of faculty and students was charged with looking for improvements the University might target in the future. In its report, issued in April 1992, the committee outlined nine critical themes, making recommendations within each one. One was cross-disciplinary education, another was the need to strengthen the first-year undergraduate experience, others urged more international study — and all of these have since taken place. This effort spawned another successful committee, chaired by English professor Burton Wheeler: the

"Task Force on Undergraduate Education." In turn, that group's work led to more changes, including the establishment of an Undergraduate Council.

In 1993, Project 21 began — the most intensive strategic planning process ever undertaken by the University. Deans and faculty, with the advice of their respective National Councils, studied each aspect of the University and developed detailed plans for the future. The Project 21 report, accepted by the board in October 1995, set an overarching goal: "to accelerate Washington University's ascent among the world's premier universities." The report identified a series of top-priority needs — adding endowed professorships, building or renovating facilities, attracting better students, undertaking new academic initiatives, improving residential life, among others — that would take more than $1.5 billion to implement. Within the schools and nonacademic areas, these goals were to frame academic and financial strategies for the coming decade.

THE CAMPAIGN FOR WASHINGTON UNIVERSITY

In an echo of the 1977 Greenbrier retreat, the trustees met in June 1996 in Williamsburg, Virginia, to consider the Project 21 findings. The board's development committee, chaired by life trustee Lee Liberman, came prepared with a recommendation: mount a giant new fund drive backdated to the time of Wrighton's arrival in July 1995 to run through December 31, 2003. Herbert Hitzeman was not on hand to organize it, since he had retired in 1990; turning over the development piece of his operation to David T. Blasingame, A.B. '69, M.B.A. '71, currently vice

Edward S. Macias. Macias, who joined the chemistry faculty in 1970, became full professor in 1984 and department chair from 1984-88. He was named provost in 1988, then interim dean of Arts & Sciences in 1994; Wrighton named him executive vice chancellor and dean of Arts & Sciences in October 1995.
David Kilper, WU Photographic Services

Campaign leaders. At the September 1998 gala kickoff of the *Campaign for Washington University* at America's Center are (left to right) Chancellor Mark S. Wrighton; John F. McDonnell, chair of the campaign's leadership phase; William H. Danforth, chairman of the board of trustees; and Sam Fox, chair of the campaign's public phase.
Joe Angeles, WU Photographic Services

Larry Shapiro.
Shapiro, A.B. '68, M.D. '71, was named executive vice chancellor for medical affairs, dean of the School of Medicine, and the Spencer T. and Ann W. Olin Distinguished Professor, effective July 1, 2003.
University of California, San Francisco

Timothy J. Ley.
Ley, M.D. '78, who joined the medical faculty in 1986, has done important research into the genetic roots of leukemia. He received the newly established Alan A. and Edith L. Wolff Professorship in Medicine in 1998.
Robert Boston, WU Medical Public Affairs

chancellor for alumni and development programs and director of the new campaign. Its goal had not yet been set, but it would be substantial — at least $750 million, with an emphasis on raising unrestricted funds. Several priorities infused this effort: attracting and retaining outstanding faculty, supporting students and giving them an outstanding University experience, and achieving world leadership in a number of important areas.

By the time of the campaign's public unveiling in September 1998, the 1995-98 leadership phase, headed by board member John F. McDonnell, had raised $541 million, including several major gifts: $100 million from the Danforth Foundation and about $40 million from the McDonnell family, its foundation and charitable trust. The public phase, led by board member Sam Fox, began with a gala kick-off dinner for more than 1,400 people at America's Center. By then, the trustees had set the bar higher, to $1 billion, and had extended the deadline to June 30, 2004. The effort was going so well that in October 2000 the board increased the goal again, to $1.3 billion. With the work of the Campaign Steering Committee, volunteers, and more than 80,000 alumni and friends, the Campaign reached its target at the end of 2002 — with another 18 months left to accomplish still more toward the $1.5 billion ideal.

ENDOWED CHAIRS, NEW ROLES FOR WOMEN

By the start of 2003, the impact of this financial infusion was evident, with every school benefiting dramatically. One highly visible change was a new wealth of endowed professorships, 115 in all at that time. Some went to deans: the Ethan A.H. Shepley University Professorship to Joel Seligman in 1999, when he became dean of the law school, housed in the new Anheuser-Busch Hall; the Bank of America Professorship in 2000 to Stuart I. Greenbaum, who had come in 1995 to head the Olin School of Business; the Edward H. and Florence G. Skinner Professorship in Systems Science and Mathematics to engineering dean Christopher I. Byrnes; the George Warren Brown Distinguished University Professorship in 2001 to longtime social work dean, Shanti K. Khinduka, whose leadership had built his school into one of the nation's best. At the medical school, the Alan A. and Edith L. Wolff Distinguished Professorship was awarded in 2002 to William A. Peck, executive

Joel Seligman.
Law dean since 1999 and the Ethan A.H. Shepley University Professor, Seligman teaches a class for undergraduates.
Joe Angeles, WU Photographic Services

vice chancellor for medical affairs and dean of the School of Medicine; Peck planned to retire from that position in 2003, giving way to Larry J. Shapiro, A.B. '68, M.D. '71, an internationally renowned geneticist and pediatrician.

With Wrighton's backing and a nudge from the University's Association of Women Faculty — whose 2000 report urged increasing the number of Hilltop women faculty in tenure-track positions — women made notable progress in garnering faculty positions and named professorships. Several became department chairs and deans: Cynthia Weese, B.S.A.S. '62, B.Arch. '65, continued as dean of architecture, a post she had held since 1993; Shirley K. Baker, already dean of University Libraries, became vice chancellor for information technology in 1995; German professor and asso-

ciate vice chancellor Gerhild Williams was named special assistant to the chancellor for academic affairs in 1997; and chief financial officer Barbara A. Feiner was also named vice chancellor for finance in 1999. Department chairs included Lynne Tatlock in German, the new Hortense and Tobias Lewin Distinguished Professor in the Humanities in 2002; Barbara A. Schaal in biology, named the Spencer T. Olin Professor in 1997, who chaired biology from 1993-97; and Lee Epstein, the Edward Mallinckrodt Distinguished University Professor of political science and professor of law, who chaired the Department of Political Science from 1995-99 and in 2002. Ann B. Prenatt was promoted to vice chancellor for human resources in 2003. The year before, Wrighton named the University's director of government relations — Pam Lokken — to the University Council.

Henry S. ("Roddy") Roediger, III.
Roediger (center), who came from Rice University in 1996 to build up the psychology department, became the James S. McDonnell Distinguished University Professor.
Joe Angeles, WU Photographic Services

The Women's Studies Program (today Women and Gender Studies) — founded in 1972, one of the first of its kind in the nation — moved forward under longtime coordinator Helen Power, A.M. '64, Ph.D. '66, then under her successor, Linda J. Nicholson, Susan E. and William P. Stiritz Distinguished Professor of Women's Studies and history, named to head the program in 2000.

Women faculty in the medical school took new roles, using an advocacy and support group — the Academic Women's Network (AWN), formed in 1991 — to seek advancement. Nerve transplant pioneer Susan E. Mackinnon became division chief in plastic and reconstructive surgery; Barbara S. Monsees, chief of the breast imaging section at Mallinckrodt Institute of Radiology; and cell biologist Helen M. Piwnica-Worms, leader of the cellular proliferation program. In 1998, geneticist Alison Whelan and

Lee Epstein.
Epstein, then chair of the political science department in Arts & Sciences, became the Edward Mallinckrodt Distinguished University Professor in 1998 and professor of law in 2000. She joined the faculty in 1991.
David Kilper, WU Photographic Services

obstetrician/gynecologist Rebecca P. McAlister became associate deans. Still, women medical faculty continued to push for proof of parity through biennial pay equity studies.

Transforming the Campuses

With the new campaign funds, an astonishing building boom began on the Hilltop Campus. The psychology building, dedicated in 1996, and the law building in 1997 were just the start. Social Work got Goldfarb Hall in 1998; Business, the Charles F. Knight Executive Education Center in 2001. Thanks to the undergraduate admissions staff, headed by associate vice chancellor John Berg, students were applying in growing numbers, and they needed housing, provided by two new residential colleges on the South 40 — six buildings in all, with faculty families living in three — and by a small-group housing complex, the four-building "Village" on the northwest corner of campus. Other buildings came to life for laboratory sciences, the Uncas A. Whitaker Hall for Biomedical Engineering, and the Arts & Sciences Laboratory Science

Barbara A. Schaal.
Schaal is known for applying molecular genetic techniques to the study of plant evolution.
Joe Angeles, WU Photographic Services

Building, with an earth and planetary sciences building under construction, and others being planned, such as a new art museum and a building for the School of Art in the Sam Fox Arts Center, scheduled to break ground in spring 2004. Existing buildings underwent extensive renovation, among them Olin Library, which acquired 17,000 square feet of space on the main level, a Technology Center, even its own cybercafé. The chancellor's residence was renamed "Harbison House," in honor of University alumni Earle Harbison, A.B. '48, and Suzanne Harbison, B.S.B.A. '49.

Parking, a perennial problem, became a thorny issue: neighbors complained about spillover into nearby streets and

Cynthia Weese.
Dean of the School of Architecture since 1993, Weese, B.S.A.S. '62, B.Arch. '65, has brought many notable international architects to campus to teach in the school.
Joe Angeles, WU Photographic Services

Patty Jo Watson.
Watson, a leading expert in cave archaeology, was named Edward Mallinckrodt Distinguished University Professor in 1993. In 2000, she received a gold medal for distinguished achievement from the Archaeological Institute of America. In 2002, she was named one of "the 50 most important women in science" by *Discover* magazine.
David Kilper, WU Photographic Services

Shirley K. Baker.
As dean of University Libraries and vice chancellor for information technology, Baker has brought the latest technology to WU's library operations.
David Kilper, WU Photographic Services

Earle and Suzanne Harbison.
The chancellor's residence was renamed for Earle H. Harbison, Jr., A.B. '48, a longtime trustee, member of the board's steering committee for Project 21, and chair of the Arts & Sciences National Council; and his wife, Suzanne S. Harbison, B.S.B.A. '49, a University volunteer and active alumna.
Joe Angeles, WU Photographic Services

Harbison House.
The house, built in 1912 by Henry Haarstick for his daughter, Emma, and her husband, Clinton Whittemore — and later named University House — was renamed Harbison House in 1999 in honor of Suzanne and Earle Harbison to recognize their longtime support for the University. The first chancellor to live in the house was Ethan A.H. Shepley.
David Kilper,
WU Photographic Services

Janite Lee Reading Room.
The School of Law library's reading room in Anheuser-Busch Hall, with its vaulted, beamed oak ceiling and cathedral windows, is the focal point of the building.
David Kilper, WU Photographic Services

the possible loss of the aging but majestic line of oaks in front of Brookings to an underground garage. The University bought and rehabilitated dozens of apartment buildings and some multi-family properties south of the University City Loop and in the Skinker-DeBaliviere neighborhood, though some area residents feared these acquisitions foreshadowed future plans for expansion. In the most controversial move of all, the University supported the expansion of the MetroLink light-rail system along the northern edge of campus in opposition to neighbors who favored an alternate route. To improve communication, the Washington University Neighbors' Council formed in 1999 with representatives from 13 neighborhoods near the Hilltop Campus.

The Hilltop building projects were paralleled by sweeping changes at the Medical Center, where a three-phase "Campus Integration Plan" unfolded after the Barnes and Jewish hospital merger in January 1996. With the need to integrate services — plus impetus from external forces, such as the demand for outpatient services and cost containment pressures created by managed care — the medical school and BJC Health System (later BJC HealthCare) embarked on an ambitious plan to tear down half the existing buildings and build or renovate others. On this reshaped map, outpatient services clustered to the north; inpatient care to the south. Both clinical and research facilities were included, among them the 11-story McDonnell Pediatric Research Building and the new Charles F. Knight Emergency and Trauma Center.

Goldfarb Hall.
Dedicated in 1998 and named for Alvin Goldfarb, BU '37, whose gift helped make the building possible, Goldfarb Hall provided needed space for teaching and research at the George Warren Brown School of Social Work.
David Kilper, WU Photographic Services

The Village.
The four-building Village housing complex at the northwestern corner of the Hilltop Campus was completed in 2001.
David Kilper, WU Photographic Services

Timothy J. Eberlein.
Eberlein, Bixby Professor of Surgery, chair of the
Department of Surgery, and surgeon-in-chief at
Barnes–Jewish Hospital, was named director of the
Alvin J. Siteman Cancer Center in 1999, as well as
Spencer T. and Ann W. Olin Distinguished Professor.
David Kilper, WU Photographic Services

THE SITEMAN CANCER CENTER IS BORN

The biggest and most innovative of these medical
buildings was the new Center for Advanced Medicine: the 14-story, $58 million ambulatory care
center opened in 2001 at the northeast corner of
campus. It represented a new vision of health care
in which complementary services are clustered in
"centers of excellence" staffed by multidisciplinary
medical teams. A portion of the building is devoted to the rapidly developing Alvin J. Siteman
Cancer Center, the culmination of a decades-old
cancer research and clinical program that took
more formal shape in the mid-1990s. In 1995,
the School of Medicine received a National Cancer
Institute (NCI) planning grant — the first move
toward recognition as an NCI-designated Cancer
Center. Then in 1996, the board of The Barnard
Free Skin and Cancer Hospital transferred effective
control of the organization, including its indigent
care, research, and community education programs, to the medical school, and subsequently its
board has been expanded to include the president
of Barnes–Jewish Hospital (BJH).

November 1999 saw the most significant changes
of all. In that month, Alvin J. and Ruth Siteman
of St. Louis committed $35 million to the medical
school and BJH — the largest gift ever for cancer-
related programs — and the budding cancer center
was named for Siteman, an emeritus trustee. After
a long search, Timothy J. Eberlein, Bixby Professor

TRANSFORMING THE CAMPUSES, 1995–2003

Under Mark Wrighton's chancellorship,
more than $1.5 billion has been invest-
ed in new construction, renovation, or
infrastructure — including some buildings still in the planning stages.

Hilltop Campus

Psychology Building (Arts & Sciences)
Completed: 1995. Cost: $28.5 million

**Music Classrooms Building
(Arts & Sciences)**
Completed: 1996. Cost: $625,000

Anheuser-Busch Hall (Law)
Completed: 1997. Cost: $40.2 million

Goldfarb Hall (Social Work)
Completed: 1998. Cost: $13 million

Student housing
South 40: Phase II: Cost: $42.9 million
**Danforth Residence House, Shepley
Residence House, and Wheeler
Residence House**
Completed: 1998
**Gregg Residence House, Lien Residence
House, and Nemerov Residence House**
Completed: 1999

"The Village" (Northwest corner
of campus)
4 buildings, one named Lucy and
Stanley Lopata House, and a parking
facility
Completed: 2001. Cost: $48.7 million
South 40: Phase III: Cost: $12.6 million
1st residence house
Completed: 2003. Cost: $12 million
2nd residence house under
construction
Completion anticipated: 2004.
Cost: $10.4 million

**Laboratory Science Building
(Arts & Sciences)**
Completed: 2002. Cost: $55.7 million

**Uncas A. Whitaker Hall for
Biomedical Engineering (Engineering)**
Completed: 2002. Cost: $33 million

276 N. Skinker Office Building
Completed: 2003. Cost: $4.1 million

Medical Campus

**Center for Advanced Medicine —
including the Siteman Cancer Center
(Medicine, BJC HealthCare)**
Completed: 2001. Cost: $57.9 million

**McDonnell Pediatric Research Building
(Medicine)**
Completed: 2001. Cost: $71.2 million

**Clinical Sciences Research Building,
4th "wing" (Medicine)**
Completed: 1996. Cost: $101.3 million

**Southwest Tower — built by BJC
7th and 8th floors (Medicine)**
Completed: 2003. Cost: $8.6 million

Major Renovations

Eads Teaching/Learning Center
Completed: 1998. Cost: $4.6 million

Olin Library
Completion anticipated: 2004.
Cost estimate: $38.4 million

**Bixby and Givens Halls in
the Sam Fox Arts Center**
Completed: 2002. Cost: $16.7 million

Under Construction

**Earth & Planetary Sciences Building
(Arts & Sciences)**
Completion anticipated: 2004.
Cost estimate: $44.1 million

Buildings Announced

**Museum Building and Earl E. and Myrtle
E. Walker Hall for the School of Art in
the Sam Fox Arts Center**
Groundbreaking scheduled: April 14,
2004. Cost estimate: $34 million

**Farrell Learning and Teaching Center
(Medicine)**
Completion anticipated: 2005.
Cost estimate: $35 million

In Planning

Engineering Building
For the departments of Electrical and
Systems Engineering and Computer
Science and Engineering

University Center (Hilltop Campus)

and chair of the Department of Surgery and surgeon-in-chief at BJH, became the Siteman Cancer Center's director. In 2001, the Siteman Cancer Center was designated as an NCI center, one of 60 in the United States.

EXPANDING INTERDISCIPLINARY PROGRAMS

One important University-wide curricular change has been the blossoming of interdisciplinary programs in every school, especially in Arts & Sciences. For years, the University had sponsored some, such as graduate programs like University College's Master of Liberal Arts (MLA) Program, or the undergraduate Text and Tradition program linking classical texts and intellectual traditions of Europe and America. Spurred by Macias' committee and then Project 21, interdisciplinary efforts grew to include such programs as biomedical engineering and, in Arts & Sciences, several new offerings for freshmen, including Medicine and Society. Social Work sponsored a community development course with Architecture, while Law created a Center for Interdisciplinary Studies.

In fall 1997, with funding from the William and Flora Hewlett Foundation, a new two-year course sequence for freshmen was born: the Hewlett Program, offering three interdisciplinary options, introduced in successive years. The *Environmental Studies* program came first, followed by *American Culture Studies* (ACS), a collection of courses on the nature of America centered around the Lewis and Clark expedition; then *Study of the Mind-Brain*, a look at cognitive science. As the Hewlett Program evolved, the offerings narrowed to ACS and Mind-Brain, while environmental studies continued as a major or minor and as the four-year Pathfinder Program in Environmental Sustainability for entering freshmen, under faculty member Raymond Arvidson. With leadership from English professor Wayne Fields and faculty member Gerald Early, the Program in American Culture Studies flourished, continuing as a part-time master's program in University College, a second major for undergraduates, and a graduate certificate program.

A recent effort, spurred by the ACS staff, has been a collaboration among the University, St. Louis Circuit Court, and Missouri State Archives to create a Web site, hosted by the University, containing 170 digitized pages of court documents chronicling Dred and Harriet Scott's landmark struggle to win freedom from slavery. In 2002, other records appeared: papers from 1809-33 involving Meriwether Lewis, William Clark, and their Corps of Discovery; a year later,

Ruth and Alvin Siteman.
In recognition of a $35 million gift from the Sitemans in 1999 to the medical school and BJH, the reorganized cancer center was renamed the Alvin J. Siteman Cancer Center.

Photos, Robert Boston,
WU Medical Public Affairs

McDonnell Pediatric Research Building.
Dedicated in fall 2000, the ten-story facility consolidated pediatric research activities, which previously were housed at five separate sites.

the group added pleadings of African-Americans who sued for freedom in state courts during the early to mid-1800s, an initiative led by history and law professor David Konig.

REACHING OUT TO THE ST. LOUIS COMMUNITY

As Wrighton suggested in his inaugural address, the University has reached out to the community with educational or social service programs. Students on the Hilltop have served as tutors, staffed soup kitchens, donated food, worked with Habitat for Humanity or the elderly; at the School of Law, the Interdisciplinary Environmental Clinic has offered free legal and technical advice. Medical students have staffed free clinics, taken part in drug and perinatal outreach, and worked with sixth- and seventh-graders through the Students Teaching AIDS to Students (STATS) Program. The University's 12 fraternities, five sororities, and eight citywide black Greek organizations have sponsored their own service projects, including Special Olympics and St. Louis Effort for AIDS. Service First, an initiative undertaken by the Office of Campus Life, has introduced incoming freshmen to community service shortly after their arrival on campus.

New science programs developed with faculty leadership. In 1991, a Science Outreach program in biology, carried out with the University City School District, got off the ground with National Institutes of Health (NIH) funding. This project, spearheaded by biologist Sarah C.R. Elgin with assistance from

---

Washington University at 150
as of February 22, 2003

Enrollment: **12,767 students**

Undergraduate full-time enrollment	**5,793**
* College of Arts & Sciences	3,551
* School of Architecture	202
* School of Art	336
* Olin School of Business	682
* School of Engineering & Applied Science	1,022

- 20,367 students applied for 1,280 freshman places in the fall 2002 class

Part-time and other undergraduates	**1,426**
Graduate enrollment	**5,548**
* School of Architecture	148
* School of Art	20
* Graduate School of Arts & Sciences	1,467
* Olin School of Business	937
* Sever Graduate School of Engineering	653
* School of Law	829
* School of Medicine	862
* George Warren Brown School of Social Work	394
* Other programs	238
Summer School enrollment	**3,485**

Wayne Fields.
Fields, director of the Program in American Culture Studies, became the Lynne Cooper Harvey Distinguished Professor of English in 1999. Fields previously served as chair of the English department in Arts & Sciences and as dean of University College.
David Kilper, WU Photographic Services

then-biology chairman Roy Curtiss, developed high school curricula in genetics and environmental chemistry. Over the years, it was sustained by funding from the Howard Hughes Medical Institute, whose support also had a major impact on the undergraduate curriculum and research program. Through Project Aria, begun in 1998, Engineering helped school districts with hands-on space engineering and science. In 2001, the University, Saint Louis Zoo, Missouri Botanical Garden, and St. Louis Science Center began an NIH-funded collaboration, initiated by biology professor David L. Kirk, to produce biology curricula for St. Louis middle and secondary students. Two programs aimed at improving local science education received National Science Foundation funding in 2002: a $10 million grant to the education department that created the St. Louis Center for Inquiry in Science Teaching and Learning; and a $6.5 million grant to Science Outreach for work with school districts under Science Outreach director Victoria May.

Programs developed in nonscientific areas as well. Social Work launched a multi-university project to give urban social service workers advanced training, while Architecture faculty worked to transform a south St. Louis neighborhood. Pulmonary specialist I. Jerome Flance, A.B. '31, M.D. '35, took on a new job after his 1998 retirement: representing the Washington University Medical Center Redevelopment Corporation in its continuing efforts to revitalize Forest Park Southeast. University College taught some 1,300 students each semester, many from the community, while other Hilltop schools — Architecture, Business, Engineering — offered classes and degree programs for adult part-time students, too.

International Programs

Meanwhile, increasing numbers of international students were arriving on campus: 479 in 1980, 753 in 1990, and 1,301 in 2003. As Wrighton said at the 2002 Commencement, "about 100 countries of the world are represented in our graduating class today." Stix International House, established in 1972, continued to serve as a focal point for international activities and to house the Office for International Students and Scholars. Students

Sarah C.R. Elgin.
In 2002, Elgin (standing), professor of biology in Arts & Sciences, received a $1 million grant from Howard Hughes Medical Institute to provide innovative laboratory research experiences for undergraduates and even younger students.

Joe Angeles, WU Photographic Services

Service First.
First-year Washington University students give chairs at Hempstead Elementary School a face-lift in the University's third Service First program in 2001. Service First introduces first-year college students to community service.

WU Photographic Services

started the Asian Multicultural Center, and some groups sponsored ethnic celebrations, such as the Chinese New Year Festival, Islam Awareness Week, or the fall Diwali festivities planned by Ashoka, an organization of Indian students.

Courses reflected this growing internationalism. Along with longtime Arts & Sciences programs

270

I. Jerome Flance.
Adams Elementary School students in the Forest Park Southeast neighborhood surround Dr. Flance. As special associate for community redevelopment in the School of Medicine, he was instrumental in the Adams School's reopening in 2001.
Robert Boston, WU Medical Public Affairs

grams going all over the world — 38 different places in Arts & Sciences alone. The University linked up with universities around the world, such as the business school's partnership in offering an Executive MBA program with Fudan University in Shanghai, China. And faculty traveled abroad on outreach missions, like the medical team organized by neurosurgeon Carl Lauryssen, which went to Nairobi, Kenya, to treat brain and spinal cord problems. At home, the affiliated hospitals began treating arrivals to St. Louis from all around the world, particularly refugees from the Bosnian conflict.

The surge in students from abroad created a new, international body of alumni and friends. An International Advisory Council for Asia, composed of 26 representatives from major Asian nations and the United States — many of them alumni or parents of students — formed in 1996 under the direction of Taiwanese business leader and trustee Shi Hui Huang, a physician and member of the medical school house staff from 1954-59. Other members included: Chia-Wei Woo, M.S. '61, Ph.D. '66, former president of Hong Kong University of Science and Technology; Ja Song, M.B.A. '62, D.B.A. '62, trustee and former president of Yonsei University in Seoul, Korea; and

Shi Hui Huang.
In 1996, Huang, H.S. '59, became the founding chairman of the University's International Advisory Council for Asia; he is now chairman emeritus and an emeritus trustee.
Joe Angeles, WU Photographic Services

— such as Romance languages, German, Russian, and comparative literature — others had gotten their start more recently, such as International and Area Studies. Additional languages took hold, including Swahili, taught through African and Afro-American Studies. Law initiated the Whitney R. Harris Institute for Global Legal Studies, directed by John O. Haley.

Students now had the chance to travel abroad for a summer, semester, or year through pro-

Carl Phillips.
An award-winning poet, Phillips is professor of English and of African and Afro-American Studies in Arts & Sciences.
WU Archives

Jeffrey C. Pike.
Dean of the School of Art since 1999, Pike, a professional illustrator and designer, has been on the school's faculty since 1983.
Joe Angeles, WU Photographic Services

Alan R. Templeton.
The Charles Rebstock Professor of Biology, Templeton applies molecular genetic techniques and statistical population genetics to evolutionary problems.
Joe Angeles, WU Photographic Services

Stuart I. Greenbaum.
Greenbaum (right), dean of the Olin School of Business, and Zheng Zukang, vice president of the School of Management at Fudan University in Shanghai, established a joint Executive Master of Business Administration program. The first class graduated in 2003.
Courtesy photo

Zhangliang Chen, Ph.D. '87, vice president and professor, Peking University in Beijing and president of China Agricultural University, People's Republic of China.

FACULTY RESEARCH AND CREATIVE ACTIVITIES BRING DISTINCTION

On the Hilltop Campus, faculty doing innovative research included Social Work's Michael W. Sherraden, whose concept for Individual Development Accounts, in which the poor participate in matched savings programs, was tested nationally and adopted in various forms by both political parties. By studying human genetic

trees, biologist Alan R. Templeton showed there were at least two major waves of human migration from Africa. Anthropologist Erik Trinkaus dated a human jawbone found in Romania to between 34,000-36,000 years ago, making it the earliest known modern human fossil in Europe; Australian architect Glenn Murcutt was awarded the 2002 Pritzker Architecture Prize, the field's highest honor, while he was a visiting professor in the School of Architecture. Pianist Seth Carlin performed internationally, and poet Carl Phillips won the prestigious Kingsley Tufts Poetry Award. Others earned recognition for their inspiring teaching, such as David Hadas in his religion and literature classes, and William Wallace in art history. In 2000, the School of Art acquired a new dean: Jeffrey Pike, who had first joined the faculty in 1983.

At the medical school, neuroscience gained in prominence. In 1991, neurologist Dennis W. Choi established a Center for the Study of Nervous System Injury and, when Choi left the University in 2002 to become Merck Research Laboratories' executive vice president, neurosciences, David B. Clifford, M.D. '75, took his place as neurology head, continuing his own research into the neurological disorders affecting AIDS patients. Neurologist John W. McDonald, who joined the faculty in 1996, pioneered spinal cord injury research and rehabilitative techniques. His surprising success in helping paralyzed actor Christopher Reeve regain some sensation and function attracted national attention.

Overall, the medical school continued to receive major support from the NIH — $328.3 million in fiscal 2002 in 701 awards — making it the third-largest recipient of NIH funds among the 125 U.S. medical schools. The Howard Hughes

Finding new treatments for spinal cord injury

Actor/director Christopher Reeve, who became quadriplegic after a 1995 horseback-riding accident, celebrated his 50th birthday in September 2002 with the announcement of a remarkable milestone: He can feel pinpricks and the touch of a cotton swab over 65 percent of his body and move his arms and legs to some extent without assistance. Reeve's intensive rehabilitation efforts were periodically adjusted based on evaluations by a School of Medicine team led by spinal cord injury specialist John W. McDonald. The team published Reeve's progress in the *Journal of Neurosurgery: Spine,* marking the first documented case of partial recovery more than two years after traumatic spinal cord injury. A simultaneous study led by University neurologist Maurizio Corbetta, and published in December 2002 in the *Proceedings of the National Academy of Sciences*, demonstrated that brain regions involved in movement and feeling appear relatively healthy and active.

Recovering sensation.
John W. McDonald (standing) has helped Christopher Reeve recover some feeling and function below his injury.
Robert Boston, WU Medical Public Affairs

Michael W. Sherraden.
The Benjamin E. Youngdahl Professor of Social Development and director of the Center for Social Development (CSD), Sherraden helped launch CSD's Global Service Institute, focused on promoting civilian service worldwide, with funding from the Ford Foundation.
David Kilper, WU Photographic Services

Medical Institute, Barnes–Jewish Hospital Foundation, and private sources provided additional significant funding. Researchers receiving these funds included pediatrician Michael R. DeBaun, studying strokes in children with sickle cell disease; an interdisciplinary team of 22 brain injury researchers, directed by occupational therapy head M. Carolyn Baum; asthma specialists Mario Castro and Robert C. Strunk; Scott Hultgren and X-ray crystalographer Gabriel Waksman, tracing the bacterial roots of urinary tract infections; John F. DiPersio and his oncology colleagues, generating animal models of cancers, particularly leukemias; and new chief of cardiac surgery Ralph J. Damiano, Jr., testing robotically assisted heart surgery.

Clinicians continued to perform important, sometimes pioneering procedures: endocrine surgeon Jeffrey F. Moley, internationally known for his treatment of medullary thyroid cancer; the adult lung transplant group, performing its 500th transplant, while the pediatric group

Triple Crown Collection.
In 2000, University Libraries acquired a spectacular collection of fine press books and ephemera: the entire output of the Kelmscott, Doves, and Ashendene presses. Their fine printing and bookmaking represented the height of the English Arts and Crafts movement at the turn of the 20th century.
David Kilper, WU Photographic Services

Ralph G. Dacey, Jr.
In 1999, Dacey became the first neurosurgeon to magnetically guide a catheter through a patient's brain to a tumor. He is the Henry G. and Edith R. Schwartz Professor and chairman of neurological surgery at the School of Medicine.
Robert Boston, WU Medical Public Affairs

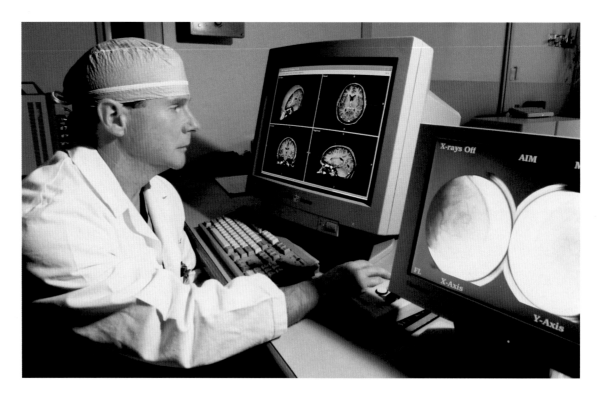

R. Gilbert Jost.
Elizabeth E. Mallinckrodt Professor and head of radiology, and director of the Mallinckrodt Institute of Radiology since 2001, Jost has written numerous scientific articles about the use of information technology in the practice of diagnostic radiology.
WU Medical Public Affairs

reached 200; Ralph G. Dacey, Jr., breaking new ground in magnetically assisted surgery; and ophthalmologists identifying new ways to treat glaucoma. Orthopaedic surgery moved to departmental status in 1993 and, chaired by Richard H. Gelberman since 1995, was growing in distinction with a patient mix that included local sports teams. Also expanding were the Institute for Minimally Invasive Surgery, founded by Nathaniel J. Soper and Ralph V. Clayman, and the Mallinckrodt Institute of Radiology, now directed by R. Gilbert Jost; the neurofibromatosis program at St. Louis Children's Hospital was one of the largest in the United States.

John DiPersio.
The Lewis T. and Rosalind B. Apple Professor of Oncology, DiPersio heads the bone marrow transplantation and stem cell biology division at the School of Medicine and serves as deputy director of the Siteman Cancer Center.
Robert Boston, WU Medical Public Affairs

Michael R. DeBaun.
DeBaun (in white coat), assistant professor of pediatrics and of biostatistics, Isaac Cornell (right), and Diamond Penn (left) play video games during the boys' blood transfusions at the Sickle Cell Medical Education and Treatment Center.
Joe Angeles, WU Photographic Services

MILESTONE EVENTS AND NATIONAL TRAGEDY

Students continued to stage annual events, such as the traditional spring Thurtene Carnival, the nation's oldest and largest student-run carnival. A much-prized honor each year was the Burmeister Award, given for best overall skit and façade production, and named for James Burmeister, A.B. '61, M.B.A. '63, M.A. '67, Thurtene adviser since 1970 and executive director of University relations and commencement.

A series of milestone events occurred during this period. In a successor event to the 1992 debate held on campus, presidential candidates Al Gore and George W. Bush took part in a "town hall" presidential debate in October 2000. For this occasion, the Athletic Complex turned into a sophisticated television set, with blazing lights, chilly temperatures, space for a 600-person live audience, and more than 1,000 journalists from around the world. In July 2002, after repeated attempts in which the University served as mission control, Steve Fossett, M.B.A. '68, became the first solo balloonist to circumnavigate the globe. Early in 2003, *Student Life*, Missouri's longest continuously publishing newspaper, celebrated its 125th anniversary.

Record-setting balloon flight. On July 2, 2002, balloonist Steve Fossett, M.B.A. '68, flying in the bright yellow *Bud Light Spirit of Freedom* capsule, became the first person to circumnavigate the globe in a solo flight — 20,482 miles in 14 days, 19 hours, and 50 minutes. Eighteen University students ran the worldwide communications efforts at Mission Control in Brookings Hall, Room 300, including (left to right) Jeremy Raphael, B.S.B.A. '02, Bryan Maddocks, Class of '04, and John Russell, Class of '04. Engineering faculty designed the capsule's heating system; and the coordination was masterminded by Judith Jasper Leicht, associate vice chancellor in public affairs.

Joe Angeles, WU Photographic Services

The University hosts another presidential debate in 2000

With a red-and-blue decorating scheme and five million watts of additional electricity, the Athletic Complex was transformed on October 17, 2000, into a brilliant stage set for the third debate of the season between two presidential candidates: Vice President Al Gore and Texas Gov. George W. Bush. Organized by the Commission on Presidential Debates in a "town hall" format, the event was moderated by Jim Lehrer of PBS and covered by more than 1,000 journalists from 300 media organizations. The television audience for the debate was estimated at some 37.6 million people. University students attended, covered the debate as student journalists, and were interviewed themselves, including Michelle Purdy, A.B. '01, A.M. '03, president of Student Union.

October 17, 2000.
Moderator Jim Lehrer (standing, right) greets presidential candidates George W. Bush (left) and Al Gore while the "town hall" debate audience looks on. In 2004, the University will host another debate — an unprecedented accomplishment.

Joe Angeles, WU Photographic Services

The University responds to September 11 attacks

The University campus grieved with the rest of the nation after the horrifying September 11, 2001, attacks on the World Trade Center and the Pentagon. At the time, Chancellor Mark Wrighton said to the University community: "Thank you for making Washington University a safe haven from hatred, for upholding the value of this community as a place where common respect and diversity are valued and where people come from all over the world to teach, learn, and create knowledge."

September 11, 2001.
On the evening of September 11, hundreds of Washington University students congregated in Brookings Quadrangle for a community gathering and candlelight vigil to remember those hurt or killed in the day's terrorist attacks. The flag flew at half-mast over Brookings Hall.

Mary Butkus, WU Photographic Services

On the morning of September 11, 2001, the University — like the nation — was plunged into grief, anxiety, horror, and anger by the terrorist events in New York City, rural Pennsylvania, and Washington, D.C. As Wrighton later said, "9/11 here in St. Louis was a beautiful, dry, crystal-clear day that began as a routine day near the beginning of our fall academic term. By mid-morning we understood that 9/11 ushered in a new and deeply troubling and challenging era." Immediately, he convened the University Council — made up of vice chancellors and deans of the eight schools, among others — for discussion. They cancelled classes for the afternoon, as faculty and counselors talked with worried students. That evening, a vigil was held on campus, with student and faculty speakers offering their reflections.

Wrighton addressed the crowd, too, asking the University to draw together during this crisis and adding that "the great expectation I have for each of you is that you will always show respect for others, both here on campus and in the community that surrounds us." He expressed the uncertainty everyone felt, not knowing yet who had been killed or injured in the attacks. In fact, as names of the victims became public, it emerged that three had University connections: Catherine Jaffe Chirls, A.B. '75, and the husbands of Nikki Stern, A.B. '71, and Elizabeth Crawford, B.F.A. '83.

A SESQUICENTENNIAL CELEBRATION

At the start of the new millennium, the University began making plans to celebrate a giant milestone in its history: its 150th anniversary. William Greenleaf Eliot would never have recognized the vibrant, nationally prominent school whose first tiny graduating class in 1862 consisted of five students, one of them his own son. How to explain such astounding success?

In part, the current Washington University is a tribute to the power of money, with the three key figures in its history setting a nearly unmatchable standard for generosity. Eliot, a minister with few personal resources, made breathtaking gifts to the young school; so did Robert Brookings, who depleted his own fortune on its behalf. Since the early 1970s, the foundation begun by William Danforth's grandfather has given an astonishing $375 million. Without these gifts and countless others, the University could not have begun or thrived; at several points, it might have disappeared altogether.

Clearly, the University is also the product of remarkable luck. In 1887, Eliot died longing for a successor to take up the cause of the struggling school; four years later, when the future looked impossibly bleak, a little-educated man named Robert Brookings joined the board, reluctantly — and his imagination awoke to the possibilities. In the 1960s, with Barnes Hospital and the medical school locked in bitter conflict and the University as a whole in serious financial trouble, Carl Cori suggested a candidate for medical vice chancellor: a quiet young physician named William Danforth, who had no administrative experience but miraculously agreed to take on the task.

Another deeper factor helps to account for the University's success. The common ingredient among these three men was faith — and not religious faith. Although Eliot's whole life was infused by his Christian convictions, he was fiercely proud of the University's liberal charter that guaranteed its students, then and forever, a secular education. Rather, Eliot, Brookings, Danforth, and other University leaders — aided by a talented, loyal, long-underpaid faculty — shared another kind of faith: a fervent belief in the transforming power of education and the importance of building a superb educational institution in the heart of the Midwest. As Danforth put it, they believed that "knowledge was better than ignorance, that humankind could be bettered by education." It was a faith strong enough to submerge personal ambition, diminish fortunes, sap time and energy, constrain family life, engulf most of a lifetime.

From that faith has evolved an institution built on noble aspirations by unselfish people with liberal ideals. Not that it has always been true to its founding principles. While admitting students who often had limited options elsewhere — women, Catholics and Jews, young people from other countries — the University closed its doors to African Americans for nearly 50 years and then approached change too cautiously. But it resisted the excesses of the McCarthy years, steered a humane course through the turbulent Vietnam era, implemented programs to right the wrongs of segregation, and never wavered during its long history in its support of academic freedom. It became, as Eliot had hoped — but in ways he never could have imagined — an extraordinary boon to St. Louis, its very own "city set upon a hill."

On February 22, 1854, a year after the University's founding, Eliot spoke with few illusions about the daunting enterprise that lay before him. "It is not only the beginning of a great work, capable of indefinite extension, but each step in its progress and the first step in its commencement involve the sacrifice both of time and money," he said. In his February 2003 letter to alumni, Mark Wrighton recalled Eliot's words, adding: "Our responsibility is to continue to extend the University's record of excellence in teaching, research, and service to society. I believe we are."

The great work has begun and flourished. Large-spirited people have sacrificed much to ensure Washington University's success. And as for "indefinite extension"? That remains the challenge for the future: The next 150 years are just ahead. Ⓦ🇺

Thomas Friedman. *New York Times* columnist and best-selling author, Friedman helped launch the University's year-long Sesquicentennial celebration with an Assembly Series lecture on the war in Iraq. He will close the year as the speaker at Commencement.
WU Photographic Services

Happy Birthday to WU. The Saint Louis Symphony Orchestra performs in Brookings Quadrangle as part of a day-long community open house that launched the year of Sesquicentennial festivities. Dubbed the "150th Birthday Party," the event attracted 15,000–20,000 visitors to the Hilltop and Medical Campuses. Robert Wiltenburg, dean of University College, served as chair of the University-wide planning committee for the event.

David Kilper, WU Photographic Services

ACKNOWLEDGMENTS

Thank you first to Chancellor Mark S. Wrighton, who asked me to write this book and make it an honest history. Both he and Chancellor Emeritus William H. Danforth were generous with their time in discussing their periods of leadership. I am grateful, too, to Robert L. Virgil, chair of the Sesquicentennial Commission, who has strongly supported this project and given helpful advice.

A splendid advisory committee, assembled by M. Fredric Volkmann and headed by Mary Ellen Benson, including Donna Boyd, Jim Burmeister, Steve Givens, David Kilper, Steve Kohler, and Carole Prietto, read every word of the book, reviewed layouts, and offered their valuable suggestions. My particular thanks to Mary Ellen Benson, the book's superb editor, who spent countless hours on the project amid her already-full schedule. In the final months, she was ably assisted by Liz Stefaniak, A.B. '00, Eileen P. Duggan, and Karen R. Daubert.

The book's magnificent contemporary photos are the work of University photographer David Kilper, who often rose before dawn to achieve such glistening effects. Other photos from recent decades were the work of University photographers Joe Angeles, Robert Boston, and Herb Weitman. The fine design is the product of art director Donna Boyd, in collaboration with Jean Lopez and Heather Needleman of Lopez/Needleman Graphic Design, with assistance from Julie Conway, B.F.A. '00, Cyndi McKenna, and Galen Harrison.

Such a book is based on research — thousands of hard-to-find documents and elusive photos. Assembling these would never have happened without the extraordinary efforts of two archivists: Carole Prietto on the Hilltop and Philip Skroska on the Medical Campus. I cannot thank them enough for their kindness, patience, and creativity. Their archival colleagues Paul Anderson and Jay Kempen provided additional assistance, as did three wonderful part-time student researchers: Abigail

Conway, A.B. '02, Jessica Sperling, and the late Amy Wilson, with the occasional help of Kevin Bastian and Andrew Broyles, A.B. '03. The Special Collections staff, headed by Anne Posega, was also helpful.

All around the University, faculty and staff were gracious in answering my questions: Rose Brower, Barbara Carrow, Jerome Cox, David Peters, and Salvatore Sutera from Engineering; David Blasingame, Denise Carlson, Rebecca Davolt, and Lee Hanson from Development; Sue Hosack and Barb Laudel, Office of Student Records; Ann Nicholson, law school; sports information directors Keith Jenkins and Chris Mitchell; Sara Hignite and Andrew McDiarmid, Gallery of Art; librarians Dana Beth, Clara McLeod, and Kay Shehan; Michael Friedlander and Martin Israel, physics; Kathleen Cook, anthropology; Henry Berger, history; Vicki Kunkler, Mallinckrodt Institute of Radiology; Rebecca Treiman, psychology; Sarah Elgin, biology; administrators Richard Roloff, Ben Sandler, and Jim Stueber; Bob Osburn, earth and planetary sciences; Mary Ann Noel, Dr. Danforth's office; Lee Fetter, St. Louis Children's Hospital; Don Clayton, Paul Manske, Garland Marshall, and Gila Reckess from the medical school; Theresa Howard with medical photos; Elaine Pittaluga, Photographic Services; Lou Anne Davidson, trustees' office; Paul Norman, grounds; Sarantis Symeonoglou and Dave Murrey, Wulfing Collection.

I have appreciated the kind assistance of others outside the University: Dennis Northcott and Duane Sneddeker, Missouri Historical Society; William Fischetti, Western Historical Manuscript Collection; architectural historian Esley Hamilton; Wade Rouse and archival volunteers at Mary Institute Country Day School; staff members, Missouri Botanical Garden, Mercantile Library, and Brookings Institution; Janice Broderick and Shelley Hagen, A.G. Edwards and Sons, Inc.; members of the Civil War Roundtable; Sharon Huffman, St. Louis Public Schools;

Scott and Nita Nordlicht for their gift of reference material; Joel Achtenberg; Mrs. Edward B. (Pat) Jones, Jesse Swanigan, and Katherine White Drescher for photos; John H. Tweedy for his help with Alice Belcher Tweedy; Gerald and Leslie Popelka about Hallowell Davis; archival staff from the Universities of Michigan, Pennsylvania, Illinois, and California; Vassar College; NASA; West Point and the U.S. Naval Academy; Oberlin College; Harvard, Johns Hopkins, Brandeis, and Princeton universities; and the Watertown Free Public Library.

One group of people gave special assistance, with lengthy interviews that dealt with their knowledge of the University or thoughts about this project: James R. Burmeister, William H. Danforth, James W. Davis, Timothy Eberlein, Lois Eliot, Michael Friedlander, Herbert F. Hitzeman, M. Kenton King, Kenneth Ludmerer, Edward S. Macias, the late Ralph E. Morrow, William A. Peck, Robert L. Virgil, M. Fredric Volkmann, Burton Wheeler, the late Gloria W. White, and Mark S. Wrighton.

Last but never least, I would like to thank my friends, all patient listeners, and my own dear family: my husband, Robert Wiltenburg, dean of University College, and our daughters Mary and Kate Wiltenburg, the "great work" of our lives. This book is dedicated to the three of them, with all my love.

In closing, let me recall what University historian Ralph Morrow said at the end of the epilogue to his monumental work, *Washington University in St. Louis: A History* (1996). "Perhaps the next historian of the University will redress my emphasis on the development of the institutional home by emphasizing the genius of those who have inhabited it." In our conversations, cut short by his death, he was cordial and encouraging about my plans; it is my hope that he would have been pleased with the result. For my part, I feel privileged to have worked on this long, exhausting, but exhilarating project.

— *Candace O'Connor*

Beginning a great work.
In honor of the Sesquicentennial, Washington University has created its own distinctive commencement gown, designed by Leslie Lambeth, lecturer in fashion design at the School of Art. Chancellor Mark S. Wrighton (left) and John F. McDonnell, chairman of the board of trustees, wear the new academic gowns at Commencement 2003.
Joe Angeles, WU Photographic Services

SELECTED BIBLIOGRAPHY

The following abbreviations have been used:
WUA Washington University Archives
WUBML Washington University Becker Medical Library

PRIMARY SOURCES

Bulletin of the Washington University Association, 1903–1912. WUA.

Compton, Arthur Holly. Papers, 1892–1962. WUA.

Eliot Literary Magazine. November 1915–May 15, 1947. WUA.

Eliot, William Greenleaf. Papers, 1847-1935. WUA.

Guze, Samuel B., interview by Marion Hunt, 1994. WUBML.

Hatchet, 1903–present. WUA.

Houston, David F. "A University for the Southwest: An Address Delivered Before the Commercial Club of St. Louis." October 31, 1908. WUA.

Hughes, David Ferrar. "Personal Log of Ensign David Ferrar Hughes, April 18, 1943–April 10, 1944." WUA.

Inaugural Addresses of Chancellors Joseph Hoyt, William Chauvenet, William Greenleaf Eliot, Winfield Scott Chaplin, Herbert S. Hadley, Arthur H. Compton, Thomas Eliot, and Mark S. Wrighton. WUA.

Irving Union. February 1869–December 1877. WUA.

King, M. Kenton, interview by Marion Hunt, 1991-92. WUBML.

Morrow, Ralph. Papers, c. 1988–1995. WUA.

Shepley, Ethan A.H., interview by William Deiss, 1970. WUA.

St. Louis Globe-Democrat

St. Louis Post-Dispatch

Student Life, January 1, 1878–present. WUA.

Washington University Alumni Directory, 1917, 1975, 1987, 1993, 1998. WUA.

Washington University Annual Catalog, 1856/1857–present. WUA.

Washington University. *The Contribution Made by Washington University in the Study and Development of Atomic Energy.* St. Louis: Washington University, 1945. WUA.

Washington University, Board of Trustees. Minutes of the Board of Trustees, 1853–1985. WUA.

Washington University Chronicle. January 1909–May 1910. WUA.

Washington University in St. Louis Magazine and predecessors, 1924 to present. (Predecessor titles: *Washington University Magazine, Alumni Bulletin, Washingtonian*). WUA.

Washington University, Office of the Chancellor. *Washington University Annual Report,* 1971/1972–2001/2002. WUA.

Washington University, Office of the Chancellor. Chancellor's Oral History Project, Thomas H. Eliot, interview by Glen E. Holt, July 6, 1979, and Thomas S. Hall, interview by Mrs. Hugh Scott, April 10, 1979. WUA.

Washington University, Office of the Chancellor. Administrative Files of the Chancellor, 1891–1998. WUA.

Washington University, Office of the Chancellor. Chancellor's Scrapbooks, 1859–1949. WUA.

Washington University, Office of the Treasurer. Files of Seth A. Ranlett, 1854–1882. WUA.

Washington University Record, 1974–present. WUA.

Washington University School of Medicine. *Outlook Magazine,* 1964–present. WUBML.

Washington University School of Medicine and its predecessors. Annual course bulletins and catalogs, 1840–present. WUBML.

Waterhouse, Sylvester. "A Eulogy on the Late Chancellor Joseph Gibson Hoyt of Washington University: Delivered at the Hall of the University, St. Louis, Jan. 20th, 1868." Philadelphia: J.B. Lippincott & Co., 1863. WUA.

SECONDARY SOURCES

Allen, Thomas G. and William L. Sachtleben, *Across Asia on a Bicycle: The Journey of Two American Students from Constantinople to Peking.* New York: The Century Co., 1894.

Barnes, Harper. *Standing on a Volcano: The Life and Times of David Rowland Francis.* St. Louis: Missouri Historical Society Press, 2001.

Beal, Graham W. J., ed. *Charles Parsons, Collections of Paintings.* St. Louis: Washington University, 1977.

Biemiller, Lawrence. "A Daring Master Plan That Has Served Washington University Exceptionally Well," *Chronicle of Higher Education,* January 15, 1992, B6-B8.

Bowling, William Glasgow. *Names That Live: An Account of the People for Whom the Buildings at Washington University Are Named and of the Benefactors Who Gave Them.* St Louis: Washington University, 1967.

Clevenger, Martha R., ed. *"Indescribably Grand": Diaries and Letters from the 1904 World's Fair.* St. Louis: Missouri Historical Society Press, 1996.

Compton, Arthur Holly. *Atomic Quest, A Personal Narrative.* New York: University Press, 1956.

Craig, James T. "Origin and History of the Collegiate Department of Washington University." Master's thesis, Washington University, 1941. WUA.

Cuoco, Lorin, and William H. Gass. *Literary St. Louis: A Guide.* St. Louis: Missouri Historical Society Press, 2000.

Eckmann, Sabine. *H.W. Janson and the Legacy of Modern Art at Washington University in St. Louis.* St. Louis: Washington University Gallery of Art, Salander-O'Reilly Galleries, New York, 2002.

Eliot, Charlotte. *William Greenleaf Eliot, Minister, Educator, Philanthropist.* Boston: Houghton, Mifflin and Company, 1904.

Fermi, Laura. *Illustrious Immigrants: The Intellectual Migration from Europe, 1930-41.* Chicago: University of Chicago Press, 1968.

Flexner, Abraham. *Abraham Flexner: An Autobiography.* New York: Simon and Schuster, 1960.

_____. *Medical Education in the United States and Canada: A Report to the Carnegie Foundation for the Advancement of Teaching.* New York: Arno Press, 1972.

Grisham, Marjorie Fox. "History of the Washington University School of Medicine." Unpublished typescript. WUBML.

Hagedorn, Hermann. *Brookings: A Biography.* New York: Macmillan, 1936.

Hexter, Jack H. *The Vision of Politics on the Eve of the Reformation: More, Machiavelli, and Seyssel.* New York: Basic Books, 1973.

Holt, Earl K. *William Greenleaf Eliot, Conservative Radical: Six Essays on the Life and Character of the 19th Century Unitarian Minister, Educator and Philanthropist, Based on the 1983 Minns Lectures.* St. Louis: First Unitarian Church of St. Louis, 1985.

Hunt, Marion. "From Childsaving to Pediatrics: A Case Study of Women's Role in the Development of St. Louis Children's Hospital 1879-1925." Ph.D. thesis, Washington University, 1992. WUBML.

_____. *A Goodly Heritage: St. Louis Children's Hospital's Centennial History 1879-1979.* St. Louis: St. Louis Children's Hospital, 1981. WUBML.

Jamieson, James P. *Intimate History of the Campus and Buildings of Washington University, Saint Louis.* Mound City, Mo.: Mound City Press, 1941.

Jerzewiak, Regina M. "History of the O'Fallon Polytechnic Institute: The Practical Department of Washington University." Master's thesis, Washington University, 1940. WUA.

Ketner, Joseph. *A Gallery of Modern Art at Washington University in St. Louis.* St. Louis: Washington University Gallery of Art, 1994.

Kimbrough, Mary, Justin L. Faherty, and David R. Brown. *Movers and Shakers: Men Who Have Shaped St. Louis.* Tucson: Patrice Press, 1992.

Kroeger, Brooke. *Fannie: The Talent for Success of Writer Fannie Hurst.* New York: Times Books, 1999.

Langsdorf, Alexander S. "The Story of Washington University in St. Louis, 1853–1953." Unpublished typescript, 1953. WUA.

Levi-Montalcini, Rita. *In Praise of Imperfection: My Life and Work.* New York: Basic Books, 1988.

Ludmerer, Kenneth M. *Learning to Heal: The Development of American Medical Education.* New York: Basic Books, 1985.

_____. *Time to Heal: American Medical Education from the Turn of the Century to the Era of Managed Care.* New York: Oxford University Press, 1999.

Milder, Benjamin. *On the Shoulders of Giants: The Story of the Washington University Department of Ophthalmology and Visual Sciences.* Marceline, Mo.: Walsworth Publishing Company, Inc., 1997.

Morrow, Ralph E. *Washington University in St. Louis: A History.* St. Louis: Missouri Historical Society Press, 1996.

Moulton, Harold G. *Robert Somers Brookings, an Address by Harold G. Moulton, President of the Brookings Institution, Delivered on February 21, 1950, at Washington University in St. Louis.* Washington University: 2nd ser., vol. 48, July 1950.

Mueller, C. Barber. *Evarts A. Graham: The Life, Lives, and Times of the Surgical Spirit of St. Louis.* London: BC Decker Inc., 2002.

Mulkey, Mab. "History of the St. Louis School of Fine Arts, 1879–1909: The Art Department of Washington University." Master's thesis, Washington University, 1944. WUA.

Pfeiffenberger, Amy M. "Democracy at Home: The Struggle to Desegregate Washington University in the Postwar Era," *Gateway Heritage,* Winter 1989–1990, pp. 14-25. WUA.

Philpott, Gordon M. *Daring Venture: The Life Story of William H. Danforth.* New York: Random House, 1960.

Pickens, Buford and Margaretta J. Darnall. *Washington University in St. Louis: Its Design and Architecture.* St. Louis: Washington University School of Architecture and the Gallery of Art, 1978.

Proetz, Arthur Walter. *I Remember You, St. Louis.* St. Louis: Zimmerman-Petty Co., 1963.

Reps, John William. *Saint Louis Illustrated: Nineteenth-Century Engravings and Lithographs of Mississippi Metropolis.* Columbia: University of Missouri Press, 1989.

Smith, Holmes. "The History of Washington University." Unpublished typescript, 1935. WUA.

Snow, Marshall. [*History of Washington University, untitled*]. Unpublished typescript, undated. WUA.

Stevens, Walter B. *St. Louis, The Fourth City 1764–1909.* St. Louis-Chicago: The S.J. Clarke Publishing Co., 1909.

Strode, William. *Washington, a University Portrait.* Little Compton, R.I.: Fort Church Publications, 1985.

Van Ravenswaay, Charles. *St. Louis: An Informal History of the City and Its People, 1764–1865.* St. Louis: Missouri Historical Society Press, 1991.

Winter, William C. *The Civil War in St. Louis: A Guided Tour.* St. Louis: Missouri Historical Society Press, 1994.

Williams, Cartus R. "History of the Law Department of Washington University: The St. Louis Law School, 1867–1900." Master's thesis, Washington University, 1942. WUA.

Williams, Robert C. "From the Hill to the Hilltop: Washington University and the Manhattan Project, 1940-46." *Gateway Heritage,* vol. 9, no. 3, Winter 1988–89, pp. 21-27.

AUTHOR INTERVIEWS

James R. Burmeister, William H. Danforth, James W. Davis, Timothy Eberlein, Lois Eliot, Michael Friedlander, Herbert F. Hitzeman, Jr., M. Kenton King, Kenneth M. Ludmerer, Edward S. Macias, Ralph E. Morrow, William A. Peck, Robert L. Virgil, M. Fredric Volkmann, Burton Wheeler, Gloria W. White, Mark S. Wrighton.

No instruction, either secta
halities, shall be allowed in any
no sectarian or partisan test sha
fessors, teachers, or other officers
hatsoever. This Article shall be